THE MYTH OF COLORBLIND CHRISTIANS

The Myth of Colorblind Christians

Evangelicals and White Supremacy in the Civil Rights Era

Jesse Curtis

NEW YORK UNIVERSITY PRESS
New York

NEW YORK UNIVERSITY PRESS
New York
www.nyupress.org

© 2021 by New York University
All rights reserved

Portions of chapter 3 appeared in an earlier form as "White Evangelicals as 'a People': The Church Growth Movement from India to the United States," *Religion and American Culture: A Journal of Interpretation* 30 (2020): 108–146. It is reprinted with permission of Cambridge University Press.

References to Internet websites (URLs) were accurate at the time of writing. Neither the author nor New York University Press is responsible for URLs that may have expired or changed since the manuscript was prepared.

Library of Congress Cataloging-in-Publication Data
Names: Curtis, Jesse, author.
Title: The myth of colorblind Christians : evangelicals and white supremacy in the Civil Rights Era / Jesse Curtis.
Description: New York : New York University Press, [2021] | Includes bibliographical references and index.
Identifiers: LCCN 2021003106 | ISBN 9781479809370 (hardback) | ISBN 9781479809387 (paperback) | ISBN 9781479809417 (ebook) | ISBN 9781479809394 (ebook other)
Subjects: LCSH: Evangelicalism—United States—History—20th century. | Race relations—Religious aspects—Christianity. | Civil rights movements—United States—History—20th century.
Classification: LCC BR1642.U6 C87 2021 | DDC 270.8/2—dc23
LC record available at https://lccn.loc.gov/2021003106

New York University Press books are printed on acid-free paper, and their binding materials are chosen for strength and durability. We strive to use environmentally responsible suppliers and materials to the greatest extent possible in publishing our books.

Manufactured in the United States of America

10 9 8 7 6 5 4 3 2 1

Also available as an ebook

For

John, Levi, Gabe, Annie

CONTENTS

Introduction	1
1. What Does It Mean to Be One in Christ? The Civil Rights Movement and the Origins of Christian Colorblindness	13
2. Creating the Colorblind Campus	49
3. Growing the Homogeneous Church	78
4. A Mission Field Next Door	109
5. Two Gospels on a Global Stage	138
6. The Elusive Turning Point: Colorblind Christians and "Racial Reconciliation"	171
Conclusion	209
Acknowledgments	221
Notes	223
Bibliography	265
Index	281
About the Author	291

Introduction

On the evening of November 24, 2014, St. Louis County prosecuting attorney Bob McCulloch announced that a white police officer would not be indicted for the shooting death of a black teenager, Michael Brown, in Ferguson, Missouri. As the nation looked on, Michael Brown's family cried out in grief and fires raged in the night. The moment produced astonishing split-screen images: the president of the United States calling for calm while buildings up and down Florissant Avenue burned to the ground. The following summer, as Black Lives Matter activists marked the anniversary of Michael Brown's death with renewed protests, one of the country's most influential evangelical pastors decided to weigh in on social media. Rick Warren shared an image of two police officers standing together, one white and one black, each holding a hand toward the camera. On each palm were the words "His life matters." The meme seemed to be a typical example of the colorblind ideology that has dominated so much of American racial discourse. But for Warren, the matter was theological. And so he added a commentary of his own:

> #AllLivesMatterToGod
> Racism isn't caused by SKIN but by SIN.
> "From one man GOD made every nation of men to inhabit the whole earth; and He determined the times set for them and the exact places where they'd live." Acts 17:26[1]

As cries of "Black Lives Matter" rang out on the nation's streets, Warren universalized and sacralized the slogan. "All Lives Matter" was God's word on America's raging racial controversy. Warren's diagnosis of the roots of racism—"SIN" rather than "SKIN"—was a pithy alliteration with a long history going back at least to the civil rights movement.[2] But what did it mean in this case? Warren implied that Black Lives Matter activists were misguided because they failed to recognize the root of sin in the human heart, a disposition that knew no bounds of color. Warren's generic invocation of sin effectively hid the reality of American white supremacy from view. His audience could imagine themselves as opponents of racism and as allies of a God-ordained racial order while sidestepping the specificity of black activists' demands. Where did Rick Warren get these ideas? How did his audience know how to interpret them? Warren worked with the tools that generations of white evangelicals had created in their adaptive response to the civil rights movement. His intervention in social media conveyed abundant meaning in few words because it expressed the colorblind theology that white evangelicals had spent the better part of five decades developing.

In the second half of the twentieth century, black evangelicals in the United States made unprecedented demands for inclusion and reform in white evangelical institutions. In response to these demands and the upheavals of the civil rights movement, white evangelicals discarded theologies of white supremacy and embraced a new theology of racial colorblindness. But instead of deploying this colorblind theology for antiracist purposes, white evangelicals used it to protect and shape new investments in whiteness as they attempted to grow the evangelical movement. They offered an individualistic message of repentance and salvation as the most potent force able to change lives and transcend racial boundaries. Seeking to address racial problems close to home through their churches, colleges, and parachurch ministries, white evangelicals emphasized the spiritual unity of all true believers in Jesus Christ, the power of the gospel to solve racial problems, and the importance of interpersonal relationships to heal the wounds of racism. As black evangelicals sought change in white evangelical institutions, they repeatedly insisted that white evangelicals' brand of colorblind Christianity failed to eradicate racism. White evangelicals often responded that black evangelicals' efforts were a divisive threat to the unity of the church. Christian colorblindness fostered communities in which whiteness often remained an invisible investment carried on under the banner of Christian unity and faithfulness to the gospel. The result was a distinctly evangelical form of whiteness.

This book argues that white evangelicals' turn to a theology of colorblindness enabled them to create an evangelical brand of whiteness that occupied the center of American evangelicalism and shaped the American racial order from the 1960s to the 1990s. While black evangelicals pressed for practical changes, white evangelicals found that colorblind theology enabled their movement to thrive and become nominally multiethnic without making substantial changes to power relations. At the outset of the civil rights era, overt associations of whiteness with godliness were commonplace. By the end of the century, such assumptions had been irrevocably shattered, but new forms of evangelical whiteness had taken their place. Expressions of racial superiority and segregationist readings of scripture became taboo. But just as importantly, antiracist interrogation of white identity and concern for racial justice remained off-limits. While professing to desire racial harmony, white evangelicals still balked at black evangelical demands and insisted that preaching a colorblind gospel would solve racial problems. Colorblind claims allowed white evangelicals to adapt to the racial revolution of the civil rights era and became key drivers of evangelical identity. Colorblind Christianity fueled the growth of the evangelical coalition even as it failed to deliver the promised gains to black evangelicals seeking an equal place in the body of Christ.

Christian Colorblindness and the American Racial Order

Rick Warren's use of scripture to critique Black Lives Matter activists highlighted an often-overlooked fact: the American racial order is religious. "Racism," wrote George Fredrickson in his classic study of the subject, "either directly sustains or proposes to establish *a racial order*, a permanent group hierarchy that is believed to reflect the laws of nature or the decrees of God."[3] These divine decrees continued to animate American imaginations even as their content changed during the course of the twentieth century. If celebration of whiteness as sacred was a frequent feature of the Jim Crow racial order, the post-1960s colorblind order immersed in evangelical religiosity took exactly the opposite stance: racial consciousness suggested a lack of Christian maturity. Those who challenged Christian colorblindness arrayed themselves against God. In this sense the colorblind racial order of the late twentieth century retained the classic features of a racial hierarchy pervaded with theological significance.

Scholars of race and whiteness have done excellent work to explore colorblind racial ideology but have been slow to recognize its religious features.[4] Implicit in much of the literature is a version of the secularization thesis. Though the crucial role of religion in racialization in the early modern period is widely understood, much of the scholarship on race in contemporary America does not account for religion's ongoing part in racial formation. Scholars of religion have shown that religion shapes the very meaning of the so-called secular.[5] This insight must be brought to bear on the American racial order. A vision that assumes religion's declining significance cannot understand race in the contemporary United States. Throughout this book, I use phrases such as "investment in whiteness" to deliberately echo foundational works in whiteness studies and critical race theory while also suggesting the limits of that scholarship.[6] Like other white Americans, white evangelicals invested in and benefited from a racial hierarchy that was often invisible to them. But I refer to an evangelical investment in whiteness in a more specific sense. White evangelicals invested in white supremacy *as evangelicals*. When they opportunistically used race to grow their churches while denying theological legitimacy to other forms of race consciousness, they gave an evangelical cast to whiteness and shaped the contours of the American racial order.

As white evangelicals fashioned a new theology of race, they created a significant grassroots symbiosis between Christian colorblindness and the colorblindness of a conservative political ascendancy in the decades after the civil rights movement. Americans read Monday morning's newspaper with the Sunday sermon ringing in their ears. When they picked up their Bibles, they did not put down their political commitments. While colorblind ideology in American politics might be expressed in idioms of national unity ("we're all Americans") or human solidarity ("we're all the same under the skin"), the idioms of Christian colorblindness—the "body of Christ," "unity in Christ," "Jesus died for us all," "we're all equal at the cross"—are at once distinct and constitutive of a sacralized racial order. To understand the durability of colorblind ideology, we must come to see that the post–civil rights era political order was both racial and religious. Though white evangelicals alone did not create the politics of colorblindness, tens of millions of white evangelicals drew on their theology to imbue those politics with a sacred character.

Scholars and evangelicals themselves have often attempted to police borders between what is theological and what is political, what is sacred and profane.⁷ Christian colorblindness obliterated these imagined borders, even if its practitioners were not always aware of its deeply political nature. On questions of race, most white evangelicals insisted that the Christian gospel working in individual hearts was the only real solution. Organized political activism for racial justice was a distraction from the real source of racial progress. So pervasive did this pietistic posture become that white evangelicals tended not to see it as a form of politics. It became, instead, the supposedly obvious Christian approach to racial tension. This stance did not reflect a general evangelical preference for antistructural solutions to social problems.⁸ Other moral concerns such as abortion energized evangelicals and as a result became opportunities for movement building and systemic interventions in the nation's political life. In contrast, in racial problems, white evangelicals tended to see a threat to their movement more than an opportunity. In consequence, they turned to a racial politics of church primacy that ably protected their investments in whiteness.⁹

White evangelicals' divergent responses to social problems—engaging systems here while eschewing them there—may tempt some observers to see the theological language of race as nothing more than cover for reactionary political commitments. Yet inquiring after the sincerity of evangelical theologies of race is a dead end, rewarding binary answers and simplistic moralism.¹⁰ Rather than imagining theological discourse as a façade, it is more useful to understand theology as one of the main ways evangelicals performed politics. Part of what it meant to be an opinion shaper in an evangelical context was to have the skill to express racial opinions in the language of biblical idiom and evangelical theology. This wasn't a sign of insincerity; it was a mark of belonging. And it was only part of a broader ferment during decades in which, as Lilian Calles Barger has written, "Across the left/right spectrum, theology was validating the religious and spiritual significance of the political."¹¹

Rather than exploring white evangelicals' racial politics of church primacy from the inside, much of the popular and scholarly literature imagines white evangelicals primarily as partisan political actors.¹² As the story goes, white evangelicals grudgingly looked on as the civil rights movement swept the land, and then they became Republicans.

Though some scholars have done excellent work to complicate this one-dimensional picture, the rise of the so-called Christian Right so dominates the conversation that the ecclesial changes the civil rights movement set in motion among white evangelicals remain underexplored and poorly understood.[13] Looking from the outside in, the popular story of white evangelical resistance to civil rights and subsequent political mobilization insists that the rhythms and preoccupations of white evangelicals' own religio-racial worlds are of little interest compared to their status as a powerful Republican constituency. In contrast, this book examines the very places white evangelicals insisted were the centers of their attention: their churches, schools, and parachurch ministries. Because evangelicals' primary racial and religious acts occurred in and through their own institutions, scholars must seek to understand those spaces, not only in the South but also in national and transnational contexts. White evangelicals insisted that these spaces, not partisan politics, held the key to America's racial destiny.

What Is a White Evangelical Anyway?

Christian colorblindness provides a useful framework to trace the changing meanings of whiteness and evangelicalism in the civil rights era. In recent years the argument that the categories of race and religion are mutually constituted has become well established among scholars of religion.[14] Yet in practice, this insight has done little to alter the analytical frames of many studies of evangelicalism, a field whose foundational works have become infamous for their inattention to race.[15] Though "white evangelical" is one of the most overworked phrases in our political and historical lexicon, to invert the phrase and speak of "evangelical whiteness" still raises eyebrows. When we begin to think through the lens of this inversion, whiteness can never be assumed; its connotations must be explained in specific contexts. Through this inversion, whiteness becomes as much religious as racial as it takes on theological, institutional, and temporal inflections. The rise and spread of what I call Christian colorblindness is one way the transformation of evangelical whiteness, and its effect on the broader American racial order, can be seen.

Christian colorblindness became an important tool of evangelical coalition building in a rapidly changing society, and it helped to form evangelical identity itself. Those who embraced Christian colorblindness found themselves inside the camp. Those who rejected it, especially black evangelicals, often found their evangelical bona fides called into question. Historians' inattention to the black evangelical story not only has hidden an important part of evangelicalism's history, but also has made it harder for scholars to discern how central whiteness was in policing evangelicalism's borders. By challenging Christian colorblindness, black evangelicals held up a mirror to the evangelical mainstream, exposing its investment in whiteness. In this sense, white evangelicalism can be understood as a religio-racial identity. Judith Weisenfeld has employed this term to describe black religious movements in the era of the Great Migration, whose members understood "individual and collective identity as constituted in the conjunction of religion and race."[16] Weisenfeld tells a story of people at the margins of American life who used this religio-racial self-fashioning as an instrument of deliberate resistance. We can imagine white evangelicalism as a religio-racial inversion of this self-fashioning: often unconscious rather than deliberate, and a means of identification with the racial hierarchy rather than resistance to it. The tangible reality of evangelical whiteness was borne out again and again by black evangelicals' efforts to belong in evangelical spaces and institutions. The intensity of their struggle in historically white evangelical spaces revealed just how *white* evangelicalism was. At the same time, the extraordinary success and influence of evangelicalism in the mainstream of American life suggested how *evangelical* whiteness had become.[17]

A generation of scholarship that attempted to locate evangelical identity in distinct theological beliefs could not adequately account for these religio-racial boundaries.[18] In recent years, scholars have described evangelicalism as an "imagined religious community," an "aesthetical worldview," and a "commercial religion" defined as much by its cultures of consumption as its theological claims.[19] As definitions proliferate, hopes for an encompassing classification able to command wide agreement recede. This is for the best. Rather than casting a totalizing definition of evangelicalism, this book approaches the movement through the category of race and the concept of Christian colorblindness. In the latter half of the twentieth century, the outlines of evangelicalism emerged not just in the fact that Christians of numerous denominations or no denomination at all might shop for the same books and listen to the same radio shows. They had come to share a common religio-racial imagination that made diverse groups of conservative Protestants intelligible to each other. They knew that God was colorblind and Christians were one body in Christ. They knew that racism was sinful and that mature Christians did not care much about their racial identities. They knew that the solution to America's racial ills was spiritual rebirth and interpersonal kindness. As they acted on these intuitions, they solidified the borders of evangelicalism and made whiteness one of its key markers.

It is helpful to bear in mind that I use Christian colorblindness to refer to something that was always in the process of becoming. Some of the constituent parts of Christian colorblindness were as old as the Christian scriptures. As far back as the seventeenth century, abolitionists used the language of spiritual equality to argue against the enslavement of human beings, while Christian enslavers replied that heavenly rewards did not alter one's earthly station.[20] In the first half of the twentieth century, racial liberals sometimes used Christian universalism and metaphors of colorblindness to protest Jim Crow. Martin Luther King and other civil rights activists spoke of the unity of the body of Christ in terms that would be familiar to white evangelicals by the 1990s. The power of Christian colorblindness was found not so much in its novelty as in its long pedigree. White evangelicals could declare that in Christ there should be no racial consciousness and claim no less a figure than the Apostle Paul as their authority and reform movements such as abolitionism as their precedent. What was new and remarkable in the second half of the twentieth century is that this avowed opposition to race consciousness, rooted in a colorblind interpretation of the Bible, became the primary *defense* of the American religio-racial hierarchy rather than a challenge to it.

Overview of the Book

The organization of this book has an hourglass shape. The opening and closing chapters take a broad view of the racial climate of evangelicalism and its intersections with the changes in American life in the 1960s and the 1990s. The four chapters in between trace narrower threads, alternating between churches and colleges to explore specific facets of change in the 1960s, 1970s, and 1980s. In their churches evangelicals worshipped, found comfort and community, and learned ways of imagining God, themselves, and others. Racial change in these spaces was fraught precisely because the stakes were so high. To explore these dynamics, I use the archives both of the nation's largest Protestant denomination, the Southern Baptist Convention, and of one of the most influential interdenominational evangelistic movements of the period, the Church Growth Movement. Colleges were sites of training for future evangelical leaders and spaces where the evangelical mainstream was constructed. Throughout the civil rights era and beyond, evangelical college students spoke more unguardedly about race than their elders, providing a particularly fertile trail of religio-racial formation across time.

White evangelicals experienced the civil rights movement as a test of the strength of their institutions and the credibility of their movement. Chapter 1 describes what the civil rights movement looked like from an evangelical perspective, and how evangelicals began to change in response to it. Black evangelicals became a more visible part of the evangelical movement in the 1960s and used colorblind theologies to challenge racial discrimination in evangelical spaces, providing a powerful impetus to change. As Jim Crow crumbled and racial norms rapidly shifted, white evangelicals sought a new way forward that would broaden the appeal of their evangelistic message and maintain the unity of their churches. By the end of this tumultuous decade, if evangelicals could not agree on the precise path forward, they could agree on one thing: the way to racial progress ran through their own institutions and the message of the gospel they carried.

White evangelical college campuses emerged in the late 1960s as key sites for the construction of Christian colorblindness. Chapter 2 describes how many white evangelical colleges began to actively recruit black students for the first time. Contested visions of what it would mean to create colorblind Christian academic communities flourished. On some campuses there was an atmosphere of crisis in the early 1970s as increasingly race-conscious black students demanded reforms and critiqued white evangelical racism. White administrators and students often responded with the emerging rhetoric of Christian colorblindness. If only students would practice Christian love and focus on what they had in common as believers, brotherhood might flourish on the Christian campus. Just a few years before, black evangelicals had used the rhetoric of Christian unity to challenge racism. Now white evangelicals used the same language to urge black evangelicals to stop demanding racial reforms. By the middle of the 1970s, most recruitment programs had collapsed.

While white evangelical colleges recruited black students, white evangelical churches embraced a very different approach. Chapter 3 traces the emergence and transformation of the Church Growth Movement (CGM). Evangelistic strategies created in caste-conscious India in the 1930s came to be deployed in American metropolitan areas decades later. During the 1970s, the CGM defined white Americans as "a people" akin to castes or tribes in the global south. Drawing on the revival of white ethnic identities in American culture, church growth leaders imagined whiteness as pluralism rather than hierarchy. The CGM allowed colorblind Christians to imagine that their segregated churches were benign expressions of American diversity in the years after the civil rights movement. In an age of white flight, the CGM helped to structure the evangelical mainstream as white, suburban, and middle class.

While the CGM enabled evangelical flight from the city, some evangelicals sought to move toward it. Chapter 4 describes the efforts of a minority of evangelicals to contest Christian colorblindness and redefine it in an era of urban crisis. In Philadelphia, Messiah College launched an urban campus in 1968 in an effort to engage the new realities that the civil rights movement had wrought. At this and other institutions, early ambitions for antiracist education and urban activism came to grief as colorblind Christians resisted the racial lessons of the American city. By the 1980s, cultural diversity, not racial justice, became the logic of these urban programs.

As white evangelical colleges continued to wrestle with questions of diversity and Christian community, evangelicals on a global stage argued over the very meaning of the gospel. Chapter 5 traces this debate from the famous International Lausanne Congress on World Evangelization in 1974 to a lesser-known conference, "Evangelizing Ethnic America," in 1985. While black and Latin American evangelicals argued that racism had to be confronted and social justice could not be separated from the gospel message, leading figures in the CGM and Southern Baptist Convention took a pragmatic approach, seeking to use race for the purposes of conversion. While concern for social justice seemed to gain ascendancy at Lausanne, the trajectory to Houston '85 signaled that colorblind Christians in the United States could become multiethnic without becoming antiracist.

By the 1990s, Christian colorblindness was a dominant force in white evangelicalism. Chapter 6 describes the flowering of the "racial reconciliation" movement in this decade and reframes it as the culminating expression of Christian colorblindness. While most black evangelicals described racial justice as the foundation of racial reconciliation, white evangelicals appropriated the rhetoric of reconciliation, discarded the vision for social justice, and doubled down on their colorblind commitments. The evangelical movement for racial reconciliation burst on the scene at the very moment a colorblind consensus in American politics became especially prominent. Evangelicals weren't merely riding this trend; they helped to create it.

The book's conclusion discusses the legacy of Christian colorblindness in the twenty-first century. Amid the Obama and Trump presidencies and the rise of Black Lives Matter, evangelicals faced the possibility that Christian colorblindness had not produced the unity and racial harmony it promised. In a new era of racial protest, the fault lines between black and white evangelicals became more starkly apparent than they had been in decades. Colorblind Christians had won the struggle to define evangelicalism and shape the American racial order. The result of their victory was an evangelicalism colored white.

1

What Does It Mean to Be One in Christ?

The Civil Rights Movement and the Origins of Christian Colorblindness

In the 1960s, Howard Jones was among the biggest names in the world of black evangelicalism. He was a rare black graduate of Nyack College on the shores of the Hudson River just outside New York City, and in 1958 he became the first African American to serve on Billy Graham's evangelistic team. Jones expanded the reach of his own ministry through preaching on the radio. On one occasion an admiring white listener invited him to her home. According to Jones, the visit became awkward from the moment she opened the door, for she had not realized Jones was black. They carried on a desultory conversation and even prayed together before Jones made good his escape. She had been a faithful financial supporter of Jones's ministry, but after that day the checks stopped coming. Jones shared anecdotes like these to dramatize what he understood as a theological scandal in evangelical Christianity. His visibility at the pinnacles of evangelicalism made him the exception that proved the rule: it was a white movement that excluded black believers. In the face of this exclusion Jones issued his clarion call: "The church must demonstrate the truth that as Christians we are one in Christ, regardless of race and nationality, and that all racial barriers lie shattered at the foot of his cross."[1] He grounded his argument in scripture. The Apostle Paul had declared, "There is neither Jew nor Greek . . . for you are all one in Christ Jesus."[2] Jones believed evangelicals' failure to practice unity in Christ was the root of the nation's racial problems and a threat to evangelicalism's future. If evangelicals could find a way to practice a colorblind gospel, revival would yield a great harvest of souls and bring renewal to a troubled land.

Jones's colorblind aspirations put him in good company. In communities across postwar America, colorblind ideals were beginning to look a lot more like commonsense fair play than dangerous radicalism. The horrors of the Holocaust and the convulsions of independence movements in the global south had dealt a severe blow to the credibility of racist ideologies. The growth of transnational black activism was both evidence of and impetus to changing racial attitudes. The rising prominence of colorblind ideals at midcentury could be seen in everything from primary school classrooms and sunbelt suburbs to the pages of academic journals.[3] Colorblind rhetoric was so appealing by the 1960s that even segregationists got in on the act in a desperate attempt to reframe their struggle for white supremacy.[4] Giving everyone a fair shot, letting Americans go as far as their dreams and hard work would take them—this wasn't the stuff of communist subversion; this was the American Way.[5] But was it the evangelical way? If it wasn't, would an evangelical gospel be credible in a changing America? As the civil rights movement began to reshape the nation's politics and public life, Jones saw that its implications for evangelicals cut especially close to home. A movement predicated on evangelization and conversion had to deliver a winning message in this new environment. A theology of colorblindness emerged not as a partisan political maneuver or an export of sunbelt suburbia, but as the result of a nationwide reckoning among evangelicals as they sought to grow their movement and make it appealing to the American mainstream.[6]

Black evangelicals played a crucial part in this reckoning.[7] Howard Jones embodied the range of forces changing the evangelical racial calculus in civil rights–era America. A black sidekick of the most famous white evangelist in the country, Jones did his part in the effort to rebrand the image of conservative Protestantism from a remnant of aggrieved fundamentalists to winsome evangelicals. Jones's very presence in such circles suggested that race was part of this rebranding effort. Colorblind theology had the potential to distinguish evangelicalism from unsavory associations and broaden its evangelistic appeal. Besides, Jones was absolutely convinced his colorblind gospel came straight from the Bible. He was emblematic of a vocal group of black evangelicals who tried to break through the exclusionary borders of white evangelicalism using the words of scripture as their calling card. Both their blackness and their biblicism were of the utmost importance. Their blackness exposed the boundaries and hierarchies of the movement. Their biblicism made them difficult to dismiss. As black evangelicals challenged exclusion, many white evangelicals searched for new ways of thinking about race. Was there a path forward that would both secure the future of their movement and save their nation from the racial crisis enveloping it?

At a time when many white evangelicals continued to imagine whiteness as sacred, Jones's call for a church that transcended the color line was a powerful solvent breaking down the invidious racial distinctions structuring evangelicalism. If in the 1950s many white evangelicals assumed that God was, as one pastor put it, the "Original Segregationist," by the middle of the 1960s such breezy assumptions had become tinged with doubt as white evangelical elites increasingly worried that the siren call of sacred whiteness threatened the credibility of their gospel message.[8] Jones's conviction that a colorblind gospel could transform Americans from racial antagonists to brothers and sisters in Christ united growing numbers of evangelicals in the 1960s. But in practice the exact meaning of unity in Christ proved difficult to pin down. A black evangelical might invoke Christian unity to claim spiritual and social equality. A white evangelical might invoke the same principle to tell black evangelicals to receive their spiritual inheritance while remaining content with their segregated earthly lot. Christian colorblindness emerged not as a full-fledged system of thought but as a theology in the making, a set of scriptures, ideas, and idioms that might be used for or against racial reform. It turned out that there were many ways to imagine the meaning of unity in Christ.

Sacred Whiteness in Evangelical Life

Howard Jones believed there was something profoundly wrong when the very churches he agreed with on almost all matters of doctrine were the most resistant to dealing with America's racial crisis. The rapid changes of the postwar era were reshaping American religion but seemed slow in coming to the evangelical world. From the 1930s, white and black Catholic activists used the Church's doctrine of the Mystical Body of Christ to promote integration. Liberal Protestants, first through the Federal Council of Churches and then the National Council of Churches, poured forth a growing body of pronouncements calling for brotherhood and racial integration.[9] But white evangelicals, wary of making common cause with papists and ecumenists, were not nearly as vocal. To be sure, there were important exceptions. In 1947, the prominent evangelical theologian Carl Henry named "racial hatred" as one of the things that troubled the "uneasy conscience of modern fundamentalism."[10] In 1948, the evangelical college ministry InterVarsity Christian Fellowship determined it would operate on an integrated basis to better demonstrate the credibility of its gospel message.[11] Because it worked on college campuses, it was one of the first evangelical institutions to see how a new generation's moderating racial attitudes were changing the evangelistic calculus. Throughout the 1950s, some missionaries and other evangelical leaders tried to sound the alarm about both how the world was changing and how evangelicals would have to change with it.[12] But by 1963, when the National Council of Churches leapt into the civil rights struggle with money, organizational heft, and a sense of theological urgency, most white evangelicals were only beginning to talk about the problem.[13]

Worse, in large swaths of evangelicalism, whiteness still seemed a sacred calling. In its most unvarnished form, sacred whiteness collapsed entirely the distinction between white and Christian identities. In its more widespread and diluted form, sacred whiteness implicitly linked white racial identity to spiritual authority and ownership of the gospel message. In either case, Jones deplored the fact that racists too often found safe harbor in Bible-believing, gospel-preaching churches. "Within their camp are outright segregationists, in pulpit and pew," he declared.[14] Perhaps Jones was thinking of pastors like Montague Cook. On the morning of September 15, 1963, Reverend Cook took to his pulpit at Trinity Baptist Church in Moultrie, Georgia, to preach the second of his two-part sermon series, "Racial Segregation Is Christian." The week before, Cook had told his congregation how important it was to remain racially "pure." As God chose the children of Israel long ago and called them to be separate, so the "white European likewise was tapped by the Almighty to carry on his Purpose" in the development of Western civilization. White people were not superior by dint of circumstance or accident. They were a divinely chosen people set apart for a sacred mission. Now in his second sermon, Cook explained how this stark vision of white supremacy squared with the teachings of Jesus Christ. He told his congregation that Jesus taught "inequality among men" and "discernment in love." It was possible to love the "negro race" without giving in to modern myths about human equality. The good people of Trinity Baptist Church could rest assured that racial equality violated God's design and was contrary to Christian principles. The "race mixers" weren't just naïve. They set themselves in open rebellion against God. For Cook, racial and religious identities were inseparable. Whiteness was not only a race; it was a calling.[15] The very morning Reverend Cook preached his sermon, white terrorists set off a bomb in the basement of a black church in Birmingham, Alabama. While Reverend Cook spoke, unbeknownst to him, the lifeless bodies of four black children lay in the rubble of the Sixteenth Street Baptist Church.

Such explosive resonances drew the attention of many Americans toward the South as the source of the nation's racial trouble and the site of white evangelical intransigence. But some evangelicals wondered if sectional scapegoating adequately captured the reality of evangelicals' racial commitments. "Let's face it," the evangelical magazine *Eternity* declared in 1964, "most evangelicals, whether they are from the North, South, East or West, are supporters of the status quo, and consequently tend to be segregationists."[16] Indeed, racial exclusion was the standard practice of white evangelical institutions nationwide. Though a handful of black students did attend white evangelical colleges and Bible institutes before the civil rights era, foreign students enrolled through white evangelicals' extensive network of overseas missions were more common than American-born students of color. The vast majority of white evangelical churches were segregated in practice and happy to remain so. Other evangelicals were members of tight-knit communities of immigrant origin where ethnicity and denominational affiliation went hand in glove.[17] For these evangelicals, it could be hard to imagine an ethical responsibility toward African Americans when they themselves were only just beginning to feel a part of the white mainstream. Rarely did a white church deliberately seek to include black worshippers. When a prospective pastor interviewed for a position at an integrated Pittsburgh church, the board asked him what he thought of black Christians attending worship services. Unaware that the church was already integrated, he generously allowed, "Well, they *do* have souls."[18] In this unusual case the man's answer was disqualifying. No doubt he readily found a job elsewhere.

A pastor in Pittsburgh pontificating on black souls—as though their existence was an open question—is a reminder that racist theologies often imagined as distinctly southern were in fact popular nationwide. Well into the 1960s, the Curse of Ham myth remained influential among white evangelicals across the country. In the ninth chapter of Genesis, Noah gets drunk and passes out in his tent stark naked. Noah's son Ham sees him in this shameful state and makes light of his father's nakedness. The unflattering episode ends with Noah pronouncing a curse on Ham's son, declaring, "Cursed be Canaan; a servant of servants shall he be unto his brethren."[19] Fanciful readings of this puzzling text imagined Ham as the ancestor of all black Africans, who were now placed under a perpetual curse of servitude. Used to justify the slave trade and chattel slavery in centuries past, in the twentieth century the curse offered a theological explanation for white rule in a segregationist order.[20] Black people's souls might be saved, but in their life on earth they were destined for subservience. As one woman put it, the Bible clearly taught the principle of inequality rather than equality. Didn't the scriptures say, "Servants, obey your masters"? The integrationists were trying to create "a mongrel race" contrary to God's design. In some inchoate way, her superiority rested in a sacred blending of religion and race. "God has made the separate races, and the white Christian is superior because of Christianity," she declared.[21] For this woman and many others, whiteness was sacred because God had made it so. As late as 1970, the national synod of the Christian Reformed Church, a historically Dutch evangelical denomination concentrated in the Midwest, felt the need to make a declaration against the Curse of Ham to counter its influence among northern evangelical laypeople.[22]

The Hamitic Curse was just one part of the broader biblical story that many white evangelicals interpreted as a divine mandate for religio-racial purity. Southern extremists like Montague Cook were not the only ones spinning these tales. Carl McIntire, the Michigan-born fundamentalist firebrand whose radio show and ministry based in New Jersey garnered millions of loyal followers, explained that "God commanded the Jewish nation to be segregated and separate." Why then were liberals carrying on as if segregation was the greatest sin? "In fact, the whole history of God's dealing with Israel in the Old Testament represents the struggle to keep them separate," McIntire wrote.[23] Reading their own experience into both the Old and New Testaments, many white evangelicals understood Ancient Near Eastern identities as directly analogous to the modern category of race. Had not God separated humanity at the tower of Babel? Then, God called Israel out as a special people and forbade them from intermarrying with the nations around them. Many white evangelicals believed the New Testament confirmed segregation as God's divine plan. Even the Apostle Paul declared that God had made all the nations and determined "the bounds of their habitation."[24] In watered-down form, the segregationist narrative of scripture held some credibility even at the center of the elite white evangelical movement. In 1963, Carl Henry, the influential theologian and founding editor of *Christianity Today*, also pointed to the Apostle Paul's words for evidence that "God has preserved distinct nations whose social components are often racial." It was undeniable that "the one human race became separated in history . . . according to color" and perhaps it was not desirable "wholly to cancel racial distinctions."[25]

Henry's struggle to reconcile the implications of scripture with contemporary racial changes was one indication of how difficult it was for white evangelical leaders to cut themselves loose from their movement's origins.[26] Henry himself was perhaps the leading evangelical intellectual charting a course away from fundamentalism, but his equivocation about segregation revealed how limited was his call to resist "racial hatred." Despite extensive efforts to rebrand fundamentalism into a more respectable movement, making a clean break with their racial inheritance was difficult.[27] When leaders edged toward colorblind theologies, they had to navigate the contested terrain of white evangelical institutions and networks with a variety of committed stakeholders. Would the successful small businessman keep writing checks? Would the elder at the local church vouch for the theological rigor of an organization? Would the pastor assure anxious parents that their child would receive sound evangelical instruction at a particular college?[28] In the civil rights era, these long-standing concerns were becoming racial questions. Colorblind theology became another wedge in the emerging split between those who continued to proudly bear the label of fundamentalist and those who sought a more socially engaged evangelical faith able to command mainstream respect.

For many white evangelicals, upholding racial discrimination remained a matter of theological fidelity. After the flagship magazine of the Bible Institute of Los Angeles published a defense of integration in 1957, reader response was immediate and overwhelmingly negative. To these laypeople, defying the norms of sacred whiteness suggested that white evangelical elites were falling away from the rigors of biblical Christianity. One Colorado man took it as definitive evidence of the magazine's drift toward a "modernistic slant" and demanded that his subscription be cancelled. Another suggested that his subscription fee could be given to the author of the offending article to "help him to buy his one-way ticket to hell."[29] These white evangelicals perceived challenges to sacred whiteness as assaults on their very identities and most basic understandings of the world. A Southern Baptist man admitted, "My faith in religion has been shaken more" by the racial moderation of white evangelical elites "than anything that has happened in many a day." Precisely because white evangelicals' racial practices were sacred, calling them into question raised a host of theological concerns. He asked, "If Southern Baptists have been wrong for over a hundred years in practicing segregation, could they not be wrong as to many other things they stand for?"[30]

White evangelicals' nationwide commitment to sacred whiteness was especially evident in attitudes toward marriage. Howard Jones wrote that the subject of interracial marriage "almost always" came up in his conversations with white evangelicals wherever he went. The specter of interracial sexual contact loomed over all evangelical discussions of integration of their churches and schools, making it a highly significant factor in the shaping of their institutions. Jones knew of a white pastor who resigned his pastorate as soon as his daughters reached their teen years, to guard against the possibility of romances with the black boys in his church. Jones wrote, "The question, 'Would you want your daughter to marry a Negro?' haunts them."[31] Here, too, many white evangelicals imagined they had scripture on their side. Were not Israel's greatest kings led astray by their marriages to foreign women? By the 1960s, most white evangelical elites well understood it was a stretch to draw a one-to-one correspondence between Solomon's legendary harem and the contemporary question of interracial marriage. They took the view that interracial marriage was certainly unwise, but they also gingerly broke the bad news to their constituents: scripture did not seem to forbid it. Carl Henry admitted that "one can hardly say that racial intermarriage is per se wicked," but nonetheless he found growing acceptance of the practice "disquieting."³² These attitudes died hard, their decline better measured in decades than years.

Though sacred whiteness could justify social discrimination, it was even more concerned with the question of spiritual authority. In American society, one might hear whiteness associated with entitlement to political rule. In evangelicalism, whiteness was often associated with doctrinal purity and theological authority. Many white evangelicals were skeptical of African American Christians exercising spiritual authority over white Christians. They were much more comfortable ministering *to* African Americans or training them for separate black ministry. Bob Harrison, a black evangelical who spent four years preparing for ministry in the Assemblies of God denomination, vividly remembered the day in 1951 when the discriminatory reality dawned on him. He and some other seniors were appearing before the District Committee of Northern California and Nevada, the board that would give them their licenses to preach in the Assemblies of God. It was, he thought, a formality. When it was his turn he bounded into the room, eager to claim his credentials and celebrate with his family waiting outside. The superintendent had other ideas. He was awfully "proud" of Bob's work, he said, but he had some bad news. "I'm sorry, my brother, but it is not the policy of our denomination to grant credentials to Negroes."³³ Harrison came to believe that white evangelicals had built "pre-fabricated" walls ready to throw up at a moment's notice to "block the path of any Negro getting too spiritually 'uppity.'" Black evangelicals who felt a calling to minister in white organizations invariably faced the same question: "Don't you think you would have a more effective ministry among your own people?"³⁴

White evangelicals took care to teach the spiritual authority of whiteness to their children as well. In 1962, the official magazine of the Assemblies of God published a story instructing young readers in the supremacy of sacred whiteness. Set in the "heart of Africa," Sarah Lewis's didactic and inspirational tale centers on Naomi, a white missionary leading a Bible school, and Tomah, an endearing but "incorrigible" African boy. While Tomah's "little black playmates" collect firewood, thereby displaying their eagerness to "help their beloved white teacher," Tomah lounges on the grass, watching the birds in the trees. Naomi finally persuades Tomah to go gather firewood. While he walks down the path to the forest, Naomi kneels down to pray for Tomah's soul. On the path, Tomah's intractable nature is demonstrated when the birds again distract him. Then he happens upon a dead tree from which he decides to get a quick armful of inferior firewood. In this moment of transgression against his white teacher, Tomah faces a life-threatening danger. Climbing up into the dead tree, Tomah encounters a black mamba, a deadly African snake. Terrified, he prays, "Oh God, save me from this awful snake. I have been very lazy and naughty but I will not be so any more. I want to be your child now. Please help me get away from this snake!" God answers Tomah's prayer and he runs back into the arms of his white teacher, tears streaming down his face, to tell her of his near-death experience. "Will God let me be His child now, Teacher?" he asks. "Will he take away my badness if I ask Him?" Naomi promises Tomah that God will make him "all clean and new." As if the symbolism thus far had not been heavy-handed enough, Tomah's spiritual guilt is presented with stark racialization as the boy's question suddenly shifts: "Will He wash the blackness out of my heart and make it white?" Naomi assures him that God can accomplish even this, but he must understand that Jesus died for him and took the punishment that he deserved. "You know you deserve to be punished for your sins, don't you, Tomah?" Naomi asks. "Yes, White Teacher, I do," he replies. So Tomah bows in prayer and asks "Jesus to come into his heart." In this uplifting tale of regeneration, the removal of Tomah's "badness" becomes inseparable from the washing of his "blackness." The evidence of his conversion is clear for all to see, for Tomah immediately goes back down the path to collect firewood, and this time he brings back an excellent bundle of wood for his white teacher.[35]

The story of Tomah's conversion offered a very different moral than the vision of Christian colorblindness that would gain popularity in the coming years. In Tomah's story, the power of the gospel is demonstrated not in its colorblind transcendence of human boundaries, but in its capacity to bring even incorrigible blackness into the fold of sacred whiteness. Such stories were not unconscious expressions of racial paternalism of the sort one might expect in an era of colorblindness; they were *celebrations* of religio-racial superiority, tributes to sacred whiteness. In this context, when black evangelicals such as C. Herbert Oliver took to the pages of evangelical magazines and declared that, in Christ, everyone regardless of color was "entitled to all the benefits of Christ's redemption, both on earth" and in heaven, it was a bold rebuke of white evangelical attitudes. While white evangelicals basked in their supposed command of biblical doctrine, Oliver counseled black evangelicals that their "hardest task and most thankless role" was to "make God's love known to those who profess most strongly to know it." People who did not claim to be Christians might be open to a colorblind gospel, but black evangelicals often found that their white counterparts were their "greatest opponents" because they were "armed with rationalizations to make their prejudices appear to be righteous."[36]

As white supremacy retained a tenacious hold on American life through the early 1960s, in many places and institutions it was still possible for white evangelicals to ignore a critique like Oliver's and celebrate their religio-racial identities with little thought that they might entail profound theological problems or bring disrepute upon their communities. But these identities, narratives, and ways of imagining the world were coming under growing pressure. The mechanization of southern agriculture, the urbanization and unionization of African Americans, their northern migration, and their growing political clout all strained the system of white supremacy. Abroad, decolonization proceeded apace, disrupting European and American assumptions of entitlement to rule. At home, scattered black activism had coalesced into a mass movement that could not be ignored. If Americans did not yet speak of a "civil rights movement," words like "racial crisis" and "Negro revolution" were in the air. For decades, white evangelicals' discriminatory practices had situated their institutions comfortably in a national climate of white supremacy. Now, though the shape of things to come was yet unclear, any sentient American knew that the racial order was irrevocably changing. Alert evangelicals understood that such a transformation could never be merely about race. It raised questions about the future of their institutions and their movement. What if sacred whiteness no longer filled the pews? As visions of a colorblind nation and colorblind gospel gained ascendancy, white evangelicals' exclusionary practices faced an unprecedented threat.

The Rise of the Black Evangelicals

The early 1960s witnessed something new in American evangelicalism: a vocal and visible group of self-described black evangelicals pushing for racial change on the grounds that it was the *evangelical* thing to do. With the founding of the National Negro Evangelical Association in 1963, black evangelicals announced themselves as a force to be reckoned with in evangelical life. Their challenge was also a portent: it exposed the fault lines that would continue to mark evangelical racial initiatives right through the end of the century. From the 1950s, small numbers of black evangelicals trained at white evangelical colleges and Bible institutes had become more visible in evangelical ministries and media. Most notably, the Billy Graham Evangelistic Association (BGEA) added Howard Jones as its first black evangelist in 1958. These men (for they were almost invariably men) were thoroughly inside the evangelical theological camp. Suspicious of liberal Protestants and often skeptical of the black church, they matched theological rectitude with a conservative social and political outlook. On the question of racism, however, they parted ways with their white evangelical brethren. They grounded their argument in scripture and accused white evangelicals of not being evangelical enough. When that didn't work, they appealed to self-interest: only a colorblind evangelicalism would thrive in the world that was coming. These black evangelicals became early vocal exponents of a kind of colorblind Christianity. Evangelicalism, they believed, had the theological and institutional resources necessary to defeat racism if only evangelicals stopped carving out a racial exception to their principles. Black evangelicals' arguments for Christian unity anticipated the discourse that would come to dominate the white evangelical mainstream in later years. At a moment when racial discrimination remained pervasive, the call to transcend race through the power of Jesus Christ troubled white evangelical consciences and appealed to their entrepreneurial evangelizing spirit. At the time, it was difficult to conceive of how the rhetoric of Christian unity might be repurposed to invest in whiteness.

By virtue of his association with Graham, Howard Jones had a more visible platform than any other black evangelical of the period. Jones first encountered Graham in advance of the famous New York crusade of 1957. Graham was searching for a way to reach the city's black population, and Jones's reputation preceded him. He had already conducted an evangelistic tour through West Africa, established himself on radio, and held pastorates in the Bronx and Cleveland. Jones liked to tell of how, as a young man, God had saved him "from the world of jazz" and called him to preach the gospel. Jones was born in Cleveland, Ohio, in 1921. His parents, part of the fledgling black middle class in the city, cultivated Howard's love for music. He became a talented saxophonist and dreamed of making it big. But, he wrote, in reality, he "was a slave to it." His high school sweetheart helped him to see the light. Wanda Young was born in Oberlin, Ohio, in 1923, a daughter of the Great Migration. From her mother she learned of Jesus and from her father she heard stories of the lynching tree and Jim Crow justice in South Carolina. When she had a conversion experience of her own as a teenager, she told Howard he would have to choose: his music or Jesus. If he chose music, he might gain fame but he would lose both his soul and the girl he loved. One night Howard insisted on going to see a popular band play, but the music left him cold. Stumbling out of the dance hall, he cried out to God. If God would forgive his sins, Howard promised, "I will serve you the rest of my life." Jazz, dancing, theater, and all kinds of "worldly" amusements had to be given up. Wanda remembered Howard rushing to her house late that night with the joyful news: "God wants me to be a preacher!"[37]

With their sights set on a life of ministry, Howard and Wanda attended the Missionary Training Institute (later renamed Nyack College) outside New York City. Wanda remembered their years there in the early 1940s as "some of the best—and worst—days of [her] life." The rules were strict, the racial hierarchy overt. On one occasion a visiting missionary declared from the pulpit, "It takes the grace of God for a white man to love a colored man." Decades later, Wanda still remembered just how the missionary said those words. "The word colored wasn't spoken," she reflected, "it was spat." The very school that was training them repeatedly reminded them that their blackness made their missionary plans impractical. They quickly learned that "while God called His missionaries, it was mostly the white mission boards that sent them." White leaders informed Howard and Wanda that the people in foreign lands would not listen to black messengers of the gospel. Howard and Wanda learned that "the white community expected [them] to know '[their] place' and to be docile, smiling Christians." Though many doors were closed to them, others opened. When the chance to go to Liberia came, Howard jumped at it, and Wanda insisted on going, too. It was no exaggeration to say that Howard and Wanda had given up their grandest dreams so that they could preach the gospel. Through all their hardships—the travel, family separations, recurring bouts with malaria—they never seemed to doubt the trade was worth it.[38]

It is altogether fitting that Howard Jones went from the improvisation of jazz to the quick-on-his-feet requirements of navigating the performance of a black evangelical identity in a white evangelical world. Both required subtlety, practice, and more practice, until the performances looked like the most natural thing in the world. In the spring of 1957 Jones received a surprising letter from an associate of Billy Graham. The New York crusade was under way, but the crowds were all white. Could Jones help solve this problem? As Jones would later tell the story of their first meeting, Graham said, "I want to integrate these meetings. But I don't know how to do it. Would you be willing to come here and work with us for a few weeks to help us with this issue of integration?"[39] Jones agreed. His advice for Graham was simple: If he couldn't get African Americans to come to Madison Square Garden, he would have to go to them. "Billy," he said, "you need to go to Harlem." Jones helped to organize successful meetings in Harlem and Brooklyn and was gratified to see Graham preach to black audiences of thousands.[40]

The effort to reach black New Yorkers led Graham to take his most controversial racial actions to date. Bringing Jones into the fold was provocative. Inviting Martin Luther King to say a prayer at a crusade meeting stoked more vitriol from Graham's opponents. And at the end of the summer he reached out directly to a national black audience with an interview in *Ebony* magazine. Graham warned that everyone "shall stand before the judgment" of a colorblind God "to answer for . . . the way in which we have treated our neighbors."[41] Graham applied the words of Jesus in the Gospel of Matthew to white evangelicals' posture toward African Americans: "As you did it not to one of the least of these, you did it not to me." With such rhetoric, Graham repositioned the racial crisis from the political arena, where white evangelicals might imagine they could ignore it, to the much more personal realm of faithfulness to the gospel. By connecting racial prejudice so closely to the meaning of the gospel, Graham's *Ebony* interview pushed far beyond the comfort zone of his white constituency. Graham also had a parting shot for those who clung to theologies of white supremacy. "There are a lot of segregationists who are going to be sadly disillusioned when they get to Heaven—if they get there." For Graham, the interview garnered positive black press even as it further cemented his alienation from his fundamentalist roots. *Ebony* lauded Graham as the "Blonde, blue-eyed evangelist" who "has launched a frontal assault on prejudice and bigotry."[42]

In some ways the New York crusade was the high point of Graham's advocacy against racism during the civil rights era. The brief collaboration with Martin Luther King, the *Ebony* interview, Jones's arrival and the preaching in Harlem—all seemed to signal that Graham might push harder on civil rights in the future. Instead, as the civil rights movement laid bare the tensions in American society in ensuing years, Graham's politics of church primacy became clearer. Reaching out to African Americans during his New York crusade was an expression of the growing belief that there should be no color line in the body of Christ. It also happened to be evangelistically useful. Such a conviction did not mean that Graham was a racial liberal. He wanted African Americans on his team both to reach black and African audiences and to carefully challenge white audiences with a message of unity in Christ. Above all, he wanted black evangelicals who agreed with him that the race problem and its solution were spiritual.

Howard Jones seemed to fit the bill. Graham later wrote that "it was decided after much prayer that although we would continue to need him and use him in our work in the States, Howard Jones' greatest contribution to the Kingdom of God could be, and ought to be, made in Africa."[43] Jones also traveled frequently to the United States to preach on behalf of the BGEA and act as a point person to the black community when preparing for Graham to come to a city.[44] All of these roles carried considerable ambiguity for a black evangelist preaching a colorblind gospel. Jones took the positive view—that his blackness opened doors for him—rather than the more cynical interpretation that his blackness typecast him into certain channels of ministry. But when he later looked back on joining the Graham team from the vantage of nearly half a century, he was remarkably unsentimental about the role he believed he had played in the organization. Graham was looking for "someone who could transcend racial boundaries; someone whose theology was sound and whose approach was nonthreatening; someone who understood the subtle intricacies, the manner and vernacular of white evangelical culture. In short, someone who was safe."[45] Jones was hitting all the right notes.

His politics of church primacy added to his credibility in evangelical circles. Jones took it for granted that structural changes in the nation's political economy were less important than ecclesial changes in evangelicalism. His approach was theologically conservative and institutionally cautious. He wanted to shore up the foundations of the evangelical house, not tear it down. Though his support for the Civil Rights Act of 1964 without any apparent reservation made him unusual in the evangelical world, he still assumed that American racism was a spiritual problem amenable, in the final analysis, only to spiritual solutions. Yet even in this respect Jones challenged his audience. While many white evangelicals placed civil rights legislation and spiritual rebirth in oppositional categories—as though African Americans eating hamburgers at Woolworth's was at cross-purposes with convincing them to say the sinner's prayer—Jones saw them as complementary. But there was no question of which was most important. "Since the race problem is basically a moral and spiritual one, we must take a spiritual approach. We shall get at the heart of the race problem by getting at the hearts of both Negro and whites, and only Jesus Christ can do that. Christ is the final answer."[46]

All of this might sound like standard-issue evangelical fare, but the challenge Jones presented to white evangelicals should not be underestimated. His status as an evangelist for the BGEA was a newsworthy event because it upended racialized assumptions about who could exercise spiritual authority. Jones believed that many people around him resented his presence. Once, at a reception honoring Graham, Jones felt his isolation keenly as the only black person in the room. He distinctly heard one white minister say, "How did he get here?"[47] Jones denounced the white church as "silent, relaxed, compromising and miserably weak" in the struggle against racial injustice. He singled out white evangelical churches as strongholds of "unchristian" attitudes in need of "strong rebuke." These were the churches that put a For Sale sign on the door at the first hint of a black family arriving in the neighborhood, while taking pride in all the money they raised to send white missionaries to black Africa. "Such hypocrisy and insincerity brings a reproach on the work of God," Jones wrote.[48] This robust sense of rebuke combined with hope for Christian unity made Jones a challenging figure in evangelicalism. His colorblind rhetoric was aspirational and convicting, designed to provoke rather than placate. Precisely because he believed in the politics of church primacy, he demanded more of churches than many of them were willing to hear. Even as his reputation expanded as an honored member of the Graham team, many white churches would not receive him. One church wanted Jones to come only on the condition that he would not "raise the issues of evangelical responsibility to blacks in our services." They had heard of his rebukes, and they didn't want to be on the receiving end of one.[49]

Evangelicals prided themselves on living by the Bible. Jones used this to his advantage, pointing out all the biblical teachings that white evangelicals were ignoring. "The Bible unquestionably is the greatest book on justice in the world," he declared, "yet these Christians, preaching the Bible, evade the race issue and close their eyes to the terrible social injustices imposed upon the Negro in this country." Then he lowered the hammer: "White evangelicals must explain before God and society how they can reconcile their love for Christ and loyalty to the Bible with race prejudice and bigotry."[50] Looking at the same scripture as his white evangelical counterparts, Jones proposed a colorblind counternarrative. Didn't the First Letter of John say that anyone who claimed to love God yet hated his brother "abideth in death"?[51] Didn't the book of James warn believers that it was sinful to show favoritism?[52] On what basis could white evangelicals claim blackness created an exception to these commands? And if white evangelicals would only open their eyes, they might see a close parallel to their experience threaded throughout the New Testament. "The Apostle Paul tells us how God took the Gentiles and Jews and blended them together into one new man, one body through Christ and His Gospel," Jones wrote. Here he identified the quintessential New Testament theme that would become central to evangelical racial discourse for the next half century.

The problem was that evangelicals couldn't agree on what these texts meant. Jones thought the upshot was clear enough: "If the Bible tells us that there is no difference in Christ, then why do we make such a differentiation between races in the church?" He wrote eloquently about the pain of worshipping in white churches. "During the service the Negro worshipper often experiences a haunting loneliness and a sense of estrangement." The alienation began from the moment of walking into the sanctuary. *If* he was allowed inside, he was likely to be greeted by "the popular 'white stare,' as though he were a creature from outer space." And though the pastor might preach about "our oneness in Christ as believers," such inspiring words only drove home the point that "there are few white Christians who really practice this truth." Despite these experiences, Jones wrote with an audacious hope for the future. "When people of different races come to the cross and receive Christ as Savior," he declared, "they become brothers in the Lord and love one another with a pure heart fervently. In their relationship as believers, racial differences are lost in the spiritual union they find in Christ."[53] That this was patently untrue of white evangelicals did not mean that Jones was naïve. He felt that the love of God he had first experienced as a young man had transformed him and altered the trajectory of his whole life. He had dedicated his career to the proposition that this transformation could be shared.

Jones played an important role in the founding of the first institutional expression of his brand of black evangelicalism. In April 1963, a group of black evangelicals gathered in Los Angeles to form the National Negro Evangelical Association (later to be renamed the National Black Evangelical Association [NBEA]). Every member of the executive committee had attended a white evangelical college or Bible institute. The group named as its first president Marvin L. Printis, a graduate of Fuller Theological Seminary.[54] Among a who's who of black evangelical leaders including Jones and the young evangelist Tom Skinner, the only woman was Ruth Lewis, the InterVarsity Christian Fellowship activist who was shortly to become one of the first black women to integrate the University of Alabama.[55] Jones was invited to give the keynote address. When his scheduling commitments threatened to make him unable to travel all the way from Liberia to Los Angeles for the conference, Printis telegrammed Jones in desperation. They had been counting on Jones's name being attached to the conference. The "entire effort [was] in jeopardy" if Jones didn't show up, Printis pleaded. "Please help us."[56] Jones made his case to the Graham team. The conference would enable him to forge connections in advance of the planned Graham crusade in Los Angeles later that year. After all, "we do want to reach the Negro people," he pointed out.[57] Jones was eventually cleared to make the trip, though not without some grumbling. BGEA staffer George Wilson complained that Jones traveled thousands of miles "for that one colored convention." He added, "These fellows ought to soon buckle down and realize that we are not made of money."[58]

The NBEA boasted that its founding conference marked "the beginning of a new day for Negro religious life in America."[59] Taking note of this new group, *Eternity* editorialized, "Though its leaders would probably deny it, the existence of the association reflects the fact that the National Association of Evangelicals has ignored the race problem and has not seriously sought any solutions."[60] Its leaders did deny it. Jones was eager to avoid any sense of rupture with white evangelicalism. "We do not see this as being in competition with the National Assn. of Evangelicals or any other group," he claimed.[61] Instead, he described the NBEA as primarily a vehicle to promote the gospel and foreign missions among African Americans. But it was also undeniably a means of increasing the visibility of black evangelicals in white evangelical discourse. One NBEA member introduced himself to the readers of a white evangelical magazine as an exotic phenomenon: "Possibly the very term 'Negro evangelical' will raise questions in your mind. Questions like: 'who are these persons called Negro evangelicals? Why have we not heard of them before?'"[62] With the formation of the NBEA, black evangelicals now had an institutional home to help explain themselves to their white evangelical brethren.

Though the NBEA would become more confrontational as the decade wore on, it is hard to gainsay the conservatism of its early years. Various strains of black fundamentalism contributed to the rise of the self-declared black evangelicals, and the NBEA's leaders had been trained in white evangelical schools. William H. Bentley, later the fourth president of the NBEA, thought this inheritance had a big impact. "Since we were trained in such institutions it was virtually unavoidable that we would as unconsciously absorb the same views as those who taught us."[63] Ronald Potter, a Wheaton College graduate who sought to move the NBEA in a more race-conscious direction, faulted black evangelicals for too often seeing "Black Christianity through White eyes."[64] Thus, there is little reason to doubt the sincerity of Jones's claim at the time of the NBEA's founding that it was not intended as a challenge to white evangelicalism. Indeed, many of the early leaders were so invested in the idea of Christian unity across racial lines that there was, according to Bentley, confusion about the NBEA's identity. If the NBEA was only for black people, "Were we any different from white Christians in whose institutions of the time we were for the most part not welcome?"[65]

The founding of the NBEA was an important institutional development for the future of evangelicalism. Though it remained a tiny organization in comparison to the mammoth National Association of Evangelicals, it served as a locus for black evangelical networking, activism, and, by the later 1960s, increasingly strong criticism of white evangelicals. Throughout the climactic years of the civil rights movement, black evangelical voices rang loud and clear in the world of evangelical media. They ensured that as evangelicals debated the civil rights movement and the meaning of Christian unity, it could not be a whites-only discussion. In the process, they provided powerful impetus for color-blind visions to overcome a legacy of sacred whiteness.

Debating Civil Rights, Debating Oneness in Christ

For most evangelicals, the civil rights movement was an occasion to double down on the politics of church primacy. While mainstream media discussed the virtues of civil rights bills in Congress, evangelicals debated the responsibilities and prospects of their own institutions in an age of racial crisis. Coverage of the movement in evangelical media had been episodic in the 1950s and early 1960s, but in 1963 there was a noticeable uptick in evangelical racial discussion as the Birmingham Campaign and the March on Washington drew national attention. "Let's not kid ourselves," *Eternity* warned its readers, "this is a revolution. And before it is over it will affect your family, your community and your church."[66] With Bibles in one hand and legislative demands in the other, black activists put white evangelical leaders in a bind. "Don't get the idea these fellas have been sitting around in cloistered studies thinking this one out," said a Tennessee minister. "The Negro has simply besieged us."[67] As evangelicals sought to calibrate their movement's appeal amid the confusion of changing racial norms, the question of oneness in Christ became a key fault line. Many white evangelicals attempted to cast an ethereal vision of unity in Christ without social implications, but most black evangelicals countered with a more concrete notion. Howard Jones thought that a colorblind gospel was a mortal threat to the discrimination he had experienced in white evangelical spaces. But as evangelicals awakened to the racial crisis, a more ambiguous reality came into view. In this contest, evangelicals would deploy theologies of racial colorblindness to elevate black voices and to silence them, to press for change and to hold the line, to break down barriers and to rebuild them. The colorblind turn might advance the interests of the evangelical church, but whether it was an instrument of black liberation remained to be seen.

In 1963, the Alabama steel town of Birmingham became a crucible refracting differing visions of churchly responsibility and Christian unity. Martin Luther King came to Birmingham not only as a radical political activist, but as a Baptist minister speaking simple theological truths. The "church is the Body of Christ," King had declared in a 1956 speech. "So when the church is true to its nature it knows neither division nor disunity." To white Christians King said, "I am disturbed about what you are doing to the Body of Christ."[68] King's arrest and confinement in Birmingham produced one of the most famous documents of the movement, which was, among other things, a theological brief against white churches. His "Letter from Birmingham City Jail" criticized churches for "commit[ting] themselves to a completely otherworldly religion which made a strange distinction between body and soul, the sacred and the secular."[69] For King, the church was at once spiritual and social, with God-given responsibilities in both spheres.

King's opponents cast a much less expansive vision of the church's responsibility amid a social crisis. The pastor of Birmingham's First Baptist Church, Earl Stallings, exemplified the dominant white evangelical sensibility. He was one of the eight white religious leaders who composed the open letter to which Martin Luther King responded from jail. Just a day after Stallings and the other clergy published the letter calling for an end to the protest campaign, a group of black activists arrived at First Baptist for the Easter Sunday worship service. Pastor Stallings made sure they were seated and he personally shook their hands. For

Stallings, opposition to the tactics of the Birmingham Campaign could coexist comfortably with a sense of Christian courtesy and welcome in the house of God.

Before Stallings knew it, his photograph was splashed across the front page of the *New York Times* and reprinted nationwide.[70] He had not intended to make a grand political statement. Nor did he want to become a lightning rod for controversy. He had merely done what he saw as his Christian duty. For taking this stance—and because a photographer captured the handshake—Stallings became a celebrated figure. Though he received many angry letters from white southerners, a much larger number of appreciative letters poured into his office from Christians all over the country. Writers praised him for his "wonderful demonstration of Christian courage and Christian love." A missionary commended Stallings for his action "heard around the world." A Pennsylvania woman wrote, "Only by such acts are we going to arrive at any positive solution for the tragic misunderstandings that are tearing apart our country."[71] The celebration of Pastor Stallings as a heroic figure exemplified the declining popularity of strong segregationist stands in the church and the growing conviction that a Christian sanctuary should be a place where all people were welcomed without respect to color.[72] But it did not necessarily connote support for black goals in the freedom struggle.

The question of the church's social responsibilities led evangelical reactions to Martin Luther King to split sharply along racial lines. Many black evangelicals deeply admired King, even if they didn't agree with him in all the particulars. Howard Jones met Dr. King for the first time at the 1957 New York crusade and crossed paths with him several times thereafter. When asked what stood out to him about Dr. King, Jones said, "It was his utter devotedness to civil rights, his utter devotedness to the task of emancipating black people. Emancipating black people from prejudice, inferior housing, inferior schools, unemployment, racism. He was a completely devoted man." Rather than seeing King as a troublemaker, Jones admired his commitment to pursuing freedom through the force of nonviolent Christian love. Jones said, "I always carried away . . . an impression of a man in a deeply reflective mood. I think he lived every moment for his cause, for our cause, indeed for the cause of all mankind."[73] In contrast, many white evangelicals found King's methods and his claims infuriating. In an indignant open letter in response to Dr. King's letter from Birmingham City Jail, Carl McIntire accused King of inventing a false gospel and imposing it on the American people by force, with the threat of civil disobedience and chaos if they didn't comply with King's whims. The true gospel was a message of sin and repentance and the regeneration of the individual heart, and the church was the proper vehicle for this gospel.[74]

McIntire was no outlier. In the summer of 1963, while the National Council of Churches threw its support behind the civil rights bill, evangelicalism's leading light sounded the alarm about the dangers of civil rights activism. In August, Billy Graham embarked on a month-long crusade in Los Angeles. On the evening of August 27, as he looked out on a crowd of 37,000 people, he spoke about the racial crisis gripping the nation. It was the day before the March on Washington for Jobs and Freedom. In contrast to later nostalgic memories of a peaceful march, dread stalked the nation's capital. Many white Americans expected violence. One white evangelical observer predicted that there would "possibly be the worst race riot in the history of the country in our capital." Amid this climate of anxious anticipation, Graham's words were bound to resonate. His voice boomed across the stadium: "I am convinced that some extremists are going too far too fast," he declared. "Forced integration will never work." The racial crisis would "not be settled in the streets but it could be settled in the hearts of man."[75] At this decisive inflection point, Graham could have embraced civil rights activists and linked his colorblind gospel with the demands coming from the streets. Instead, he borrowed language from segregationists and framed the gospel as an alternative to black aspirations for freedom.

Some black evangelicals were appalled. Marvin Printis, in his new role as NBEA president, called Graham's words "trite and demoralizing," and he charged that Graham "consistently fails to appreciate the intensity of this great social dilemma which cries out to be met headon [sic].... To preach regeneration as the only answer to such a pressing social ill is to so oversimplify the Gospel that it could never appeal to the people of the earth now in the throes of a revolutionary movement, including the Negroes."[76] This intra-evangelical spat carried on in full public view illustrated the institutional importance of the NBEA. The United Press International wire report described Printis as the head of a 20,000-strong black evangelical organization. Whether the NBEA had really secured such a large membership mere months into its existence is doubtful but beside the point. Rather than a lonely critic, Printis suddenly appeared to be speaking on behalf of a major evangelical constituency unhappy with evangelicalism's biggest star. Having made himself a lightning rod with his criticisms of Graham, Printis eventually exited the presidency, which was assumed by the less threatening figure of Howard Jones. Though Jones did not always agree with Graham's decisions, he never aired his disagreements publicly. With a Billy Graham associate in the office, everyone could rest assured there would be no more sensational headlines describing NBEA attacks on "America's Pastor."[77]

The day after Graham's warning against "forced integration," the March on Washington went forward without support from white evangelical leaders. On the steps of the Lincoln Memorial, King spoke about Christian unity in a more secular idiom. He declared, "I have a dream my four little children will one day live in a nation where they will not be judged by the color of their skin but by the content of their character."[78] In this iconic moment, King articulated the ur-text of colorblind America. Though he might have deplored the uses that would be made of this phrase in later decades, the sincerity of his hope was not in doubt.[79] It was a hope infused with eschatological longing. To imagine black and white children walking hand in hand in Alabama was "Thy kingdom come" translated into the American vernacular. While many white evangelicals put their hopes in a heavenly tomorrow, black activists insisted Christian unity could be made tangible today. As the Reverend James Lawson said, "The Christian favors the breaking down of racial barriers because the redeemed community of which he is already a citizen recognizes no barriers dividing humanity."[80] For King, the great failure of white Christians was their refusal to bring this spiritual yearning down to the level of the concrete where they lived.

With everyone from white Protestant ministers and Jewish rabbis to President Kennedy himself now speaking of civil rights legislation as a moral imperative, some white evangelical leaders fretted about their movement's image. "The massive demonstration was void of official evangelical representation," *Christianity Today* admitted in the days after the March on Washington. "Our folks are sympathetic with solving the race problem," one leader was quick to say, "but we feel that this wasn't the way to go about it." The editorial plaintively asked, "But what *is* the way?"⁸¹ Exhibiting a profound uneasiness, many white evangelicals could not bring themselves to proactively support the movement, yet they also worried that the evangelical church was somehow failing in its responsibility. For some, the very existence of the civil rights movement was prima facie evidence that the church had missed the mark. If evangelicals had been doing their job, spiritual solutions would have solved the problem before it emerged as a crisis on the nation's streets.⁸² Many white evangelicals found themselves in the position Martin Luther King thought so exasperating: "I agree with you in the goal you seek, but I can't agree with your methods."⁸³

When white evangelicals did critique their movement's inaction, they were often careful to clarify that their proposed solutions fell squarely within the politics of church primacy. *Eternity* criticized white evangelicals for being "ostrich-like with [their] heads in the sand" while a revolution swirled around them. "For too long we've contented ourselves with platitudes," instead of taking decisive action, the magazine lamented. But moving beyond platitudes did not necessarily mean joining the civil rights crusade. Instead, white evangelicals needed only to enlarge their vision of the body of Christ: "if there are Negroes living in your community, these Negroes are as much the spiritual responsibility of the church as the whites are."⁸⁴ And white evangelicals' responsibility extended beyond the church walls. If a black family moved into a white neighborhood, white evangelicals must love them. In fact, the editorial implied that people who failed to love African Americans might not be true Christians at all. Lack of love was a serious problem because it got in the way of preaching the gospel. *Eternity* asked its readers to consider if they were forcing their neighbors into "a Negro ghetto where they have neither the chance nor the inclination to hear the saving gospel of Jesus Christ?" If white evangelicals did not bring them the message, how would they hear? Somehow, white evangelicals could be at once "ostrich-like" with "heads in the sand" and also the only reliable bearers of the gospel message to the black community.⁸⁵

The bombing of the Sixteenth Street Baptist Church in Birmingham that September added to the pressures white evangelical leaders felt. In Grand Rapids, Michigan, three hundred Calvin College students marched in support of a civil rights law. The editor of the student newspaper declared that the "middle ground" had vanished and they now faced a stark choice: "One either actively protests injustice to the black man or hates him."[86] The black evangelical Bill Pannell watched the news in horror. The bomb, he wrote, "shattered more than brick and plaster.... It blistered my evangelical conscience." After Birmingham, Pannell felt he "could no longer be a standard evangelical Christian, content merely to preach a typical evangelical Gospel." He had to find out how the gospel connected to the life-and-death struggles of the contemporary racial crisis. After Birmingham, "the illusion was over."[87]

In the aftermath of the bombing, *Christianity Today* published the most forceful denunciation of the white evangelical mainstream ever seen in its pages to that time. William Henry Anderson Jr. accused white evangelicals of being more easily awakened by "threat to profit or property" than moral appeal. Accordingly, Anderson was not above appealing to self-interest. He warned that inaction during the racial crisis "could so discredit the evangelical cause as to bring it to disrepute and oblivion." What was to be done about this looming public relations disaster? The very first thing evangelicals ought to do, he suggested, is "assert the oneness of all believers in Christ." Anderson's forceful denunciation of evangelical indifference combined with such a seemingly esoteric solution was characteristic of some white evangelicals' halting steps toward colorblind theologies. "We may never be able to rid ourselves of the consciousness that the man to whom we are speaking is Negro," he admitted. "But we can stop hurting our fellow in Christ."[88] For Anderson, oneness in Christ was not an abstraction at all. It was an urgent project that revealed God's work to the world. Through Jesus, God reconciled people to himself and to each other. If white and black evangelicals would better demonstrate this in the United States, they would not only secure evangelicalism's credibility, but help black people as well.

Though the events of 1963 jarred the conscience of some white evangelicals, most continued to evince a remarkable ability to combine social pessimism with spiritual utopianism. As Sam Boyle, a pastor in the Reformed Presbyterian Church of North America, put it, "Humanistic liberals, with no faith in the Bible God and nothing to offer sinners except the mirage of a socialistic Paradise of good will, are marching with the Negroes and going to jail." Boyle believed evangelicals had a better prescription for what ailed the nation. Instead of the "many absurd and extreme statements and demands" of "the Negro . . . determined . . . to force himself on the white majority," evangelicals had to "confess fearlessly the Bible truth that in Christ there is no racial inequality." The solution to the racial crisis would come from those who realized that "man's sinful nature" was the root problem, and conversion the final cure. Only then could the truth that "ye are all one in Christ Jesus" be made real.[89] It is tempting to dismiss Boyle's views as convenient white excuses for inaction. But in fact, the elevation of spiritual over social solutions united many evangelicals across the color line in this period. NBEA secretary Joseph Brown lamented that "many Negro seminary students have been hoodwinked into believing the non-biblical dream of social peace through human efforts." In contrast, he said, even though black evangelicals such as himself had felt the pain of discrimination, they maintained that "the New Birth" was more important than "social justice."[90]

While Congress continued its marathon debate of the civil rights bill, Billy Graham prepared to go to the epicenter of the racial crisis to present an evangelical answer to the nation's troubles. He was going to hold an integrated crusade in Birmingham. Amid controversy and heightened security, Graham arrived for an Easter Sunday service at the Legion Field football stadium, one year after the drama of April 1963. Preaching to a mixed crowd of 35,000, Graham delivered a classic gospel sermon while steering clear of Birmingham's racial troubles. The service drew widespread acclaim across American media.[91] Described as the largest integrated gathering in Alabama's history, pundits and pastors and ordinary Alabamians pronounced it a key step in the healing of Birmingham. The city's moderate mayor declared that "Billy Graham has brought out the best in us," a measure of praise conspicuously lacking for black activists. For many evangelicals, the Graham crusade was a prototypical example of productive racial action. No demands were made, no boycotts launched, no injunctions defied. Instead, ordinary people, black and white together, worshipped God and experienced real human contact. Howard Jones wrote that the crusade had been a powerful demonstration of the unity that was possible in Christ.[92] At the altar call, some 4,000 people came forward. A white woman who found herself sitting beside an African American for the first time in her life said, "When she put out her hand to shake mine and smiled, I couldn't refuse."[93] Such anecdotes painted a seductive portrait of racial progress that possessed great appeal among white evangelicals and the broader American public.

Graham's Birmingham crusade met with a euphoric response because it represented something very unusual: integrated worship. As churches became sites of protest in Birmingham and elsewhere, congregations engaged in heated debates about whether to admit black members. The audacity of black activists who picketed churches and engaged in "kneel-ins" deeply offended many white evangelicals. For white evangelicals who believed in the spirituality of the church, a sphere held separate from state and politics, it seemed that crass political aims were polluting sacred space.[94] Yet the arguments of those opposing an open-door policy betrayed a growing sense that sacred whiteness was losing its power to persuade. While the old claims of Jim Crow as a sacred order continued to be made, far more important were appeals to social custom, protection of children, and, perhaps above all, the financial health of the local church. After all, integration might cause major donors to stop writing checks.[95]

To be sure, white evangelical advocates of church integration had their own set of self-interested arguments—protecting the movement's reputation, the credibility of foreign missions, and the watching eyes of the younger generation—but oftentimes they supported integration because they felt their personal faith commitments left them with no choice. One man at First Baptist Church of Tallahassee, Florida, who had thought his mind was made up in favor of segregation, declared, "In a spiritual experience God turned me around and said, 'Don't you ever again in all your life hold the view you have been holding.'" From that moment he became a supporter of an open-door policy. A week after the church refused entry to five African American worshippers, another man at First Baptist went from an intractable opponent of integration to a supporter after getting down on his knees to pray and seeing, in his mind's eye, the five black activists outside the church and Jesus Christ himself standing at the pulpit. "What is he going to do?" he asked himself. "Is He going to turn them away?"[96] The man knew the answer, and so he knew what he had to do. Supporting an open-door policy did not necessarily make one a racial liberal, or a supporter of the civil rights movement as such. Indeed, the experiential power of such personal encounters with Jesus may have strengthened evangelicals' conviction that racial progress came through such life-altering mystical experiences rather than divisive protests.

In 1964, white evangelical media published profiles of integrated churches as models of Christian leadership on a difficult issue. The tone of these articles assumed white readers all over the country would be unfamiliar with integrated worship, fearful or awkward around black Christians, and generally full of questions about what to do. These articles also began to articulate a vision of Christian colorblindness to challenge segregated churches. Iola Parker's profile of an integrated church in Pittsburgh described Harriet Davis, a nearly saintly black woman—always patient, always kind, always forgiving—as the key actor in the integration drama. Meant to be complimentary to African Americans while assuaging white fears, the portrait had the effect of demanding black perfection in integrated spaces. Parker based her case for church integration on colorblind sentimentality rooted in the consciousness of children. In one pivotal scene, Harriet and Iola listen to the church children's choir on Christmas Eve, "a black and white checkerboard of little faces." Then Iola whispers, "It is the little children, like these, who will finally straighten out this racial mess, isn't it?" Harriet replies, "Bless their little hearts. They don't know there's any difference in black and white." As Parker zooms out from this intimate scene, she asks the reader, "Need they ever know? They never will—unless we tell them. And are we so sure there *is*?"[97]

Other evangelical advocates of church integration admitted it was not as simple as Parker implied. In "The Case of the Colorblind Church," Judi Culbertson suggested that it would take years of painstaking efforts and deliberate planning for the average church to become integrated. She believed the experience of Philadelphia's Tenth Presbyterian Church bore this out. By 1964, the congregation had already been integrated for over a decade and had "20 Negro members who participate in church life as deacons, quartet members, as Sunday school superintendents." But Culbertson pointed out that Tenth Presbyterian had several unique advantages that other churches might not have. The pastor worked for years to make sure the congregation was "spiritually prepared" for the change, and integration occurred "before the Negro Revolution really got started, before every action of the Negro community was scrutinized with such concentrated suspicion and fear." Tenth Presbyterian also benefited from its status as a downtown church with a "large commuting congregation" that made for "less social mingling." For ordinary community churches in the throes of the revolution, integration was likely to be a much harder sell. Nonetheless, integration had to be pursued, not because it was expedient but because it was right. "Racial discrimination, no matter how many good excuses we may have for it, is wrong in the eyes of God," she wrote. Like Howard Jones, Culbertson appealed to the New Testament example of Jewish and Gentile believers becoming united. It would take years of laborious work "on a personal basis" to change attitudes. She portrayed church integration not as complementary to political liberalism but as a hedge against it. It was urgent to begin the work of integration now so that African Americans would have solid Bible-believing churches to attend as black churches moved toward "a liberal social thrust." Pulpit and choir exchanges were one place to start.[98] As timid as such appeals might appear today, in 1964 they represented a significant challenge to sacred whiteness.

Black evangelicals continued to be among the most robust proponents of colorblind theology as they attacked their exclusion from white evangelical spaces. King A. Butler, pastor of St. John's Missionary Baptist Church in North Carolina, declared, "For a Christian (white or colored) to deal with another person on the basis of color is to eliminate the grace of God." In Butler's view, only those who had experienced the grace of God through saving faith in Jesus Christ were prepared to solve America's racial problems. So total was the reorientation of one's identity upon turning to Jesus Christ that race should no longer even be mentioned in the church. Butler went on, "Where Christ is supreme, our hearts and minds will bend to His will. And then, yellow skin, red skin, white skin, or black skin will not be a motivating factor for our relationships with one another."[99] NBEA secretary Joseph Brown agreed. "The solution to America's race problem is the 'grace' problem," he wrote. "If all true Christians would both tell and live this glorious gospel of the grace of God, the race problem insofar as black and white saints are concerned would vanish into the shadows of the past."[100]

Though black evangelicals could lapse into vague platitudes as easily as white evangelicals, there was a nuance to their views often lacking among their white counterparts. Brown portrayed black evangelicals as a people caught between the liberal civil rights movement, which had positive social concern but lacked proper doctrine, and white evangelicalism, which had correct doctrine but was disastrously deficient in social concern. While black evangelicals often advocated unity in Christ as the foundation of social equality, white evangelicals often described unity in Christ as a *substitute* for equality. As Billy Graham's father-in-law, L. Nelson Bell, put it, the church faced "the urgent necessity of removing all barriers to spiritual fellowship in Christ, without at the same time attempting to force un-natural social relationships." Black evangelicals found these distinctions exasperating. Joseph Brown criticized white evangelicals for claiming to be faithful to scripture while practicing discrimination. How could they preach "Sonship only through faith in Christ" and then "ignore the black man who is a *brother* in Christ"? He put his finger on the vital and uncomfortable question of what exactly unity in Christ meant. "The Negro evangelical," he wrote, cannot "understand how we are one in Christ but socially inferior." Brown shared all the conservative doctrine of his white evangelical peers, so his critiques of the movement hit close to home: "Apparently, some believe that Christianity is only a white man's possession."[101]

Despite Brown's complaint, many white evangelicals went on insisting that unity in Christ had no bearing whatsoever on the question of social equality. "Just because I don't want to socialize with them," one Georgia woman said, "in no way means I don't care about their souls."[102] For some white evangelical leaders, such care for the soul was the acid test. Leroy Gardner of the *Evangelical Beacon* told his readers that they had a responsibility to preach the gospel to "the American Negro" just the same as anyone. But that was their only responsibility. "Social and economic discrimination" were matters of "personal prerogative." Behind the evangelistic imperative was the persistent assumption that white evangelicals owned the gospel. Gardner described the black church as a veritable hellhole of heresy, emotional excess, and immoral behavior. Thus, if white evangelicals didn't preach to African Americans, how would they hear the gospel? "You'll find Negroes congenial by nature and receptive to any friendly gesture," Gardner assured his readers. And besides, "it is not necessary to socialize with the Negro; just witness to him."[103] With such bald pronouncements some white evangelicals tried to give the narrowest possible definition to oneness in Christ.

Other white evangelicals testified it was through social encounters on an equal footing that their views were transformed. Judi Culbertson wrote, "I have been amazed to talk to person after person who, when they got to really *know* one Negro well, found that their abstract prejudices and fears were greatly dissolved."[104] Even passing encounters might be employed as racial lessons for evangelical audiences. A Colorado woman wrote that on two separate occasions when she had car problems on a busy highway "the white people buzzed right by" while "it was a Negro who came to our rescue." Drawing on white evangelicals' shared familiarity with the parable of the Good Samaritan, she asked, "Does this remind you of any particular Bible story?"[105] White evangelicals put a lot of stock in such experiences. They fit well with their view of how social change occurred. The evangelical governor of Oregon, Mark Hatfield, wrote, "Ultimately, the solution must be found in the hearts and minds—and actions—of each of us as individuals."[106] If some critics saw such individualizing rhetoric as an excuse for inaction, many evangelicals understood it as a call to supply the essential spiritual and moral force without which legal change would be hollow.

The remarkable trajectory of Bob Harrison's career seemed to illustrate the possibilities of this gradual and church-based method of change. After the Assemblies of God rejected his ordination in 1951, Harrison had persisted in the orbit of white evangelicalism and was eventually rewarded for his pains. In 1960, he joined Howard Jones to conduct crusades in Africa on behalf of the BGEA. In 1962, he became a part-time Graham Associate and finally received the ordination denied to him a decade earlier.[107] Like Jones, Harrison was deeply conservative. There was little theological daylight between him and Graham. At an Assemblies of God conference, Harrison spoke to his overwhelmingly white audience "as an American Christian who happens to be a 'man of color.'" He said, "I cannot help but emphasize that although political and economic pressure can help curb the racial problem, only Christ and His gospel can solve it."[108] Such rhetoric invoked race for the purpose of deemphasizing racial justice activism, assuring white evangelicals that a colorblind gospel fulfilled their evangelistic mandate and promoted racial progress. By emphasizing the primacy of spiritual solutions to racial problems, Harrison was able to overcome his outsider status as a black man in a white movement.

But as the sense of racial crisis deepened in 1965 and beyond, it became increasingly clear that black evangelicals' colorblind appeals might trouble some white evangelical consciences and open up ministry opportunities for men like Harrison and Jones, but that did little to promote decisive action on behalf of black freedom. Howard Jones believed his call to transcend race through the power of Christ was the crucial missing ingredient in the civil rights revolution he supported. To his surprise, many white evangelicals used the same spiritual claims to oppose that very revolution. While Jones sang Martin Luther King's praises, most white evangelicals believed King had missed the mark. As one Pennsylvania woman put it, "The problem is not skin but sin and Christ is the cure." She believed King's radical politics and protests failed to deal with the real problem of sin in the human heart.[109] "Often when thinking of the civil rights movement my heart has bled for the Negro who has been treated so unjustly," one white evangelical declared. "But over and over again the word of Christ comes to me: What shall it profit the Negro if he gain all the civil rights guaranteed him but lose his own soul? The latter is the dynamic work of the Church—it is committed to this one great task, and the sooner we get to it the sooner will injustices be solved."[110] The beloved community of civil rights activists' dreams would not come about through direct action or federal legislation. Instead, evangelical churches would save souls. If this traditional message was taking on a new veneer of colorblind inclusion, the goal remained the same: growing evangelicalism and saving America, one heart at a time.

Conclusion

When clergy from all over the United States came to Selma, Alabama, to participate in the voting rights campaign of 1965, white evangelical leaders were absent. In fact, in the days after police in Selma assaulted nonviolent protestors, and white supremacists bludgeoned to death pastor James Reeb, Clyde W. Taylor, the secretary general of the National Association of Evangelicals (NAE), was busy knocking down rumors that the NAE was lobbying for voting rights legislation. "The official stand of the NAE on the whole race issue, including Selma," he wrote, "is that we do not take a stand on it. We are neither for nor against."

In a telephone conversation with an evangelical who wanted the NAE to support the civil rights movement, Taylor's assistant explained, "The NAE has a policy of not becoming involved in political or sociological affairs that do not affect the function of the church or those involved in the propagation of the gospel."[111] This was false. In fact, the NAE was not just an umbrella group for white evangelical denominations, it was a lobbying arm with a history of political entanglements.[112] But in the face of the most grotesque and deadly forms of racism, the nation's leading body of white evangelicals declared its neutrality. If such a stance alienated some black evangelicals, it effectively maintained the unity of the NAE's white constituencies. The story was similar at the Southern Baptist Convention (SBC). Southern Baptist elites, careful not to get too far ahead of their constituents and seeking to hold the convention together at nearly any cost, continued to welcome Montague Cook and men like him as brothers in Christ. During the civil rights era, the convention deliberately remained in fellowship with overtly white supremacist churches.[113] As far as the NAE and the SBC were concerned, the life-and-death struggle of African Americans to live in freedom took a backseat to the goal of maintaining the unity of white churches.

The most high-profile evangelical response to the Selma crisis came from Billy Graham. Reprising his role in Birmingham the year before, when Graham heard of the violence in Selma he began planning an evangelistic crusade in Montgomery. As the Graham team prepared for the crusade Howard Jones was at his post in Liberia but planned to return to the United States shortly. "I would like to be with you and the team for these meetings," Jones wrote. "I have arranged my schedule, Billy, so that I can be with you in Montgomery, that is, if you should need me." Besides assisting with the evangelistic enterprise, Jones was finishing up his book on the race problem and he believed he could gain helpful insights in Montgomery. Jones seemed to be aware he was making a big request. In a separate missive to Graham's right-hand man, Walter Smyth, Jones wrote, "I do not know if I have the right to ask" to come to Montgomery. In both letters, Jones went out of his way to emphasize that his intentions were appropriately evangelical. He wanted to bring the message of the gospel to black and white Alabamians alike. He was sure that "Christ is the answer," and he praised Graham's "courage" and his ability to "ease racial tensions."[114]

Without saying it outright, Jones was promising not to stir the pot. His desire to be in Montgomery was not an idle curiosity or a civil rights project; he would be there as a loyal Graham evangelist. A full week later, Jones received his answer in a terse telegram: "Team feels due to extremely tense situation you should not plan on crusade, as requested." The following week Graham himself followed up: "I am not sure that it would be wise for you to come to Montgomery just now."[115] Jones's exclusion from the Montgomery crusade was a plain and simple effort to appease white supremacist opinion. The presence of a black evangelist would indeed have raised tensions. Graham believed it would be worthwhile to preach the gospel without such controversy. The evangelistic calculus was changing, but in Montgomery, Alabama, in the spring of 1965, Christian colorblindness was still a bridge too far. Sacred whiteness still held sway there and could still be placated. The incident had the shape of a parable outlining the future of Christian colorblindness. Jones was the black supplicant seeking inclusion, and Graham was the white evangelical power broker gauging the comfort level of the white majority and the imperatives of evangelization to determine the terms and pace of that inclusion.

The later 1960s tested the limits of Howard Jones's endurance. He bluntly described his anguish about racial discrimination in evangelicalism. "White evangelicals often tell me how much they love colored people. But I shudder when I hear this," he said. If they loved people, they would act on their behalf. "If our Lord were here in earthly body he would be walking the streets of the ghettos ministering to the poor." Instead, most of Jesus's white evangelical followers "bypass the Negro and his problems like the priest and the Levite passed by the wounded man in the story of the Good Samaritan." But Jones never yielded in his hope for the future, and his message never wavered. Through the gospel of Jesus Christ, black and white evangelicals could "realize their oneness in Christ as believers" and change the world together.[116]

As black evangelical frustration with white evangelicals increased in the later 1960s, their criticisms became more pointed and more race conscious. George M. Perry, the third president of the NBEA, declared that Billy Graham–style evangelicalism was no longer relevant for black Americans. "We believe in the content of the message, but we can't go along with its suburban, middle-class white-orientation that has nothing to say to the poor nor to the black people."[117] This was a hard-hitting attack on the white evangelical turn toward Christian colorblindness. If Graham, of all people, was not actually preaching the colorblind gospel he claimed, what hope was there for white evangelicalism to transcend the racial divide? Jones's dream of evangelical unity across racial lines would play out in the years ahead not in the pages of magazines but in the church sanctuaries and college classrooms of the evangelical movement. The civil rights movement had set the stage for the real battle to come in evangelicalism. The struggle for racial justice and colorblind Christianity would be won or lost in white evangelical institutions themselves. There, as a new generation of black evangelicals demanded inclusion while insisting on the importance of their blackness, the next chapter in the rise of Christian colorblindness was written.

2

Creating the Colorblind Campus

Founder's Week, 1970, Moody Bible Institute (MBI): it was the most important week of the year for the storied college founded by the famous nineteenth-century evangelist D. L. Moody. Melvin Warren and Leona Jenkins knew a public protest at this time and place would have maximum impact. Warren and Jenkins might have fit the profile of hundreds of other recent graduates of the college, but for one important difference: they were black. On a cold day in February, Leona Jenkins stood on the doorstep of the college holding a large handwritten sign—"Woe unto you, hypocrites"—while Melvin Warren ceremoniously ripped their diplomas and tossed them in a trashcan. Warren told the media the protest was designed to draw attention to the "institutional white racism" of Moody Bible Institute. It certainly did that. To the administration's chagrin, national media picked up the story and soon MBI faced a blizzard of accusations surrounding its history of segregated dorms and other forms of discrimination against black students. White students and administrators responded defensively. The dramatic protest had hit its mark and raised a potent question. Were white evangelical colleges places of Christian community for all people, or were they yet another site where investment in whiteness was cloaked in the name of Jesus?[1]

As the MBI protest indicates, white evangelicals grappled with the consequences of the civil rights movement close to home as they confronted fraught questions about the nature of their own institutions. The historian Adam Laats has written that white evangelical colleges often faced two imperatives that were in tension.[2] They aspired to rigorous and respectable academic standards equal to secular schools. They also tried to stay on the straight and narrow evangelical path, creating campus environments that reinforced faith rather than undermining it. During the 1960s, race began to figure into both these imperatives in ways it never had before. The cultural and legal changes the civil rights movement produced made nondiscrimination on the basis of race part of what it meant to be a modern academic institution. Equally important, some white evangelicals began to wonder if opening the door of evangelical higher education to black Christians was now part of what it meant to be an evangelical college. By the end of the decade, efforts to build Christian academic communities had to account for these rapidly shifting racial norms.

The resulting attempts of white evangelical colleges to recruit black students reveal Christian colorblindness in formation. What would it mean to have a colorblind campus instead of a white campus? Rather than imagining that white administrators suddenly launched a clearly defined plan in the late 1960s to remake their campuses in a colorblind vein, it is more helpful to consider how the events of that tumultuous decade caused them to take actions whose outcomes were unknown and often unforeseen. Christian colorblindness on the white evangelical campus was not a static theology brought to bear to solve the problem of racial integration. It was, instead, a contested idea emerging through negotiation and conflict between newly arriving black students and overwhelmingly white student bodies and administrations. Warren and Jenkins's protest shined a light on a crucial factor in these negotiations: the rising expectations and racial consciousness of a generation of black students arriving on white evangelical campuses in the wake of black power. They would insist that white evangelicals accept them not only as brothers and sisters in Christ but also as *black* people. Such demands stoked controversy and spurred white evangelical students to embrace the language of Christian colorblindness.

Before the Recruitment Era

If white evangelical colleges were going to recruit black students, they would have to face the matter of sex. It was bad enough that some good Christian kids might find ways to defy the rules and engage in sex outside of marriage. It was far worse if that sex could conceivably be interracial. In 1963, *Eternity* magazine asked some white evangelical college administrators about their institutions' policies on interracial dating and marriage. "Definitely not permitted," wrote one. "No dating allowed," wrote another. "We counsel against such relationships," said a third, but "do not legislate." At times, "some very frank and forceful counseling" was required to keep young people from making a tragic mistake.³ It was because of sex, more than anything else, that many white evangelical colleges that enrolled black students here or there before the 1960s often saddled them with discriminatory policies. Besides bans or counseling against interracial dating, black students might be forced to live off campus or be encouraged to attend evening classes distinct from the daytime courses of white students living on campus.

Despite these limitations, handfuls of black students, like those who went on to found the National Black Evangelical Association, did attend white evangelical colleges in the 1940s and 1950s. Bill Pannell attended Fort Wayne Bible College in the late 1940s and, though a generation older than the black students of the civil rights era, emerged as an important voice on their behalf. Thoroughly embedded in evangelical networks, Pannell worked for Tom Skinner Crusades and Campus Crusade for Christ before going on to a long career as a professor at Fuller Theological Seminary. Students like Pannell found that their social interactions were almost invariably fraught with the specter of interracial contact. Pannell recalled the nervousness of registration day and the cheerful housing question: "would it be all right to put you in with a fine Negro student?" Pannell, who had grown up in small-town Michigan surrounded by white people, was quite sure he knew as little about black people as anyone else at Fort Wayne Bible College. But he was black, so he would room with a black student, and that was that. On the dating question, he remembered, the explicit ban didn't come until later. While he was enrolled, "they simply smiled uneasily and hoped for the best. But you got the message anyway."⁴

Bob Harrison grew up in such a conservative environment in the circles of San Francisco fundamentalism that when the time came to apply to a college in pursuit of his dream of entering the Christian ministry, he could think of no more prestigious place than Bob Jones University in Greenville, South Carolina. After making inquiries, he was shocked when he received the following reply: "Under no circumstances will we accept a black as a student at Bob Jones University." No matter, he reasoned, that was the South. Everyone knew racism was a problem down there. So he would go to the local Assemblies of God school across town, Bethany Bible College. In what Harrison later recognized as foreshadowing, the president of Bethany looked surprised to see him. "You realize that when you enroll you'll be our first Negro, don't you?" Harrison, young and naive, thought being first might be great. He enjoyed his first semester, and since the college was nearby, he could commute from home. But Bethany was in the process of relocating south to Santa Cruz. He couldn't commute that far. He would have to live in a dorm with white students, and that meant that the administration had a difficult decision to make. In the end, a workaround was found: Harrison was assigned a Filipino roommate. During the remainder of his college years, Harrison gradually became more aware of a peculiar quality to many of his social encounters. He came to believe that the fear of him "mixing socially with white girls" and, God forbid, marrying them was the "unspeakable, unthinkable" thing to which "everything else was really incidental."[5]

A controversy at Wheaton College demonstrated just how volatile the question of interracial dating could be and how it served as a barrier to becoming colorblind institutions. Wheaton's president, V. Raymond Edman, asked the Division of Social Sciences to draft a statement on race relations. Much work and eight drafts later, in the summer of 1960 the Department of Sociology and Anthropology submitted a "Wheaton College Statement on Race Relations" for the president's approval. This fascinating document set forth a theological and sociological justification for a colorblind campus. In a remarkably nondefensive and self-critical tone, the statement told Wheaton's story as a declension narrative. It described the school's noble abolitionist beginnings as sadly forsaken as the college reacted against the social gospel and "settled into a defensive position" in the early twentieth century. The professors affirmed that Wheaton had been right to emphasize proper doctrine and separation from the moral contagions of modern American life but, in doing so, had tragically lost its sense of Christian responsibility on racial matters. Though explicit racial discrimination was not written into Wheaton's policies, the statement admitted that "in practice" people of color, "especially Negroes, were for a time excluded from admission." Then when several black students enrolled in the 1940s and 1950s, "they were restricted in regard to housing and certain social activities." The statement bluntly declared that "evangelical white people have tended to regard colored peoples as inferior and have so treated them," despite no scientific or biblical basis for this prejudice. Turning Wheaton's claim of fundamentalist separation from worldly evils on its head, the report declared, "Distinctions based on social categories are of this world's system. . . . In Christ Jesus there is no segregation." Did not Colossians 3:11 make this plain?[6] This colorblind reading of scripture enabled the professors to directly attack sacred whiteness and declare it unchristian. Ironically, in just a few years, similar colorblind logic would be used to tell black students to be quiet about the racial discrimination they faced.

Fatefully, the draft statement submitted to President Edman included this unassuming recommendation: "That rules governing dating and permissions for marriage be uniform for the whole student body."[7] The self-critical tone of the statement might have been difficult enough for the administration to accept, but this little proposal was explosive indeed. Edman, acting as if he had just come into possession of the nuclear codes, forwarded a single copy to the Executive Council with strict instructions to read it one at a time and then return it to him in "the utmost confidence." It would be best, he advised, "that no word whatever be said about it, even to our families."[8] It was one thing to suggest that Wheaton had made some mistakes. It was another thing altogether to propose, going forward, that Wheaton should affirm interracial romances. Professor Merrill Tenney wrote back to Edman, urging that the document be kept under wraps until it was given further study. Interracial marriage was not a sin, he admitted, but it sure was foolish. "Will some of the parents of our students regard a tacit approval of interracial marriage as a danger to their children?"[9] To ask the question was to answer it. The following fall, a full 14 months after giving the draft statement to the president, its creators were in the dark about what had happened to it, so they asked President Edman for a follow-up meeting. The following year, when one faculty member published an article that echoed the sentiments of the draft statement, the board of trustees demanded an explanation for his recklessness. President Edman made sure the statement on race relations never saw the light of day.[10] In the early 1960s, making a biblical argument on behalf of social equality could land one in a world of trouble at white evangelical colleges.

A 1963 *Eternity* magazine survey of white evangelical colleges and Bible institutes found that their story was Wheaton's story writ large. Black enrollment in the dozens of colleges surveyed was 0.5 percent. Editor William J. Petersen perceptively noted that the average white evangelical college had worked very hard both "to attain its academic standing and maintain its evangelical testimony." Historically, the presence of black students seemed to be a threat to both. Few African Americans were academically prepared to go to college, and few white evangelical parents were enthused about sending their children to a place that raised the specter of intimate interracial social contact. A black pastor suggested that if a white evangelical college simply added the word "inter-racial" to its promotional material, "our people would know that it was for them too." But Petersen doubted that white evangelical colleges "would be willing to risk alienating some of their constituency by the use of such a loaded word." Still, he believed the time had come to accept the risk of change. A white evangelical college should "go out of its way to encourage Negro young people to attend." This meant removing discriminatory policies that made black students feel unwelcome. Petersen suggested schools should not stop at trying to create a level playing field. They should launch new scholarship programs specifically for black students. Wasn't it ironic, after all, that it was often easier for an international student from Africa to enroll in a white evangelical college than for an African American thousands of miles closer to home to do the same?[11]

If Petersen's suggestions were ahead of where most white evangelical colleges were prepared to go in 1963, they did anticipate the changing reasoning that emerged during the course of the decade. The legal, moral, and cultural influence of the civil rights movement made integration increasingly hard to resist. The related theological transformations within white evangelicalism, meanwhile, were turning the lily-white college into a potential credibility problem instead of a wholesome marker of evangelical bona fides. What if these white institutions signaled not only high academic and moral standards, but also an unchristian attitude of discrimination and disregard for fellow Christians? By the late 1960s, more and more white evangelical administrators were asking questions like these.

Recruitment Begins

In the late 1960s, many white evangelical colleges launched unprecedented campaigns to enroll black students. White evangelicals' desire to keep in step with the changing times and demonstrate Christian concern prompted recruitment, but what black inclusion in these institutions would really look like was up for debate. The recruitment era was more than a literal enrollment of black students. It was a mood, a tenor of the times shaped by black power and the new legal regime of the Civil Rights Act of 1964. Colleges receiving federal funds had to submit yearly reports of the racial composition of their student bodies and demonstrate compliance with nondiscrimination in employment and student admissions.[12] Colleges that had allowed a handful of black students to attend over the years began in the late 1960s to discard discriminatory policies and launch new recruitment initiatives. Northern white evangelical colleges were not always ahead of their southern counterparts. Wayland Baptist College in Plainview, Texas, had admitted its first black student in 1951 and had integrated dorm housing during the 1950s. Georgetown College in Kentucky integrated in 1955. Many other Southern Baptist colleges integrated in the early 1960s.[13] But admitting black students was not the same as seeking them out. Proactive recruitment designed to enroll significant numbers of black students in this period was primarily a project of white evangelical colleges outside the South. Even at institutions that didn't experience significant increases in absolute numbers of black students, the zeitgeist of the moment was often evident as the race-conscious mobilizations of the new generation of black students challenged white evangelical campuses. White administrators' recruitment efforts were, ironically, race conscious in their own way as well. They believed visible display of an integrated campus would bolster claims of Christian unity and demonstrate evangelical concern for the racial crisis.

The trend toward recruiting black students in the late 1960s was far from uniform. Some schools tried to shut out the noise and continue much as before. As late as 1972, Dordt College in Sioux Center, Iowa, had no nonwhite students at all.[14] Others moved to action at different times and with varying degrees of commitment. Though the national context informed the move toward black recruitment, the specific spurs to action varied from one institution to another. In some cases, white student bodies took the lead in calling for change. That is what happened at Messiah College, a small evangelical institution in rural Pennsylvania. In the spring of 1967, the college welcomed John Howard Griffin, the white author of the popular book *Black Like Me*. The book chronicled Griffin's escapades after he purposely darkened his skin in order to pass as a black man in the South for six weeks in the fall of 1959. In a talk given to a large crowd of Messiah students, Griffin urged them to confront the problem of racism. Conscience-stricken students demanded action. One student raised a challenge that hit home: if Messiah students thought integration was good for the South, it ought to be good for their own dorm rooms too. Students launched a fund-raising drive to pay the tuition for a black student. The following semester Edna Curry, an African American woman from Gulfport, Mississippi, enrolled as the college's lone black student.[15]

For other colleges, racial tensions in local metro areas provided a sense of urgency. In 1966, Dr. Martin Luther King launched his fair housing campaign in Chicago, and the West Side experienced rioting that summer. The following year, nearby Wheaton College launched a new "Compensatory Education Program." The initiative brought 12 black students to campus with the help of financial aid and large amounts of loans.[16] At North Park College in Chicago proper, proactive recruitment began in 1967 and resulted in over three dozen black students at the college by the fall of 1969, a dramatic change from prior years.[17] In Grand Rapids, Michigan, racial polarization around crime and school busing, coupled with controversial school segregation in the Christian Reformed Church, gave impetus to new recruitment planning at the denomination's flagship Calvin College.[18] In the spring of 1970, a small interracial group of Calvin students formed a Committee for Black Enrollment to push the administration to recruit black students. "The plight of the black man is the nation's most severe domestic problem," the committee's president declared. Yet "the college is for the most part ignoring the problem." Meanwhile a faculty committee recommended that for the first time Calvin begin actively recruiting students beyond the Christian Reformed Church, a key step if Calvin was to have any hope of becoming more racially diverse.[19] One of the few black students at Calvin before the new recruitment got under way pointed out that the black residents of Grand Rapids were well aware of Calvin College. They simply didn't want to go there. They viewed the school with "cynical contempt," he said.[20] Later that year the US Office of Education awarded a $15,000 planning grant "to develop a program of assistance to black students," and in the fall of 1971 black enrollment at Calvin doubled.[21]

For many colleges, the tumultuous spring of 1968 was a moment of truth. Confronted with Dr. King's assassination and major rebellions in urban centers, they believed that their own institutions could meet the challenge of racial hatred and violence. At Bethel College in St. Paul, Minnesota, faculty pressure in the wake of Dr. King's death led to the creation of a Minority Recruitment Committee. In the fall of 1970, the college welcomed 10 black men, most of them from the local metro area, as its first cohort of black students.[22] At Eastern Baptist College in suburban Philadelphia, the president established an Advisory Committee on the Disadvantaged in 1968 to explore how Eastern could help "nonwhite" people. By the following year Eastern had nearly two dozen black students enrolled. Though the rapid social changes of the 1960s made recruitment of black students a matter of institutional self-interest, college leaders conceived of their efforts as expressions of Christian love. As Eastern's president declared, their "orthodox words of truth must become Christly deeds of concern and sacrifice."[23]

This was easy to say and hard to do. Dr. King's death both motivated recruitment and exposed hostility to black concerns among white evangelical colleges' key constituencies. On the Sunday after King's assassination, as troops patrolled American cities, words of commemoration and grief rang out at memorial services all over the country. One of these memorial services occurred at Wheaton College. An ecumenical gathering of faith leaders praised the late civil rights leader, and the president of Wheaton College, Dr. Hudson T. Armerding, also gave some remarks. That's when the trouble started. Evangelical media broadcast the news that Wheaton College had hosted a memorial service for Dr. King, and dozens of letters poured in from confused and angry white evangelicals. Timothy LaHaye, a San Diego pastor who would gain fame as the coauthor of the apocalyptic fiction series *Left Behind*, found it "incredible that a Christian college could participate in honoring an out-right theological liberal heretic whose 'non-violent' demonstrations resulted in the deaths of seventeen people." He went on to hint that this episode could affect his ability to recommend Wheaton College to his congregation in the future.[24]

Pastors, professors, Wheaton alumni, and ordinary churchgoers complained that Dr. King associated with communists, believed a false gospel, and propagated violence and disorder. "What is happening to our Christian colleges?" asked one woman.[25] A student at Covenant College in Tennessee was upset that the college flew its flag at half-mast in the days after Dr. King's death. "To make a martyr out of a man who so encouraged strife and violence in America through his actions, while he talked peace, is the height of hypocrisy," she wrote. "I feel that Covenant College has let down its moral standards."[26] Most white evangelicals objected to King's civil disobedience as an affront to law and order, and a denial of the sufficiency of the gospel. President Armerding quickly disavowed any support for King's methods and noted that the college had not sponsored the memorial service but merely allowed the community to use its chapel.[27] Even as white evangelical colleges launched a new era of black recruitment, expressing sympathy with black aspirations risked alienating their white constituency.

Sometimes, black students became unwitting pioneers of racial integration at white evangelical colleges. That is what happened to Dolphus Weary and his friend Jimmie Walker. The two young men wanted to get out of Mississippi, so a basketball scholarship to Los Angeles Baptist College came as a lifeline.[28] When they arrived in the fall of 1967, they were shocked to discover that they were breaking the color line, becoming the very first black students to live on campus. They had escaped the closed society of Mississippi only to find themselves more isolated than they had ever been. When they walked around the town of Newhall there were no black faces to greet them. Black students in such difficult circumstances responded in various ways. Weary decided to embrace the role that had been thrust upon him. If he was a black ambassador to a little corner of white evangelicalism, then he would play the part to the full. He cut his hair to avoid any appearance of militancy. He took care to obey the rules and stay away from troublemakers. He focused on his studies. And perhaps most importantly, he remembered, "We never dared to date white girls. We'd been told up front that was a no-no." In short, Dolphus Weary and Jimmie Walker, like so many black students on white evangelical campuses, were trying to walk what Weary called a "tightrope." He wanted to be himself, but he knew his actions never represented him alone.[29]

Weary's memoir veils the psychic toll this tightrope must have exacted, but King's murder in the spring of Weary's second semester marked a turning point in his approach to being a black student on a white evangelical campus. When he heard the news that King had been shot, he retreated to his dorm. Then he heard a commotion down the hall and went to investigate. The radio report had just confirmed King's death, and white students were laughing and celebrating. Weary suddenly remembered he was not alone. Where was Jimmie? He found him in his room, radio on. The two black men shared a silent moment of grief. Then they "talked into the night—the only two blacks for miles around." For the rest of the semester, Weary was on a mission. He spoke up about racism. He courted controversy and took it upon himself to educate his white peers. No longer merely students, he and Jimmie had become "teachers ... on a campus dominated by white people."[30] For the small number of black students on white evangelical campuses by the late 1960s, change could not come soon enough.

In 1969, as recruitment efforts gathered steam, Nancy Hardesty took stock of what had changed since *Eternity*'s 1963 survey and what still needed to be done. Hardesty, destined to become a controversial figure as a leading evangelical feminist, also took a progressive approach to questions of race in the evangelical community.[31] A new survey showed that in six years white evangelical colleges had made small strides. The overtly prejudiced responses seen in the earlier survey seemed to have gone out of style. But Hardesty wondered how much had really changed. In 1963 the student bodies of white evangelical colleges were 0.5 percent black. Now, the figure had edged up to 1.5 percent.[32] This number was still smaller than the number of international students of color drawn to white evangelical schools through missionary contacts and scholarships. At this pace, it would take more than half a century for black student enrollment at white evangelical colleges to become equal to their proportion of the American population. None of this was to say that secular campuses were doing a good job at racial integration. A large survey of state universities and colleges nationwide had recently found black enrollment at these historically white institutions clocking in at about 2 percent. Amid ample evidence of racism and administrative cluelessness on mainstream campuses, the 1968–1969 academic year was the epicenter of the black student revolt.[33] But Hardesty worried that white evangelical colleges seemed to lag behind even this meager standard. As institutions committed to the gospel of Jesus Christ, should they not be leading the way toward racial integration?[34]

Hardesty had some ideas for how white evangelical colleges could become leaders rather than followers in racial change. Issued as black recruitment efforts were gathering momentum, had her suggestions been widely followed the outcomes on white evangelical campuses might have been quite different. First, she declared that colleges had to stop caving in to fear and the pressures of wealthy donors. If recruiting black students made someone stop writing checks, that money wasn't worth having anyway. Second, Hardesty called for a new sense of Christian responsibility on the part of white evangelical colleges and churches. "Christ loved and died for all men. Because of this, our institutions should be the first to accept all men regardless of the color of their skin." Instead, she lamented, "we have been among the last." Hardesty used the rhetoric of Christian colorblindness to shame white evangelicals for their failure to live out their own professed beliefs. She insisted that this colorblind theology ought to motivate practical actions that reordered the campus environment. That would mean serious recruitment not simply of black students, but of black faculty. They would have to establish "special remedial programs" for incoming black students who found the academic standards challenging. The entire student body would have to be taught "the whole story, not just the 'white' view." History courses would have to change. Sociology courses would be revamped. Classes on everything from the Bible to evangelism would have to be built anew to weed out prejudiced interpretations. One thing was sure, Hardesty wrote. "Christ is calling us to do more. Will we answer His challenge?"[35]

Crisis

Most recruitment efforts did not take Hardesty's suggestions to heart. Almost without exception, black recruitment campaigns produced controversy on white evangelical campuses. Black students were invited into the Christian academic community under the rubric of help, outreach, and mission. Most white administrators seemed to believe the task at hand was to open up access to their institutions so that black evangelicals could also benefit from all that they had to offer. White students and administrators tended not to reckon with how much their own institutions would need to change to make this work, or how much they might have to learn from black students. As African American Christians at the margins of white evangelical institutions called for systemic reform and insisted they could be both black and evangelical, they encountered criticism and discrimination. White evangelicals often insisted that unity in Christ was already a reality and that black Christians attacked such unity when they raised questions of systemic reform on the Christian campus. While Hardesty's colorblind theology led her to believe systemic reforms were necessary, many white students and administrators used the same theological language to tell black students to be quiet. After all, if they were all united in the love of Christ, why did they have to keep talking about race? If their spiritual identities transcended their earthly ones, weren't the people demanding race-based reforms the real troublemakers? In the crucible of these encounters, a brand of Christian colorblindness took shape that justified inaction.

The white response to the formation of black student groups in the late 1960s and early 1970s demonstrated the growing pull of colorblind theology on white evangelical campuses. Despite the fact that these groups were almost invariably open to all students, rumors swirled that the groups were militant and separatist, a threat to the unity of the body of Christ. Even when black students carefully described their groups as efforts to build interracial understanding, many white students indignantly asked why race-conscious groups belonged on a Christian campus at all. At Philadelphia College of Bible, the new black student group stressed that its purpose was "BROTHERHOOD and UNITY," but even this failed to stop the rumor that the new group excluded white students.[36] At Nyack College in New York, the student newspaper announced, "Contrary to popular opinion, the Afro-American club is for everyone."[37] In the face of white students' discomfort, one black student group drily announced that they didn't "intend to instigate riots" so white students ought to remain calm.[38]

Black students found solidarity and community in black student groups, and they used them to make specific demands for institutional reform. Common pleas included the hiring of black faculty, the establishment of black studies programs, curriculum redevelopment, opportunities for cultural activities, and black worship expressions in chapel services. While many of these demands overlapped with the black revolution taking place on secular campuses, the stakes on white evangelical campuses were even higher. Black students insisted that their demands went to the heart of whether these white evangelical colleges would truly build Christian communities. As the Black Student Union (BSU) at Messiah College declared, "Messiah, don't be called a racist Christian institution."[39] The way to avoid this designation was to support the BSU's demands for practical race-conscious reforms.

Black students did not speak with one voice. Some students simply tried to quietly fit in as best they could. Some found their experiences on campus difficult but believed they were still better off than they would be at a secular campus. Others joined white students in expressing colorblind rhetoric. At historic Taylor University in the fall of 1970, black students used a special chapel service to assure the white majority that they were not like the black students on many college campuses who insisted on forming a "black clique." Instead, they declared, they "believe in Taylor" and wanted to "be completely integrated into the college environment."[40] Many black students felt misunderstood and typecast. As one student said, "I frankly resent being constantly singled out." Administrators had even invited him to dinner at their homes, where he heard questions like, "What does the Negro in America want?" His reply: "how should I know? I only know what one person wants—and that's me!"[41] Other black students grudgingly accepted the role of racial teacher. One black student declared that he was willing to answer questions, but only if "the other blacks refuse to talk to you." He had "developed the talent or curse (call it what you will) to be black enough to answer your questions and white enough to make you feel comfortable."[42]

A vocal minority of white evangelical students on these campuses supported black demands and called on their fellow white students to repent of racism. As Eastern Baptist College began to experience racial tensions in the spring of 1970, a white student named Phil Jenks put the blame squarely on white students and administrators. He pointed out that black students were objects of spectacle, curiosity, and fear, yet white students still blamed them for separating themselves and not fitting in. Jenks drew a cartoon in which a black student stands in a padlocked display case, his hands against the glass, looking distressed. Above him, as if on a theater marquee, are the words "Now Showing! Eastern's 24

'Blacks'!" A white man meant to embody the college looks on in annoyance at the black student: "Whaddaya, some kind of segregationist militant or something?" he asks. Even sympathetic white students, however, often couched their concern in a form of Christian colorblindness that sidestepped institutional reform. After excoriating white students and administrators for the racial climate on campus, Jenks's proposed solution was a "revival" of Christian love.[43] Like most white evangelicals, Jenks conceived of racial tensions as a lack of interpersonal kindness rather than a systemic problem.

Students like Jenks were invariably overshadowed by a larger number of white students who did not understand black students' concerns or who actively resisted them. Many white students found black students' activism bewildering and responded defensively. Steve Heise, the editor of the Messiah College student newspaper, declared, "I must ask if racism really exists on our campus or if one faction among us is CAUSING it to develop." He accused black students of trying to inject racial controversy into issues that he believed had nothing to do with race. Perhaps, he suggested, the real problem was not white racism but "some of the things some of the Blacks are doing and saying on our campus." The BSU at Messiah had called for both the hiring of black professors and the establishment of a black studies program. It demanded—and received!—an apology from the white student body for its racism. Heise believed this behavior was not just disagreeable but harmful to Christian unity. In the Christian academic community, those who sought to draw attention to racism were the real purveyors of racial tension. "We must get back to the point where race is no issue and skin color is overlooked," he pleaded.[44]

Heise's decision to publicly launch a direct attack on black students was rather unusual. More often white students made a more elaborate theological case for why black students should stop talking about race. After black students at Nyack College participated in the national Black Solidarity Day in the fall of 1970, a white student responded with a series of indignant questions. "Isn't it true that Jesus' sacrifice was for all men? Isn't it true that those that take Him as Lord and Savior become part of His Body? . . . Didn't Jesus break down all barriers with what He did on Calvary? If the response to these questions is yes, why then in a so called Christian school where everyone is supposed to be . . . part of Christ's body . . . are there words in our vocabulary such as Black Brother, White Brother, and so on?" For this student and many other white students, race-conscious language wasn't merely unhelpful. It was unchristian, and it called into question the maturity of black students' Christian faith. Anyone who "persists in using racially charged language with regards to another child of God had better sit down with God and re-evaluate his or her form of Christianity," he concluded.[45]

The colorblind assumptions of white students collided with a new generation of black students who insisted on celebrating their blackness. Shaped by the civil rights movement and black power, many black students took pride in their blackness and refused to hide it. White students often found this baffling. Rod Alexander, a black student at Covenant College in Tennessee, wrote that he didn't expect many of his readers to understand the point he was trying to make, but "the AFFIRMATION OF OUR BLACKNESS AND OUR HUMANITY IN BLACK IS A BEAUTIFUL, LONG-AWAITED GIFT FROM GOD." Alexander pointed out that he was not an opponent of Christian unity. But he refused to play by white evangelical rules. "Unfortunately," he wrote, "this white evangelical concept of 'oneness' with black people conspicuously capitulates to America's game entitled, 'To be one with us, you must be like us.'" For many white students such talk seemed maddeningly vague. What exactly were they doing wrong? A white student explained that he couldn't understand Alexander's affirmation of his blackness "because I don't even know what it means for me to affirm my whiteness."[46] Another white student wrote, "I am white and proud of it. . . . If you are white, yellow, black or red, I'm proud of it." Like many white students, he imagined whiteness and blackness as mirror images of each other, incidental identities that didn't matter in comparison to "what's inside . . . the state of the heart. Christ has broken down the walls between us; let's not build them again."[47]

Black students repeatedly tried to explain that they weren't trying to build walls. They were trying to find a way to exist in white institutions, and it was extraordinarily hard to do so because their very presence was coded as divisive. Black students often felt that they were welcomed on campus only so long as they submerged their identities and embraced white normativity. At Bethel College, one black student said, "Bethel as a whole doesn't seem to want blackness here. . . . They want the blacks to conform to white society."⁴⁸ At Messiah, a black student declared, "Whites are often able to accept Blacks as people, but not as Black people." Some black students testified that Messiah wanted "shuffling Niggers" who would not challenge the superficial niceties of the campus environment. "Change at Messiah must come from the authorities," they declared, but "the campus wishes its minority groups to be quiet and unseen."⁴⁹

Most provocatively, black students often insisted that the way they were being treated called into question the Christian identity of their colleges. "How can Messiah be a Christian college," they asked, "when it tears apart the personalities and feelings of Black students?"⁵⁰ Because many black students sincerely believed in the unity of the body of Christ and had expected to find it on a Christian campus, they felt their disillusionment all the more keenly. "As long as I am part of the Body," wrote a black student, "you cannot say 'I do not know any blacks and when I go home and begin my life vocation I will not know any blacks, so why should I read or learn about their problems?' My problem is your problem. If I am hurting, you, as a part of the Body must feel it. This is scriptural!" She concluded, "There will be no middle ground until whites allow other races to be who God made them to be and you stop trying to melt us into a wishy-washiness of whiteness."⁵¹

This "wishy-washiness of whiteness" was often invisible to white students and suffocating to black ones. Even as many white students insisted that race ought not be important among people united in Christ, black students testified that they were objects of fear and fascination on their campuses, alternately shunned and put on display. Barbara Bowser, a black woman who attended Houghton College in rural New York in the 1970s, recalled her searing experiences. The questions: "does your color rub off? Is your hair wiry?" And the fears: a student told her she couldn't come to her house because her father hated "colored people." While the college claimed it was a welcoming community, she spent her freshman year feeling "terrified" in her white dorm. "I had to stay really close to the Lord to keep from committing suicide," she concluded.⁵² In other cases, black students reported feeling as though they were constantly watched in the dorms. In one instance, two dozen white students looked on in fascination as a black student did her hair.⁵³ "This isn't the Bronx Zoo and we're not on display," said one black student.⁵⁴ In short, black students faced extraordinarily confusing environments. On the one hand they were expected to be no different from white people, while on the other hand they felt reduced to stereotyped stock characters of essentialized blackness. It is not surprising that they often responded with anger and disillusionment.

White administrators were often little better than the students. Armerding, Wheaton College's president, weakly admitted that "the black students here on campus perceive a problem in their being here," but he seemed to think the causes of the problem were mysterious.[55] At Calvin College, president William Spoelhof came up with the idea of inviting the black students to a "special" dinner featuring "soul food." Maybe, he suggested, "a black student would play or sing or perform some way." But he had doubts about his plan because he didn't know the students, or even how many there were, and worried that a dinner might "provoke a whole series of demands and open up too early a whole can of worms."[56] The episode could serve as a metaphor for the entire era. The president thought he could establish rapport with black students if he fed them soul food and allowed them to perform their blackness through stereotyped entertainment, but he hoped he could pull off the event without any demands being made upon the college. Too often, white administrators cast black students as troublemakers rather than trying to understand the sources of their frustration. At North Park College in Chicago, the board of directors noted in 1970 that "the younger students are a new breed. They and the black students make it difficult to enforce the rules."[57]

It didn't help that white administrators often shared the presumptions of innocence common to many northerners and northern institutions.[58] With the Jim Crow South as a foil, it was easy for leaders of white evangelical colleges to imagine that they had always been welcoming institutions. As one Wheaton public relations official put it, Wheaton "has a history of demonstrated concern for treating persons on the basis of their individual merit, irrespective of race or color." It could take pride in its "cosmopolitan student body" and the outreach efforts of its students to poor people of color in nearby Chicago.[59] This sense of complacency and self-satisfaction was a barrier to the kinds of reforms black students demanded. White administrators were more likely to be mystified by black discontent than to understand its causes.

Some colleges were more proactive than others in trying to reform their campus environments. Among the most aggressive was Messiah College. In the years after Edna Curry's arrival in 1967, larger cohorts of black students had followed in her footsteps. In the spring of 1972, Messiah formed an interracial committee of faculty and students to study discrimination and draft a statement of policy for the college.[60] For decades, no such institutional policies had appeared necessary; now, in the aftermath of the civil rights movement, they seemed urgent. In characteristic evangelical fashion, the committee's work was at bottom a theological project. Among its first and most important tasks was the laborious drafting of a "Theological Prelude to the Study of Racial Discrimination." The committee undertook an extensive fact-finding mission, interviewing students—especially black students—and commissioning a detailed survey to measure racial prejudice among students, faculty, and staff. The committee found that "overt racism is relatively uncommon at Messiah College," but "unvoiced prejudices ... appear to be rather widespread throughout the white community." The committee found extensive "closemindedness" and "cultural isolation rooted in apathy and ignorance."[61]

More is known about the racial climate of Messiah because the administration was more willing than most to try to understand it. At other institutions where the record is silent, the climate is likely to have been worse. Though white students and administrators spoke the language of unity in Christ, grotesque indifference to the black experience was built into campus cultures and traditions. At Nyack College in New York, the 1968 freshman class initiation week "ended with the bang of the auctioneer's gavel Friday night. After proving their worth by various feats and tests of endurance, the frosh slaves were auctioned off."[62] That fall the black student population had surged to more than 20, including three of Howard Jones's daughters. The black students formed an Afro-American Society, but what they thought of the "slave auction" was not recorded. Similar "Slave Day" events, such as one at Messiah College in 1978, were widely seen as innocuous fun.[63] Such activities went on with the full support of the college community. They were not underground hazing activities. They were ostensibly harmless traditions proudly reported on in college publications.

To become welcoming places, these and other practices would have to change. As white evangelical colleges felt the ground shifting beneath their feet, they found it difficult to keep up. Decisions that might not have drawn a raised eyebrow a decade before could suddenly blow up into major controversies. That is what happened at MBI when the school invited the fundamentalist preacher John R. Rice to Founder's Week for 1971. Rice was the editor of *Sword of the Lord*, a popular newspaper that blasted Billy Graham's more ecumenical brand of evangelicalism and called for separation from the godless ideologies of modern America, including racial integration. It almost beggars belief that President Culbertson could not have known that Rice advocated racist views. But just a few short years before, that fact would have been unlikely to be counted against him. In the new world the civil rights movement wrought, with increasingly vocal black evangelicals among the voices in MBI's orbit, it mattered a great deal. Culbertson was slow to realize this. Just months after Melvin Warren and Leona Jenkins's protest of MBI racism, Culbertson reached out to Rice as a "Dear Brother" whose presence at Founder's Week would bring him "real joy." Rice agreed to come and MBI duly announced his inclusion in the lineup of speakers.[64]

Then some MBI students reportedly alerted Culbertson to Rice's racist screeds, including a defense of the white supremacist Bob Jones University, which Rice published just weeks before Culbertson's invitation.[65] It is likely Culbertson had more on his mind than the concerns of a few students. He had received an anonymous letter purporting to be from a "radical group" threatening to unite Students for a Democratic Society, Black Panthers, and other radical organizations to launch "one of the biggest demonstrations Chicago has ever seen." If Culbertson didn't disinvite Rice, "we are coming," it warned, and MBI's reputation would be "destroyed."[66] Jealous of the institution's good name, Culbertson held back a letter finalizing the details of Rice's visit. Instead, the next day he sent Rice a brief note explaining that Rice's segregationist editorial gave him no choice but to rescind the invitation. "It was our hope to put the emphasis upon . . . the fundamentals of the faith, but now . . . your article has shifted it to civil rights." MBI could not let stand any impression that it supported a segregationist stance.[67]

Even at this late stage, Culbertson continued to think of Rice's anti-black hatred as separable from the core of Christian doctrine. This kind of thinking angered black students and inflamed the sense of crisis on white evangelical campuses. In a more fulsome explanation that Culbertson elected not to send, he was more explicit about what was at stake for MBI: "Our announcement of your coming has set up a flood of [illegible] and the threat of reprisal." The city was "seething" with racial tension, and MBI could not risk being associated with Rice.[68] The response to Culbertson's decision paralleled the anger directed at Wheaton College after the memorial service for Dr. King. While Culbertson appears to have had a great deal of support from faculty, administration, and black evangelicals, many Rice supporters and Moody alumni wrote to express their frustration with the decision. Some threatened to withhold funds. Others wondered if they could still trust Moody to stand for the fundamentals of the faith.[69] Culbertson's response emphasized MBI's colorblind bona fides. As he put it in a letter to a pastor critical of his decision, "Through times of changing social mores the policy has always been to emphasize the salvation from God by which all men who believe are made one in Christ."[70]

Colorblind theology like Culbertson's led white evangelical colleges both to distance themselves from the racism on offer from places like Bob Jones University *and* to look with alarm at black students' race-conscious protests. Black students felt the bind that campus environments put on them. "We are loved for being ignorant and hated for being militant," said one black student.[71] As much as white administrators feared black students' activism, the demands black students made at evangelical colleges were usually not radical. They amounted to the claim that they ought to be able to be both black and Christian. At Wheaton College, President Armerding and other leaders described black students as radical, yet their demands were measured: black studies, curriculum reform, clarification on the interracial dating policy.[72] Many white evangelical students and administrators experienced these claims as radical and disorienting because they made so little distinction between their own racial and religious identities. As one white administrator at Wheaton confessed, "The college has allowed itself to think that white culture is the only Christian culture."[73]

The lingering appeal of sacred whiteness on the white evangelical campus made black students' attraction to black power all the more shocking. Some black students defended the black power movement wholeheartedly and tried to craft Christian forms of black power or black nationalism. Many, like John Skinner, a black student at Nyack College, embraced some of the language of James Cone, if not all his conclusions, and insisted "Black Theology" had something to teach white evangelicals who had imbibed "a theology of the oppressor." Such views were anathema on a colorblind campus. Skinner diagnosed the situation in 1972. As African Americans became more race conscious, whites increasingly threw the charge of racism back at them in a bid to delegitimize black power and displace racism from a white problem to a black problem. As long as blacks continued "pointing their finger at the oppressor who happens to be white, the oppressor will continue to call blacks racists. I ask you, who is the true racist and who will do something about racism?"[74] Ronald Brown, a black student at North Park, said he would not allow the college to "assimilate" him. To those upset about the perceived separatism of the Black Student Association, Brown simply quoted Stokely Carmichael. The association was going to be a black organization, led by blacks. Brown rejected the charge that this posture was antiwhite. Instead, it opposed white paternalism. In another article titled "Help Wipe Out Fascist Oppressors"—published in the student newspaper!—Brown called for a revolution, by force if necessary.[75]

Bill Pannell gave voice to the new militancy of young black evangelicals like Brown and Skinner. Few were more thoroughly engaged in white evangelical networks than Pannell, so when his book *My Friend, the Enemy* came out in the awful month of April 1968, just as the urge for black recruitment gained ground, it came as a shock to many.[76] Pannell relentlessly attacked white evangelicals for their racism and spiritual pieties amid a deadly struggle. The promise of salvation "gives little balm when viewing the bloodied form of a twelve-year-old lying face down on Newark's cold pavement," he wrote. "But what would my white brother know of this? He taught me to sing 'Take The World But Give Me Jesus.' I took Jesus. He took the world and then voted right wing to insure his property rights."[77] This was the kind of critique, taking in questions of class and economy, that had rarely been heard in evangelical circles up to this time. Acerbic, sarcastic, and angry, Pannell pulled few punches. "I have grown weary," he explained, "of that kind of love which is altogether willing to accept me as long as I remain a nice Negro—humble, patient and understanding. Well, I am none of these."[78] While many evangelicals wanted to speak of division, mistrust, and misunderstanding, Pannell spoke of white oppressors, the black oppressed, and a gospel message bigger than white evangelical claims of ownership. "What right," he asked, "has the oppressor to demand that his victim be saved from sin?" Pannell pointed out that white evangelicals were eager to engage in all sorts of moral crusades. "But mention the inhumanity of a society which with unbelievable indifference imprisons the 'souls of black folks,' and these crusaders begin mumbling about sin. All right. I'll play the game, my brother. Whose sin shall we talk about?"[79]

Pannell even defended black power. In a country organized around "white power," African Americans were now doing what immigrant groups had always done to secure their progress: banding together in ethnic solidarity and "meeting power with power." When immigrants did it, people called it uplift and personal responsibility. But as soon as black people applied the same strategies, "shouts of 'foul play' rise from my conservative friend." Pannell's attention to power and social context cut through the emerging assumptions of colorblind theology. He seemed to sense that white evangelicals were in danger of exchanging one antiblack view for another. "You can ignore a man in several ways," he wrote. "You can refuse to 'see' him by insisting that he be a man and not a Negro ('I never think of you as a Negro. To me you're just as good as I am') or you can overlook him by relating to him as a Negro and not a man ('Negroes are so full of fun, so graceful and happy, so child-like in their approach to life')."[80] If the latter view was in decline, the former was in the ascendancy. Both, Pannell thundered, were functions of white supremacy. The *Evangelical Beacon* accused Pannell of "supersensitiveness" and "extreme views" but admitted that the book should cause white evangelicals to "confess our sins of prejudice" and "consider man as man regardless of color." This simple colorblind takeaway suggested the reviewer might have missed Pannell's point entirely. A white evangelical college student declared, "When I finished [it] I wanted to find every black person I know and apologize."[81] But for every white student who was awakened to a new understanding of the black experience, there were many more who reacted negatively. The resolution to the racial crisis on white evangelical campuses would come not by listening to voices like Pannell's, but by silencing them.

Retrenchment

As white students reacted against race-conscious black students and white administrators rejected demands for far-reaching institutional reforms, they gave to colorblind theology a distinctly reactionary cast. Howard Jones had used the claims of unity in Christ to press for racial change and inclusion. Now the same claims were deployed to maintain whiteness at the center of evangelical colleges. The decline of the first wave of recruitment efforts was a widespread phenomenon by the middle of the 1970s. On some campuses, early black recruitment campaigns collapsed in the wake of white resentment and black disillusionment. Black power advocacy on white evangelical campuses was not only a measure of the radicalism of incoming students. It revealed the deep disappointment of students who arrived on evangelical campuses expecting to find acceptance in a Christian community. For some, a semester on such a campus was a radicalizing experience all by itself, but white administrators seemed rarely to understand this. In some cases, administrators deliberately pulled the plug on recruitment programs when it became obvious their institutions were ill-prepared for black students. A common struggle at all institutions was the indifference or hostility of most of the student body. As one white student declared, "I am tired of being made to feel guilty about minority students. They're cramming this minority business down our throats!"[82]

In nearly all cases, the resources and staffing devoted to the recruitment and retention of black students proved insufficient. While committees established to study these issues almost invariably sounded the alarm about the need for more funding and more cultural opportunities for students of color, such resources were hard to come by. Too often, a committee on "minority concerns" or some other similar title was merely the administrative backwater where such concerns went to die. Questions recorded in committee minutes spoke volumes: "Is this a venting committee?" "Are we powerless?"[83] At North Park, the Committee on Disadvantaged Students admitted that one of the problems was that white students and administrators knew next to nothing about black people or black culture and were doing "little or nothing about remedying this deficiency."[84]

Faculty often dragged their heels, especially when urged to hire black professors or make changes to their classes. At a tense meeting between black students and white faculty at Wheaton College in the spring of 1970, faculty members asked what they should do. "Shut up and listen" was the reply. President Armerding described the faculty response as variously "guilt-ridden . . . unimpressed . . . [and] alienated."[85] Even when college leaders pushed for change they often faced pushback from faculty jealous of their prerogatives. When Armerding urged Wheaton professors to incorporate a more multicultural focus into their classes, one responded that the "contributions of the more 'primitive' cultures" should certainly be included, but "not to the point of over-reacting with making superficial connections."[86]

When administrators honestly faced a realistic assessment of how much their institutions would need to change to become welcoming to African Americans, it could be dispiriting. One official at Calvin College declared, "I think the fact is that it's not going to happen."[87] The lack of substantive action spoke volumes to black students. As one Wheaton administrator confessed, "if you think that you do not consider white culture superior to black culture, yet you continue to know nothing about their culture, then you may be a member of a racist community."[88] For most white evangelical students and administrators, the presence of black students proved far more difficult than they had imagined, in part because it forced them to encounter their own whiteness. Thinking about whiteness was theologically disturbing for many evangelicals, for it raised the possibility that their faith was not unmediated divine truth but was instead a culturally and racially conditioned religiosity.

While many of the factors causing racial retrenchment on white evangelical campuses were indigenous to these institutions, the turn away from black demands also reflected the palpable fatigue evident in American political life in the 1970s as bipartisan white activism against busing and affirmative action marked the boundaries of the civil rights movement's gains. Then, too, there was simply a lot going on. As one white evangelical leader put it, "After Vietnam, ecology, women's lib, Watergate, and the energy shortage, it is difficult indeed to remember back to the 'olden days' in 1968, when the problem of race relations was in focus and near the top of everyone's list of interests or concerns."[89]

By the middle of the 1970s, the alienation and cultural disconnect that black students experienced on white evangelical campuses were becoming widely known among black evangelicals, which further discouraged enrollment. By 1974, "after many hours of conversation" with students of color attending white evangelical schools, Bill Pannell "concluded that evangelical schools as they now exist are inadequate to train minority leaders effectively." Their culture was suburban, middle class, entirely out of touch with the realities of a world of urban injustice. Students of color didn't fit in, Pannell said, and tended "to view the atmosphere of an evangelical campus as make-believe, where make-believe whites try to absorb a make-believe theology for a fantasy world."[90] The difficulties for black students were so obvious and consistent that the National Black Evangelical Association sponsored a *Handbook for Black Christian Students*, which was intended to guide students on, as editor Ruth Lewis Bentley subtitled the booklet, *How to Remain Sane and Grow in a White College Setting*.[91] Her guiding principles for the book were that black students needed Jesus and they needed each other. She had seen black students lose their faith altogether in the face of racism on college campuses. Bentley counseled black students to band together and find a solid Christian identity in their "redeemed blackness."[92]

Bentley gathered a team of black evangelical contributors who promoted Christian race consciousness by incorporating strains of black power, black theology, and black nationalism. One essay discouraged black students from spending too much energy trying to educate white students. The most likely outcome was emotional exhaustion for the black student and little change on the part of white students. Instead, the black student should pursue academic excellence and the building up of a black student group while encouraging white students, in an echo of Stokely Carmichael, to work against "the oppressive structures and the white racism" of their own community.[93] Another essay discouraged interracial dating on the grounds that it harmed black families and disrupted the ongoing "psychological liberation" the black power movement had initiated. "The first and most important step in rebuilding the black nation," wrote Ronald Potter in one of his contributing essays, "is developing strong black Christian families." These black families would counter American standards of beauty and value, while interracial couples would continue to harm the psychology of black women and children. In contrast, "Nation-building within the black family will bring about health for the black man, the black woman, and the black child."[94] Though designed as a handbook for black students on white campuses, it could easily be read as a brief for attending a historically black college.

The retreat from black recruitment left some colleges with fewer black students at the end of the process than at the beginning. At Bethel, the sudden presence of black students had stirred ugly (and false) rumors that the school was lowering academic and theological standards.[95] In 1972, the school dismissed six students for violating the code of conduct. Four of the students were black, meaning that an extraordinarily high proportion of the black students were expelled. Controversy was so intense that Bethel simply canceled its black recruitment campaign outright. By the spring of 1975, 0.4 percent of Bethel's students were black.[96] Wheaton College shut down its Compensatory Education Program and began a new initiative in 1970 that targeted black students from backgrounds deemed more likely to fit in at Wheaton. By 1980, Wheaton had a grand total of 20 black students, less than in the early 1970s. Black enrollment at Calvin peaked at 50 students in 1974–1975 and declined thereafter. By then, some Christian Reformed activists ministering to African Americans in poor urban neighborhoods felt they could no longer recommend Calvin College to prospective black students. The insensitivity and abuse were too great. President Spoelhof was resigned to the outcome. "It could be that we just are not geared for the minority student. I hate to arrive at that conclusion, but it could be true that in our specific situation there are simply insurmountable difficulties."[97]

The unique histories and ethnoreligious identities of many white evangelical colleges complicated their integration efforts. Bethel was Swedish Baptist, Calvin was Dutch Reformed, Messiah was German Anabaptist, and Moody was nondenominational fundamentalist. In 1972, a Christian Reformed Church report revealed that every member of the governing boards of Dordt College and Calvin College was ethnically Dutch. Even all the maintenance workers at both schools were white. An ostensibly humorous bumper sticker on sale in the Calvin bookstore was emblematic: "If yer not Dutch yer not mutch" [sic].[98] Into the 1980s, admissions officials at colleges such as Houghton and North Park seemed more concerned about maintaining the denominational character of their student bodies than in becoming more diverse. For denominations that were almost entirely white, these recruiting priorities had racial implications. Moreover, nearly all schools drew on donor bases and prospective student populations that had felt the influence of fundamentalism and sacred whiteness through the first half of the twentieth century. These influences whitened evangelicalism theologically and narrowed its social ambitions. The arrival of black students in the 1960s required nothing less than theological reformation and a new communal identity. By the middle of the 1970s, white evangelical campuses scaled back expectations for racial change. Lyle Hillegas, the president of Westmont College in Santa Barbara, California, admitted that the school "had particular difficulty in getting blacks." Hillegas said the school's Hispanic and Asian students seemed to "fit in better." Black students, he said, "easily become isolated" and seemed to reject even the well-intentioned actions of white students. In spite of all the college's efforts—serving soul food, trying to include them in the planning of social events, featuring a "Black Emphasis Week" in chapel—Hillegas concluded, "I do not think we have succeeded at all." David McKenna, president of Seattle Pacific College, believed white evangelical colleges were being asked to bear the brunt of a broader problem. They served an overwhelmingly white constituency. Yet they faced pressure from the government and from some evangelicals to diversify, even as "the evangelical Christian community has not provided us with a black evangelical base from which to draw." Colleges were being asked to solve a problem that only the larger evangelical community could resolve.[99]

Conclusion

For white evangelical colleges, becoming more diverse was not just a matter of changing curriculum and hiring new faculty. It meant redefining the body of Christ. While the black revolt on mainstream campuses produced significant systemic changes such as the rise of departments of African American studies, on white evangelical campuses black students' demands were both more modest *and* less likely to be met. White administrators pleaded institutional poverty. Not unreasonably, they pointed out that many of their institutions simply did not have the resources that a large secular college could deploy. This was true, but the theological and social context mattered too. Administrators at white evangelical schools were trying to manage environments that they needed to sell to donors, alumni, and prospective students not just as academically rigorous and in keeping with the times, but as wholesome Christian spaces where community centered in Christ was enacted. Many stakeholders in white evangelical colleges believed the very notions of black studies programs, affirmative action, black student groups, and the like were antithetical to that vision of Christian community. Using the rhetoric of Christian colorblindness, white evangelicals could express a desire for unity without engaging in systemic reform. The uneasy silence that descended on white evangelical campuses marked the solidification of the colorblind Christian campus as a space of white normativity and nominal integration.

In environments where whiteness had become an implicit marker of theological rigor, becoming an inclusive academic institution raised core questions about Christian community and the nature of evangelical identity. By their very presence, black students revealed the symbiosis of whiteness and Christianity that had been so invisible to its practitioners. Anne Gilliam, a black student at Messiah College, exposed the racial theology of her institution in 1973. Like many black students, she had arrived with high expectations of a Christian community that could transcend race. During her four years there, she had become disillusioned. She now saw her role differently. "My job," she wrote, "is to show the white Christians here that they have been living a lie in the form of Jesus Christ. He has been a white Christ with white middle class values, and I am neither white nor am I middle class."[100] Gilliam's four years at Messiah came at the height of the civil rights era ferment on white evangelical campuses. By the middle of the 1970s, racial tensions declined and token integration reigned. It seemed that many colleges had managed to put the genie back in the bottle. But beneath the surface, the struggle for an evangelical faith beyond the investment in whiteness would continue.

3

Growing the Homogeneous Church

While white evangelical colleges made new efforts to recruit black students, white evangelical churches moved in a very different direction. Colorblind Christians faced a simple conundrum: overt church segregation had come into disrepute, but proactive church integration remained extremely difficult.¹ In this climate, the teachings of the Church Growth Movement (CGM) emerged rather suddenly in the 1970s as a popular strategy for starting and growing evangelical churches within the United States.² The CGM taught that socially homogeneous churches grew fastest. As the CGM's founder, Donald McGavran, declared, "Men like to become Christians without crossing racial, linguistic, or class barriers."³ "Show me a growing church," Professor C. Peter Wagner wrote in 1974, "and I'll show you a homogeneous . . . church."⁴ Critics worried that this was just another way of justifying segregation. The black evangelical activist John Perkins wrote that it seemed awfully "convenient" for white evangelicals to suddenly discover after the civil rights movement that "homogenous [sic] churches grow fastest!"⁵ Church growth theorists insisted their ideas did not offer any support for American segregation. After all, the origins of their movement were not to be found in the struggles of the civil rights–era American South, but in Donald McGavran's work on the mission field of central India in the 1930s. Though the CGM as a popular American phenomenon was a long time in coming, when it burst on the scene in the 1970s it helped to reify American evangelicalism as white, middle class, and suburban. Through the CGM, ideas generated by American missionaries in the global south in the 1930s circled back to the United States, where white evangelicals applied them in thousands of local churches in the 1970s and beyond.

In CGM practice, white middle-class suburbanites in the United States effectively became "a people"—a distinct cultural group with a strong sense of ethnic identity and loyalty—not unlike the Kikuyu in Kenya or the Bhil in India. In this way church growth theorists came to understand white identity in the United States not as racial hierarchy but as cultural pluralism. Instead of resisting American white supremacy, white evangelicals could invest in it to grow their churches in an era of white flight. Ironically, the race-conscious strategies of the CGM had great appeal to colorblind Christians. Precisely because whiteness was normative and often invisible to white evangelicals, these investments appeared to them as innocuous rather than discriminatory. The CGM offered white evangelicals absolution for their monochrome congregations and the promise of church growth without uncomfortable racial diversity that might disrupt their religio-racial identities. In a post–civil rights movement age when colorblind Christians dared not defend segregation outright and, indeed, no longer wanted to do so, the CGM enabled white evangelicals to recast their segregated churches and ongoing appeals to white identity as faithful evangelism rather than racism.

David Hollinger has suggested that American Protestant missionaries in the twentieth century created an accidental "boomerang effect." They set out to change the world and ended up transforming the United States.[6] The CGM was the evangelical corollary to this boomerang effect. Throughout the civil rights era, evangelical missionaries around the world had warned that racism at home hindered the cause of Christ abroad. These concerns made foreign missions a seemingly progressive force for evangelical racial change in the United States.[7] But the CGM revealed a different side to this missionary influence, one that doubled down on the appeal of whiteness in an age of pluralism. In its creative insistence that the power of group identity—even whiteness in the United States—could be harnessed to grow churches, the CGM demonstrated the potency of transnational exchange and the vitality of an American evangelicalism eager to borrow, appropriate, and repurpose changes in American culture for its own enduring goals of evangelization. To understand how white evangelical churches adapted to the civil rights movement, a church growth seminar turned out to be a far more revealing site of activism than a Republican Party meeting.

The Origins of the Church Growth Movement

CGM founder Donald McGavran lived an extraordinary life. His career, stretching across most of the twentieth century, profoundly shaped

American missionary practices and American churches.[8] Along the way, McGavran charted a course from the liberal Protestantism of his early years to an evangelicalism more suited to his crusading spirit. Born in India in 1897, he was the son and grandson of missionaries to that country. He set foot in the United States for the first time in 1910. He remained in the United States into young adulthood, receiving his undergraduate education at Butler College in Indianapolis. While at Butler he came under the influence of the Student Volunteer Movement, an influential missionary coalition that recruited college students for the foreign mission field.[9] Inspired by the SVM, McGavran decided to become a missionary.[10]

McGavran's outlook in the 1920s was broadly ecumenical rather than fundamentalist. He was a member of the Disciples of Christ, a Protestant denomination focused more on Christian unity than on litigating the so-called fundamentalist versus modernist battles of the era.[11] Before returning to India as a missionary in his own right in 1923, McGavran earned a bachelor of divinity degree at Yale Divinity School. He then took advantage of a furlough between 1930 and 1932 to complete coursework for his PhD in religious education at Union Theological Seminary and Columbia University.[12] Trained in the power centers of liberal Protestantism, McGavran would later say that in his younger years he had "counted" himself as "one of the enlightened."[13] In his early years in India he worked comfortably in the fold of liberal Protestant missions. McGavran and his missionary partners declared the good news of Jesus Christ, established schools to educate the poor, and built hospitals to care for the sick. But hard experience upset his youthful self-satisfaction, and he began to wonder to what end all his efforts were pointing.

By the mid-1930s, McGavran became increasingly concerned about the stagnant condition of the missionary-founded churches. Why weren't they growing? In search of answers, he began to shed the liberal theology he had learned at Yale and Union. The most formative intellectual influence driving McGavran's shift was a Methodist missionary to India, J. Waskom Pickett. In 1933, Pickett published *Christian Mass Movements in India*, a study that anticipated much of McGavran's later thought. Pickett and McGavran had come of age in the era of the "white man's burden." European imperialism meant not only soldiers, railroads, and resource extraction. It meant European and American missionaries seeking to save, educate, and uplift populations imagined as uncivilized.[14] Pickett challenged some of these paternalistic assumptions and emphasized the importance of contextualizing Christianity in indigenous cultures. He criticized the individualism of Western missionaries and called for a more evidence-based approach to missions. It was not enough for missionaries to be well intentioned. They also had to assess whether their missionary methods were working. Pickett insisted that if Western missionaries discarded their paternalism and individualistic assumptions whole populations could turn to Christianity without disrupting indigenous social bonds and cultural autonomy.[15]

McGavran was enthralled. His own experiences seemed to confirm Pickett's ideas. The people of central India were not becoming Christians. Churches were not growing. Why not? "We have rendered lip-service to Evangelism," McGavran wrote, "but have been too busy to practice it."[16] He believed part of the problem was that the good works the mission stations were doing separated Indian Christians from their communities.[17] Children attending missionary schools might become good Christians, but in the process they also became like their teachers. These conversions cut them off from their culture. After McGavran wrote a glowing review of Pickett's book, the two men worked together in 1936 to prepare a "Mass Movement Survey" of church growth in central India. McGavran believed the report demonstrated an unprecedented opportunity for "rapid growth along castewise lines."[18] After McGavran's self-described awakening, he worked as a missionary in India for nearly two more decades and tried, by trial and error, to implement his new ideas about evangelism. He also studied other mission agencies in India to understand why some churches were growing and some were not. He came to believe there was nothing more important than the questions of how people become Christian and how churches grow. All human beings faced an eternal destiny, he knew, and only the good news of Jesus Christ's death and resurrection could save them. It was incumbent upon missionaries to use the best possible methods to bring the greatest numbers of people into the Christian fold.

In the spring of 1954, McGavran toured several states in East and Central Africa in a bid to gain a more global perspective on church growth. As he prepared for the journey, he was finalizing the manuscript of a book he hoped would shatter the complacency of Western missions. He had submitted it to the publisher and anxiously awaited word of its acceptance. He worried that he would be forced to shorten the book, but he didn't know how he "could cut out so much pure gold."[19] He sent his manuscript off to Pickett for advice, declaring "there is no one in India whose judgement I value more highly."[20] In April he set out for Africa. His travel notebooks and letters reveal a keen observer, a man eager to soak up all the information and experiences he could. As he journeyed by boat from Karachi to Kenya he enthused, "The adventure has really begun."[21] Traveling "by ship, plane, train, car, foot, lorry, truck," McGavran made his way through Kenya, Uganda, Rwanda, Burundi, and Congo.[22] In Uganda he took in a Sunday service at Kampala Cathedral. "I was the only white man present," he noted.[23] While traveling, McGavran commented on food and fashion, politics and geography, and, of course, the past and prospects of Christian missions in the countries he visited.

He arrived in Nairobi amid the Mau Mau revolt. The British colonial government had declared a state of emergency in October of 1952 and embarked on a brutal counterinsurgency campaign.[24] McGavran observed a European settler community "built up in a land which they consider *is their own*." He thought immigrant Indians "stir up the Africans to create trouble and to run the Europeans out" with dubious promises of solidarity among people of color. Meanwhile, "The Europeans hang desperately on to the idea that they are going to rule Kenya." They promised a fair deal to Africans and Indians, but "the Europeans themselves will decide what is a fair deal. And the Africans (the tiny educated minority) boil and bristle at this taking of their best lands by the Europeans—and their best jobs by the Asians—and plan to throw them both out!! What a mess," he concluded.[25] If McGavran's assumption that Indians were stirring Africans up showed his paternalism, his recognition of legitimate African grievances about land expropriation made him more insightful than many British and American observers. In Britain and the United States "Mau Mau" usually signified atavistic and senseless violence.[26] McGavran took a more nuanced view than Europeans invested in colonial projects as such. He could afford a more detached perspective about declining European power because what really mattered to him was "the state of the church and its growth." The political context could affect the church, but it was no match for "the power of God and men dedicated to his service."[27]

McGavran concluded his African trip more confident than ever that the ideas born in India were applicable throughout the global south. Whether in caste-conscious India or amid the independence conflicts of colonial Africa, people needed to hear the gospel in a way that resonated in their culture and preserved their sense of belonging in their social group. He published *The Bridges of God*, a sharp rebuke of traditional Western missionary practices, the following year. The question of how people became Christians stood at the center of the book. Like Pickett, he argued that Western missionaries were too often blinkered by their individualistic assumptions. Human beings' social bonds and sense of peoplehood were crucial assets in the quest to evangelize the world. These forces were the "bridges" God wished to use to bring vast "People Movements" into his kingdom.[28] McGavran believed that rather than orienting missionary activity around a paternalistic mission station that plucked a few individual converts out of indigenous society now and then, missionaries ought to invite whole groups to encounter Christ en masse without giving up their culture and group identity. In places like India, the invitation to become Christian should not compel people to relinquish their caste identities. Rather than understanding caste as an obstacle to the formation of Christian churches, missionaries had to start seeing castes as pathways for God's work. Christianity could spread further and faster *along* caste lines than *across* them.

In 1955, McGavran had no thought of applying these ideas to the United States. In fact, he explicitly contrasted the "homogeneous" and "individualistic" populations of the "West" with the "castes, clans, and peoples" of the rest of the world. McGavran noted that the "intense battle against race prejudice" in the United States caused many missionaries to reject ideas of racial difference and racial consciousness. "But to ignore the significance of race hinders Christianization," he wrote. "It makes an enemy of race consciousness, instead of an ally. It does no good to say that tribal peoples ought not to have race prejudice. They do have it and are proud of it. It can be understood and should be made an aid to Christianization."[29] With his focus set on foreign missions,

McGavran believed that these evangelistic strategies were not relevant to the "modern" societies of Western Europe and the United States.[30] As American elites declared opportunity for all as a national creed and imagined a consensus in American life on everything from labor and capital to religion and patriotism, it was easy for McGavran to assume the United States had moved beyond the intense communal bonds and prejudices of so-called premodern peoples.[31]

If McGavran had looked a little more closely, he might have seen the reality of prejudice and discrimination that undergirded the imagined consensus in American society. He might have seen a religious landscape that sacralized hierarchy with every bit as much fervor as the caste system with which he was so familiar. By the time *The Bridges of God* went to press, the gathering force of the civil rights struggle was beginning to expose white evangelicals' religio-racial commitments. One of the nation's most popular evangelical pastors offered an example. Under W. A. Criswell's preaching, the First Baptist Church of Dallas, Texas, had grown to become one of the largest congregations in the country. Even Billy Graham was a member. Criswell liked to speak his mind, and he had no use for cowards. At a pastors' conference in February 1956, Criswell vigorously defended segregation. His words struck such a chord that the governor of South Carolina invited him to speak to the South Carolina legislature a few days later, with the expectation that he would reprise his performance. When Criswell stood before lawmakers on the afternoon of February 22, he did not disappoint. His address effectively combined Southern Baptist identity and white supremacy as a single edifice. Criswell accused integrationists of attacking everything "we love as good old Southern people and as good old Southern Baptists." There was no line between Christianity and whiteness; they made each other. Integrationists violated the sanctity of his home and struck at his deepest commitments as a white southerner and a Southern Baptist. "Some of these things are personal," Criswell said. "Some of them belong to the inside of your heart and your soul." But he insisted he had nothing against black Christians and did not feel superior to them. He believed human nature dictated that people, black and white alike, were happier among their own "kind." Segregation was preference, not hierarchy.[32] Such attitudes could become fertile ground for McGavran's race-conscious evangelism if he ever decided to mine them.

The Yale historian of Christianity Kenneth Scott Latourette called *The Bridges of God* "one of the most important books on missionary methods that have appeared in many years."[33] Another reviewer called it "revolutionary."[34] The Christian and Missionary Alliance, the evangelical denomination that had trained Wanda and Howard Jones, made it required reading for all its new missionaries.[35] Amid favorable reviews, some active missionaries offered critiques of McGavran's ideas. A missionary to Burma faulted McGavran for failing to pay sufficient attention to the workings of political power. "Isn't it significant," he asked, "that almost all the 'People Movements' have been among minority ethnic groups that have to some extent been dissatisfied with their lot?"[36] Other reviewers accused McGavran of compromising the gospel by accommodating social divisions and hierarchies—especially caste in India—for the sake of producing converts.[37] When, over a decade later, McGavran's ideas became popular among white evangelical pastors and church planters in the United States, these criticisms would loom large.

Some of the ideas that would make the CGM so alluring and controversial in the decades to come could already be seen in the drafting stage of *The Bridges of God*. An early version of the manuscript had an illustration showing how much money missionaries could expect to spend for each convert gained in different parts of India. This was the "cost per Christian."[38] Evangelicals knew they could not serve God and mammon, but McGavran was sure mammon could be used to serve God. The naked pragmatism of his approach made some Christians queasy. During the manuscript stage of McGavran's second book, one reviewer worried that his language almost made it seem as though he would "make the business of Church-growth a *real business-enterprise*, to be treated as Ford or Pontiac." He warned McGavran that he might be too caught up in "the modern trend of American business-thinking."[39] Another commenter wrote that McGavran seemed to advocate "growth for growth's sake."[40]

McGavran, in typical fashion, was buoyed by the enthusiastic reviews and undeterred by the criticisms. By the time *The Bridges of God* was published he was nearing 60 years of age, but he was ready to launch a second career. He embarked on a world tour, studying church growth in Latin America and East Asia. For a few years, McGavran became something of an itinerant evangelist for his church growth theories, with teaching stints at several American colleges and seminaries. During this late 1950s interregnum between McGavran's missionary career in India and his later prominence as the founder of the CGM, he gave his most sustained attention to the problem of racism in the United States.

McGavran's Theology of Race

The United States to which McGavran returned in the 1950s was a society infused with religion. As the country mobilized for the Cold War, pastors and politicians defined America as a Christian nation in opposition to atheistic communism. Politicians competed to display their religious patriotism, adding "under God" to the Pledge of Allegiance and making "In God We Trust" an official national motto. Billy Graham skillfully mixed American nationalism and evangelical revivalism in his crusades, becoming a national celebrity. Movies such as *The Ten Commandments* and *Ben-Hur* were epic blockbusters, reminding Americans that they stood on God's side in an eternal struggle between freedom and tyranny. Church membership soared. By the end of the decade, more Americans than ever before claimed a religious affiliation.[41]

The geography of American Christianity was changing too, as metropolitan areas experienced rapid demographic and economic transformations. Discrimination and agricultural mechanization in the South pushed millions of African Americans to try their fortunes in northern cities, moving the center of gravity of black Protestantism from the rural South to the urban North.[42] The Great Migration changed the landscape of African American religion and presented a challenge to the segregated white churches of northern cities. White evangelical churches actively contributed to the dislocations of white flight, exacerbating an era of disinvestment from center cities.[43] In the early twentieth century, the fundamentalist movement had thrived in cities such as Chicago, Philadelphia, and Boston.[44] Now their white evangelical descendants were leaving the city. What was the responsibility of local churches in a moment of such rapid and divisive racial change? McGavran wrestled with this question during a six-month sojourn in Indianapolis in 1958.

When McGavran had last lived in Indianapolis while attending Butler College, the city boasted integrated schools and a large black population. But from the 1920s, city leaders began to enact Jim Crow–style segregation as the African American population grew.⁴⁵ By the 1950s, segregation of housing, schools, churches, and employment networks was standard practice in the city. After arriving early in 1958, McGavran planted himself at Second Christian Church, a black congregation. He was surprised to find that he was the only white member of the church, and he promptly drafted an audacious plan for a member exchange program among white and black churches in the city. Mature believers in each of the respective churches would be chosen to temporarily attend a church of another race, thereby enhancing understanding and brotherhood, and breaking down the walls of segregation. McGavran convinced the leadership of Second Christian Church to support his idea and sent a letter to dozens of churches in the city. He received a thoroughly discouraging response. White churches were not impressed with an outsider who presumed to know how to fix their churches during a six-month visit. Nor were they charmed by McGavran's blunt criticisms. He called the very notion of "coloured" and "white" churches a "satanic condition." Though his outrage at racial division was palpable, his efforts in Indianapolis bore little fruit.⁴⁶

The following year, he took up residence in Des Moines, Iowa, where he was a visiting professor at Drake Divinity School. Again the indefatigable missionary pestered the local congregations to promote church integration, and again he was rebuffed. It seemed that white Christians in northern cities had little appetite for the kind of brotherhood McGavran espoused. Though Des Moines had a much smaller black population than Indianapolis, white supremacists in the city nonetheless sought to intimidate those who challenged segregation. After a white pastor sold his house to an African American, a cross was burned on the pastor's front lawn. As McGavran sat down to write the following day, he was in no mood to make excuses for his fellow white Christians. He was "certain that among the cross-burners were members of white churches." And he was equally convinced that these Christians had never experienced genuine fellowship with African Americans as fellow believers in Christ. They had not shared meals or sat in the same pew or sung the same songs together. They had not encountered each other on grounds of spiritual equality. As a result, they vented their racial opinions "immorally, and ludicrously." While paying lip service to brotherhood, they had never actually experienced it. Instead, they indulged in "sub-Christian stereotypes."⁴⁷

McGavran paired his outrage at white Christians with a paternalistic mindset toward black Christians. He wrote that white Christians in Des Moines "have no first-hand knowledge of the strong bearing the burdens of the weak, or of the culturally advanced joyfully fellowshipping with the culturally retarded and being accepted by them. Of this part of the cross they have no comprehension." Most Christians were familiar with the Apostle Paul's instruction to bear the burdens of the weak, but McGavran's deployment of this idea in the context of the racial controversies in Des Moines made strength and weakness not just spiritual characteristics, but racial ones. McGavran seemed to indicate that white Christians could retain their assumptions of cultural superiority even as they embraced spiritual union with black believers. The work of Christ on the cross brought all human beings together and opened up the possibility of brotherhood that transcended race. Yet white people, as such, were "strong" and "advanced" and would enact brotherhood through their willingness to bear with the "weak" believers of color.[48]

Despite—or because of—his missionary experiences, McGavran seemed to approach African Americans with an attitude at once accepting and colonialist. With this posture he tapped into a long American tradition of paternalism both racial and theological. Many Americans imagined white Christianity as a masculine and rational agent of uplift for black Christianity imagined as feminine and emotional. In the nineteenth century, sympathetic observers often portrayed African Americans as naturally religious, the better to emphasize their dignity in the face of suffering. By the early twentieth century, the flip side of this assumed religiosity came to the fore. African American religion supposedly revealed the primitivism and emotionalism intrinsic to blackness.[49] Whiteness carried connotations of theological maturity and biblical literacy, while blackness implied irrational spiritual exuberance. William J. Petersen, executive editor of *Eternity*, perfectly captured this sensibility in 1963. While urging white evangelicals to break down "race barriers," he offered an instructive history lesson for his readers. The "American Negro" had been "set adrift spiritually by the American white" after the Civil War. The result was a century of isolation. Black churches lacked "the counsel and economic aid" of white churches. Bringing the story up to the present, Petersen spun a woeful tale of black religious damage: "they are still struggling without ways or means, the illegitimate offspring of the marriage of a slave culture and the Christian church. Their father is dead and their mother has disowned them."[50] With such rhetoric Petersen put a spiritual twist on the motif of black impairment then popular among historians and social scientists, who argued that slavery and Jim Crow had wounded the black psyche and deformed black culture.[51] Many white evangelicals found it easier to perceive African American Christians as subjects of pity and missionary charity—the children of a white "mother"—than as equal partners in a common faith.

In 1961, McGavran drew on his experiences in Indianapolis and Des Moines to produce an article manuscript titled "End Segregation in the Churches Now." He shopped it around to Christian magazines including the evangelical *Christianity Today* and the more liberal *Christian Century* before another evangelical periodical, the *Christian Herald*, agreed to publish it. The core of the article was a restatement of his member exchange program. Despite its failure in Indianapolis and Des Moines, McGavran apparently thought the idea still had merit. The article provided a fascinating window into McGavran's thought in a moment of transition. In his missiology, he remained focused on places like India and Latin America. When he turned his attention to the United States, he saw in the system of segregation a social injustice and a theological scandal. He did not immediately draw a connection to the evangelistic ideas he advocated for the global south, though the dots were there for connecting. If caste-based movements for Christ were useful in the caste-conscious society of India, why not race-based movements for Christ in a country as obsessed with race as the United States? After the theological and cultural earthquakes of the 1960s this question would impress itself on McGavran and his followers. But these unimagined changes lay in the future. For now, McGavran offered an optimistic faith in the power of Christian fellowship to break down racial barriers.

McGavran believed there was a latent desire for brotherhood among American Christians that only needed to be awakened. There were just a few practical problems to overcome, and his member exchange program could solve each of them. People didn't want to be "oddballs" by going to an integrated church, and they didn't want their kids to develop interracial romances. McGavran hinted at this last possibility rather than stating it outright. He also understood that, all too often, integrated worship in the era of white flight was a temporary phenomenon signaling a neighborhood in transition from white to black. He described "the irresistible march of Negroes to take over white residential areas," as if black homebuyers were a force of nature reshaping the metropolitan landscape. "Integrated worship," McGavran observed, "often occurs in churches lying in the path of Negro steamrollers." It was a revealing metaphor. Steamrollers flatten and crush, overwhelming whatever is in their path, leaving an empty surface in their wake. McGavran's metaphor seemed to display an assumption of white Christian entitlement in the American city.[52] Were white evangelicals as eager for "brotherhood" as McGavran claimed? The pervasiveness of sacred whiteness seemed to challenge his optimism. The intractable core of fantasy and fear at the center of this theology—interracial sex—was a significant barrier to church integration. Rather than attacking white fear and entitlement head-on, McGavran sought to manage it through methodological innovations: *don't* send teenagers; *do* send older couples or a young family; make sure the commitment has an end date.

McGavran's project was necessarily race conscious, but in important ways it anticipated the methods colorblind Christians would use in the years to come. Rather than seeking systemic reforms, McGavran presumed there was a Christian consensus for brotherhood that could be stirred through a voluntary program of interpersonal interaction. The goal of these interactions was a new consciousness of the spiritual reality of Christian unity rather than a change in power.[53] Through his member exchange program, Christians could become conscious of their unity in Christ. In doing so, they would paint a picture of the destiny of humanity. "It would please the Lord Jesus Christ to see men from every tribe and kindred and tongue and people worshipping Him together in America, today," McGavran wrote. He borrowed this language from the seventh chapter of John's Revelation, the apocalyptic conclusion to the Christian scriptures. In other words, McGavran wanted American Christians—through their interracial worship—to present to the world nothing less than a foretaste of the end of time.[54]

Growing the Movement

In 1961, McGavran took a new position at Northwest Christian College in Eugene, Oregon, as the founder and director of the Institute of Church Growth. He set up shop at a desk in the library and called his one-man operation an "Institute." But the small size of the venture belied the growing scale of McGavran's influence. His board of advisors included the president of the University of Oregon and also the state's governor, Mark Hatfield.[55] In 1962, McGavran brought together key thinkers from the Southern Baptist Convention, the Assemblies of God, and the American Bible Society for a dialogue later published by Harper & Row as *Church Growth and Christian Mission*. Eerdmans, the major evangelical publishing house, launched a church growth book series, and in 1964 McGavran's institute received a grant from the Lilly Endowment to promote the study of church growth in Latin America.[56] McGavran also founded the *Church Growth Bulletin*, a new monthly periodical initially delivered free to thousands of key missions executives and missionaries around the world. During the 1960s he forged close ties with the Evangelical Foreign Missions Association (EFMA) and the International Foreign Mission Association, organizations responsible for well over half of the total number of Protestant missionaries sent from the United States. Wade Coggins of the EFMA wrote that his organization "has given the fullest possible backing to Dr. McGavran." Annual church growth seminars at Winona Lake, Indiana, in partnership with the EFMA, brought together dozens of missionaries and mission agency executives each year. A single seminar might routinely draw representatives from over a dozen denominations and mission boards. McGavran was becoming known as "a rather key man" that groups such as the National Association of Evangelicals would do well to develop closer connections with if they wanted to grow their influence with independent churches. Growing numbers of evangelical seminaries were using McGavran's books in their curriculums and some denominations made his work required reading for new missionaries.[57]

Though McGavran's work was primarily associated with the evangelical wing of American Protestantism, in the early 1960s he still hoped to influence a broad cross-section of Protestants, both evangelical and mainline. He had some temporary success. In the summer of 1963, the World Council of Churches' Department of Missionary Studies held a consultation on "The Growth of the Church" and asked McGavran to lead some of the sessions. The consultation produced a statement that advocated church growth and evangelism in terms remarkably similar to McGavran's, and it explicitly praised McGavran's "pioneering work" at the Institute of Church Growth.[58] McGavran in this period was at his most winsome and charismatic as he enthused, "A new world community has come into being, based not on might, wealth, color, or continent, but on a common faith in Jesus Christ and the scriptural teaching that in Him there is neither Jew nor Greek, slave nor free, white nor black, but one great brotherhood of man." He declared that "Christianity... must be purged of its present image as the white man's religion."[59]

As late as 1964, McGavran was still trying to bring the two poles of American Protestantism together in a common evangelistic enterprise. He held out hope that his institute could be a place where the National Council of Churches (NCC) and the evangelical mission organizations could come together. Evangelical leaders warned McGavran in no uncertain terms that it would be impossible for them to work with the NCC. McGavran's dalliances with liberal Protestants left some evangelicals concerned about his reliability. Clyde Taylor, executive secretary of the EFMA, reassured a worried correspondent, "As a result of his prolonged past associations with these people [i.e., liberal Protestants] he has picked up much of their vocabulary. However, he is an out and out evangelical."[60] McGavran may have sought allies wherever he could find them, but he knew who his friends were. By the end of the 1960s, as the World Council of Churches emphasized social action over evangelism, he would write off liberal Protestants and focus all his energies on the evangelical movement.

In 1965, McGavran moved to the influential Fuller Theological Seminary in California, an institution closely associated with efforts to renew an evangelical intellectual tradition and gain mainstream respectability.[61] He was invited to serve as the founding dean of the new School of World Mission, with a mandate to hire a faculty. There was competition as well as trepidation among evangelical seminaries about the prospect of catching a big fish like McGavran. Clyde Taylor cautioned that McGavran's institute might "swamp" the school to which it became attached. "This is pretty much his own show," he warned. Another comment Taylor made as McGavran sought a new home for his institute might just as well have summed up the restless energy of McGavran's entire career. "Actually," Taylor wrote to Norman Cummings, "you and I know that we do not have any real control over Dr. McGavran."[62] The move to Fuller meant that McGavran had more resources at his command and could dramatically expand the scale of his church growth operations. He was perched in an important role at one of the most powerful evangelical institutions in the country. He did not intend to let the opportunity go to waste.

The CGM, now poised to go mainstream, was an identifiable body of thought still closely associated with McGavran in particular but embraced by a growing cross-section of American evangelicals active in foreign missions. The movement might have seemed paradoxical at a glance.[63] It put a great deal of hope in both quantification and the working of the Holy Spirit. It criticized individualistic missions' strategies but insisted that the goal of missions was the salvation of individuals' souls. It paid attention to the latest scholarship in the fields of anthropology and sociology but did so in service of an evangelical conversion agenda. Yet in all these ways the movement was not as unprecedented or paradoxical as it may have appeared to some observers. Evangelicals had always been eager capitalizers on the latest trends and the CGM was no different. Indeed, the movement bore a striking resemblance to what Timothy Gloege has called the "corporate evangelical framework" and "consumer" religion pioneered decades earlier by figures such as Henry Crowell and James Gray.[64] Despite being embedded in this tradition, McGavran came to believe he was launching nothing less than a new academic discipline. He told his students he taught them the "science of church growth."[65] The factors that caused some churches to grow and others to stagnate could be measured. Best practices could be standardized and reproduced, leading to more converts. Mysterious supernatural processes revealed through divine revelation in the scriptures could be advanced through scientific and sociological principles. This melding of spirit and strategy, of piety and pragmatism, did not make the CGM an outlier in evangelicalism. On the contrary, this Christian modernism was characteristically evangelical and key to the movement's success.[66]

By the time McGavran moved to Fuller, the civil rights movement was reaching its apex. Whatever blind spots might have been reflected in his cross-racial member-exchange scheme, McGavran's enthusiasm for the freedom struggle distinguished him from most white evangelicals. During the height of the Selma campaign, he wrote a letter to Martin Luther King with an idea. He thought Dr. King ought to commission an artist to paint a scene of Jesus Christ's arrest in the garden of Gethsemane. Make it large, make it public, and put it on public property next to the courthouse in Selma. This would be no ordinary painting. Christ would be "darkskinned," his opponents "white skinned" and "leading police dogs." In the faces of disciples beaten to the ground the viewer would recognize the "martyrs" of the civil rights movement. And in the faces of Christ's oppressors, one would discern the likeness of Bull Connor of Birmingham and Jim Clark of Selma. "Expect it to be cut to ribbons," McGavran wrote. After white racists destroyed the first attempt, the art project would resume at an out-of-the-way black-owned property. It would become a "pilgrimage place" and a site of "educational pressure" and "international attention."[67] On another occasion he urged King to distribute a pro–civil rights pamphlet via an "air drop." The pamphlets would be tucked in envelopes marked "AIR MAIL FROM GOD" and hurled from planes over strategic cities.[68] Alongside these whimsical suggestions, McGavran offered more tangible supports: financial contributions to King's Southern Christian Leadership Conference, prayer, and assurance of Christian solidarity across the color line.

Besides sending supportive letters to Dr. King, he sent scathing letters to King's opponents. After white mob violence against school integration in Grenada, Mississippi, in September 1966, McGavran wrote to the town's mayor. The white residents of Grenada brought "shame and disgrace" on the South. "You have no chance to win," he declared. "God Himself wars against you. Turn from your evil ways while there is yet time."[69] These letters marked McGavran as an unusual white evangelical leader and revealed his crusading spirit.[70] Once he took up a cause as his own, there were very few shades of gray in his mind. His strong support for the civil rights movement showed the ongoing influence of his early grounding in liberal Protestantism and of his decades of mission work, which had brought him face to face with the oppression of marginalized groups around the world. These complexities defy attempts to paint him as a reactionary segregationist. Indeed, he was much more progressive on questions of race than most white evangelicals of his time, and far more comfortable with cultural diversity than most white Americans. But nothing mattered more to McGavran than converting people to Christianity. He remained ready to pick up any tool to accomplish that end. New developments in liberal Protestantism's approach to global missions and profound changes in American culture and politics were about to turn McGavran in a more conservative direction and open the door for the CGM to come home to the United States.

Bringing the Movement to the United States

When McGavran finally soured on the kind of liberal social activism the civil rights movement represented, it was not primarily because of events at home—the rise of black power, urban riots, protests against the Vietnam War—though these did affect him.[71] Much more concerning to McGavran were the changes in American missionary activity abroad. The decisive turning point came at the fourth assembly of the World Council of Churches held in Uppsala, Sweden, in 1968. He believed the liberal churches were "quietly scuttling" the historic mission of the church, which was evangelization. Liberal Protestants still used the language of Christianity, but now "salvation" meant political and social liberation, and "mission" meant doing good works.[72] McGavran wrote of 1968 as the moment the scales fell from his eyes and he realized how dire the cause of world evangelization had become. He had long had his differences with liberal Protestants, but he had not realized just how far they had moved from a traditional evangelistic missionary enterprise. McGavran had always insisted that Christians ought to do good works and care about injustice. It was on that basis that he supported Dr. King's desegregation campaigns. But Uppsala left him shaken and fearing the spread of a form of Christianity emptied of its supernatural evangelistic heart. He described the "capture" of the World Council of Churches "by men who are not in the least interested in discipling the nations." After Uppsala, McGavran more or less gave up on reaching mainline Protestants. He was determined not to "water down" his church growth message to appeal to Protestants who did not even agree on the church's mission.[73] Henceforth, McGavran became an advocate of evangelism at almost any cost.

McGavran echoed the conservative turn in American politics after 1968, but for him the root of the shift was the theological battle between evangelism and social justice. As he critiqued liberal Protestants, he more forcefully insisted on the absolute priority of evangelism over social concern. "Where Christ is enthroned in the heart," he declared, "social amelioration follows."[74] The man who had so enthusiastically supported the campaigns of Martin Luther King in 1965 was harder to recognize after 1968. This crucial turning point, rooted in international missiology rather than domestic politics, paved the way for McGavran to fully support the use of his church growth ideas in the United States. If, in 1958, segregated churches were a "satanic condition" that undercut the authenticity of the gospel, by the early 1970s Protestantism's emphasis on social justice seemed ready to drown out entirely the message of the gospel as McGavran understood it. He increasingly began to frame evangelism and social justice not as complementary but as competitors. The implications were stark. If evangelism and social justice were at odds, then attacking racism as McGavran had in Indianapolis and Des Moines in the 1950s might harm church growth. Maybe racial loyalties in the United States could, instead, be used to make evangelism more effective.

For the CGM to become a major force in American churches, it was not enough for McGavran and other evangelicals to be concerned about the missiology of liberal Protestants. Their view of American society had to change as well. The cultural and political convulsions of the civil rights movement provided ample material for this change. As early as 1963 Daniel Patrick Moynihan and Nathan Glazer had declared that the great American melting pot was an old-fashioned idea. The rise of black power further shifted perceptions about race consciousness and assimilation. As the 1970s dawned, a new era of cultural pluralism seemed to be at hand. In 1971 Michael Novak described the "unmeltable ethnics" who weren't WASPs and didn't want to be. This so-called ethnic revival made the United States look a lot more like the rest of the world than McGavran had imagined just a decade earlier.[75] Perhaps Americans' enthusiasm for ethnic consciousness and origin stories indicated that a deep-seated sense of peoplehood remained operative even in the United States.

In 1967, Wade Coggins, of the Evangelical Foreign Missions Association, noted that "up to now, church growth research and training have been aimed toward the missionary front. What about pastors in the U.S.? Should they not be equally interested and equally in need of this philosophy and emphasis?"[76] M. Wendell Belew, of the Southern Baptist Convention Home Mission Board, was asking the same question. Belew attended a McGavran-organized church growth symposium in 1964. He found the principles electrifying but was "disturbed" that they were not being applied to the United States. From Belew's perspective, much of the CGM thought aligned with what Southern Baptists were already doing. In the 1950s the Home Mission Board had established a Language Missions Division to provide funds and missionaries to establish Southern Baptist churches in immigrant and foreign-language communities. Southern Baptists were well aware of peoples' felt attachments to their group identity. Belew became a key figure synthesizing CGM thought and translating it for the nation's largest Protestant denomination. In books like *Churches, and How They Grow* and *Missions in the Mosaic*, he engaged with McGavran's ideas while seeking to approach church growth from a distinctly Southern Baptist perspective. While McGavran increasingly brooked no compromise on his core ideas, Belew adopted a more moderate tone, praising the CGM as a positive force but cautioning that there was more to the life of the church than numerical growth, and that the church needed to minister to physical as well as spiritual needs. For his part, McGavran called Belew "one of the great leaders of missions."[77]

McGavran, after describing the United States as "homogeneous" in the 1950s, now joined Belew in speaking of American society as a "mosaic" rather than a melting pot. And he forged connections with Southern Baptists who were trying to reach that mosaic. As early as 1963 he led a church growth seminar focused on growth within the United States. The Language Missions Department of the Baptist General Convention of Texas, a part of the Southern Baptist Convention (SBC), held a conference focused on Latino church growth. McGavran encouraged the audience of Latino pastors to be unabashedly different from the white Southern Baptists who had helped start their churches. "God has called you Latins to serve the 1,100,000 Latins," McGavran declared. "God calls you to make your churches much warmer, more friendly, more Latin than the Anglos, more Spanish, more Mexican, more tortilla, sombrero." But "What about the Anglo Churches and Anglo Christians? Forget about them! . . . Act as if they did not exist. . . . Do not follow Anglo patterns."[78]

Following McGavran's logic, Southern Baptists had remarkable success. By 1978, the SBC claimed over 2,200 congregations of "minority ethnic identity."⁷⁹ In a convention that prided itself on the independence of the local church, Southern Baptist efforts could promote the cultural autonomy of ethnic churches. During the 1970s McGavran praised Southern Baptists as the most successful practitioners of cross-cultural evangelism. While many denominations had little success diversifying, Southern Baptists added new ethnic congregations at a rapid clip. McGavran's Homogeneous Unit Principle—the idea that people liked to worship with people like themselves and should not have to cross boundaries of race, class, or language in order to become Christians—seemed intuitive to Southern Baptists. But such praise inadvertently highlighted the ambiguity of Southern Baptists' multiethnic turn. The SBC had long been a quintessential expression of segregationist Christianity and white southern identity. Did the embrace of church growth principles represent a repudiation of that segregationist past, or a refinement of it as the era of ethnic revival and multiculturalism dawned?

Perhaps because of their intimate acquaintance with the long history of Southern Baptist segregation, some Southern Baptist leaders found much to be cautious about in CGM thought. They didn't want church growth ideas to enable overt racism. Francis Dubose, professor of Missions at Golden Gate Baptist Theological Seminary, called the Homogeneous Unit Principle downright "Machiavellian," an approach to evangelization in which "the ends justify the means." Dubose admitted that the principle did seem to work, and he allowed that it could be helpful in some cases, especially for minority groups. But "the situation of the majority is fundamentally different," he insisted. Separation into homogeneous units was built on an ongoing history of "ostracism." Despite such concerns, some Southern Baptist leaders were wholeheartedly enthusiastic about McGavran's thinking. In *Design for Church Growth*, Charles Chaney and Ron Lewis encouraged churches to be "absolutely ruthless" in pursuit of numerical growth. Every church growth initiative was to be evaluated by a single pragmatic question: "Does it work?"⁸⁰ A 1981 Home Mission Board report put the racialized reality of this question in perspective when it admitted that "the overall church expansion of Southern Baptists is dependent upon trends in [sic] white population."⁸¹

As the nation's largest Protestant group variously adopted, resisted, and repurposed McGavran's ideas for their use, McGavran wanted his church growth principles applied to the cities from which so many white Protestants were fleeing. His "overriding conviction" about such work was that the populations of America's cities should be treated as distinct peoples. "It is of vital importance," he wrote to Southern Baptist missions professor Cal Guy, "that black populations, Porto Rican populations, Portuguese populations, etc., be regarded as special sub-cultures and churches which fit those cultures be planted amongst them—led by their leaders, operated at their level of culture."[82] Here were early indications that McGavran was willing to think of American minority groups in terms similar to "peoples" in the global south. But it is telling that he first thought in this way about people of color in the United States, not white Americans. Soon enough, his disciples would apply the same logic to the white majority.

The idea that homogeneous churches were effective vectors of Christianization was not new to the American context. White Protestants in the nineteenth century had sounded the alarm about the supposed threat of mass immigration and proposed home missions, complete with foreign-language churches for distinct ethnic groups, as a solution. Leading proponents of these home missions efforts often justified the work in explicitly xenophobic and racist terms as a nation-building project.[83] Getting the immigrant masses into churches was a form of quarantine on the way to eventual assimilation and Americanization. McGavran and the leading CGM theorists exhibited no institutional or personal memory of these American antecedents. In contrast to the overt Anglo-Saxon Christian nationalism of earlier American home missions advocates, the CGM described homogeneous churches as a purely evangelistic enterprise. CGM theorists consistently located the origins of their movement overseas and showed remarkable disinterest in questions of American decline or ascendance. For them, homogeneous churches were not instruments of national renewal or assimilation; they were ends in themselves because they understood them to be effective at converting people to Christianity. And while an earlier generation of mission churches had been launched in an era in which white supremacy was the avowed ideology of American public life, the CGM gained its ascendancy in a dramatically different context, in the aftermath of a civil rights movement that made integration and diversity the supposed American creed.[84] Because of this, CGM advocates imagined homogeneous churches not as waystations to assimilation but as healthy expressions of pluralism.

At Fuller Seminary, McGavran began gathering around him a team of followers who would spread his ideas. Among these, no one was more important than C. Peter Wagner. He was a missionary in Bolivia when he first heard the name Donald McGavran. He read *The Bridges of God* and concluded that "this fellow McGavran is a fanatic."[85] After all, if McGavran was right, much of the modern missionary enterprise was a waste of time. But Wagner gradually came to embrace McGavran's thought and in 1971 joined him on the faculty at Fuller. McGavran and Wagner established a close working relationship and friendship. Wagner, ever the loyal pupil, jealously guarded McGavran's reputation as the founder of the CGM and defended him against his critics. In his voluminous writings, Wagner interpreted the CGM for an American evangelical audience of pastors, professors, and church planters. As comfortable quoting Moynihan as the Apostle Paul, Wagner combined sociological analysis and spiritual revelation in an effort to make church growth theory the dominant methodology of the evangelical church in the United States.

In the fall of 1972, Wagner and McGavran cotaught a church growth class designed for leaders of American churches. Among the attendees was Win Arn. Inspired by the teaching, Arn promptly quit his job and founded the Institute for American Church Growth. Arn and other self-styled church growth experts taught church planters to conduct demographic analyses of local communities, taking note of factors such as per capita income and racial composition. A new church ought to have a clear idea of the sort of people it was trying to reach. They encouraged established churches to examine their membership records, graph changes over time, and set targets for future growth. Church growth manuals taught pastors how to create mathematical charts and calculate their "Annual Growth Rate (AGR)" and "Decadal Growth Rate (DGR)." These graphs were "as important to a student of church growth as a compass is to a sailor or a stethoscope to a physician," the manuals lectured.[86] Wagner suggested a "rule of thumb" that membership growth of 25 percent in a decade was "poor," while 100 percent was "good," 300 percent was "outstanding," and 500 percent was "incredible."[87] Church growth experts taught that in theory any church anywhere could grow.

In practice, as American cities continued to hemorrhage middle-class residents, locating new churches in growing suburbs was an obvious path to success.

By the middle of the 1970s when evangelicals used the phrase "Church Growth Movement" with capital letters, they were talking about a specific network of people and institutions. The institutional Church Growth Movement had its locus at Fuller Seminary and included organizations like Arn's Institute for American Church Growth and magazines like *Church Growth America* and *Church Growth Bulletin*. From there the CGM's influence spread to many evangelicals who embraced the ethos of "church growth," if not the jealous movement-building prickliness of the cadre of Fuller professors. Some denominations, like the Nazarenes, embraced McGavran's teachings wholesale and aggressively trained their pastors in it, while others selectively adopted strategies they found useful.[88] As if the growing influence of their movement wasn't enough, church growth theorists had a tendency to take credit for success wherever they found it. Though superstar pastor Robert H. Schuller founded his Garden Grove Community Church in Orange County, California, in 1955 without the influence of McGavran, CGM materials tended to describe Schuller as a man who made them look good, a successful religious entrepreneur who had "intuitively" understood their principles before they were widely known.[89]

It is not surprising that the movement would want to claim Schuller as its own. His church boasted thousands of members and innovative methodologies. Attendees were welcome to come inside or enjoy the service in the comfort of their cars parked in the "drive-in area."[90] Schuller's influence radiated outward through his national Hour of Power television show and his Institute for Successful Church Leadership. Among Schuller's most famous trainees was Bill Hybels, who went on to found the influential megachurch Willow Creek in suburban Chicago. Schuller's first book, for which Wagner wrote the foreword, was a veritable alphabet soup of self-help and positive-thinking pep talk from the very first page. Schuller promised readers "results . . . optimism . . . success . . . higher levels of accomplishment than you ever dreamed of . . ." all brought to life by "real possibility thinking!" With chapters like "Seven Principles of Successful Retailing," "How You Can Sell Your Ideas Successfully," and "Three Keys to Certain Success," Schuller invited pastors to jump into the religious marketplace and make their dreams come true. The CGM's positive appraisal of Schuller is a striking indicator of its comfort with the use of sleek marketing and business practices to sell the gospel. In these moments the CGM looked like nothing so much as an invitation to treat religion as another consumer good in the modern capitalist economy.[91] American consumers had high standards and many options on a Sunday morning. Churches needed to sell themselves or they would lose market share.[92]

As Wagner, Arn, and other popularizers of church growth theory extended McGavran's "peoples" approach to the white American middle class, the missiological language of McGavran's earlier work took on a more scientific sound. They talked about "homogeneous units" rather than "peoples." Though the Homogeneous Unit Principle sounded technical, it was an elastic term that could refer to numerous kinds of group affinities. Win Arn's organization stressed this principle as the axiomatic foundation for church growth. "Almost without exception," proclaimed *Church Growth America*, "a common characteristic of healthy, growing churches is a membership composed of basically one kind of people, be it defined culturally, ethnically, economically, educationally, linguistically, occupationally."[93] Arn warned against a church mismatching a pastor and its congregation. "People want their pastor to be 'like' them," he explained. Those desiring a "successful ministry" ought to make sure the "pastor and church fit the same basic homogeneous unit."[94] Though church growth theorists insisted they opposed segregation and racism, these instructions were all but explicit warnings against the danger of integration and cultural pluralism in a local church. When Wagner taught a church growth seminar at Wheaton Graduate School in the summer of 1972, his final exam included this question: "How could an integrated church in a segregated society retard evangelism?"[95] For students steeped in the idea that effective evangelism was priority number one, the message was clear. Wagner and Arn made no distinction between, say, a poor immigrant congregation that did not speak English and a wealthy white congregation in a prosperous suburb. Both were equally entitled to homogeneous worship with people like themselves, lest the spread of the gospel be impaired. Both were positive expressions of the diversity of the kingdom of God. In effect, if people like W. A. Criswell existed, Wagner and Arn did not want to know.

Some church growth literature openly described racial integration as a threat to the health of American churches. C. Peter Wagner's 1976 book, *Your Church Can Grow*, devoted a chapter to an "autopsy of a dead church." Zion Evangelical Free Church, a white congregation of several hundred in the Austin neighborhood of Chicago, closed in the summer of 1969. It had appeared healthy just a few years before. What went wrong? Wagner declared that he had examined the "corpse" and had the "diagnosis" in hand. Zion Free Church came to a sorry end because of a terminal case of "ethnikitis." Church leaders had failed to "understand and apply the homogeneous unit principle" before it was too late. As a result, the church became a "victim" of the changing racial demographics of the Austin neighborhood. As white residents moved out, the church's attendance rapidly dwindled from 350 to 30. In a desperate bid to save itself, Zion partnered with Circle Church, a new multiracial church in the neighborhood. This effort was doomed, Wagner informed his readers, because it involved a mixing of homogeneous units. Trying to merge a young, hip, multicultural church and a staid, traditional, white church produced "symptoms" of disease "almost as inevitably" as a blood transfusion mixing type A and B. A worship leader with sideburns showed up at Zion, causing offense. Some young women from Circle Church arrived in miniskirts, causing an uproar. And "the heaviest donor in the church left as soon as he heard that blacks would be welcome."[96] Wagner grouped all these phenomena together as examples of cultural incompatibility. The white supremacist, like those who objected to miniskirts and long sideburns, apparently deserved a homogeneous unit congregation. Over 20 years after McGavran wrote that the racial prejudices of "tribal peoples . . . can be understood and should be made an aid to Christianization," Wagner was directly transferring this pragmatic use of racism to American churches in an age of white flight.

As the CGM burst on the American scene, evangelical opponents quickly emerged. Paul D. Simmons, professor of Christian ethics at Southern Baptist Theological Seminary, castigated church growth experts for pursuing evangelism at the expense of social justice. He pointed to the Hour of Power TV show as a characteristic example of how evangelicals had gone wrong. Schuller's show "has all the sweet smells of success but no hint of the scandal of the cross. It seems pure Hollywood rather than the simple but demanding Gospel." Schuller offered "style but little substance, preaching comfortable Christianity and substituting middle-class morality for disciplined service." And the church growth experts seemed perfectly content with this shallow product, because it brought bodies into the pews. Simmons believed evangelicals ought to demand more of themselves and their potential converts. "We get our credentials not from the Chamber of Commerce," he archly observed, "but from the Lord of the Cross. We must not produce churches without souls, programs without conscience, love without justice, religious experience without conversion, salvation without a cross."[97] For some evangelical critics, the CGM represented nothing less than a perversion of the gospel.

Another trenchant critic was the Mennonite theologian John Howard Yoder.[98] In a 1973 symposium, Yoder faulted the movement for what he viewed as overconfidence in methodological innovation and lack of concern for social ethics. Paraphrasing the humorous critique of the Latin American evangelical C. René Padilla, Yoder wrote, "Church Growth people assume that you can make Christians the way you make cars and sausages."[99] The drive to measure and analyze and systematize made some evangelicals concerned that the spiritual process of evangelization was being turned into a mass production enterprise. Yoder also directly tackled the racial and theological implications of the Homogeneous Unit Principle. "Building the church in a racist culture in southern Mississippi, you can only win people if you accept racism," he argued. But "if you have accepted the institution of racism as the condition of your operating," was such a church even Christian?[100] Yoder argued that the message of the New Testament was that God broke down the wall of division between Jews and Gentiles. This was not a singular historical event; it was the essential ongoing ethical and theological principle of Christianity. "The breaking down of the wall between two ethnic groups," Yoder argued, "*is* the gospel. It is not a fruit of the gospel; it is not an *object lesson* in the gospel; it is not a *vehicle* of the gospel, it *is* the gospel." A church that was not growing "across cultural barriers ... to incorporate people of all kinds" was not being true to God's purposes.[101]

Black evangelicals spoke up, too. Howard Jones argued that "many white Christians" were using supposed cultural differences between black and white Americans to "excuse themselves from accepting blacks into their churches." He believed Wagner's arguments for homogeneous churches in an age of pluralism gave room for unchristian segregation to continue. Jones described a New Testament church that was united together without losing its God-given diversity. "Our churches today need to exhibit that same racial oneness if they are to effectively meet the spiritual and social challenge of this hour." Bill Pannell wrote that Wagner's methods seemed to be a recipe for a church that followed social change rather than leading it. Evangelicals were good at making converts, but they didn't challenge them to be countercultural, "and so a good Christian remains a 'good American.' And 'good Americans' do not believe in intermarriage."[102]

Criticisms of the racial implications of CGM methods were only part of a broader critique of the movement as a trendy but vacuous phenomenon more concerned with success than faithfulness. In a satirical take appearing in *Eternity* in 1976, "Pilgrim and his family" visit the "Chapel of the Winns," otherwise known as the "First Church of the American Dream." The church's ample parking lot has its own pastor. The former used-car salesman "groups people together by type of car," thus creating a sense of "togetherness" even before escalators whisk the visitors up to the enormous sanctuary. The founder and senior pastor of the church, a certain Wyatt W. Winn, is a TV-preaching, globe-trotting salesman for Christ who is rarely present at his own church. The administration of such a large congregation requires the formation of a "Consortium of Church Management," a body made up of Dr. Winn and his seven sons. It is duly called "the Board of Winners." As the service begins, Pilgrim and his family are overwhelmed. The music is grand, and the sermon is delivered with all the polished flair of a Hollywood performance. By the time the service is over Pilgrim is feeling ambivalent. He asks an official "welcomer" if a sense of personal human connection is lost amid the bigness and efficiency of a gigantic church. The welcomer assures Pilgrim that each new convert is assigned to a group called a "Winner's Circle," thus satisfying the need for connection. The family, somewhat dazed, leave the First Church of the American Dream carrying their copy of Pastor Winn's autobiography, *Winning Is the Name of the Game*. It was like the welcomer said: "You just can't argue with success."[103]

The managerial ethos, the relentless drive for numerical growth, the accommodation of visitors' comfort—all these made some white evangelicals nervous. Yet in ways that even many critics of the CGM often didn't realize, these concerns had racial implications. Black evangelicals such as the community organizer and "racial reconciliation" activist John Perkins were particularly concerned about how the pursuit of success in a racist society came at great cost to black people.[104] What did it mean for a church to be successful in a moment in which the white middle class was willing to sell their houses, start new private schools, and build new churches to maintain their advantages over—and distance from—African Americans? On one occasion a friendly interlocutor suggested to Wagner that there might be something uniquely troubling about homogeneous *white* churches. "In erecting an all-white church there's an inescapable aura of offense to blacks," he noted, a reproduction of the racial divisions cutting across every part of American life. "Shouldn't the church embody the answer to our racial situation?" he asked. Wagner responded with a non sequitur, "My position is that culture is not sinful."[105] Wagner looked at white domination and appeared to see nothing more than cultural distinctiveness. To see otherwise would disrupt the business of church growth. From a pragmatic perspective, locating churches in communities bearing the brunt of the middle-class exodus was a fool's errand. If pastors wanted their churches to grow, the simplest bet was to locate them where populations of middle-class potential donors were growing. Whether white evangelicals admitted it or not, this was a racialized bet.

McGavran believed this was a bet worth making. When he wrote that "men like to become Christians without crossing racial, linguistic, or class barriers," he meant it prescriptively as well as descriptively.[106] Homogeneity was what people wanted, and evangelicals ought to give it to them. It was a fact of human nature that evangelicals could embrace and use for their purposes. This was not to say that racial prejudice aligned with Christian ethics. McGavran made a clear distinction between what he called "discipling" and "perfecting." In the discipling stage the new convert heard and accepted the message of Christ's death and resurrection for sins. The "perfecting" stage, in which the new believer gradually learned and embraced Christian ethics, was chronologically and theologically secondary to the first priority of discipling. Insofar as white evangelicals embraced this thinking, it meant that the life-and-death struggles of African Americans against systemic oppression were in the secondary category.

McGavran's pragmatic efforts to defend the priority of evangelism in the 1970s took him into some dark waters. In a forum debating the Homogeneous Unit Principle, he imagined that "if all the whites in Tennessee were pagan and all the blacks were Christian, and if 'becoming Christian' meant joining a black Church and giving up white culture, whites would become Christians very slowly, if at all." The principle of this unsettling hypothetical scenario was that "all men should be able to become Christians without feeling they are betraying their race." McGavran drove the point home further, clarifying that he was thinking specifically of white Americans' investments in their racial identities. "We do not want white men to feel that the only way they can follow Christ is in multi-racial and multi-language congregations." He warned that "people movements all around the world languish and often die" because mixing homogeneous units created "mongrel" congregations. In contrast, a homogeneous unit church "liberates its own people without raising difficult questions of cross-race dining, marriage and the like."[107] McGavran's evocative use of the word "mongrel" aligned with long-standing white supremacist rhetoric about the dangers of racial mixing and interracial marriage.[108] In the white supremacist imagination these practices spoiled so-called racial purity and invited communist infiltration or a one-world government. In McGavran's imagination, these practices were mortal dangers to church growth. On their face, McGavran's words could give aid and comfort to white nationalists in the United States. But his mind was still back in India. He understood himself to be defending a peoples-based approach to evangelism, not a hateful American political ideology.

Conclusion

By the end of the 1970s, the CGM had completed its surprising journey. Launched by American missionaries in the 1930s and imagined as an ally of the cultural integrity of "tribal" peoples, it was now being successfully deployed in the quintessentially modern consumer culture of the world's capitalist superpower. "Evangelicals from all points on the ecclesiological continuum agree," wrote *Eternity* editor Robert T. Coote, that "the Church Growth Movement is 'hot,' the debate it has stirred is getting hotter, and evangelicals around the world—not just those in the U.S.—are going to have to deal with it." The CGM had become "too big to ignore."[109] Despite white evangelicals' often oppositional rhetoric toward American culture, they had proved to be zealous appropriators of the latest trends. The ethnic revival gave to church growth experts a language to justify whiteness as pluralism and a certain cachet as religious anthropologists attuned to the cutting edge of demographic and cultural change. Yet the CGM did not usher in a truly multicultural American evangelicalism. Instead, it helped to create the evangelical mainstream as white, middle class, and suburban. For colorblind Christians, the CGM enabled the ongoing invisibility of race in church spaces. And here, perhaps, was the core irony of the CGM's embrace of whiteness as peoplehood. Race-conscious church growth leaders offered a language of justification for local congregations where whiteness was an unmarked category, an identity so normative it seemed not to exist.

In the decades after the civil rights movement, as white evangelicals turned to the new "science" of church growth, they were dealing in race whether they knew it or not. The church growth theorists mistakenly believed it was possible to capitalize on white identity apart from racial hierarchy. While whiteness as a benign piece of the American mosaic sounded appealing to some, it was an obtuse reading of the very meaning of whiteness in a society so long structured on white supremacy. Amid national backlash to the gains of the black freedom struggle, white evangelicals described their pursuit of church growth as an expression of their faith in the power of the gospel. It was also a solid investment in the enduring advantages of whiteness. But even as the CGM catalyzed white evangelicalism's suburbanization, there were other evangelicals who believed God had called them to go to the American city. Their efforts to deal with urban problems in the 1960s and 1970s marked the next phase in the struggle to define Christian colorblindness.

4

A Mission Field Next Door

In the spring of 1968, Messiah College, the small higher education institution of the Brethren in Christ Church, announced it was about to add a distinctive feature to its portfolio: a campus in the heart of Philadelphia. At a glance, Messiah might have seemed to be an unlikely candidate for a venture into the city. The college was located in the farmlands of south-central Pennsylvania 90 miles west of Philadelphia. Most students came from rural white communities and were unfamiliar with the city. In the 1950s and early 1960s students portrayed the college as a rural idyll whose wholesome atmosphere "can be felt floating through the air here on our beautiful campus." The college was a refuge, a sanctuary. Just a few years later the civil rights movement and urban uprisings gave new meanings to the cloistered campus. By 1966 one student wrote that the "beauty and tranquility" around them served only as a "reminder of a clamoring, tumultuous world" beyond. The president of Messiah College, D. Ray Hostetter, came to believe that the events of the 1960s marked a decisive shift demanding new approaches in evangelical higher education. He wrote that it was "absurd" to think that Messiah provided adequate education for its students if it did not prepare them to be "where the action is" in urban America. Hostetter forged a partnership with Temple University to establish a Messiah College satellite campus in North Philadelphia. The new facility proudly opened its doors in the fall of 1968. Just as many white Americans were escaping the city, Messiah sought to move toward it.[1]

Messiah's foray into Philadelphia pushed against the tide of the rapidly suburbanizing white evangelical mainstream. As early as 1963, a student at Olivet Nazarene University in Illinois pointed out that most evangelical college students came from rural and suburban backgrounds and after finishing their studies sought out "the comfortable life of the suburbs." These choices were as much theological as economic. "We must rid from ourselves this notion that it is somewhat sub-Christian to be near the heart of the city," the student wrote.[2] But as the 1960s wore on, this notion seemed only to grow. Through white evangelical eyes, cities emerged as the epicenter of a palpable descent into moral chaos and anarchy. *Christianity Today* editorialized, "We are appalled at watching metropolitan areas roar into ruin while human pack rats carry off people's hard-earned property.... We are sick of hearing that civil-rights injustices triggered all this insane violence."[3] Watts 1965, Chicago 1966, Newark 1967—as uprisings shook one city after another, the racial crisis appeared to be a crisis of the American city.[4] The uprisings were the explosive exclamation points on the quieter reckonings happening every day on residential streets: a new next-door neighbor; sudden signs on neighbors' lawns; urgent calls to sell before it was too late; declining attendance at the local church as congregants headed for the suburbs. White evangelical colleges joined the exodus. Institutions such as Calvin College, the Bible Institute of Los Angeles, and the Philadelphia College of Bible moved from city centers to more spacious campuses, usually in the suburbs. Urban America had become a fount of wickedness, a place to be feared.[5]

Messiah's Philadelphia plan raised important questions about evangelicalism's relationship to the city. A zealous evangelical movement sending thousands of missionaries overseas could hardly ignore urban America. As *Christianity Today* put it, "Our words are empty when we talk to the black man about love and brotherhood and then withdraw into our all-white churches to pray for the lost in the Congo."[6] If white evangelicals' claims of Christian love were to be credible, something also had to be done about the mission field next door. Could white evangelicals embrace Christian colorblindness and the changing American city at the same time? What might Christian colorblindness in an urban form look like, and could it provide white evangelicals a path back into the city?

Rather than uniting evangelicals around a common vision, Messiah's initiative became a flashpoint of intra-evangelical conflict. President Hostetter's careful efforts to expand the horizons of evangelical education intersected with the emergence of what historian David Swartz has called "the evangelical left."[7] These radical evangelicals dreamed of an antiracist faith rooted in urban America. At the center of the movement was the Canadian-born and Yale-educated Dr. Ronald Sider.

Sider sought to enact this more progressive brand of evangelicalism in an institutional context, serving as director of the Philadelphia campus during its crucial formative years. But establishing an evangelical antiracist agenda in an urban setting proved to be more difficult than Sider and other evangelical leftists had imagined. Their commitment to assailing racism made the Philadelphia campus a flashpoint for controversy and alienated them from white evangelical constituencies.[8] The turmoil Messiah's Philadelphia plan produced suggested that the American city loomed as a profound threat to the construction of colorblind white evangelicalism. In the city racial inequality and systemic oppression were viscerally apparent, seeming to stretch to the breaking point professions of Christian unity and faith in the efficacy of interpersonal kindness. At times, Christian colorblindness in urban America dissolved into incoherence as white evangelicals exhibited attitudes of fear, pity, and defensiveness. The meaning of Christian colorblindness in the city, much less its viability as a vehicle for evangelical urban living, remained in doubt.

Contesting Christian Colorblindness in the City

Messiah's plan to expand into Philadelphia drew on both its evangelical sensibility and its Anabaptist tradition. On the one hand, as Messiah's ethnoreligious distinctiveness began to break down and the college entered an emerging white evangelical mainstream in the 1950s and 1960s, students absorbed the assumptions of nascent colorblind Christianity.[9] On the other hand, the pacifist theological tradition of the Brethren in Christ Church and its history as a persecuted minority continued to encourage a critical distance from American nationalism.[10] In contrast to leaders at institutions such as Wheaton College, who proudly defended "the Christian and American way of life," Messiah's leaders were more likely to question the claims of the American state and less likely to reflexively oppose radical forms of protest.[11] Some Brethren in Christ leaders were cautiously supportive of the civil rights movement. Yet, as in other evangelical denominations, the civil rights era exposed a significant divide between leaders and laity. While some Brethren in Christ leaders engaged the rapidly changing racial and social context of the 1960s, most ordinary Brethren in Christ folk in the pews felt the influence of fundamentalism and the strong pull of colorblind theology. If Messiah's Anabaptist heritage made it possible to imagine the creation of a Philadelphia campus in a moment when most white evangelicals wanted nothing to do with urban areas like North Philadelphia, Messiah's evangelical inheritance also shaped the boundaries of the project and ultimately oriented it toward a colorblind vision that proved difficult to sustain in Philadelphia.

Messiah College began planning its Philadelphia campus early in 1967. After holding talks with several universities in Pennsylvania, President Hostetter chose Temple University because of its urban location and its commitment to the project. It was the first partnership of its kind between a state university and a private Christian college. Messiah secured a large grant from the US Office of Education to purchase and renovate several rowhouses on North Broad Street adjacent to the Temple campus. In the earliest years of the Philadelphia campus, over 300,000 dollars of federal funds poured into the project. The influx indicated the potential some observers saw in this innovative experiment. Hostetter believed the world had changed, and Messiah had to change with it. Despite the problems of the nation's urban cores, he understood America's increasingly diverse metropolitan areas were going to drive the nation's economy and culture in the decades to come. The college had long been committed to instilling an ethic of Christian service in its students, but Hostetter believed the changes of the 1960s had rendered that effort "farcical" if it did not prepare students to face the "great problems in urban society." The new Philadelphia campus would be an academic boon for Messiah College, and a chance for white evangelical kids from rural America to encounter the "inner city." Messiah could no longer afford to stay behind the ivied walls of the rural campus.[12]

The choice of location was audacious. It meant that Messiah College would be entering an urban neighborhood shaped by a recent history of systemic oppression and severe racial tension. In the fall of 1963, a white rookie patrol officer had shot Willie Philyaw to death outside a white-owned discount store about half a mile from the future site of the campus. The officer claimed the young black man lunged at him with a knife, but community members pointed out that Philyaw was handicapped and suffered from epileptic seizures. One eyewitness claimed Philyaw was experiencing a seizure in the moments before the shooting. The slaying incited two nights of violence as black residents broke store windows along Susquehanna Avenue and attacked white pedestrians. The officer was cleared of any wrongdoing. The exoneration infuriated many black Philadelphians, who were already battling pervasive employment and housing discrimination. One longtime resident said, "This community is like a lighted stick of dynamite. It could blow at any minute." The spark came the following summer. On the night of August 28, 1964, police arrested Odessa Bradford after she refused to get out of her stalled car at 22nd Street and Columbia Avenue. After the officers dragged Bradford to a police wagon, gathering crowds pummeled them with bricks. That night, a false rumor swirled through the community that Bradford was pregnant and had been beaten to death in police custody. Rioting spread through a large swath of North Philadelphia in the following days as black residents systematically targeted hundreds of white-owned stores along Columbia and Ridge Avenues. All told, two people died in the uprising, hundreds were injured, and white-owned properties sustained millions of dollars in damages.[13]

Rural white students from Messiah's main campus would enter this charged environment to experience an "urban semester." The rowhouses would be both a residence and academic center for Messiah students. After spending their first two years at Messiah's main campus, students could attend the Philadelphia campus and take courses at Temple to finish their studies.[14] While earlier generations of urban initiatives were often frankly paternalistic in their intention to uplift racialized populations, Messiah's planning for the Philadelphia campus demonstrated the growing norms of colorblindness. President Hostetter and other leaders used coded language and made no explicit mention of race in written documents. This was remarkable in light of the realities of the neighborhood around the proposed campus. While it was possible for the program to work, it was clearly a complicated venture fraught with potential for misunderstandings, fear, and counterproductive exchanges. How would Messiah students feel about living in the neighborhood? How would residents feel about the students' presence in their community? The extant planning documents do not address these sorts of questions and appear remarkably sanguine about the potential challenges.

In the Philadelphia campus Hostetter invested grand hopes. Alongside the academic and cultural benefits, a characteristic evangelical missionary impulse animated Hostetter's vision. Students from "rural backgrounds" would awaken to "the social problems of the inner city" and become involved in ministry in the community around them. They would take their faith and learning and apply it to the real-world problems of the modern city.[15] Dr. Hostetter envisioned rapidly increasing enrollment, with support from foundations that would be eager to invest in the unique project. More enrollments would mean more "prestige," which in turn would lead to more donations. He proposed the construction of a new high-rise to house 150 students at the Philadelphia campus.[16] For Hostetter, the campus was nothing less than a new way to do Christian higher education in the United States. Through its partnership with Temple, Messiah could offer the academic resources of a large university combined with the tight-knit Christian community of a small evangelical college. The campus at once expanded Messiah's academic imprint and engaged social problems with evangelical conviction.

The Philadelphia campus officially opened its doors in September of 1968. Dr. Hostetter's upbeat vision belied small beginnings. The student newspaper described the campus as a "pilot program" in which a grand total of 12 students were enrolled for the fall semester. Some of these students promptly wrote an article describing their culture shock—the smells, the noise, the subway, the anything-goes atmosphere of Temple University, and "black people . . . lots of black people."[17] On the other hand, students commented that the rowhouse living-learning environment made for a close community and sense of camaraderie, all the more so because the poor black neighborhood and large secular university just steps away from their front door seemed so different from home. After visiting the campus for a couple of days, one student described it as a "family" atmosphere and declared that he had "never been more impressed or proud of anything this college has undertaken."[18]

Positive reports helped to grow enrollment at the Philadelphia campus, which reached 43 by the fall of 1972.[19] Students consistently described their experience as an opening up to the world: the pluralistic atmosphere of Temple together with its myriad academic offerings, the cultural opportunities of center city, the social needs of the community around them. The uniqueness of a rowhouse campus made the entire experience intense, immersive, and, for some, life-changing. While students in rural Grantham attended class in a staid, homogeneous environment, the Philadelphia students often felt that they were experiencing real life—and doing it together. "Students practically run the Center," one student noted. "They do all the cooking, maintenance, and secretarial work" and lived alongside professors and their families. "Being together so much and having to pull together to keep the Center running smoothly helps to foster a real sense of community." Some students had the feeling that they were not just getting an academic degree; they were experiencing "a kind of community-style living not quite available" at the main campus.[20]

Ronald Sider, who became acting director of the Philadelphia campus in 1971, envisioned Messiah's program as a model that dozens of evangelical colleges could follow.[21] Indeed, Messiah helped to inspire other evangelical urban education initiatives across the country, and some administrators seeking to establish urban training programs at their own institutions wrote to Sider for advice.[22] But more than direct imitation, the proliferation of such programs reflected the tenor of the time, a moment in which experimentation seemed possible. In 1968, Barrington College in Rhode Island partnered with Cross Counter, Bill Iverson's ministry in Newark, to establish an Urban Field College that would give students "the gut experience of living and working in the city." The student newspaper reported that "much of the work involves intimate contact with the black community and with social and poverty problems of the inner city."[23] The program, though small, drew evangelical students from as far away as Taylor University in Indiana, Davidson College in North Carolina, and Covenant College in Tennessee to experience a semester of urban ministry and gain college credit in the process.[24] In 1970, a small group of evangelical activists and college students, primarily from Wheaton and Trinity colleges, founded the Urban Life Center in Chicago. This program, too, drew college students from around the region to "work and live among minorities in order to feel the heat of oppression and discrimination" while gaining course credit through a partnership with Roosevelt University.[25] In 1971, Westmont College launched an Urban Semester program in nearby San Francisco to provide "vital educational experiences" for evangelical students while "exposing them to the multiple needs and potential" of the city.[26] Though different in their particulars, these programs had common features: a residential center in an urban neighborhood white evangelicals ordinarily tried to avoid; hands-on ministry experience across boundaries of race and class; and accreditation. Such immersive education experiences would, it was hoped, raise up a new generation of evangelicals prepared to constructively engage modern urban America.

But at the Philadelphia campus, Messiah College quickly discovered how difficult the implementation of such projects could be. In the fall of 1972, Messiah's growing cohort of black students put racism on the school's agenda more than ever before. Black Student Union (BSU) calls for institutional reform at Messiah included immediate changes at the Philadelphia campus. The BSU demanded that the college hire a black director for the Philadelphia campus, subject to their veto.[27] Administrators responded that they had been looking for a black director for over a year, but that the market for black evangelical educators was extremely competitive. The board reiterated its commitment to pursuing a black candidate with "greater vigor" but also cautioned that the search depended on finding a "qualified candidate." The BSU also demanded that the Philadelphia campus do more to serve the needs of the community around it. Hostetter responded that this was a great idea, but "not something that happens by fiat." He counseled that ministry to the community was an individual decision for each student to make. "White students have failed here," he admitted, "but have the Blacks as well become oriented to service?" He encouraged them to take the lead in ministering "in the inner city."[28] While the resource constraints Messiah operated under were real enough, some of the BSU's demands were controversial not because they were expensive but because they represented a different way to think about racial consciousness and Christian responsibility in the city. Hostetter transformed the BSU's call for a systemic change in the operation of the Philadelphia campus to an invitation to individual students to volunteer for service.[29]

Dr. Sider was more sympathetic to black students' demands. Though he was not the black director the BSU wanted, he was eager to use the Philadelphia campus as a center for antiracist training. Animated by his Anabaptist tradition, Sider was antiwar, antiracist, and an irrepressible advocate for evangelical forms of social justice activism. He went on to write popular books, such as *Rich Christians in an Age of Hunger*, challenging the orthodoxies of American capitalism and its nexus with evangelical Christianity. While serving as director of the Philadelphia campus, Sider sought to awaken white students and faculty to the cause of racial justice. He deliberately made white students uncomfortable in a bid to expose their racism. In contrast to most Messiah administrators, he wrote very directly about the fraught racial context of the campus. He viewed the campus's location—amid "the excitement and confrontation of the black inner city"—as "ideal for 'consciousness raising.'" He believed "Church and society desperately need a new generation of young people with the courage to confront racism, structural injustice, and the still festering urban crisis." But this wouldn't happen by reading books in the comfort of the classroom "safely isolated from both black persons and the urban ghetto." The way to produce real change was to push evangelical students into face-to-face encounters with the realities of urban injustice and the experiences of people unlike themselves.[30] Sider's own experience living in a majority-black neighborhood shaped his perspective. "Most of what I know about oppression," he said, "I've learned from black Americans."[31] He wanted other white evangelicals to have similar learning opportunities, and the Philadelphia campus seemed ideally situated to provide them.

In the summer of 1972, Sider began to implement this vision in earnest. He and Philadelphia campus administrator Merle Brubaker led an 11-week "seminar on urban problems" at the Philadelphia campus. There were 19 black and 13 white students from a dozen colleges around the country who enrolled in a course, "Models of Christian Ministry in the City."[32] Reverend Randy Jones, a black evangelical, taught the class. A draft of introductory remarks for the summer seminar has Jones declaring, "I have heard Christian blacks say to white audiences: 'If it were not for the love of Christ, I would take a gun and shoot every white face in this room.'"[33] A skit continued this confrontational theme. For the students to succeed in the summer program, Sider and Jones insisted, they would have to confront white racism and black anger. Reading requirements included the autobiography of Malcolm X and James Cone's *Black Theology and Black Power*. A midterm exam encouraged students to use black liberation theology to critique a white Christian who said "we don't need a white theology or black theology. . . . Christ died to make us one. God is color blind." Such exercises suggest how aware progressive evangelicals were of the growing power of colorblind theology as a reactionary force among their evangelical brethren.[34] In addition to confronting racism, a wide-ranging curriculum of field trips, service-learning opportunities, and lectures exposed students to both individualistic and more structural approaches to Christian ministry in Philadelphia.

In an attempt to awaken the broader white evangelical community to racism and urban problems, an interracial group of students in the summer seminar conducted programs at seven suburban and rural churches around the Philadelphia region. These performances used skits, personal testimonials, and music to try to implicate white congregations in the problems of the city. Putting an evangelical twist on the Johnson administration's Kerner Commission report, which examined the causes of urban uprisings, the speakers told these evangelical congregations the church bore special responsibility for the ghetto.[35] It had disengaged from the city and failed in its mission. Most churches responded positively to the program, but the directness with which it confronted white racism offended at least one of the congregations. Dr. Sider felt compelled to defend the program to the pastor of the church and to Messiah administrators. In a letter to President Hostetter, Sider implied that the congregation was offended only because it was racist.[36] He continued to believe "confrontation and vigorous honesty can be instruments of the risen Lord, who is still in the business of converting the worst of sinners—like white evangelical racists."[37]

The summer program's challenging style was surprising because the advertising for the seminar featured evangelical clichés and racial paternalism. "As foreign mission fields are less open to American personnel and as the desperate need of American cities becomes increasingly obvious," a brochure stated, "the possibility for increased service in the city will arise." The pamphlet cast the American city as a space analogous to a foreign mission field, allowing students to imagine themselves as spiritual superiors to a needy population.[38] While the text noted the seminar would feature black lecturers, the accompanying images made white evangelicals appear as rescuers for a childlike and helpless black population. On the front cover, a white woman posed with two small black girls. Innocent and endearing, the female children allowed prospective students to visualize the objects of their ministry in the most nonthreatening and ego-boosting terms. On the opposite page of the brochure, a skinny black boy, perhaps 10 years of age, gazed out over a rubble-strewn empty city lot. The exclusion of black adults in the brochure pictures was probably not a conscious decision, but it communicated an unmistakably paternalistic message. Though the brochure likely appealed to some of Messiah's white evangelical constituency, it fell far short of the tone Sider wished to convey. Rather than challenging colorblind Christians to learn from black perspectives, the brochure seemed to invite white evangelicals to minister across the color line in a way that reaffirmed white leadership in evangelical spaces.

The summer program had been small and voluntary. Sider wanted to do something bigger to deliver a message of Christian racial consciousness to Messiah's whole student body. Drawing on the same biblical texts colorblind Christians used, Sider imagined them as a call for "a glorious oneness in the multiracial body of Christ." Rather than assuming racial identities ought to dissolve in this union, Sider wanted "the black Christian" to be "proud of his blackness and African heritage." He insisted that making multiracial unity a reality required "incredibly difficult work." Instead of declaring unity to be so, white Christians had to do the hard work of preventing "their churches from fleeing to suburbia when neighborhoods change."[39] Beginning in the fall of 1972, he led a program that brought the entire freshman class of Messiah College to the Philadelphia campus for weekend seminars on racism. Titles of lectures included "Racism and Its Effects," "Black Power," "Black Consciousness," and "Black Evangelicals."[40] Students watched black films and had the opportunity to attend black churches in a whirlwind weekend of racial education and exposure to the unfamiliar city. This effort to implement an antiracist vision on the still-fledgling campus ultimately produced a backlash against the Philadelphia campus and what it seemed to represent.

According to Merle Brubaker, the goals of these weekend seminars were twofold: to make students "aware of the problem of white racism both institutional and personal" so that they would see antiracist work as a Christian imperative; and to get students interested in enrolling at the Philadelphia campus. But the more Sider and Brubaker pushed the first goal, the more the second goal seemed to suffer. The seminar program took an aggressive approach. Speakers denounced white racism and demanded that white students repent. Many students, fresh off a bus from rural Pennsylvania and in the city for the first time, were bewildered to say the least. In a review of the freshman visits, Brubaker reported that many students seemed to feel "threatened" by the experience.[41] The outcome of the freshman seminars was so ambiguous that faculty were soon debating whether the weekends in Philadelphia made the students "more or less racist." One freshman wrote, "I think this was a total waste of time. I was sick of being called a white racist all weekend." Another student was "VERY DISGUSTED!" by the "black bias" of the program. Others had positive feelings about the experience, and some were ambivalent. "At first I thought it was great that we were bringing [racism] out in the open," one student wrote. "By now, I'm almost sick of talking about it."[42]

Challenging the assumptions of white students could have unpredictable effects, leaving them confused by the experience and stumbling toward a colorblind theology to defend their religio-racial identities. Some students insisted that the racial consciousness they experienced in Philadelphia showed a lack of Christian maturity. One student declared, "Black Christians are more like Black Panthers with a little Christ thrown in."[43] The implication was that white Christians were just plain and wholesome Christians unburdened by racial consciousness. For students who had never had occasion to think much about their whiteness, just 48 hours in North Philadelphia could be enough to make them "sick" of race talk. Though most of them came from backgrounds of racial exclusion and white domination, their personal experience in those environments was one of innocence, not animus. They had barely had any contact with black people their whole lives and now strangers were suddenly telling them to repent of their racism. Instead of reckoning with how race had formed their identities and practices, some students came to believe that their own lack of racial awareness attested to their strong Christian faith. Here was whiteness in evangelical form.

The weekend seminars proved to be a short-lived experiment for the freshman classes of 1972 and 1973. Acquiescing to white students' discomfort, the administration at the main campus backed down. Freshmen would no longer be required to take a trip to the Philadelphia campus. Sider admitted that the antiracist nature of the weekend seminars "clearly conflicted" with the goal of making the Philadelphia campus appealing to Messiah students, but he complained that the main campus should not have unilaterally made the decision to end the trips without his input. He insisted that something needed to replace the seminars. "If the college is serious about attracting more black students," he wrote, "then there has to be serious, massive effort made to get to the racism which incoming freshmen inevitably bring with them." But, he concluded, he wasn't sure the college was actually "serious" about increasing black enrollment.[44] The decision to shut down Sider's antiracist training for Messiah freshmen indicated the core tension at work: while Sider wanted to build an antiracist program and let the chips fall where they may, Messiah could not risk an open rupture with its constituency of colorblind Christians.

Sider in this period was something of a bull in a china shop, one minute launching bold initiatives on the Philadelphia campus, the next embarking on a new project to organize a left-wing evangelical coalition nationwide. His growing profile as a national leader of progressive evangelicals added to the radical reputation of the campus and risked embarrassing Messiah in the eyes of its constituency. In 1972 he led a quixotic "evangelicals for McGovern" campaign. In the fall of 1973, he organized an interracial gathering of progressive evangelical activists in Chicago that resulted in the Chicago Declaration of Evangelical Social Concern. The declaration critiqued American nationalism, materialism, racism, and militarism, and the evangelical church's complicity in all these forces. The large contingent of black evangelicals, including John Perkins, Bill Pannell, Ruth Lewis Bentley, and Clarence Hilliard, pushed for a particularly strong statement against racism. "We deplore the historic involvement of the church in America with racism and the conspicuous responsibility of the evangelical community for perpetuating the personal attitudes and institutional structures that have divided the body of Christ along color lines," the declaration announced. "Further, we have failed to condemn the exploitation of racism at home and abroad by our economic system." With its attention to structural injustice and the reality of white racism in the evangelical church, the declaration directly challenged the colorblind theology of most Messiah students.[45]

Though Sider's efforts produced a backlash, extended immersions in black neighborhoods were more likely to produce lasting change in young white evangelicals' attitudes about colorblindness and the American city. Some students embraced these experiences and became newly conscious of their status as white people. For one white Messiah College student, news headlines about racial controversies were abstractions until she spent the summer of 1971 in a black neighborhood in Brooklyn, New York. "I encountered situations which made me very much aware of my 'whiteness,'" she wrote. "Feelings of uneasiness and insecurity were strong and continuous," she admitted. "I clearly did not fit in with the people of this urban community." Now she could imagine how it felt to be a person of color in the United States or at her own college campus. She wrote that her summer in Brooklyn changed her "attitude toward black people and their demands." She no longer believed black students were stirring up unnecessary racial trouble. Instead, she saw that her colorblind assumptions did not describe the reality black students experienced.[46] A Westmont student's journal entry while in San Francisco said it all: "I felt just a tiny wave of what it was like to be black in white America." Wrote another, "Today I found myself swimming in an ebony sea for the first time in my life."[47]

Students often felt the tension of trying to align these new experiences with colorblind and paternalistic assumptions. One veteran of the Urban Field College in Newark wrote about how touched she was when a girl hugged her and said, "We're going to miss you." From her experience she concluded that "no matter who you are or what color you are . . . love and concern overcome all barriers." She had developed friendships with people in the city, "and that was very precious to those of us who had, previous to our experience in Newark, little contact with blacks." These personal encounters weren't just feel-good stories; they were the basis for reevaluating her beliefs. In Newark, "You actually see the vacant tenement buildings, the poverty, the prejudice and the injustice that you have heard so much about . . ." and learn "how our society has built in prejudice into our institutions." If she had come with a paternalistic intention to save benighted people, she had quickly learned that "the blacks are getting it together by themselves." Now that she had become aware of racial injustice, her job was to go back to her own people and "inform and change the attitudes of the white community."[48]

Bill Iverson, the director of the Urban Field College, lamented that such open-minded students were the exception. When he went to Barrington College to try to get students excited about coming to Newark, he "found out good ol' white . . . Bible-believing, born again" students were "full of fear." An astute observer of his white evangelical constituency, Iverson put his finger on the most salient feature of this fear. It wasn't just that students were afraid of being mugged (although they certainly were!). They most feared the disruption of their identities and understanding of the world. "White people are so afraid of black people," Iverson wrote, and they were especially afraid of Newark because "Newark makes the Wasp a minority, and he (together with Mom and Dad) are [sic] afraid to 'walk a mile in those shoes.'" In contexts of white domination, Christian colorblindness seemed to be a coherent and viable response to racial division, and it ably protected investments in evangelical whiteness. Outside these majority-white spaces, in a city like Newark, Christian colorblindness seemed to fracture, leaving students' religio-racial identities exposed. But if only students would give the program a try, they could be delivered from their fear. Iverson wrote, "To expose someone with fear to Newark people where they live is to teach love anew, cast out fear, and transform the person's whole perspective, not to mention the value system."[49] Some white Messiah students had these sorts of awakenings at the Philadelphia campus. After just a month in Philadelphia in 1971, Jan Whitworth described how she had wished she was "a couple of shades darker."[50] Randy Rhoad wrote that simply going across the street to McDonald's on his first night in Philadelphia made him understand "how it felt to be in the minority!"[51] Though uncomfortable, such feelings compelled students to see themselves from new perspectives. Some of these students described their experiences in Philadelphia as life-changing. Rather than acting as saviors bringing the light of the gospel into the darkness of the modern city, they found that they had much to learn from urban America.

Sider and his leadership team were learning too. In advance of the 1973 summer seminar on urban problems, they sought to discard the paternalism that had affected the program in 1972. A planning document stated, "Seek opportunities for whites to work with whites . . . avoid the superiority complex." Appropriate pictures in the ad brochure would help prospective students to expect black leadership. The 1973 brochure used more egalitarian images and declared that "painfully honest black-white confrontation is a basic ingredient of the summer!"[52] As might have been predicted, it turned out that the market for this kind of honesty was painfully small. Individual positive experiences of Philadelphia did not overcome the broader sense of alienation from the city that most members of the Messiah community felt. A 1974 survey of hundreds of Messiah College students found that fully half the student body had "no interest" in the Philadelphia campus, and 75 percent had no intention of enrolling there. "I hate city life," one student admitted.[53]

Faculty and administrators' attitudes often matched those of students. Though the Philadelphia campus had strong support from President Hostetter, much of the leadership of the college was unsupportive or actively hostile. Year after year, Philadelphia administrators brainstormed how to get colleagues at the main campus on board with the Philadelphia project. One Philadelphia administrator wrote that "rumor" and "innuendo" about the Philadelphia campus flourished in rural Grantham. "The Campus gained a reputation, not completely undeserved, as being a 'dangerous place' where persons were verbally put up against the wall and confronted with their racial views." Such tactics left students "angered, frightened, and resentful." Enrollment remained low throughout the 1970s, reaching 45 in 1976. Staff turnover was high. In the spring of 1974, Jay Basler, the director of student development at the Philadelphia campus, noted that he was the fifth person to hold the position in just six years. The resources invested in the campus were not commensurate with the expected outcomes. Administrators lived on-site in a dormlike atmosphere that often felt detached from the black neighborhood around it. For most white evangelical educators, it was no place to settle down with a family. Basler believed the college either needed to make a more intensive effort to find people willing to live at the center or had to commit the resources to provide alternative housing arrangements. "My family wishes to leave at the earliest possible date," he concluded.[54] As Messiah's venture into Philadelphia risked foundering on colorblind Christians' hostility to it, whether the campus could be sustained remained an open question.

The Imagined Mission Field Next Door

As Messiah grappled with the challenges of running an institution in North Philadelphia, most white evangelicals continued to pull away from the city. "What should disturb every Christian," wrote one white evangelical college student, "is the smug 'Let-the-big-city-go-to-hell' attitude of so many of us who have never lived in the big city." This indifference was a matter of concern for white evangelical leaders, who wondered what it meant for the credibility of their movement. One evangelical scholar lamented that in the predominant evangelical mindset "it is almost as if God had abandoned the city or never had anything to do with it."[55] The city was the place where God was not. Evangelicals might bring God into the city, but God was not indigenous to it. And that meant that the people living there were lost and without hope. When challenged with the realities of racial oppression in urban America, many white evangelicals insisted the real problem was the spiritually needy people who lived there. This imaginary city was a crucial impediment to constructive evangelical engagement with urban problems. When white evangelicals like Sider promoted structural notions of injustice and racism, they found themselves isolated from the very constituencies they most wanted to influence. Colorblind Christians might pity the city, but they rarely wanted to learn from it.

Perhaps they could send missionaries to the city instead. Some black evangelicals positioned themselves to fill this role. Tom Skinner gained a national profile in 1966 as a black evangelist that white evangelicals could trust. Just 24 years of age that summer, Skinner's meteoric rise owed much to his ability to leverage his childhood experiences into an inspirational tale of uplift from the rough-and-tumble streets of New York. Black evangelicals like Skinner faced a conundrum: how to mobilize white evangelical help without ratifying negative stereotypes of the city and the people who lived there. Black evangelicals challenged, accused, and confronted white evangelicals, but they also deliberately played on white evangelical pity to garner resources for their ministries. No one managed this balancing act more adeptly than Tom Skinner. His relationship to white evangelicalism in the late 1960s and early 1970s can be read as an embodiment of the white evangelical connection to the mission field next door.

Skinner described himself as the former hardened leader of a notorious Harlem gang of 129 members. He boasted that his mixture of toughness and strategic thinking had "every one of them eating out of my hand" and they never lost a gang fight. He claimed he enforced discipline in the gang with brutal efficiency. He "had personally broken the arms and legs" of two would-be quitters, and he claimed to have 22 notches on his blade, one for each of the people his knife had cut.[56] All of this supposedly happened before his sudden conversion to evangelical Christianity at the age of 14!⁵⁷ Exaggerated or not—Howard Jones didn't believe Skinner was telling the entire truth—evangelicals ate up this tale of redemption.⁵⁸ As Skinner traveled the country speaking at Messiah and other white evangelical colleges, the sensational details of his biography were widely repeated. The doubtful veracity of all the particulars is wonderfully symbolic: whether or not Skinner really was a sadistic teenager breaking bones and slashing flesh in a ruthless urban jungle, that's exactly what white evangelicals imagined the ghetto must be like. To white and black audiences alike, gritty Harlem roots signaled the authenticity of Skinner's blackness and his identification with black struggles.⁵⁹ And it fit comfortably into a tradition of evangelical conversion narratives. The more gratuitously sinful one's former life could be shown to be, the more glory abounded to the grace of God.⁶⁰ For white evangelicals, the evil escapades of Skinner's adolescence testified to the power of the gospel and signaled that when they supported Skinner they were tapping into an authentic conduit to the ghetto.

Skinner offered a bridge between white evangelicalism and the black city. It had long been the case, as Bob Harrison complained, that black Christians were encouraged to minister among their own people and steer clear of challenging white entitlement to spiritual authority. But white evangelicals did not imagine Skinner's evangelistic crusades in the ghetto through the traditional parameters of segregated ministries. In fact, when Skinner came to town for a crusade, local white evangelical college students were encouraged to help out.⁶¹ They needed only to support Skinner to know they were doing something meaningful about the nation's racial troubles and the urban crisis. He was less an outcast from white evangelicalism, as Harrison had sometimes felt himself to be in the 1940s and 1950s, and more an envoy. Said *Christianity Today*, "Skinner has created great interest among evangelicals who worry vaguely that they might be missing the boat."⁶² In this project Skinner's blackness was crucial, enabling him to act as a liminal figure, white evangelicalism's black ambassador to the ghetto.⁶³ By the summer of 1967, *Christianity Today* told its readers that Skinner deserved their "fullest support."⁶⁴

To get that support, Skinner knew which buttons to press. While trying to raise funds from white evangelicals, he portrayed the black ghetto as a site of pity and desperate need.⁶⁵ In a major address before an audience of thousands of evangelicals at the 1969 US Congress on Evangelism, Skinner described black urban dwellers as "a crippled people, a people who are crippled economically, socially, politically, and psychologically."⁶⁶ And in his 1968 book, he described black churches as bastions of excessive emotionalism and spiritual immaturity, led by ministers given over to sexual immorality and hypocrisy.⁶⁷ As a result, he claimed, "There is hardly any Christian witness in the ghetto."⁶⁸ There's little reason to suppose Skinner's hostility toward the black church was insincere, but it also proved useful. It flattered white evangelical views of the city. Skinner did not doubt that white evangelicals had the correct theology on the point that mattered most—salvation through faith in Christ—and he asked them to help him bring their theology to the ghetto. And the beauty of it was that they wouldn't have to go there themselves. They could just support Skinner, confident that he wouldn't go off on any wild social causes. *Christianity Today* approvingly noted that Skinner "plays down social insurgence in sermons because he feels that reform may take 'sixty years' but that regeneration through Christ can help now."⁶⁹ To put it baldly, converted Negroes were not rioting Negroes.

None of this meant that Skinner made white evangelicals entirely comfortable. In fact, his cultivation of white evangelical sympathy gave him a platform from which he launched increasingly scathing criticisms of white evangelical racism and indifference. It wasn't every day that a black evangelical got extended speeches printed in *Christianity Today*. With his blending of entreaty and confrontation, Skinner did. In the same speech in which he asked for help for a "crippled people," he declared, "Large numbers of us as black Christians have discovered that in the minds of some of our brethren 'fellowship' usually means a paternal relationship; if we act as they expect us to act, and if we say what they want us to say, and if we believe what they want us to believe, then we can have fellowship. My friend, that is not fellowship; that is psychological slavery."⁷⁰ Skinner's increasingly radical tone was evident at InterVarsity Christian Fellowship's 1970 conference in Urbana, Illinois. Messiah students were among the 12,000 young people gathered when Skinner famously challenged students to embrace Jesus Christ as liberator, a militant revolutionary Christ who brought spiritual and social freedom. The problem was that "most evangelicals in this country who say that Christ is the answer will also go back to their suburban communities and vote for law-and-order candidates who will keep the system the way it is," Skinner declared.[71] One Messiah student wrote that Skinner "almost forced one to consider his own life style and the necessity for change in a radical way." For at least some Messiah students, Skinner offered an inspiring call to dedicate their lives to "the One true revolutionary—Jesus Christ."[72]

While Skinner called for revolution and Sider urged white evangelicals to resist white flight and confront their own racism, most white evangelicals acted to protect their economic and institutional investments. The urban crisis was the occasion for major statements of concern from bodies such as the National Association of Evangelicals (NAE) and the Southern Baptist Convention (SBC), but neither group had the power, nor the inclination, to coerce their constituencies to implement the statements at the grassroots level. The SBC, at its 1968 annual meeting, adopted "A Statement Concerning the Crisis in Our Nation." It called on Southern Baptists to "undertake to secure opportunities in matters of citizenship, public services, education, employment, and personal habitation." The statement blandly acknowledged "our share of responsibility" for the racial crisis, and concluded with a call for "courageous actions for justice and peace. . . . Words will not suffice. The time has come for action."[73] The NAE, too, tepidly suggested that "we must find ways of expressing our interest in our neighbor's physical welfare as we express our concern for the welfare of his soul." The rest of the statement hedged and qualified this grudging admission of the need for social action. Evangelicals must remember, the NAE declared, that all the outward manifestations of crisis were only "symptoms of a deeper disease." Evangelicals knew what that disease was—"man is a sinner inclined to evil"—and they knew its cure: "Jesus Christ as the only savior of sinners."[74]

Calls for action were aspirational. Implementing them was not easy. A 1968 in-house survey of Southern Baptist churches in "transitional areas" of racial change found "negligible" outreach to African Americans despite deliberately designing the study to find churches engaged in such outreach. "The overwhelming majority of respondents did not feel that a ministry to Negroes was a reasonable possibility for their church," the report concluded. "Churches have written off the Negro as not their responsibility." In a paradox characteristic of colorblind Christianity, white evangelicals paired these overtly racial decisions with a profound inability to see their own racial investments. The report charged that "many Southern Baptists are no more aware of . . . the importance of race in their actions and attitudes than fish recognize that they swim and survive in water."[75] While evangelical leaders called for action, many laypeople resented efforts to make them think about race. One man no doubt spoke for untold numbers of white evangelicals with his frustrated response to yet another sympathetic article on the racial crisis in an evangelical publication: "There is too much propaganda about Negroes. I'm tired of reading about them."[76] Another man in a Chicago suburb became incensed when some evangelicals pushed for racial integration in his neighborhood. "Where am I supposed to go now?" he asked. "I moved here to get away from them. . . . If you people are going to be shoving this down our throats, I'm not going to church anymore. My house is my God. I have $20,000 invested in that house, and my house is my God."[77] C. W. Scudder, a professor at Southwestern Baptist Theological Seminary, deplored this abdication of evangelical responsibility. "As long as people run from Negro neighbors," Scudder warned, "the black wave will continue to move across our cities, engulfing churches and other institutions. And as long as the black wave keeps moving, our churches will have to keep on moving." Though Scudder evoked racial panic with his metaphor, it was the white evangelical flight from the city that really scared him. He questioned "how long . . . God could keep on blessing a church that ran from people." He feared the answer.[78]

Black evangelicals continued to try to implicate white evangelicals in the urban crisis. They insisted that white evangelicals were not bystanders to it, but creators of it. In February 1969, Southern Baptist leaders held a meeting with black pastors from Atlanta and New York to dialogue about the Crisis Statement. Pastor Earl Moore of New York said the only word he could think of when reading the Statement was "duplicity": the duplicity and "pious platitudes" of a "white church that has tied its destiny with the destiny of the nation." Moore deliberately provoked discomfort in his listeners by invoking the circumstances of his parishioners back in New York City. Though he was unimpressed with the Statement, at least he could read it. Many in his church could not.

They were products of schools that "annihilated them before they had a chance to come out and face the world." Until Southern Baptists acted as "prophet" against, rather than enabler of, a racist nation that destroyed black lives, "this Crisis Statement won't mean a thing." Toward the end of the meeting, a black layman from New York spoke up. John Grant had grown up in Savannah, Georgia. He had made it out and done well for himself. But on a recent visit to his childhood home he encountered old friends who had not been so fortunate. Grant felt an overwhelming "anger" and "hate" boil up inside. "How is it," he asked himself, "that people who are supposed to be so religious, and so righteous and so God-loving and so kind, and who can say as they read the Bible, 'how could they do this to Christ', and in the meantime these same people are crucifying Christes [sic] everyday of their lives."[79]

Many white evangelicals resisted such images. They saw the city through the lens of pity and spiritual need, not social injustice. Those who dared to call attention to the structures of urban inequality usually faced accusations that they were straying from the straight and narrow path of evangelicalism. Wheaton College's Inner City Ministries branch of the Christian Service Council became the subject of "many innuendos" when it failed to maintain a singular focus on the desperate spiritual plight of city residents. Amid rumblings that it had become too concerned with social issues, the group reaffirmed its commitment to a spiritual mission. When it described people in the city trapped not only in poverty but "behind walls of bitterness," dying not just from hunger but "from lack of love," it aligned itself with appropriate evangelical visions of the pitiful city. White evangelicals routinely portrayed the urban poor as people cut off from normal human affection and knowledge of God. But "those who have been touched by the love of Christ . . . no longer live a hopeless life. They know that someone cares for them."[80]

Imagining the problems of the city as spiritual and individual frequently led to moralistic judgments about the people white evangelicals encountered. After a visit to an evangelical "rescue mission" in Chicago, a Moody Bible Institute student described the "fleshy body-shells" of the men, whose "dull eyes peer out from skulls once occupied by operative minds."[81] A 1967 photo essay in the student newspaper titled "Tares among the Social Wheat" offered a "graphic portrayal of social decay" in the neighborhoods around Moody.[82] The title, ripped out of context from a parable of Jesus, perhaps unwittingly implied that physical impoverishment made one a "tare" that would be burned up in the final judgment.[83] At MBI, students saw the urban crisis up close as the neighborhood around the institute deteriorated. The Cabrini-Green Homes, just a couple blocks from the MBI campus, would become nationally notorious as an example of public housing gone wrong. Yet MBI's institutional culture was one of siege, a white Christian oasis amid the disorder of the city. Moody hired a private security force and fostered an environment that felt insulated from its neighbors.[84]

While every Moody student had a "Practical Christian Work" assignment with a ministry in the city, many of these activities were focused on evangelism and work with children. Social action to ameliorate physical hardship was more controversial. Some students thought MBI did a lot of ministry in the "inner city" black community, but students were thrust into such work without cultural awareness or preparation.[85] The social distance between campus and neighborhood remained vast. This troubled some students. One student wrote perceptively about the culture shock MBI students experienced when they got to the city and urged students to become true "citizens of Chicago" rather than sequestering themselves on campus. There were periodic calls to move beyond their "stained-glass ghetto" and reach out to the "slum world, not 100 feet from MBI." Moody students were being trained to "reach lost people—everywhere. . . . Yet our own neighbors are left untouched."[86]

The disconnect between white evangelical institutions and the city was so stark that sincere efforts to move toward the city sometimes fell comically short. Houghton College, in western New York, had ambitions remarkably like Messiah's. Though a rural institution, it wanted to build connections to the city. In 1969 Houghton merged with Buffalo Bible Institute, creating a new extension campus closer to Buffalo. Houghton's leaders had high hopes for what the so-called Buffalo campus would accomplish. The initial long-range plan called for rapid expansion to accommodate 1,200 students.[87] Like Messiah, Houghton imagined the campus as a way to enhance both its academic curriculum and opportunities for rural white students to gain valuable urban experiences. "The emphasis envisioned will provide broad opportunities for social service—Christian concern confronting the ills of urban society," one fund-raising document stated.[88] In reality, Houghton's new campus was not located in Buffalo at all. Instead, it was in the leafy suburb of West Seneca. Five years after the 1969 merger, Houghton College had 1,200 students on its main campus and only 80 at the so-called Buffalo campus. The college began to scale down its plans. Rather than a full-fledged branch campus, the West Seneca location would be an "extension" site providing an "urban laboratory" for students from the main campus with relevant majors such as social work. It could also serve as a continuing education site for nontraditional students in the Buffalo region.[89]

In a 1974 application to the US Office of Education, Houghton's president noted that the college was trying to follow the example of Messiah's Philadelphia campus, which had secured significant federal funding.[90] Among Houghton's goals, the application explained, was to "explore the needs and create the corresponding programs for the black community" in nearby Buffalo.[91] In light of the stated intentions at the time of the merger, one might have assumed that such program development would have occurred years earlier, but the barriers were formidable. Houghton was a rural college catering to the evangelical Wesleyan Church and its overwhelmingly white constituency. It lacked cultural and institutional ties to the more diverse population of Buffalo. The attention to difference that successful programming required did not come naturally to these colorblind Christians. Worse, Houghton's students tended to see the city as a godless place. When one student dared to suggest they might "see God's glory" in the city, he had to overcome entrenched negative attitudes. He assumed that for his audience the city evoked the biblical cities of Sodom and Gomorrah and all manner of evil associated with them. "Few of us like the city," he admitted.[92]

At Messiah College, pulling back from mandatory antiracist education did not solve the problems of the increasingly embattled Philadelphia campus. Even if students no longer had to worry about being "put up against the wall and confronted with their racial views," long-standing fears of the city continued to hold them back. One veteran of the Philadelphia campus remembered how rumors about the dangers of the city made him "ready to crawl under my bed and stay there." When he first arrived, in his imagination, "Everyone who passed me was a mugger or worse."[93] Students who dared to go to Philadelphia sometimes pushed against stereotypes of the "big bad city." As one Philadelphia student put it, "You won't get mugged. Come on, folks, give the city a chance before you condemn it." Another student admitted that those accustomed to the bucolic Grantham campus might at first be taken aback by the "fortress" character of the Philadelphia campus, with its "barred windows" and "careful locking" of all the doors. But this was more than made up for by the close-knit community the living environment fostered.[94] Another student had heard bad stories from the Philadelphia campus that made her "very apprehensive" about going there. But she found the reality less frightening than she imagined. She came to believe that the Philadelphia experience was a vital opportunity for Messiah students to "achieve social awareness."[95] These students knew their endorsement of the Philadelphia experience pushed back against a rising tide of hostility.

Rather than unifying the Messiah community, the Philadelphia campus became a fault line that produced recurring controversies about Christians' role in the modern city. For President Hostetter, the campus promised to make Messiah more competitive in the marketplace of higher education and reduce white students' cultural isolation. These goals did not necessarily align with the antiracist agenda of the evangelical left. For Sider, the campus was a center for antiracist education and an urban training ground for the evangelical community nationwide. He imagined the Philadelphia campus as the leading wedge that would remake the main campus in a new multicultural and antiracist image, shorn of its investments in whiteness. As he contemplated this vision, he knew "there would be questions from the traditional constituency and, alas, changes in it. But is it too much to hope that there are also many evangelical parents who would like their children to attend a college that gives flesh to the biblical view of the body of Christ?"[96]

It was too much to hope. As faculty resistance and student defensiveness undercut efforts to turn the Philadelphia campus into a major evangelical center for racial education and urban ministry, the grand hopes for the Philadelphia campus seemed to be in danger. A 1976 internal evaluation of the Philadelphia campus reported grave concerns. While most of those who actually attended the campus characterized their experience as positive, the program lacked staffing and funding, and enrollment still had not met expectations. The problems of resources and logistics seemed to reflect a deeper theological and ideological disconnect between the two campuses. The report admitted that "a bad image" of the Philadelphia campus as "a center for radical ideas" had emerged on the main campus at the outset. The weekend racism seminars for incoming freshmen reinforced that perception and had "negative effects," the report declared. Moreover, fears of North Philadelphia were pervasive. Parents of Messiah students expressed "anxiety" for the safety of their children in the city. It seemed that an "urban institution" had "little or no appeal" for most Messiah College families. Most remarkably, the report declared that many Messiah students and administrators viewed the Philadelphia campus as a "threat" instead of an opportunity. While Messiah tried to run an urban campus, most of its white evangelical constituency wanted to avoid the city. The ideal that white students would be missionaries to the black neighborhood around them while pursuing their academic goals gave way to the realities of isolation and mistrust. There was "very little interaction between the students and the members of the community," the evaluators admitted. Much of these negative dynamics might have seemed predictable, but the colorblind commitments of Messiah and its white evangelical stakeholders made it difficult to reverse course. In 1975, Ron Sider stepped down as director of the Philadelphia campus.[97]

The same radical moment that opened space for black students to protest conditions on white evangelical campuses in the early 1970s made room for creative urban experiments in evangelical higher education. But the closing of that sense of experimentation in the second half of the decade was palpable in evangelical settings, as in the nation at large. In the 1980s, the Philadelphia campus became not a center of evangelical antiracism but a site where students could consume urban experiences and gain cross-cultural exposure as part of a liberal arts education. Diversity was domesticated for white evangelical students. Enrollment peaked at 80-odd students, only a little more than half the number Hostetter's aborted high-rise proposal alone would have housed. The declining academic rationale for the Philadelphia campus hastened the turn toward diversity as a consumable experience. As the main campus expanded its offerings, growing numbers of academic majors could be completed without ever attending the Philadelphia campus. Even majors that seemed to be a natural fit for the campus, such as social work, faced challenges. A student survey revealed that large numbers of Messiah students did not even consider majoring in social work because it required attending the Philadelphia campus for two years.[98] When the college relocated the engineering program to Grantham in 1991, in a single stroke a quarter of the students at the Philadelphia campus no longer had an academic reason to be there. Rumors circulated that the campus would close down.[99]

In response to these changes, the college cast about for ways to keep the Philadelphia campus relevant. Messiah continued to offer black and Puerto Rican cross-cultural courses in a short January term that combined academic instruction with a 12-day stay in a black or Puerto Rican home. Some students enjoyed these immersion experiences while others felt deeply uncomfortable. Philadelphia campus director Don Wingert nurtured dreams of refocusing the campus toward outreach to the North Philadelphia community, or perhaps an urban training and conference center for evangelicals nationwide. Of course, these ideas were not new, and they remained only dreams. Rather than embracing these more ambitious goals, the college doubled down on making the Philadelphia campus an outpost for cross-cultural experiences for Messiah students. Students would come to Philadelphia for cultural enrichment and a broadening of their horizons. Rather than being directly confronted with charges of white racism, as in the early 1970s, they would be invited to explore an unfamiliar culture.

Students who attended for these purposes were frequently very glad they had done so, but their tales of adventure and cultural awakening in the big city rested uneasily alongside reports of crime and danger. As crime rates reached new highs in the 1980s and early 1990s, students and their parents were as fearful of North Philadelphia as ever. One student who enjoyed the January cross-cultural course in 1987 criticized fellow students who were so afraid of the city they "wouldn't go anywhere out of reach of the Messiah facilities."[100] But this fear ought not to have been surprising. Articles in the student newspaper featuring racialized reporting of crime against Messiah students fueled fears.[101] The administration did not adequately address the Messiah community's fears of the city, leaving students ill-prepared to make an informed decision about attending the campus or what to do when they got there. One student described being "thrown into the atmosphere" after a "lackadaisical" orientation of one hour.[102] In 1991, the director of student life at the Philadelphia campus said the "apprehension of parents and students" continued to be one of the major challenges he faced. But the reality of life in North Philadelphia was almost always less scary than students imagined. "I expected to see a good deal of crime and violence," one student reported, but "I haven't seen as much as I expected." In the absence of adequate institutional support, students relied on spiritual resources to overcome their fears and assure anxious friends and relatives. "I just told [my mom] that this is where I feel God wants me to be right now," one Philadelphia student declared.[103]

Messiah students' colorblind understanding of the city continued to be a formidable obstacle to productive action in it. Colorblind theology's emphasis on face-to-face interaction mediated through evangelical institutions too often rendered invisible the systemic inequality and discrimination of America's metropolitan areas. Colorblind Christians looked to the city and saw pitiful people caught in a web of bad habits, broken families, and despair. In a passionate plea to reach out to the city, Messiah student Howard Tripp described his experiences. "I've driven through Camden a few times," he declared, "and I've been deep into the heart of Harrisburg many times." He had even taken a walk in Harlem! "If you have been to one inner-city, you have been to them all," he informed his readers. They were all "crying out for love and hope." Tripp called on Messiah students to sacrificially expend their resources on behalf of these poor people. "The[y] all need to experience the love of Christ, and that can only come from interaction with Christians." In Tripp's imagination, the residents of places like North Philadelphia would not encounter Christians until people like him ventured into their neighborhood.[104]

Conclusion

In the early 1970s, as Americans of means left cities in droves, Messiah moved toward it. As most white evangelicals sought to put a lid on the uncomfortable tensions raised by the civil rights movement, Dr. Sider and black Messiah students put white racism at the top of the agenda. In the aftermath of Sider's tenure Messiah consigned the radical moment to the past but found itself in possession of an urban campus and partnership with a major university that was unique among evangelical colleges in the United States. Rather than leveraging this institutional distinctiveness into a chance to be a leader in evangelical urban higher education, Messiah let the campus wither on the vine. Though Messiah began the campus with ambitious hopes, it did not provide sufficient institutional support to the fledgling program. The campus relied on personalities—notably the backing of Dr. Hostetter during his long presidency—rather than broad-based investment from ordinary white evangelicals. Turning the campus into the major evangelical urban center it might have been would have moved the college away from what was emerging during these decades as its core constituency: colorblind Christians.

The antiracist possibilities of evangelical activism in the city proved incompatible with the priorities of the white evangelical mainstream as it took shape under the aegis of Christian colorblindness. The 1976 evaluation had called the Philadelphia campus a "threat" in the minds of many Messiah students and faculty. And, indeed, it was. Raising the specter of race in explicit and systemic terms put the Philadelphia campus out of step with the construction of a colorblind Messiah College. In this respect it was a microcosm of white evangelicalism's relationship to the city. The city, with its race and radicalism, remained the strange and colorful other against which white evangelicals could define the normative Christian experience. That this normative experience was white and middle class was at once obvious to outsiders and nearly invisible to insiders. Ron Sider had tried to make white evangelicals see that the urban crisis was also a crisis of white evangelicalism. Rejecting Sider's claims, white evangelicals kept their psychological and physical distance from the city. With Christian colorblindness ascendant, the crisis of the evangelical investment in whiteness showed no sign of abating.

5

Two Gospels on a Global Stage

In July 1974, over 2,700 evangelicals from all over the world gathered in Lausanne, Switzerland, for the International Congress on World Evangelization. The Ecuadorian theologian C. René Padilla spoke for evangelicals from the global south who longed for social justice in societies ravaged by poverty, Cold War conflicts, and decolonization struggles. Padilla confronted the American delegation and attacked what he called "Culture-Christianity" based on "the American way of life." He accused American evangelicals of selling a cheap brand of Christianity that called individuals to salvation without placing the ethical demands of Christ upon them. In this system, "The racist can continue to be a racist, the exploiter can continue to be an exploiter." Padilla understood the gospel differently. He argued that the purpose of the gospel was to produce a "radical reorientation" of one's entire life, not merely the salvation of one's soul. The gospel challenged the oppressive systems of society—including those of the United States—creating "an open break to the status quo of the world."[1] Padilla's speech was a sensation. It seemed that a global, socially concerned evangelicalism was ascendant and ready to make its mark on the United States.

A very different conference over a decade later indicated the surprising trajectory of the Lausanne Movement in North America. On April 15, 1985, the Convocation on Evangelizing Ethnic America began in Houston, Texas. This Lausanne-sponsored conference deliberately excluded black evangelicals who might have echoed Padilla's words. It focused on a different understanding of the gospel: the salvation of individual souls through faith in Christ. Dominated by the agenda of the Church Growth Movement (CGM), the Houston conference sought to use ethnic loyalty as an evangelistic tactic to reach America's increasingly diverse population. If Lausanne stirred hopes for an antiracist and socially concerned evangelicalism, Houston symbolized the emergence of an evangelicalism that could be multiethnic without being antiracist.[2]

This tale of two congresses suggests the ways in which issues of race and class had become integral to the most basic question evangelicals could ever ask: what is the gospel? Dueling answers to this question played out at Lausanne and in the decade beyond. On one side were a radical contingent of global south evangelicals, joined by a smattering of black evangelicals and American Anabaptists such as Ron Sider and John Howard Yoder, who argued that the gospel announced the creation of a new countercultural community. The evangelistic task incorporated both the proclamation of salvation to all *and* liberation for the oppressed. Padilla called it "integral mission." The black evangelical pastor Clarence Hilliard called it "theological blackness." They insisted that the gospel, when faithfully embodied in the local church, created a concrete redistribution of power that challenged the dominant social system. Race was a central concern to these evangelicals because they believed the gospel proclaimed a new community of God that was fundamentally incompatible with racial oppression. Racial justice was a matter of fidelity to the gospel. On the other side were colorblind Christians, led by the American Church Growth Movement, who argued for a gospel of personal salvation. Evangelism meant proclaiming salvation for sinners. Its social implications came later. For these evangelicals, race could be used as a methodological tactic to enhance the evangelistic enterprise insofar as it proved useful. But ethical commitments about race ought not interfere with the proclamation of the gospel. The Lausanne Congress served notice that in the aftermath of the civil rights movement and the rise of liberation theology, to talk about the gospel was to talk about race.[3]

Many observers thought that Lausanne showed a new day of social concern had arrived for global evangelicalism. But in the ensuing decade colorblind Christians in the United States fought to commandeer and control the legacy of Lausanne and its institutional powers. These elite debates mattered because they set agendas for whole denominations and priorities for the use of concrete resources. The dispute was contentious because all involved knew how much was at stake: the outcome would shape the course of evangelicalism for decades to come. The promise of an evangelicalism that viewed race through the lens of justice and Christian community gave way to an evangelism-first approach that viewed race opportunistically, as an evangelistic tool. Colorblind Christians could accommodate, or even embrace, these episodic uses of race because they did not challenge whiteness or make antiracism a core matter of Christian discipleship. As the CGM expanded its reach across more institutions and denominations in the late 1970s and 1980s, Lausanne-sponsored events with prominent church growth influence became yet another source of tension between white and black evangelicals in the United States. As the CGM reached the peak of its popularity in the 1980s and groups like the Southern Baptist Convention took an increasingly multiethnic turn, it furthered the suspicion among some critics that white evangelicals had a seat for everyone at the table—except black evangelicals.

Lausanne '74: A Victory for Evangelical Social Activism?

The Lausanne Congress on World Evangelization is widely regarded as a vital moment in the history of modern evangelicalism. The evangelical historian Mark Noll puts its importance for evangelicals on par with Vatican II's role in the reshaping of Catholicism.[4] Billy Graham conceived the Congress as an evangelical counterpoint to the 1968 Uppsala meeting of the World Council of Churches. Graham joined Donald McGavran in being concerned about the direction of missionary activity in liberal Protestantism. In Graham's view, radical political action seemed to have replaced the preaching of the gospel. The Lausanne Congress would attempt to cast an alternative global evangelical vision for the mission of the church. There had never been such a large and diverse meeting of evangelical leaders.[5] The leading lights of the CGM were there, and so, too, were their critics. If the theme of Lausanne was the future of global evangelism, the most controversial vector for that theme was the growing influence of the cadre of church growth activists based at Fuller Seminary.[6] The CGM arrived in force at Lausanne, prepared to spread its message of evangelistic pragmatism, which, in the United States, had come to mean accepting whiteness as a legitimate form of peoplehood. Padilla and other radicals were determined that the CGM would not become an American export that reinforced the ruling status quo in their own countries. At stake was the very meaning of the gospel in a world of racial and economic oppression.

The CGM shaped the early planning stages of the Lausanne Congress.[7] At a meeting in August 1972, Ralph Winter, McGavran's colleague at Fuller, urged planners to focus on evangelism from the church growth perspective. The planning committee promptly assigned to McGavran's School of World Mission and the Missions Advanced Research and Communication Center (a Winter-led cooperative project of Fuller Seminary and the evangelical charity World Vision) the task of preparing data for conference participants on "unreached populations" around the world. This all but guaranteed that the CGM's priorities would play a major role at Lausanne.[8] The sheer size of the Lausanne conference presented political and logistical challenges. With thousands of participants and just as many perspectives and priorities, whose voices would be heard? The most coveted assignment was a plenary speech from the main stage with the entire Congress assembled to hear it. Organizers distributed some plenary speakers' papers to participants in advance so that their spoken addresses could build on the feedback they received from hundreds of interlocutors all over the world. Only 11 speakers were honored with this opportunity—all of them men.[9] Two of them—Donald McGavran and Ralph Winter—were CGM activists from Fuller. No African Americans received plenary speaking roles. Two other speakers—the Latin American missiologists C. René Padilla and Samuel Escobar—used this high-profile stage to attack the CGM. In the aftermath of the Congress, both factions sought to claim victory.

Billy Graham's Congress-opening speech on July 16 pleased CGM advocates. Graham was far too much the politician to place himself in a narrow corner associated with a particular school and movement. But the broader theological thrust of his message positioned him firmly on the side of the CGM. In recent years, McGavran had been sounding the alarm about not only the threat of theological liberalism from without, but also the danger of social concern within evangelicalism. Graham's speech parroted McGavran's concerns, even if Graham did so in a style more winsome and ecumenical than McGavran could ever muster. Graham sought to connect Lausanne to a long and noble history of missionary activity that he believed liberal Protestantism had derailed. He described the New York and Edinburgh missionary conferences of 1900 and 1910 as great moments of evangelistic enthusiasm. But a "small cloud on the horizon" at Edinburgh would soon become a "cyclone that swept the world." That cyclone was the social gospel.[10] Christians became preoccupied with the here and now, with people's stomachs more than their souls, and turned away from the most important task of the church. Instead of proclaiming the good news of Jesus's death and resurrection for the forgiveness of sins, Christians sought to redeem social structures. Graham's declension narrative cast the Lausanne Congress as a restoration. Lausanne, Graham said, must recapture the theological clarity of Edinburgh and the evangelical conviction that the social gospel had squelched. To be sure, Graham believed that evangelicals ought to do a better job caring for material needs and addressing social problems. But he insisted on the priority of evangelism. Converting human beings to faith in Christ was the church's core mission. Positive social effects would follow conversion.[11] McGavran could not have put it better himself.

The day after Graham opened the Congress, McGavran took center stage in the evening plenary session. He had received over 1,000 responses to his written paper, but he was not one to back down in the face of criticism. He used his speech to defend the theological, ethical, and chronological priority of evangelism over social action. "The most potent forces for social change," McGavran emphasized, "are Bible reading, Bible obeying churches." Conversion was the wellspring of social justice. Focus on evangelism, and you'll get social justice too. Focus on social justice to the detriment of evangelism, and you'll get neither. He insisted that "calling people to repent and become disciples . . . is the most important political act that anyone can perform." As he addressed a crowd of evangelicals from every continent, McGavran positioned himself as an ally of the global south. He urged missionaries to be attuned to the diverse "mosaic" of peoples around the world, and said he took special pleasure in the recent rise of missionaries from Africa, Asia, and Latin America. Instead of a one-directional flow from Europe and the United States to the global south, there was a growing multidirectional evangelical expansion across the world. This was all for the good, because "God accepts all cultures as equally valid vehicles for the Gospel." Americans and Europeans did not have a corner on Christianity. The gospel did not wash out cultural integrity and promote Western colonialism; instead, it brought to the fore the "latent beauties" inherent in every culture.[12]

McGavran's defense of non-Western cultures was a creative way for him to promote the primacy of evangelism in opposition to the Latin American radicals. If every culture had good and bad in it, missionaries ought to think very carefully about the ethical demands they placed on potential converts. Were their instructions essential to Christianity or were they cultural norms the missionaries brought with them? McGavran reminded his audience that the New Testament seemed to present a very simple set of requirements for conversion: repent, believe, and be baptized. But missionaries were constantly coming up with additional obligations of personal piety ("quit drinking, stop smoking") and social justice ("attack slavery, renounce child labor, stop segregation"). McGavran believed this was unbiblical and counterproductive. Let people trust in Jesus. The ethical improvement would come later.[13]

The next morning, C. René Padilla issued a blistering denunciation of McGavran's perspective. The Ecuadorian-born Padilla reflected the growing links between Latin American evangelicals and evangelicals in the United States. He had attended Wheaton College in the 1950s and became involved in InterVarsity Christian Fellowship, the evangelical college ministry. After his undergraduate years Padilla returned to South America with the task of launching InterVarsity chapters there. In 1970, he became a founding member of the Latin American Theological Fraternity, an evangelical organization that sought to join evangelism and social justice together, avoiding the poles of left-wing liberation theology and right-wing American evangelicalism.[14] At Lausanne, Padilla matched form and substance in his plenary speech, choosing to deliver his broadside in Spanish.[15] His English-speaking listeners would have to make do with a translation.

Because Padilla did not name names or engage in personal attacks, the full significance of his celebrated speech has often been misunderstood. He did not merely critique a broadly defined American evangelicalism. He attacked the CGM in particular as an influential and damaging incarnation of American Culture-Christianity. Padilla critiqued McGavran's theology because he believed it undergirded an unholy alliance with American practices. Instead of providing a comprehensive alternative to the problems of American society, American "Culture-Christianity" was so captured by the American way of life that it was blind to its evils. This blindness caused American evangelicals to use for their own evangelistic purposes social ills which they ought to have been resisting. In a tone of incredulity, Padilla said Americans even tried "to integrate racial and class segregation into [their] strategy for world evangelization." Lest anyone doubt he had McGavran in mind, Padilla went on to attack the Homogeneous Unit Principle (HUP) as just another name for segregation: "The idea is that people like to be with those of their own race and class and we must therefore plant segregated churches, which will undoubtedly grow faster." Padilla did not call these views misguided. He declared them profoundly unchristian. He turned to the rhetoric of unity in Christ and the classic texts of Colossians 3:11 and Galatians 3:28 to support his position.[16] While many colorblind Christians used these same texts to express their desire to transcend race, Padilla deployed these verses quite differently. Rather than pointing only to a changed consciousness and a future heavenly state, he saw a picture of the church as a prophetic counterculture that transcended social divisions in the here and now.[17]

While McGavran argued that conversion to Christianity should take place without any sense of social displacement, Padilla believed if conversion did not change one's relationship to society it was not real conversion. Churches that did not reorient the social life became "an instrument of the status quo." They preached "a gospel that the 'free consumers' of religion will want to receive because it is cheap and it demands nothing of them." In this acerbic image the CGM reduced the sacred evangelical faith to another product in an endless marketplace of American consumption. Instead of challenging society, the CGM tried to "produce the greatest number of Christians at the least possible cost in the shortest possible time!" Padilla feared the drive for quantification and efficiency gave undue attention to material forces at the expense of the Spirit's work. Worse still, this kind of consumer religion came with dire social costs. Padilla believed some churches did not deserve to grow. Some compromises were not worth making. Questions of race and class could never be reduced to mere evangelistic tactics without doing violence to the oppressed. McGavran described a chronological progression from conversion to ethical development, but Padilla insisted that "without ethics there is no repentance." The gospel was tangible and earthy, affecting every dimension of life and society. He believed reconciliation with God and reconciliation between people were two inseparable parts of the gospel. Sacrificing one for the sake of the other fatally undermined the whole gospel.[18]

The other major Latin American critic to deliver a plenary address was the Peruvian InterVarsity Christian Fellowship leader Samuel Escobar.[19] Like Padilla, Escobar understood the church as "a radically different community" that ought to have "a revolutionary effect" in society. The call to follow Christ was an invitation to join a distinct community that stood on the side of the poor and offended the powerful. As Escobar saw it, the CGM seemed to turn this distinctiveness on its head. Instead of being an alternative community, it gave in to "the demonic forces at work" in society that caused "racism, prejudice," and "oppression." Escobar suggested that accommodating segregation to achieve faster church growth amounted to a denial of the true nature of the church. Then, in an extremely confrontational rhetorical move, he paraphrased the words of Jesus as recorded in the Gospel of Matthew: "Woe to you zealous evangelists, hypocrites, for you traverse sea and land to make a single proselyte, and when he becomes a proselyte, you make him twice as much a child of hell as yourselves."[20] While the CGM prided itself on protecting the supreme task of evangelization against the inroads of liberal social concern, Padilla and Escobar insisted that the decoupling of evangelization and social justice produced a distorted gospel not worth peddling.

The intensity of these criticisms disconcerted McGavran and his allies. They thought of themselves as standing apart from Americans who imposed a cultural Christianity on the rest of the world. They understood themselves to be allies of the global south. They wanted people to be able to become Christians without giving up their cultures or becoming Western. McGavran had spent decades critiquing American missionary practices. Now his movement stood accused of being an exporter of American Culture-Christianity. The Latin Americans' critiques did not come out of the blue. Padilla had written publicly against the CGM before, and in 1971 McGavran wrote to Padilla in hopes of converting him to the CGM cause. While McGavran described his missive as a plea for common ground, according to the historian David Kirkpatrick, Padilla saw McGavran's letter "as an attempt to silence him" and apparently did not respond.[21] Despite previous clashes, the severity of the blowback at Lausanne surprised Wagner. Everyone, he believed, had come to the Congress with an agenda. McGavran wanted to focus on the "3 billion" globally who were not Christians. Winter wanted to provide a sense of urgency for cross-cultural evangelism. Wagner wanted better "goal setting and measurement" in the task of evangelization. But it turned out others had agendas too. Wagner ruefully noted that he had "assumed Cong. of *evangelization* would agree that evangelism was top priority." But this was not the case, or, at least, not evangelism in the way Wagner understood it. In fact, Padilla and Escobar were just as committed to evangelism as Wagner. They just disagreed about the gospel message.[22]

Forty-eight hours after Padilla's address earned a standing ovation, Ralph Winter tried to turn the Congress back toward the CGM's priorities. His speech was influential in popularizing the idea of "unreached people groups" and drawing evangelicals' attention toward the need for cross-cultural evangelism to convert them.[23] He envisioned a global evangelistic effort using the HUP. But in a world full of ethnic hatreds and strife, Winter's call for homogeneous unit evangelism and the Latin Americans' call for social justice seemed directly at odds. Winter spent the whole second half of his address defending the HUP as a legitimate method that did not betray the unity and purpose of the church. What Padilla and Escobar described as sinful accommodation of racism, Winter called smart strategy.[24] He pointed to his own biography to make his case. The former engineer turned missiologist described himself as a typical white American Christian raised on the dogma that integration was good. In his mind, that meant that everyone should become like him and go to a white Christian church. But God had taught him that unity in the body of Christ did not mean conformity. Now he stood before his diverse audience as a humble convert to cultural pluralism in the body of Christ. By framing the question in this way—integration as conformity and homogeneity as pluralism—Winter described the HUP as the only way to protect diversity. Through local homogeneous congregations the rich tapestry of the body of Christ would be preserved.

Winter claimed that his view forbade segregation or any attempt to promote a sense of superiority among one group of Christians against another. Instead, it protected "Christians of one life style" from being "proselytized to the cultural patterns of another." He believed there was nothing wrong with churches that "deliberately seek to attract a certain social level." It was wrong to exclude people outright, but "it is a fact that where people can choose their church associations voluntarily, they tend to sort themselves out according to their own way of life pretty consistently. Some call this de-facto segregation. And if it is necessarily an evil, 99 out of 100 churches are involved in this evil." Winter insisted that evangelicals ought to see this phenomenon as a healthy sense of peoplehood rather than "wringing our hands about the fact that the worship services of the world Christian community are 'the most segregated hour of the week.'"[25]

Winter seemed unaware that he was perilously close to repeating—almost word for word!—decades-old arguments in support of racial segregation. In fact, one of the most pervasive tropes white evangelicals employed before and during the civil rights movement was that segregation implied no indignity to black people and was consistent with spiritual equality. W. A. Criswell's famous speech to the South Carolina legislature (see chapter 3) was a characteristic example of these claims. He said that he did not have an attitude of superiority and the segregation of his church did not insult African Americans. For evidence, Criswell had pointed to the thriving black religious scene in Dallas. Didn't he know many black preachers, and couldn't some of them preach even better than he could? Let them do it over there, in their churches. Didn't the pastor of St. John's Baptist Church, colored, drive a fancy black Cadillac? Good for him. Let him do so, over there.[26] Winter appeared to be unable or unwilling to explain how his vision of churches deliberately seeking "a certain social level" differed substantially from segregationist stances of old. Predictably, some of the white South African delegation at Lausanne appropriated Winter's speech as an endorsement of apartheid. Winter claimed he was appalled, but he had little reason to be surprised.[27] At a time when many evangelical churches remained functionally closed to African Americans, church growth theorists did not explain how their vision was meaningfully distinct from the long-standing theological logic of evangelical segregationists.

Black evangelicals were at Lausanne, too, though they seemed to make little impression on the proceedings. Representing only around 4 percent of the 600 American attendees, African American evangelicals did not become major players at the Congress in the way Padilla and Escobar did. Major black evangelical names who might have joined the radical contingent, such as John Perkins and Bill Pannell, were not in attendance. But there were a few black evangelicals present who were more than happy to rock the boat, no one more so than Clarence Hilliard, a pastor at Circle Church, a predominantly white but interracial congregation on the west side of Chicago.[28] Born and raised in Buffalo, Hilliard attended Buffalo Bible Institute then earned his B.A. from Houghton College after its 1969 merger with Buffalo Bible Institute. Hilliard moved to Chicago to attend Trinity Evangelical Divinity School and not long thereafter was hired to replace Melvin Warren as the black pastor on Circle's leadership team.[29] At Lausanne, Hilliard helped lead a workshop, "Urban Evangelization among the Poor," in which he joined other participants in urging evangelicals to develop systemic solutions to social problems.[30]

Hilliard was among some 500 delegates who formed a Theology and Radical Discipleship Group to advocate a more socially conscious gospel. The white South African's eager appropriation of Winter's speech was an embarrassingly pointed example of the problems the radicals saw in the gospel of personal salvation. In their view the HUP just dressed up segregation for a new era. They did not bother responding to the church growth activists' claims that they were actually promoting pluralism and cultural autonomy. Perhaps the claim was hard for them to credit based on their own experiences. Padilla and Escobar, for instance, had seen firsthand how American funding for the Latin American Theological Fraternity had come along with attempts by Wagner and others to control the theology and agenda of the group.[31] Such efforts to promote American leadership could easily be read as theological and cultural paternalism.

Neither side got all of what it wanted at Lausanne. The CGM could be pleased with the focus on unreached people groups, while the Latin Americans could claim victory for the stronger-than-expected social justice emphasis. As much as the social justice message of Padilla and Escobar thrilled many participants from the global south, many were also intrigued by what the Americans had to offer. As Brian Stanley has written, "Many delegates might have left Lausanne more enthused by the sharply statistical vision of 'unreached people groups' adumbrated by Donald McGavran and Peter Wagner than by the pleas of the radical evangelicals for an integration of ministries of justice, mercy and evangelism."[32] Wagner claimed over 600 people showed up for his workshop on goal setting and measurement.[33] The Congress expressed its consensus in the Lausanne Covenant, a declaration of global evangelical principles. A five-man committee, including Escobar and headed by the British evangelical John Stott, was responsible for drafting the Covenant. Though all Congress participants had an opportunity to submit amendments, much of the hard work of reconciling competing demands fell to the tactful diplomacy of Stott. Over successive drafts, the Covenant's language on social justice became stronger. In its final form, the Covenant affirmed that "faith without works is dead" and expressed "penitence both for our neglect and for having sometimes regarded evangelism and social concern as mutually exclusive." Still, the document read like the committee-made compromise it was, embracing a series of qualifications: "Although reconciliation with other people is not reconciliation with God, nor is social action evangelism, nor is political liberation salvation, nevertheless we affirm that evangelism and socio-political involvement are both part of our Christian duty." The Theology and Radical Discipleship group released its own statement "repudiat[ing] as demonic the attempt to drive a wedge between evangelism and social action." The gospel was "Good News of liberation, of restoration, of wholeness, and of salvation that is personal, social, global and cosmic." Stott, ever the diplomat, announced that he intended to sign both the Covenant and the radicals' declaration.[34]

Clarence Hilliard was among the radicals who declined to sign the Lausanne Covenant. Despite the unexpectedly strong social justice plank, he could not in good conscience endorse the document. He believed the Covenant did not take a strong-enough stand against the "false dichotomy" of evangelism and social justice, a dichotomy that he believed promoted injustice against African Americans and other oppressed people. He also took aim at the Congress's treatment of the South African delegation. According to Hilliard, some of the South Africans at Lausanne suggested they should agree on a statement of "unity and brotherhood," a simple step that "the overwhelming number of whites" was unwilling to take. From Hilliard's perspective, even as the Congress produced a statement about reconciliation and social justice, it failed to deal forthrightly with a case of "dehumanizing and demonic attitudes" among white South Africans right in its midst. For Hilliard, this was disqualifying. The lack of black evangelical participation also disturbed him. He did not believe the Graham-aligned black evangelicals could be trusted to advocate for the interests of the poor and the oppressed. Hilliard pointed out that major black evangelicals who might have challenged Graham's perspective were conspicuously absent.[35] Lausanne leaders pushed back against Hilliard's claims, claiming ignorance of the South African controversy, and suggesting they had made every possible effort to get African Americans to attend. But black leaders seemed unresponsive. Letters went unreturned. The major figures Hilliard had in mind had in fact been invited but chose not to come. Their absence, and the debate over the meaning of that absence, was a telling indicator of the distance between black and white evangelicals. Where white leaders saw a planning committee that had done all it could to secure black attendance, Hilliard saw a white-controlled process that reeked of "plantation politics."[36]

The Battle to Claim Lausanne's Legacy

In the years after the Lausanne Congress, evangelicals competed to define its legacy. Everyone seemed to agree that something important had happened there, but what was it? If Lausanne came to be seen as an endorsement of the radicals' gospel of a new community, it would boost the prospects of a more socially concerned and antiracist evangelicalism. If it was seen as favoring colorblind Christians' gospel of personal salvation, the CGM's evangelism-first approach and racial pragmatism would gain additional credibility. The struggle for legitimacy between these two visions overlaid practical questions of how the new resources and networks Lausanne established would be used. Colorblind Christians had absorbed some tough criticisms at Lausanne, but in the ensuing years they regrouped and spun the Congress in their favor.

In the immediate aftermath of Lausanne, news reports tended to portray it as a win for the Latin Americans. "Lausanne in '74 marks a strong turning of the evangelical tide toward the importance of sociopolitical involvement as an indispensable part of proclaiming the Bible message," wrote Russell Chandler of the *Los Angeles Times*. "The third world flexed its muscles" and "stole the show," said *Eternity*.[37] But by the fall of 1974, Samuel Escobar worried that Wagner and other American evangelicals were already commandeering the meaning of the Lausanne Congress. The continuation committee formed during the Congress notably declined to include Escobar and Padilla. In October, a larger permanent committee was announced, made up of 46 people from 28 countries. Regional quotas ensured a diverse group. Included among the nine-member North American regional committee were Wagner and Manuel L. Scott, a prominent black pastor in Los Angeles.[38] Though the Latin American challenge had been heard loud and clear at the Congress itself, Escobar believed the selection of people to serve on the committee showed a determination to "silence some trends and voices." He thought "it would be a pity if the impact of the Congress is manipulated by the more closed and triumphalistic sectors of Evangelicalism."[39] A. J. Dain, the Anglican assistant bishop of Sydney and chairman of the committee that planned the Congress, agreed that Lausanne's emphasis on social justice had "shattered some of our North American brethren," but he believed the message had resonated among evangelicals all around the world. It was to be expected that "whenever a prophetic word is spoken there will always be some opposition and some misunderstanding," he noted.[40]

While Escobar viewed Lausanne's sense of global evangelical unity and concern for social justice as the essential legacies of the Congress, Wagner was busy trying to portray these same concerns as "torpedoes" that nearly sunk the evangelical ship. At a follow-up Lausanne meeting in Mexico City in 1975, participants sparred once again over the meaning of the gospel and Americans muscled their way into obtaining over a quarter of the seats on the global committee. Wagner wrote that he and his allies had successfully beaten back the initiatives of the radicals and preserved the priority of evangelism at the center of the Lausanne Movement.[41] Escobar wrote that Wagner's article "really upset" him. In his view it represented a "concerted effort on the part of the conservative elements that are in charge of *Christianity Today* to change the meaning and direction of Lausanne." In this they would fail, Escobar believed, because evangelicals around the globe were so affected by Lausanne exactly because it was not "an American jamboree, but rather a world form of evangelicalism. And this is what our friends from Pasadena [i.e., CGM leaders] cannot accept."[42] Padilla took to the pages of *Christianity Today* to fire back at Wagner. He suggested Wagner's cohort still needed to learn how to listen rather than leading a "backlash" against the radicals. "It is high time for American evangelicals . . . to face the criticisms that are being leveled outside the United States against their 'successful' techniques for evangelism and church planting," Padilla wrote.⁴³

The critiques came from inside the United States too. In the aftermath of Lausanne, Clarence Hilliard became a vocal critic of the Congress and the CGM leaders who sought to use it for their evangelistic purposes. Hilliard's dissatisfaction stemmed from theological concerns similar to those of Padilla and Escobar. But Hilliard approached the problem from the perspective of African American Christianity and the new black liberation theology. Hilliard grounded his theology of the gospel in two key passages of scripture. In the fourth chapter of Luke's Gospel, Jesus announced his purpose by quoting Isaiah the prophet: "The Spirit of the Lord is upon me, because he has anointed me to preach good news to the poor. He has sent me to proclaim release to the captives and recovering of sight to the blind, to set at liberty those who are oppressed, to proclaim the acceptable year of the Lord."⁴⁴ And the Apostle Paul, in his first letter to the church at Corinth, described Christ's death on the cross as a counterintuitive demonstration of God's power. Not many of the Corinthian believers, the Apostle wrote, "were wise according to worldly standards, not many were powerful, not many were of noble birth; but God chose what is foolish in the world to shame the wise, God chose what is weak in the world to shame the strong, God chose what is low and despised in the world, even things that are not, to bring to nothing things that are, so that no human being might boast in the presence of God."⁴⁵ Hilliard's innovation was to insist that these passages must be translated and applied to the American system of white supremacy. What did Christ's liberation mean in a racist society? What did it mean to "shame the strong" in a society that privileged whiteness and stigmatized blackness? With questions like these, Hilliard gave a relentlessly racial cast to these beloved passages of scripture.⁴⁶

For Hilliard, only a race-conscious gospel could call a racist society to repentance. In a system built to dehumanize blackness and uplift whiteness, Americans couldn't know what it meant to take up their cross and follow Jesus unless they confronted race. More than any other major evangelical figure, Hilliard embraced James Cone and black liberation theology. "To be black," Cone had written, "means that your heart, your soul, your mind, and your body are where the dispossessed are." Hilliard agreed. He looked at Jesus proclaiming liberty for the oppressed and concluded that blackness was the most potent symbol Americans had to understand Jesus and his message. Jesus, Hilliard said, was "black theologically." Jesus Christ "came into the world as the ultimate 'nigger' of the universe. He moved to the bottom of the social order, and his people and his culture rejected him. Christ's situation sounds like that of Any Black Person, Anywhere, U.S.A." More scandalous still, Hilliard insisted that "we as his followers are . . . to become niggers with him. . . . The black Christ calls the world to become black, to deny everything for what can only be a nigger's death—the cross."[47]

This was not a form of black self-loathing. Hilliard understood it as a theological mandate for every Christian in America, regardless of their phenotype. Theological blackness was a choice, not a birthright. One became black by following Jesus. One became white by pursuing success and turning away from the poor. All Christians had a responsibility to resist "the siren call of the system to move up the social ladder." A status quo–affirming, success-oriented way of life was the "theological whiteness" Jesus struggled against. When Jesus said "deny thyself and follow me," the message translated to white Americans was "deny their theological whiteness."[48] A church "true to their Lord" would "so identify with oppressed blacks that they would, in the eyes of the system, cease to be white."[49] Hilliard's casting of Jesus as black drew on a long African American tradition that associated black suffering with the sufferings of Christ, that linked the Roman cross to the American lynching tree.[50] The shocking imagery at the end of Countee Cullen's "Christ Recrucified" (1922) is suggestive of the tradition in which Hilliard operated:

> Christ's awful wrong is that he's dark of hue,
> The sin for which no blamelessness atones;
> But lest the sameness of the cross should tire,
> They kill him now with famished tongues of fire,
> And while he burns, good men, and women too,
> Shout, battling for black and brittle bones.[51]

The life-and-death stakes of black suffering in a white supremacist country made Hilliard unwilling to accept the tactics of the CGM and its allies. He described whiteness and blackness not as incidental racial identities but as theologically significant categories. Whiteness was nothing less than a heresy. Those who parleyed with it in an effort to make Christian converts perverted the gospel. Hilliard wrote, "It is harder for the average white person to receive the purposeful call of God than it is for a camel to go through the eye of a needle. But although the gospel of Jesus Christ will still send the rich, white, young ruler away sorrowful, most prominent evangelistic efforts take him in."[52] Here Hilliard alluded to the famous story of the rich young ruler who was unwilling to sell his possessions to follow Jesus.[53] In Hilliard's version, crucially, the story is racialized. The wealthy man becomes white, and to find salvation he must divest from his racial entitlement in addition to his wealth.

While Hilliard remained within the evangelical camp and insisted on the necessity of conversion through faith in Jesus Christ, he believed white evangelicals were cheapening its meaning, turning it into a selfish personal transaction between the individual and God. Hilliard called out McGavran by name and criticized his gospel of personal salvation for failing to disrupt the social order. "Specialists in getting quick, easy decisions for a strange, mystical, theologically white Christ are rapidly increasing," he wrote. "These persons peddle a Jesus easy to accept, a Jesus who demands very little commitment of energy, money, life." Hilliard directly connected this transactional gospel to the denigration of racial justice. In a racist society like the United States, "a Jesus easy to accept"—a Jesus easy to sell—was inevitably a racist Jesus. In the evangelical mainstream, "The horizontal dimensions of the Gospel are presented as optional, not intrinsic to it," he pointed out. "That is what frustrated some of us who attended" the Lausanne Congress.[54] The idea that a single-minded focus on evangelism could be harmful to African Americans was not new. In the nineteenth century, the antilynching activist Ida B. Wells criticized the famous evangelist Dwight Moody for accommodating white racism in his popular revival meetings. On another occasion she said, "Our American Christians are too busy saving the souls of white Christians from burning in hellfire to save the lives of black ones from present burning in fires kindled by white Christians," she wrote.[55] Now, Hilliard charged Moody's spiritual descendants with the same crime.

Hilliard's claims were not original, but they were shocking. White evangelicals found it easy to dismiss liberals for their latest theological adventurism. But now a self-described evangelical brought a black

Christ to the pages of *Christianity Today*, the flagship publication of white evangelicalism. Colorblind Christians did not like what Hilliard had to say. His critique was so far outside the evangelical mainstream that few people, certainly not McGavran, bothered to listen to him. Dr. John Gratton, a professor at Wheaton, wrote that Hilliard "seems to have merely moved Christ from one social level to another and in the process lost sight of him as the Son of Man who meets all men where they are."[56] Colorblind Christians were comfortable imagining God reaching out to all people equally. They rejected the idea that God stood especially on behalf of the oppressed—and the disturbing notion that in the United States this was a racial category.

At the very moment Hilliard brought his message of a black Christ to a national evangelical audience, events at his church had become an object lesson in how contentious the message was. Indeed, by the time *Christianity Today* published "Down with the Honky Christ," Clarence Hilliard had been fired. The trouble started some months before, when Hilliard presented a sermon draft very much like the article that later appeared in *Christianity Today*. If anything, the sermon was more scathing, criticizing Billy Graham by name. Hilliard saw the battle in American evangelicalism as nothing less than a struggle between two different gospels. "One must realize," the sermon draft reads, "that another gospel is being preached—the gospel of the system, the gospel of the status-quo, the 'honky' gospel." He accused Graham's evangelism of being "nebulous, almost contentless," presenting a "Lord and Savior Jesus Christ" who didn't actually place demands upon self-satisfied defenders of the status quo. It was the custom at Circle Church for the entire leadership team to pre-approve sermons. But the white leadership of the church refused to allow Hilliard to preach such an explosive message. This opened up a broader debate about authority in the church and the nature of the interracial project. In the ensuing conflagration, both the white senior pastor David Mains and Hilliard told the church board they could not continue as pastors under the circumstances. The white-dominated board made its choice. The board asked Mains to stay on and asked Hilliard for his resignation. Hilliard left Circle, taking the entire black membership of the church with him. He soon started a new church on the west side, but the fallout from Circle Church lingered. If even a progressive evangelical church deliberately trying to be interracial could not abide Hilliard's theological blackness, what hope was there for evangelicalism writ large?[57]

If Hilliard's race-conscious gospel suggests some of the diverse possibilities inherent in evangelical theology, it also stands as a marker of the road not taken. The CGM was much more successful than radicals like Hilliard in gaining bureaucratic control of Lausanne functions. In 1976, the Lausanne committee formed four "working groups" to continue its mission. The committee named Wagner the chair of the Strategy Working Group, whose mandate included "investigating the growth of evangelization worldwide; continuing to gather information about unreached peoples and making it available to church and mission leadership for study ... and the convening of consultations to develop and share strategies for evangelization among particular peoples or groups."[58] Wagner could not have asked for a better assignment to use the infrastructure of Lausanne to promote his church growth ideas. Meanwhile, the Theology and Education Working Group began planning a consultation on the HUP. Remarkably, after all the attention given to social justice at the Congress, the first major Lausanne-sponsored event in the ensuing years not only sidelined the radicals' concern for social justice; it enhanced the credibility of the CGM's most controversial evangelistic method. With Wagner at the helm of one working group and church growth priorities dominating the deliberations of another, the CGM was effectively using the resources of Lausanne to advance a gospel that invested in whiteness.[59]

Held from May 31 to June 2, 1977, in Pasadena, California, the consultation on the HUP featured a five-man Fuller team, including McGavran, Wagner, and Winter, arguing on behalf of the HUP. Five invited scholars took the opposing view. Padilla reluctantly came to reprise his criticisms, as did John Howard Yoder. John Stott agreed to serve as chairman and worked to resolve differences between participants.[60] In advance of the meeting, the Fuller team produced a description of the HUP that can reasonably claim official status: "Men like to become Christians within their own homogeneous units, without crossing linguistic, class, or race barriers. The homogeneous unit principle affirms that far from being contrary to Christian practice, that mode of becoming Christian is normal, Biblical and should be allowed and encouraged."[61] This idea—and its far-reaching ethical implications—structured the debate.

The Fuller team cast themselves as defenders of the rights and cultural integrity of minorities while describing their opponents as paternalistic at best. Wagner suggested that "much of the ethical opposition" to homogeneous unit congregations "may turn out to be a subtle and thinly-disguised manifestation of racism."[62] Wagner and Winter accused their opponents of expecting everyone to join their own white churches and become carbon copies of themselves. Yet, even as church growth theorists described whiteness as a force for assimilationist racism, they also continued to imagine whiteness as a part of the American mosaic entitled to its own autonomy. If whiteness should not assimilate, neither should it be diluted. Despite the manifest risk of white nationalists appropriating such logic, church growth activists continued to insist on whiteness as peoplehood.

This sensibility was most clear in McGavran's remarkable paper, in which he argued that white solidarities in the United States were every bit as ethically legitimate as black solidarities. This was the conference at which he warned against "mongrel" congregations and advocated homogeneous congregations so Christians could worship "without raising difficult questions of cross-race dining, marriage and the like" (see chapter 3).[63] His description of "cross-race dining" as something to avoid was surprising. As all the consultation participants knew, the New Testament described the sharing of meals between Jewish and Gentile followers of Jesus as a major point of contention in the early church. When Peter refused to eat with Gentiles, Paul famously rebuked his actions as contrary to the Gospel.[64] McGavran appeared to believe Peter was in the right after all. The rest of the Fuller team followed McGavran's lead. Ralph Winter repeated the same claims that had appealed to South Africa's apartheid defenders three years before, and Wagner insisted that if a church mixed homogeneous units, the community around the church would probably not find the gospel very appealing. "If, on the other hand, the congregation decides to remain homogeneous, the evangelistic potential will increase accordingly."[65]

The opposing team assembled for the consultation struck a moderate tone in response to the Fuller cohort. In light of McGavran's explosive racial commentary, it is notable that the critics did not push back more forcefully. Black evangelicals who might have critiqued McGavran more vehemently were not invited, though Bill Pannell, a fellow professor at

Fuller, was present as a consultant. Harvie Conn, a former missionary to Korea and professor at Westminster Seminary, argued that McGavran and his colleagues were glossing over the overwhelming theological thrust of the New Testament: the creation of a new people of God drawn from every culture and nation. This new kind of community at once honored diversity and transcended it. The critics faulted the Fuller team for turning the sociological *fact* of group affiliation into an ironclad *prescription* for church growth. When Fuller professor Charles Kraft wrote that "homogeneity is, to my way of thinking, a fact," John Stott drily noted, "So is sin!"[66]

For Robert Ramseyer, a longtime missionary to Japan, the spread of the gospel along ethnic lines might make strategic sense but was theologically and ethically fatal. "When the boundaries of a church are identical with those of a previously existing ethnic unit, it becomes very difficult to talk of the new people of God, of the newness of life which frees and liberates." At times McGavran and his colleagues imagined the homogeneous unit as an elastic concept; it might be based on race or language, or even common occupation or educational level. These human solidarities were so strong that they formed an organic unity broken only at great cost. Yet the community of God that the New Testament described did not constitute a new organic unity. Nothing was more important than salvation through Jesus Christ, but the shared experience of salvation did not create a homogeneous unit. In two brutal sentences Ramseyer cut to the heart of church growth activists' paradoxical claims. "Our friends from Fuller speak a great deal about those who would reduce the church to a drab cultural sameness and uniformity. Yet it is precisely this school of thought which seems unable to think of the congregation except in terms of cultural sameness—homogeneity."[67]

Though everyone seemed to agree that the HUP raised profound ethical questions in the American context, and those questions were at the center of the consultation, the people with the most at stake were not invited to participate in a meaningful way. How different the consultation might have looked if someone like Clarence Hilliard had been invited. But the Fuller team's goal for the consultation was not so much the sharing of diverse ideas as the spread of the ideas they already held. Padilla sensed this posture and later called the meeting "terrible." He believed the Fuller professors "had made up their mind" and weren't interested in a real exchange of perspectives. "They didn't listen. At all," he remembered. John Stott vented his displeasure to his diary: "it saddened me that when René Padilla got up to speak, they (quite unconsciously, no doubt) put down their pads and pens, folded their arms, sat back and appeared to pull down the shutter of their minds."[68]

The consultation produced a public statement that allowed the Fuller team to claim the HUP had the endorsement of the Lausanne Movement. The statement celebrated "substantial areas of agreement" while acknowledging "points of tension and disagreement which still remain."[69] It endorsed homogeneous congregations as acceptable in certain contexts but declared that any kind of apartheid or denial of membership on cultural grounds was impermissible. Participants agreed that homogeneous churches often grew faster, but seemed no closer to agreeing about whether such churches exacerbated hatreds or helped to resolve them. The statement described a "painful dilemma" of trying to choose between "the struggle for reconciliation" on the one hand or "numerical church growth" on the other. Nonetheless, it affirmed that it was wrong to try to grow a church in a racist homogeneous unit without challenging the racism of the group.[70] Leighton Ford, brother-in-law of Billy Graham and chairman of the international Lausanne committee, invited the global evangelical church to build on what the consultation had accomplished. Now, Ford believed, "the homogeneous unit principle, properly interpreted and carefully implemented, can be translated from the realms of musty theory to dynamic strategy."[71] The CGM's most controversial tactic—the very one the Latin American radicals had blasted in their celebrated speeches at Lausanne—now had the official imprimatur of the Lausanne Movement.

The consultation on the HUP bolstered church growth experts' enthusiasm for using race as a strategic tool of evangelism. In 1979, C. Peter Wagner published the most robust defense of the principle ever produced. Building on the rhetorical strategies deployed at the 1977 consultation, Wagner opportunistically positioned himself against colorblind Christians. He argued that it was time for evangelicals to discard their ostensibly "colorless" theology and embrace the flourishing of multiple "colorful" theologies. He urged them to see that they were culturally located, "Western," not bearers of a universal theology unencumbered by culture.[72] Wagner even quoted James Cone in his defense.[73] For theology to have integrity and meaning, it had to be contextualized in culture. Wagner argued the HUP provided space for healthy theological pluralism to flourish and assimilation to Western norms to be resisted. He suggested that the spiritual unity of the church could be expressed at the supra-congregational level. Interracial and cross-cultural fellowship between congregations rather than within them preserved the essential unity of Christians without harming church growth.

Because of its seemingly paradoxical embrace of diversity and homogeneity, *Our Kind of People* could provoke whiplash in its readers. One reviewer wrote that the book was so "schizophrenic" he "hesitates to criticize it for fear of having completely missed the point."[74] Wagner's deployment of liberation theology and cultural pluralism to bolster his own vision of evangelical conversion could easily come off as opportunistic rather than sincere. Tom Nees, a white pastor of a church in Washington, DC, savaged the book for "reducing conversion to a personal, private religious experience" that allowed Christians to ignore the social demands of Christianity, including its call to break down racial divisions. Nees condemned the HUP as an ecclesial version of the old Supreme Court doctrine of separate but equal. Nees wrote, "The answer is neither assimilation nor homogeneous units, but groups of Christians whose differences are celebrated and whose lives are enriched by a unity within diversity."[75]

Wagner's professed concern for the cultural integrity of American minorities might have come as a surprise to an ordinary white evangelical who picked up the book after glancing at its cover. The publisher of *Our Kind of People*, John Knox Press of Atlanta, promoted it as a salve for white evangelical guilt. The back cover of the original paperback edition offered this extraordinary description of the book's contents: "OUR KIND OF PEOPLE attacks the Christian guilt complex arising from the civil rights movement and puts it to rest with a skillful mixture of scriptural precedent and human psychology. In doing so, Wagner transforms the statement that '11 A.M. on Sunday is the most segregated hour in America' from a millstone around Christian necks into a dynamic tool for assuring Christian growth." In this framing, Wagner's defense of homogeneity was important not because of what it did for evangelicals of color but because it helped white evangelicals feel better about their segregated churches. Wagner's thoughts within the book were more nuanced, but the slippage between Wagner's argument and the selling and use of that argument is precisely the point. While Wagner theorized about cultural pluralism and contextual theology, ordinary white evangelicals could interpret it as license to *not* think about race. So long as they did not literally bar the doors of the church to people of color, their local homogeneous congregation was good. Wagner's sunny optimism about church growth and unyielding focus on individual conversion smacked of the kind of success orientation and privatized religion that, in Hilliard's view, epitomized theological whiteness.

By 1981 Wagner admitted the HUP was "risky" and "can support racism" but insisted that when "properly applied" it could "be an effective force to reduce racism."[76] The caveat of proper application was doing a lot of work in Wagner's writing. When Tom Nees went to a CGM seminar, he reported his experience:

> During the seminar we used a medical analogy to describe impediments to church growth: Healthy churches grow, sick churches do not. . . . If a church is not growing it must be because of certain diseases which church growth diagnosticians have identified. The first disease, and the one afflicting more churches than any other ailment, was defined as "ethnicitus," the disease that begins when a congregation finds itself in a racially changing community. Rather than being seen as an opportunity to demonstrate the universalism and cross-cultural possibilities of the Christian faith, integration was described as a deadly threat to normal congregational life and certain death to church growth.[77]

This was not a rogue popularization of CGM thought.[78] Despite its claims of Christian pluralism, the CGM effectively supported an all-too-familiar feature of the white evangelical imagination: racial integration as spiritual threat. The HUP was not in fact being widely used to promote the flowering of diverse colorful theologies. Instead, young and energetic white pastors, armed with church growth principles, looked with strategic eyes to prosperous suburban communities and sought to target white middle-class families as their growth demographic. This was the era in which some of the most influential churches of the 1990s and early twenty-first century got their start. Bill Hybels, founder of Willow Creek church in suburban Chicago, received training and fundraising support from superstar pastor Robert Schuller. Rick Warren, after training under C. Peter Wagner at Fuller, chose Orange County as the site of his Saddleback Church. From the start, he dreamed that his church would one day have 20,000 members.[79] Warren and his leadership team created a composite character representing the precise kind of person they wanted their church to reach. He was an upper-middle-class white man.[80] To someone like Clarence Hilliard grappling with impoverishment, violence, and racism on the west side of Chicago, these strategies and dreams appeared to have little to do with the gospel of Jesus Christ.

The evangelism-first efforts of the CGM and its successful co-option of the North American wing of the Lausanne Movement led to growing disenchantment among evangelicals around the world. At the 1980 Lausanne Consultation in Pattaya, Thailand, many delegates expressed their alarm at what historian Brian Stanley has called "a resurgent strategic pragmatism" that slighted social concerns.[81] Meanwhile, in the United States, the CGM all but ignored the concerns of black evangelicals. In a 1981 interview for the movement magazine *Church Growth America*, McGavran discussed the CGM's successes and its prospects. The movement had already had a profound effect on American evangelicalism. It had influenced the nation's largest Protestant denomination, the Southern Baptist Convention, and smaller denominations such as the Nazarenes. But so far, most of the movement's influence was concentrated in white churches. McGavran explained that this was because "most devout believing pastors" were white, and as they learned about church growth principles they "naturally" tried to convert "their own kind of people" first. McGavran saw a great future ahead for the movement as it spread to other groups making up the diverse "mosaic" of the United States. "The minorities," he explained, "are virtually untouched by the church today." He urged Christians to pray for the "penetration" of all these "untouched" groups. He declared that African Americans and other people of color in the United States were "growing up unchurched" and were effectively "Christo-pagan." At no point in this astonishing interview did Donald McGavran acknowledge the existence, much less the value, of black churches and other nonwhite expressions of Christianity.[82] The black evangelical activist John Perkins had seen enough. At the height of the CGM's influence, he blasted white evangelicals for "not bothering with breaking down racial barriers, since that would only distract us from 'church growth.' And so the most segregated, racist institution in America, the evangelical church, racks up the numbers, declaring itself 'successful,' oblivious to the . . . dismemberment of the Body of Christ."[83]

Houston '85: Evangelizing Ethnic America, Excluding African Americans

McGavran's denigration of the black church was not anomalous, and Perkins's criticisms proved prophetic. Indeed, the leading lights of American evangelicalism were about to embark on a new evangelistic project from which they would deliberately exclude black evangelicals. Early in 1981, the North American Lausanne committee began planning a National Convocation on Evangelizing Ethnic America, to be held in Houston in the spring of 1985. Conference planners turned to the Southern Baptist Convention, widely regarded as leading practitioners of evangelism to people of color, for expertise. As Wagner put it, "The Southern Baptist Home Missions Board has more experience and a better track record for evangelizing minorities than any other denominational agency in the U.S."[84] But the Home Mission Board of the SBC had long-standing contrasting approaches to ministry among African Americans as opposed to other groups. One division worked with black Baptists, and the entirely separate Language Missions Division worked with other people of color and foreign-language groups, an organizational structure first set in place during Jim Crow. The Lausanne committee asked Oscar Romo, the Hispanic longtime leader of the Language Missions Division, to chair the planning committee, and organizers promptly reproduced the logic of the Home Mission Board's organizational structure. The initial steering committee "unanimously agreed that the principal focus of the Convocation should be those ethnic groups whose language and/or culture is other than English." This meant that the conference would include a focus on "Native Americans, Hispanics, Asians, Europeans, Middle Easterners, Internationals, Caribbean, and Deaf," as well as "Non ethnics" who were interested in cross-cultural evangelism. It would *not* include African Americans. Reflecting the influence of the CGM (Wagner was on the steering committee), the proposed conference would "research the ethnic realities of the United States" and "provide data . . . discuss models, methodologies and progress" in evangelizing "American ethnics." The ultimate goal was "greatly increasing the evangelistic ministry to unreached individuals and people groups in the United States." The steering committee set up a diverse central planning committee made up of Hispanic, Asian, European immigrant, and "Anglo" Americans (including one woman!). There were no African Americans on the committee.[85]

In effect, organizers chose to exclude black evangelicals from the conference and then created an after-the-fact definition of "ethnic America" to fit their discriminatory decision. As early as April 1982, before the establishment of a permanent planning committee, Wagner explained to Lausanne chairman Leighton Ford that he and other leaders deemed it necessary to exclude African Americans not just from the Convocation's definition of "ethnic America," but from the planning of the event entirely. Wagner claimed he initially "had no idea at all of excluding American blacks" but as he talked with other leaders "all except one" believed in "the wisdom of keeping them separate." Wagner explained that "experience has shown that whenever a joint project is conducted with all included, the American blacks almost inevitably take control of the project." Wagner and his fellow white evangelicals, of course, never dreamed of controlling a project. Black Americans, he warned, "understand power and know how to use it." It would not be fair to the other ethnic groups to have black people dominating the agenda. Besides, African Americans were already a "reached" people group, with large numbers of Christians, and they did not seem to be interested in cross-cultural evangelism. White evangelicals were very interested in it, so it was only proper that they should plan the conference. Behind the baldly discriminatory logic of the decision was the ongoing debate about the meaning of the gospel. Wagner feared that black evangelicals would get in the way of the evangelistic focus of the conference and he didn't want persuasive voices for social justice to be present in the planning process.[86]

As planning for the conference began in earnest, some black evangelicals heard about it and protested their exclusion. In September 1983, Bill Pannell, Wagner's colleague at Fuller, wrote to Paul Landrey, a member of the planning committee, to protest. "As could be expected," he wrote, "there was no Black evangelical speaking for this conference and I suspect there were none in any significant leadership positions either."

Tongue in cheek, Pannell noted that this seemed curious in light of the fact that "Dr. C. Peter Wagner... reports to be sensitive to the contribution the Civil Rights Movement made to our understanding of ethnicity." Pannell called for an end to the exclusion and for "significant Black involvement in this important event."[87] The following month Wagner wrote that the North American Lausanne committee "needs to move fairly rapidly" on a plan for a separate "Convocation on Evangelizing Black America" to "defuse some of the potential criticism of Houston '85 from black leaders who may feel that [the North American Lausanne committee] is ignoring them."[88] Such a scheme raised as many questions as it answered. Why did black evangelicals need a separate conference? And why were white evangelicals trying to plan that one too?

A year after Pannell first raised the issue of black exclusion, with no substantive action taken to remedy the problem, Leighton Ford wrote letters to Oscar Romo and Robert Coleman. As the chairmen of the Houston '85 planning committee and the North American Lausanne committee, respectively, these men had the power to change course if they wished. Ford reiterated the suggestion that "we probably should have a consultation on evangelizing black America." He wrote that his "main concern is that our black evangelical brothers and sisters feel confident that they are important to us and we to them in the total task of world evangelization." He was "concerned lest the perception of our black evangelical friends be that intentionally or otherwise they have been left out."[89] Had black evangelicals been privy to the discussions taking place behind the scenes in the planning of Houston '85, they would have been anything but confident that they were important to their white brothers and sisters.

As the controversy threatened to spill into the open, Wagner expanded on his justifications. He explained that the decision about whether to include black evangelicals was extensively discussed because the steering committee knew it could generate controversy. Some of the "denominational executives" described past "unpleasant experiences" trying to work with African Americans. "The black American culture," Wagner declared, "is by nature far more aggressive than that of most other minorities and as a result committee meetings tend to be dominated by the blacks." Other ethnic groups, "even top leaders," were "intimidated by outspoken blacks." It was better to simply exclude them than to try to work together under these circumstances. Wagner sent this incriminating letter to Ford, Romo, Coleman, and Landrey. It does not appear to have generated pushback.[90] Here was a telling picture of what could happen when colorblind Christians opportunistically deployed race-conscious strategies. Though happy to assemble a diverse board and promote ethnic evangelization, they pointedly excluded the very people whose experiences as racial minorities might cause them to have meaningful disagreements with the conference agenda. In doing so, they laid bare the tangled religio-racial process of exclusion. There was a theological logic to it—Wagner and others were determined to keep their evangelistic focus at the center of the conference—but the exclusion was explicitly racialized. African Americans, as such, were to be excluded. When the boundaries were drawn and black evangelicals found themselves on the outside, it was not only as advocates of social justice but as black people.

Wagner's antiblack sentiment aligned with rather than contradicted his enthusiastic embrace of the ethnic revival in American life. As Matthew Frye Jacobson has argued, the ethnic revival facilitated a redefinition of whiteness around immigrant roots and diverse ethnic identities, at once decentering black struggles and claiming white innocence.[91] Wagner's actions seemed to reflect a genuine feeling of hostility toward African Americans that he did not possess toward other groups. He kept in his files a *Time* magazine article describing the more progressive turn of the National Baptist Convention, USA, after the replacement of its longtime conservative leader, Joseph H. Jackson. The comedian Dick Gregory declared, "You're the strongest, biggest, blackest organization there is. Use it!" Wagner underlined this quote and scrawled across the top of the page, "Why isn't this a racist statement?" Despite Wagner's explicit praise for a "colorful theology" and declaration that race consciousness was positive, he seemed to recoil when he saw these same attitudes in African American Christians. "Are US blacks," he wondered, "more racist than other US ethnic groups?"[92]

In an attempt to defuse controversy, the planning committee decided to ask each of the participating denominations to "send one key black pastor to come as an 'observer' to the Convocation." These black pastors would gain the benefits of seeing "how this sort of thing is done" and "hopefully accept the challenge of holding a similar convocation" for black America. At the conference these black pastors would hold their own meeting to explore this possibility. Wagner, Ford, and other leaders had specific ideas about which black leaders should be invited and who should be in charge. Wagner also wanted to make sure that he and Robert Coleman opened the meeting and explained "how previous similar events have been handled."[93] Leighton Ford, wanting to avoid an open break between Lausanne and black evangelicals, seems to have been the driving force for setting up a black caucus at Houston. Wagner wanted to humor him for political reasons if nothing else. "I'm sure you can see what Leighton is after," Wagner told another committee member, "and that we must do what is necessary to support him."[94] After writing to a few black evangelical pastors to ask them to come to Houston, Wagner could breathe a sigh of relief. "I think," he told Romo, "we are in the clear as to our black situation."[95]

On April 15, 1985, the Convocation on Evangelizing Ethnic America began. After all the controversy in the planning process, the conference itself seemed to be a roaring success. Like the organizers of the conference, evangelical media portrayed it as a groundbreaking opportunity for evangelicals to come to grips with the new America—a multiethnic mosaic of cultures in need of the gospel in their communities.[96] With nearly 700 registered attendees and over three dozen denominations represented, it was an important gathering of a broad cross-section of American evangelicalism. In his keynote address, Wagner declared, "The teeming multitudes of all colors, languages, smells, and cultures are not just a quaint sideline in our nation. They *are* America." The task at hand, Romo said, was to "evangelize" these groups, not "Americanize" them. The venue hosting the Convocation, South Main Baptist Church, illustrated what Wagner and Romo had in mind. Amid a changing neighborhood in the 1960s, the white leadership of South Main determined not to flee the city. Now, the church was made up of four congregations: Korean, Cambodian, Hispanic, and "Anglo." A few times a year the congregations came together for a combined worship service. It was stories like this that convinced Wagner the HUP could be a positive force for social ethics as well as evangelism.[97]

The conference celebrated evangelical denominations making major strides in ethnic outreach. The growing numbers of Asian and Hispanic Southern Baptist congregations were held up as a model. The Assemblies of God, too, had over 1,000 Hispanic churches by the end of 1987.[98] The Nazarenes, a small and historically white denomination, were another example of what evangelicals could accomplish if they committed themselves to church growth. Facing stagnating membership numbers, the denomination had gone all in on church growth theory, seeking training from McGavran and Wagner in the 1970s.[99] By 1987 the Nazarenes reported that over half of their recent church plants—some 250 congregations—were "ethnic." This included 94 black churches, making the Nazarenes a leader in adding black churches to a historically white denomination. What the conference leaders did not say is that the Nazarenes were the exception that proved the rule. Most evangelical denominations remained overwhelmingly white. And despite the Nazarenes' rapid turn toward ethnic church planting, the denomination reported that only 4 percent of its total membership was "ethnic."[100]

The one discordant note in the Houston conference was the ongoing tensions borne of the exclusion of African Americans. Black pastors duly held a meeting to begin planning a black convocation, but not without demanding a "formal apology" from Houston '85 leaders. Leighton Ford claimed he was "grieved and sorry for any misunderstanding." Wagner said, "I don't think we realized it would be this controversial." Neither man publicly owned their deliberate actions. Bob Harrison, now a veteran of more than three decades of ministry in white evangelical spaces, noted that the whole episode was symptomatic of the disconnect between black and white evangelicals. African Americans, Harrison pointed out, did not just want to be invited to events. "What we'd like is to be in on the ground level."[101]

In the ensuing months, as the "black task force" formed at Houston began planning a black convocation, its first order of business was to seek accountability for the mess at Houston '85. It promptly drafted a scathing resolution condemning the exclusion of African Americans from the Convocation. The resolution declared that planners had "deliberately" chosen to exclude black Christians, a decision that was "insensitive" and "unchristlike." The Bible demanded that "Black Americans and other minorities be accepted and treated as peers." The failure to do this produced a sense of "rejection" and "abandonment" and could only "weaken the sense of unity and equality in the body of Christ." The resolution demanded that the North American Lausanne committee take "immediate conscious steps and make public pronouncements to counteract an apparent philosophy and attitude which treats Black Americans and other minorities simply as an appendage."[102] Houston '85 had exposed a divide in evangelicalism that, a generation after the height of the civil rights movement, appeared to be growing. Evangelical elites, in pursuit of a gospel of personal salvation, were eager to make their movement multiethnic. But an antiracist gospel remained outside of most evangelical imaginations. An evangelicalism in which black evangelicals could participate *as black people* with distinctly black concerns remained only a distant dream.

Conclusion

The period between Lausanne '74 and Houston '85 coincided with surging church attendance in many evangelical denominations, a growing trend of large congregations that would come to be called megachurches, and the increasing visibility of evangelicals in the nation's culture and politics. Steven P. Miller has called this "the age of evangelicalism."[103] It might more accurately be labeled the age of *white* evangelicalism. Even as more Americans claimed the evangelical label, African American evangelicals felt increasingly beleaguered and alienated from the community with which they had so much in common. They saw the national retreat from the ideals of the civil rights movement, but little evidence of concern from their fellow Christians. As white evangelicals celebrated a revival and helped usher in the Reagan Revolution, the heady mixture of growing churches and growing influence signaled the ascendancy of investments in evangelical whiteness.

Black evangelicals who asserted that their black experience mattered to the body of Christ continued to trouble the white evangelical mainstream. "When I insist on being black," Bill Pannell wrote, "I find myself once again a nonperson." The Houston fiasco had deepened a climate of distrust. Pannell wrote that by the end of the 1980s, "The North American version of the Lausanne movement was widely perceived to be racist to the core." When yet another Lausanne Congress took place in Manila in 1989 with little black evangelical participation, Pannell called it "the most telling insult to our sense of Christian selfhood in all the years we have ridden in the back of the white evangelical bus." What was behind this pattern? "Was this exclusion of black evangelicals at a conference overwhelmingly represented by people from the two-thirds world a mere oversight? A matter of culture?" Pannell thought not. "Perhaps there was a concern about power and a related fear that if black evangelicals from North America got themselves together and made some alliances with other men and women of goodwill from other parts of the globe, a new network might emerge, one closer to the ethos of the oppressed than is currently represented by any Euro-American association."[104]

By the end of the 1980s, black and white evangelicals alike harbored a growing sense that the questions raised by the civil rights movement had not been successfully resolved. Token integration here and homogeneous growth there seemed to have left black and white evangelicals as far apart as ever. Power remained in white hands. Theology was still colored white. For most ordinary white evangelicals, racial justice seemed like a distraction from the pure message of the gospel. Pannell thought his white evangelical counterparts "were especially upset that I would insist that the kingdom of God has something to do with justice." Not only that, a chasm separated black and white understandings of the civil rights era through which they had lived. Many white evangelicals had yet to make their peace with the civil rights movement. Pannell wrote, "Some of these Christians have never forgiven Martin Luther King, Jr., for dispelling their cozy view of themselves or the value system of their parents." While white evangelicals tended to see the 1960s as an age of chaos and moral decline, Pannell remembered "those great years when democracy crept up on this country, led by a black Baptist preacher from the Deep South."[105] Black evangelicals' claims about a gospel that "has something to do with justice" added to their reputation as troublemakers. Their priorities disrupted the logic of what Clarence Hilliard called theological whiteness. Obvious signs of disunity and growing black evangelical impatience—combined with colorblind Christians' discomfort with both—would lead to a new movement of "racial reconciliation" in the 1990s. But whether this movement would be any more successful at severing the link between Christian colorblindness and the evangelical investment in whiteness remained to be seen.

6

The Elusive Turning Point

Colorblind Christians and "Racial Reconciliation"

In the summer of 1995 hundreds of thousands of white Christian men were filling American football stadiums and, to nearly everyone's astonishment, publicly repenting for racism. The black evangelical writer Edward Gilbreath offered a vivid portrait of the atmosphere at these events.[1] "The legion of masculine voices sings, shouts, chants, cries. Frisbees, footballs, and plastic-foam planes constantly zoom overhead.... And between speakers, the stadium spontaneously breaks out into deafening macho chants: 'We love Jesus; yes, we do! We love Jesus; how 'bout you?'"[2] This was Promise Keepers (PK), a men's movement that had suddenly become the leading exemplar of what many commentators were calling "racial reconciliation."[3] PK urged men to live by seven promises, including a pledge to "reach beyond racial and denominational barriers to demonstrate the power of biblical unity."[4] When a PK conference came to Three Rivers Stadium in Pittsburgh in the summer of 1996, a local black columnist went to see what all the fuss was about and found the sight "surreal." From the stage, "a multi-racial cadre of speakers confronted 45,000 mostly white males with the legacy of racism and their complicity in maintaining it." Remarkably, the men seemed to listen. They promised "to take the spirit of racial reconciliation back to their neighborhoods and their all-white churches where serious soul-searching has to begin." The columnist didn't have to be an evangelical Christian to believe that the sight of 45,000 men engaged in "handwringing and spontaneous male bonding across racial lines was an inspiring image in an age of racial polarization."[5]

Widespread fears of racial division provided powerful impetus to racial reconciliation discourse in the 1990s. The alienation of black evangelicals from major evangelical movements like Lausanne and the Church Growth Movement (CGM) seemed to some evangelical leaders like a problem that could hamper the growth of evangelicalism and threaten its credibility. To prevent this possibility, black evangelicals had to be made to feel more welcome than they had been thus far. To a greater degree than ever before, leading white evangelicals turned to the arguments Howard Jones and other black evangelicals had been making for decades: that interracial fellowship was an essential demonstration of the truth of the gospel; that church segregation harmed Christian credibility; that unity in Christ—now called racial reconciliation—was no longer optional for faithful Christians.[6] At the same time, a series of surprising events—from Klansman David Duke's candidacy for the governorship of Louisiana in 1991 to the Los Angeles riots of 1992—reminded Americans of the continued power of race and racism. Racially polarized reactions to the Nation of Islam–sponsored Million Man March and the O. J. Simpson trial in 1995 added to fears that the nation was dividing into hostile racial camps. These racial divisions in evangelicalism and in American society motivated white evangelical leaders to act.

Precisely because Americans feared racial division, the 1990s witnessed the growing dominance of a bipartisan, theologically infused colorblind consensus in American politics. Most white Americans believed a firmly colorblind approach to policy and public life—where character rather than skin color counted—would be the surest path to ending racial division.[7] If there was more racial tension in the 1990s, the solution was not more racially conscious policies (to reduce inequality), but fewer (to reduce racial consciousness). Americans, skeptical of government solutions in a neoliberal age, looked to churches and other civic institutions to promote racial progress. Much has been made of white evangelicals' growing power in the Republican Party in these years. This partisan story overlooks the deeper synergy taking place in the 1990s between Christian colorblindness and the colorblind consensus in American political life. Evangelical racial reconciliation movements were the perfect fit for an era of diminished expectations. The racial wealth gap might be stubbornly impervious to change, but Americans could rid prejudice from their hearts. The characteristic patterns of Christian colorblindness remained at the center of the racial reconciliation movement. What was different in the 1990s is that these values aligned white evangelicals with the tenor of the times. When they said racial healing was a matter for the heart, not the state, their message rang true.

Racial Reconciliation as Radical Christianity: John and Vera Mae Perkins

Before "racial reconciliation" became a common turn of phrase in the 1990s, it was a challenge to white evangelicalism coming from the margins.[8] Its most prominent advocates were black evangelicals like the community organizer John Perkins. He used the concept to promote a kind of radical Christianity that called for spiritual, social, and economic liberation. By the early 1970s, John and Vera Mae Perkins had already been ministering among the poor in Mississippi for over a decade, and John was using their story as "a testimony to the ministry of reconciliation between white and black people carried on today by God's Holy Spirit." John wanted white evangelicals to know that "yes, you can do something; yes, there can be racial reconciliation," and his own life proved it.[9]

The oppression of the Jim Crow Deep South had indelibly shaped John and Vera Mae. Born in Depression-era Mississippi into a family of sharecroppers, John saw a limited set of choices. "We could stay, accept the system and become dehumanized niggers; we could go to jail or get killed; or we could leave for the big city."[10] While the Perkins clan was known around town for their bootlegging and quick resort to violence, Vera Mae's family owned a little piece of property and led a more stable existence. Vera Mae recalled a childhood under the protective umbrella of her parents, mercifully shielded from the full realities of the Jim Crow system. But looking back, she saw how the twin forces of racial and economic oppression had "molded and formed everything, what we ate, what we thought, how we acted, how we prayed."[11] John's path was rockier. His mother died when he was an infant, and his father left the children with their grandmother. When John was a teenager, a police officer killed his older brother. Seeing no future in Mississippi, he escaped to California. He found a good job and married Vera Mae, who joined him in Pasadena. Then he had an evangelical conversion experience. Over the next few years John wrestled with a growing conviction that he should go back to Mississippi and share in the struggles of his people. At first he didn't want to go. He and Vera Mae were well situated in California and had a growing family to care for. But in the spring of 1960 they packed up their life in Pasadena and returned to Mississippi.

John and Vera Mae initially understood their task in characteristically evangelical terms. As John put it, "I believed that if people would come to know Christ their lives would be changed and everything would be okay."[12] The first project they started was a Bible study. But their experiences living alongside poor black Mississippians broadened their view of their mission. The Bible study morphed into an educational institute. When John realized that many of their neighbors couldn't read, the institute offered remedial education. When Vera Mae saw the need for childcare, she started a day care center, which became a Head Start program in 1966. From there their ministry—called Voice of Calvary—expanded into an ever-wider array of programs and activism, from food co-ops to voter registration drives. For 10 years, they worked to bring a gospel of spiritual and economic liberation to poor black people in Mississippi. Though distinctly Christian in his approach, John attempted to build black economic self-sufficiency through co-ops, which were in keeping with the temper of the times. A friend said, "He's a Bible-believing fundamentalist, but he's for black power."[13] John said he was "using a Black Muslim approach to reaching people," instilling an ethic of self-help and self-respect in a poor black community.[14] "I have often thought," Vera Mae said, "if [John] had never become a Christian, he would have been a Muslim, with their strict devotion and discipline and he would have risen right to the top."[15]

John Perkins had never been a separatist, however, and he made use of white volunteers at Voice of Calvary. An important turn in what racial reconciliation meant to Perkins began in a Mississippi jail cell in February 1970. Just a few days before Christmas in 1969, he and others associated with Voice of Calvary launched a spontaneous boycott against white-owned stores in Mendenhall. The boycott dragged on for weeks as the white community resisted black demands for paved streets, employment, an end to police brutality, and integrated schools. One February evening, police arrested Perkins when he went to pay bail for jailed boycotters. White police officers hauled him into the jail and beat him there for hours. As he passed in and out of consciousness, he saw the faces of the police officers "twisted with hate. It was like looking at white-faced demons," he recalled. For all the bitterness Perkins had toward white people, he looked into those faces of hatred and discovered he "just couldn't hate them back."[16] As Perkins recovered from his physical wounds in the ensuing months, he believed God also healed him of the invisible wounds of white supremacy. He found a new capacity to forgive. As he thought about white police officers who couldn't find their worth without beating a black man, he realized in a new way how white supremacy damaged white people. As the years went by, his vision increasingly focused on bringing people of all backgrounds together to experience solidarity with the poor and the oppressed.

Perkins drew on these experiences to articulate a comprehensive evangelical vision for racial reconciliation, which he shared in his books and in speeches around the country. Perkins embedded racial reconciliation in a broader ethic of Christian community development and grassroots activism rooted in a theology of incarnation. As Jesus Christ had emptied himself of his power and made himself flesh to draw sinners to himself, so Christians had to be incarnate—physically present in the place of need. This was the principle of relocation. Rather than separating themselves from the poor, buying the best house they could afford, Christians must live in the communities they sought to help. Once there, guided by an organic sharing of needs, Christians could give freely of their resources and skills. This was the principle of redistribution. Poor communities needed more than money. They lacked businesses, social capital, educational services, and more. Through the body of Christ these resources were to be redistributed from those who had to those who lacked. Only in the context of these demanding principles—relocation and redistribution—could the third component, reconciliation, truly occur.[17]

Perkins never claimed any of this was easy. Christian love, he liked to say, was not "a smile" and a "lollipop." It was measured by one's willingness to lay down one's life for the good of the community, much as Christ had laid down his life. Instead of pursuing a comfortable existence within the confines of the American Dream, all Christians were called to a life of sacrifice, to "love our neighbor in a way that liberates him from poverty and oppression, either spiritual or physical." Perkins wrote in quite arresting terms about how demanding this Christian life could be. "Responding to the call of God is like a trap," he wrote. "It's like walking into a closet and shutting the door and finding out that there is no doorknob on the inside. You just can't get out."[18] Perkins wasn't one to sugarcoat things—neither the costs of reconciliation, nor how badly white evangelicals failed to bear those costs. For evangelicals who thought they could bypass the problem of race, Perkins always had the same message. "Our day calls for a gospel that reconciles black and white, for unless we preach a gospel of reconciliation we preach no gospel at all," he declared.[19]

In John Perkins's theology, racial reconciliation was much more than friendship across the color line. It was a kind of radical Christianity, a strategy for liberation that was at once spiritual, social, and—most controversially—economic. When Perkins called for racial reconciliation he declared war on the American Dream. He believed Christianity turned the normative aspirations of middle-class Americans on their head. Americans pursued upward mobility; Christians chose solidarity with the poor. Americans valued safety and security; Christians chose to share in the suffering of the marginalized. Americans sought personal success; Christians sacrificed for the good of the community. No wonder this demanding message of racial reconciliation had trouble catching on. He admitted that real examples of the racial reconciliation he envisioned were few. After decades of reconciling work on the margins of evangelicalism, Perkins sometimes wondered if much had changed. By 1993, he declared, "Something is wrong at the root of American evangelicalism."[20]

The Black Evangelical Demand for Racial Reconciliation

In the late 1980s and early 1990s, black evangelicals made a renewed push for racial reform in white evangelical institutions. Often carried out under the banner of racial reconciliation, black evangelicals challenged white evangelicals to accept a vision that had much in common with John and Vera Mae Perkins's brand of radical Christianity. As they had for several decades, black evangelicals linked justice, power, and economics in evangelical institutions to more subjective measures of racial harmony. They insisted that reconciliation required real reform. Some white evangelicals embraced this critique; many rejected it and appropriated the language of reconciliation to restate their colorblind commitments and protect the status quo in their institutions.

By the end of the 1980s, leaders in the National Association of Evangelicals (NAE) and the National Black Evangelical Association (NBEA) were grappling anew with the alienation between their constituencies. As the NAE sought to find common ground with black evangelicals, it sent Darrell Anderson of the Social Action Commission to attend Atlanta '88, the black evangelism conference that had grown out of the exclusion of African Americans at Houston '85. Anderson took his role as liaison seriously and reported his observations of an "excellent convention." He was quite pleased with the prevailing attitude of the black leaders in attendance, though he noted Tom Skinner was still causing mischief. What Anderson meant by this can be gleaned from a similar report he wrote when he attended Destiny '87, a separate conference that featured many of the same African American leaders. Some of the speakers were still "rehashing the past," Anderson complained. "For some reason," he reported, "there seems to be a need for blacks to address these feelings, even in 1987. They still feel discriminated against." Mystified, Anderson noted that he had "no way of determining how much" of this feeling of discrimination "is real and how much is feared."[21]

Anderson was an ironic liaison, unwittingly exemplifying the gulf between the predominantly white NAE and the black NBEA. He resented what he considered to be black evangelicals' misuse of Christian language. "Some insist on making 'righteousness' into 'social righteousness' and reconciliation a term to balance all things," he complained. He wished black evangelicals would be quiet about their "slavery days" and tales of mistreatment. Such talk was counterproductive. On the bright side, though, Tony Evans's sermon was "absolutely outstanding, and never once brought up the subject of black/white or any reference to it whatsoever."[22] Anderson's report contained an ominous suggestion of disagreement about the very meaning of racial reconciliation. Did it have redistributionary intent, as in Perkins's vision—a force to "balance all things"—or was it merely a new way of saying what white evangelicals had been saying for decades: that racial identities ought to be submerged in Christ?

In the spring of 1989 representatives from the Social Action Commissions of the NAE and the NBEA began planning a gathering to discuss racism in the church.[23] The brochure for the event—tagline "Unity in Christ: A Consultation on Racism"—repudiated Anderson's reactionary colorblindness and described racism as a serious and growing problem in church and society that "undermines the Body of Christ and the reconciling spirit of the Gospel." The consultation was scheduled to begin immediately after the NAE board meeting so that board members could attend, an opportunity every one of them declined.[24] The consultation had some tense moments as black evangelical leaders spoke about their frustrations with the evangelical movement. A follow-up meeting in January finalized the language of a public declaration against racism. The document cast a vision for reform that would be all but unrecognizable in the friendship-based racial reconciliation popular later in the decade. The statement called on "the white evangelical church" to "repent of its sin of racism"; to "examine its doctrine, policies, institutions, boards, agencies and para-church entities"; to "exert pressure for economic justice by witnessing within its own power structures"; to "remove the institutional barriers which hinder progress for blacks and other people of color"; and "to make restitution and repair as soon as possible." This was nothing less than a direct assault on the precepts of Christian colorblindness. In this black evangelical vision, racial reconciliation was *a result* of justice. The absence of top NAE leaders from the meeting had allowed black evangelicals and their progressive white evangelical allies to craft a blunt statement against white evangelical racism, but it also raised obvious questions about how much support such a statement had at the top of the NAE, much less among ordinary white evangelicals.[25] The NAE and the NBEA continued to dialogue throughout the decade, but the practical changes that the 1990 statement demanded remained elusive.

The call for racial reconciliation gained a wider hearing after the Los Angeles riots in the spring of 1992. The riots seemed to provide a wakeup call and an important object lesson in the dangers of racial division. But they did not unite evangelicals. Robin McDonald, a black evangelical and director of the Capitol Hill Crisis Pregnancy Center in Washington, DC, wrote that the riots exposed the church's failure to practice the ministry of reconciliation God had entrusted to it. Not for the first time or the last, black evangelicals found the pain of a racial crisis compounded by the indifferent or insensitive responses of white evangelicals. As McDonald faced the fallout from the trial of the police officers who beat Rodney King, she found that her white friends' "subtle denial of the racial implications of the incident cut deeper than the verdict itself."[26]

Los Angeles opened old wounds and new opportunities. In temporarily making the state of American race relations front-page news, the riots led to publishing platforms for black evangelical authors. The following year brought a flood of evangelical racial reconciliation books with black authors or coauthors, including Raleigh Washington and Glen Kehrein's *Breaking Down Walls*; Spencer Perkins and Chris Rice's *More Than Equals*; Bill Pannell's *The Coming Race Wars? A Cry for Reconciliation*; and John Perkins's *Beyond Charity: The Call to Christian Community Development*. Though the books were quite different in their particulars, each of them used the unrest in Los Angeles to emphasize the urgency of the racial reconciliation task. *Breaking Down Walls* and *More Than Equals* served as bridges between the more radical vision John Perkins had espoused since the 1970s and the more popular forms of racial reconciliation emerging in the 1990s. Rather than castigating white evangelicals as the most grievous bastion of American racism (as Perkins did in 1982), these books insisted that the evangelical church was the nation's only hope for racial progress. They challenged white evangelicals, to be sure, but their predominant focus was reconciliation one friendship at a time.

Bill Pannell, however, continued to promote a more comprehensive vision of racial reconciliation that defied dearly held white evangelical commitments. No evangelical of the era wrote with more clarity and sophistication about the tangled intersection of race, evangelicalism, and politics than did Pannell. He perceptively diagnosed an American society caught in an "in between moment" in the 1990s. A generation after the civil rights movement, Americans were eager to believe the country had made a great deal of racial progress, yet feared the undeniable evidence of ongoing racial animosity. Especially after the L.A. riots, Pannell believed that the "fundamental contradiction" between the promise and reality of American life had made "the theme of reconciliation . . . a dominant one in our time." He thought this mood gave evangelicals an opportunity. If met boldly, the challenge of reconciliation could be "the finest hour for the church. Reconciliation is a biblical word. It is *our* word, and its ministry *our* enterprise."[27] But because Pannell had a more robust reconciliation agenda than most white evangelicals, he took a bleak view of what the church was doing with its opportunity. The CGM had expanded evangelicalism's numbers but led to an ethical dead end. "After all the turmoil of the past twenty-five years at home and abroad, and after all the noise about evangelism and growing churches," the "unfinished agenda of North American evangelicals was to deal with our own version of Reconstruction," he wrote.[28] Reconstruction was a potent metaphor implying that a reordering of power and resources must precede reconciliation. Colorblind Christians didn't see it that way. Pannell was a voice crying in the wilderness.

In October 1993, black evangelicals had a surprising opportunity to bring their concerns directly to the white evangelical mainstream. *Christianity Today* (*CT*) published a cover story featuring interviews with dozens of black evangelical leaders under the provocative headline "The Myth of Racial Progress." Black evangelicals took the chance to try to explain to their counterparts how their understanding of racial reconciliation differed. J. Deotis Roberts, a professor at Eastern Baptist Seminary, explained that many black Christians stayed away from the evangelical label because "it usually refers to a one-dimensional view of Christianity—a spiritual, privatized, vertical view. The term usually carries with it the idea that race relations are expected to be based on a sentimental love without real consideration for social justice." Black Christians could not embrace that agenda. They had "known the Bible as a means of oppression as well as a source of liberation." They could not "assume that all Christians get the same message from reading the Bible." African Americans needed more than sentimental love. "There can be no genuine reconciliation," Roberts declared, "without liberation and social transformation."[29]

Black evangelicals also challenged white evangelicals' self-image as people who desired racial harmony. In fact, declared Morris E. Jones, pastor of Immanuel Evangelical Baptist Church in Indianapolis, "White evangelicals have done little or nothing to help America heal the wound of racism." Glandion Carney of InterVarsity Christian Fellowship agreed. "There has been very little fruit from the pledges of racial reconciliation." Evangelical "organizations continue to be white in their structure and avoid issues that concern the cities. Nothing has come from our great words." Peggy L. Jones, senior pastor of Macedonia Assembly of God Church in Saint Paul, Minnesota, sometimes wondered why God wanted her to minister in the painful world of evangelicalism. She wrote, "My heart still cries out to God. When will my people no longer be seen by white evangelicals as a threat? As less than? When will we be allowed to be equal with you and not oppressed by you? It is expected that the secular world continues to oppress, but not the body of Christ." Robert Suggs of Grand Rapids Baptist College agreed. He recalled that when he was the pastor of a black church in Rochester, New York, he "frequently got a call from the white pastors in the area." Another black family had visited a white church and the pastor was trying to steer the family to Suggs's church. To Suggs, these practices were blatantly contrary to the gospel. In his view white evangelicals hadn't repented, and it appeared they didn't intend to do so.[30]

Ironically, the difficulty white evangelicals had in submitting to this black evangelical critique could be seen in the pages of the same issue. Alongside black evangelical voices, *CT* offered "models of reconciliation," inspiring and hopeful stories of the evangelical church in action. One of these profiled a wealthy, white, suburban Atlanta church that had committed half a million dollars and 600 volunteers to help "revitalize the low-income African American neighborhood" of Summerville. As part of the effort, one Sunday morning a busload of wealthy white suburbanites attended an African American church service. "When the service is dismissed," *CT* reported, "a question hangs over everyone: Will people connect over cookies and coffee in the Fellowship Hall?" As the bus headed back to the suburbs, its riders unanimously agreed that a connection had indeed been made (readers could only guess how the ordinary members of the black church felt about it). One of the white visitors said, "I was surprised at how much we had in common. They're people just like us. They seem to have the same concerns we do, such as wanting their kids to be the best they can be or wanting to learn more about God." In a story ostensibly about the commitment of concrete resources to produce positive racial change, the focus shifted to the white suburbanites' subjective sense of reconciliation ("Will people connect over cookies and coffee in the Fellowship Hall?") and sympathy ("They're people just like us").[31] Possibly the initiative would become a long-term partnership producing tangible changes in power and resources in metro Atlanta. But *CT* appeared to be remarkably uninterested in such questions. Instead, it used the very frame of sentimentality that black evangelicals critiqued.

Because colorblind Christians did not conceive of race as an ideology of power in a hierarchical society, it seemed to them arbitrary and unfair for black evangelicals to single out white evangelicals in a call for repentance. As one reader put it, there wouldn't be any progress without both sides realizing that "there's enough sin to go around for all of us." Another reader allowed that black evangelicals had made "a convincing call for action to the White church." But he was "struck by an equal failure or blind spot in the Black church: that of grace. When are we Whites to be forgiven?" he asked. "Black church, where is your grace?" In these responses colorblind Christians deployed cherished theological concepts—it was by grace, evangelicals knew, that people are saved—and reinterpreted them to express entitlement to forgiveness apart from restitution. "The resentment expressed in your article toward white evangelicals was unchristian," another reader wrote. "The church is not perfect," he admitted, "but the real enemy" were the "elite voices of liberalism" that slandered evangelicals as racist while "pretending to be the savior of society and the black community, persuading them to resent 'white evangelicals.'" Though black evangelicals spoke in the evangelical idiom of sin and repentance, the reader saw lurking behind them the specter of liberal politics.[32] Black evangelicals had forcefully argued their case. Was anyone listening?

Church Growth and Racial Reconciliation

As the push for racial reconciliation began to influence evangelical churches, it did not overturn an enduring focus on church growth. Though there were glimmers of an emerging interracial church movement, largely homogeneous churches remained the overwhelming norm.[33] Racial reconciliation drew a great deal of attention in the 1990s because it appeared to be a new phenomenon. Meanwhile, observers often overlooked the profound influence of the CGM precisely because it had become so widespread and uncontroversial. Insofar as churches embraced racial reconciliation, they often did so in the name of evangelism and church growth. The turn of the Southern Baptist Convention (SBC) toward racial reconciliation received much comment. The reason for it—the imperatives of evangelization in a diversifying America—was less widely understood. Talk of homogeneous units seemed increasingly out of step with the times; more and more church leaders spoke the language of reconciliation. But they did so not in pursuit of the black evangelical vision of justice and liberation but as the latest innovation designed to defend and grow the evangelical movement.

On July 10, 1990, Donald McGavran passed away at the age of 92. His death marked a symbolic end to the heyday of the CGM. But if CGM activism no longer had a clear institutional locus, that was partly because its basic approach had become so broadly accepted. *CT* reported in 1991, "After a wave of church-growth bashing in the seventies, many of the movement's ideas have become virtual givens in today's discussions of church vitality. Demographic charts and membership projection graphs have found their way into pastors' studies and board meetings in churches of almost every description." Overlooking black evangelicals' consistent criticisms of the CGM, *CT* falsely reported that "outright critics are now hard to find." It took a while, *CT* explained, for evangelicals to "become comfortable with success." But the CGM had helped evangelicals join the "successful mainstream," and they were now getting used to it.[34]

The priorities of the CGM had carried the day, even if some of its most strident language had increasingly come to be seen as toxic. By the last years of his life, even McGavran became wary of the phrase "church growth." It had become encrusted with connotations of ruthless pragmatism and an implied insult to small churches. McGavran's principles didn't change, but his followers' words did. As racial discourse shifted, evangelical observers modified the history of the CGM to suit the needs of the time. *Christianity Today* falsely claimed that McGavran's Homogeneous Unit Principle was only ever meant as descriptive. Critics had supposedly misinterpreted McGavran and turned it into a prescriptive plan for homogeneous church growth.[35] These claims had no basis in fact but tried to ascribe racial innocence to the white evangelical mainstream. The CGM's influence was undeniable; it had effectively won the struggle to define the church's mission. But by the 1990s, it was inconvenient to admit that such a popular movement had so aggressively portrayed church integration as a threat to church growth.

Celebrity pastors trained in CGM principles modified its most controversial features in the 1990s and helped to diffuse its ideas across the evangelical mainstream. Rick Warren, whose Saddleback Church had grown to 10,000 members, spoke now of "church health" more than "church growth" and dedicated his best-selling *Purpose Driven Church* to "bi-vocational" pastors of small churches. Bill Hybels of Willow Creek disavowed the Homogeneous Unit Principle and naturalized the whiteness of his congregation, almost as if he had located the church in a wealthy suburb by accident.[36] Hybels spread his "seeker sensitive" church growth approach through the Willow Creek Association, which boasted over 700 affiliated churches by the summer of 1994.[37] These developments garnered less news coverage than the racial reconciliation turn, but they were more indicative of where the white evangelical mainstream was going.

The nation's largest Protestant denomination, the Southern Baptist Convention, took the lead in embracing the language of racial reconciliation. But the process was more ambiguous than its boosters admitted, reflecting continuity with church growth principles and the ongoing priority of growing the evangelical ranks. In 1988, Richard Land took the helm of the convention's Christian Life Commission. Land was thoroughly on the conservative side of the battles that had roiled the convention through the 1980s. Moderates called it the conservative takeover. Conservatives called it the resurgence, a return to the solid foundation of the Bible. As head of the Christian Life Commission, Land had the power to nudge Southern Baptists toward engaging issues he deemed important. When he announced that "race relations" was the first item on his agenda, it came as a surprise. Land explained it this way: "only Nixon could go to China." Just as Nixon's anticommunist bona fides gave him political space to craft an opening to communist China, so Land's credibility as a staunch conservative in the SBC allowed him to "speak about racism and the conservatives cannot dismiss me as a wooly-headed liberal."[38] If Land had his way, the SBC's future would be multiethnic.

The following year, the Home Mission Board (HMB) of the SBC began a new initiative to start black Baptist churches. As late as 1981 the HMB had frankly admitted that the convention was hostage to demographic trends among white Americans. It assumed that in areas where white population growth stagnated, "the prospect for church expansion . . . will be much slower than was possible in earlier decades."[39] But by the early 1990s the HMB was launching some 150 new black churches each year and projected that the convention's future growth would come primarily from people of color.⁴⁰ The CGM's logic of homogeneous churches continued to inform these efforts. In the SBC, planting black churches was particularly fraught. Did it demonstrate racial progress, or did it reflect the convention's long history of segregation and discrimination? The growing numbers of African Americans in the convention raised new doubts about the sufficiency of a homogeneous growth strategy. Did the SBC have to answer for its racist past? Were white Southern Baptists ready for a multiethnic convention, and could black Americans trust the SBC? For the sake of the gospel and the future of Southern Baptist life, wasn't racial reconciliation required?

Questions like these led Southern Baptists to adopt a historic "Resolution on Racial Reconciliation" at their 1995 annual meeting, acknowledging the SBC's ties to slavery and apologizing for racism perpetrated "in our lifetime." The 150th anniversary of the SBC's founding provided the occasion for the apology, but it was not the cause. The roots of the racial reconciliation resolution were in the work of Southern Baptist church planters who deemed an apology necessary to promote evangelization in urban black communities. An October 1993 meeting of Directors of Mission, who were working in areas with large African American populations, crystallized the need for action. They appointed a "racial reconciliation task force" to draft a statement of repentance. Jere Allen, the executive director of the Washington, DC, Baptist Association, spearheaded the effort. Seeking to drum up support for a "Declaration of Repentance," Allen argued that "if we, as Southern Baptists, are to effectively evangelize Blacks we need to publicly declare our repentance in regard to our beginning and our lack of bold and significant involvement in the 1960s Civil Rights Movement."⁴¹ In a separate letter to Richard Land, Allen pointedly noted that he and his colleagues ministering in cities such as Washington, DC, were "affected by what some Blacks perceive as racism on the part of people related to the SBC."⁴² An apology, he thought, combined with an explicit mention of slavery, could go a long way toward removing the distrust.

Apologizing to African Americans so that they would be more likely to come to your church was a reasonable motivation in the context of evangelical theology, but it hardly made for good press. Nonetheless, the early draft of the apology Allen circulated said the quiet part out loud: "Regardless of how much progress we think we have made in Race Relations, we are nevertheless perceived by many Blacks and non-Blacks as a racist denomination. This negative perception is an obstacle toward our efforts to evangelize, plant churches, and minister among Black people, especially for those called to minister in the metropolitan cities." This was not a particularly auspicious beginning for an apology. The draft declaration went on to admit that "our relation to persons of African descent has been less than ideal." The draft acknowledged Southern Baptist complicity in slavery and declared, "We publicly repent and apologize to all persons of African descent for condoning and perpetuating individual and systemic racism in our lifetime" and "we ask for the forgiveness of our brothers and sisters of African descent."[43]

By the spring of 1994 the statement had garnered widespread assent from Southern Baptist Directors of Mission in urban areas, but one of the members of the task force still thought it would be a miracle if the full convention passed it as a resolution.[44] Just one month before the SBC's 150th anniversary meeting in June 1995, Land's Christian Life Commission hosted a "racial reconciliation consultation," which extensively edited and rewrote the Declaration of Repentance into a form that Land and others hoped would pass at the full convention meeting.[45] The Land-approved version removed some of the most overtly self-interested language of the earlier draft, and it more bluntly acknowledged that Southern Baptists' embrace of slavery had "crippled from the beginning" the convention's relationship with African Americans.

On the floor of the convention, only one messenger (the term for SBC delegates) dared to speak fulsomely against the resolution. He thought the statement unfairly indicted "the great men who founded the convention." But Gary Frost, second vice president and the first African American to hold such a high position in the SBC, believed the resolution was urgent. "Our nation is being ripped apart by hatred," he said. "I believe it's up to the church of Jesus Christ to begin the process of true reconciliation." Observers estimated the resolution passed with 95 percent support.[46] Some newspapers covered the story with the kind of headlines Southern Baptist leaders were hoping for. The SBC had taken "a bold step" and "black pastors agree[d]" it was "a great day."[47] After the vote, Frost spoke from the stage: "On behalf of my black brothers and sisters, we accept your apology and we extend to you our forgiveness in the name of Jesus Christ."[48]

If only it were so easy. Southern Baptist messengers passed the racial reconciliation statement with little drama, but reaction from around the country was mixed. An unusual volume of letters poured into the office of the president of the convention. Many were positive, but others resented the idea that Southern Baptists were apologizing for their ancestors.[49] In fact, the resolution had pointedly only apologized for racism "in our lifetime" but this distinction was lost on some critics. One man complained that Southern Baptists seemed to be "elevating political correctness to the status of scripture." If Jesus and Paul didn't even denounce slavery, who did Southern Baptists think they were to get up on a high horse and condemn their ancestors? "Heaven forbid that all this was a ploy to recruit black churches" to the convention, he concluded. For others, the resolution marked a turning point in Southern Baptist history. Rick Warren, whose books would soon blow up the religious best-seller lists, called it "our finest hour."[50]

For black Southern Baptists who had labored within the convention for racial change, it was a moment to savor. One black pastor remarked that the statement would be an effective tool to overcome black distrust.[51] But others were more skeptical. E. Edward Jones, head of the National Baptist Convention, declared that black Baptists would "need more than an apology." As far as he was concerned, the civil rights movement was still an ongoing project. Instead of helping in the struggle, the Southern Baptists were trying to steal their members. The apology came "pretty late in the day," said another black leader.[52]

If, in the months leading up to the meeting, even many insiders in the SBC doubted such a resolution could pass, what accounted for the easy adoption of this sweeping statement of racial reconciliation? It was of a piece with the larger turn toward black church planting in the 1990s. As *CT* argued, when push came to shove, the desire to grow the evangelical movement was stronger than historic racial divisions. But those familiar with the nuances of Southern Baptist and white evangelical life in the United States knew there was more to the story than the near-unanimous approval the racial reconciliation statement implied. Even in 1995, there were still churches where black worshippers were not welcome. Eddie Jones knew as well as anyone the real state of play in the Southern Baptist heartland. He was an African American pastor who, in 1983, founded Mississippi's first black Southern Baptist church. Jones believed that to at least some degree most pastors in the SBC had absorbed the message of racial reconciliation. The challenge now, he said, was "getting it down to their congregation in a way in which they won't lose their job."[53]

As Southern Baptists turned to racial reconciliation as a church growth strategy, Christian colorblindness was also coming into its own in evangelical popular culture. In 1992, the evangelical pop star Michael W. Smith released "Color Blind," a rollicking tune in which Smith repeatedly asked, "Why can't we be color blind?" "The only race would be the human race," he sang, "and all these barriers would be erased." For a pop star crossing boundaries between sacred and secular music, this was no place for an elaborate theological statement. But in the opening lyrics of the song, Smith echoed a touchstone for millions of Christian listeners when he sang,

> There's not a world of difference
> out in the world tonight
> between this world of people
> red, yellow, black and white.[54]

The lyrics recalled a classic children's song, "Jesus Loves the Little Children," and its indelible words "red, brown, yellow, black and white, they are precious in his sight." Rooted in sentimentality and the idea that a change of perception could somehow resolve systemic problems, Smith's song was a popular encapsulation of evangelical racial theology. That the song was so deliberately constructed in the register of black musical traditions highlighted the paradoxes often at work in colorblind aspirations.

No one better demonstrated the power of Christian colorblindness in evangelical popular culture than Christian rap group DC Talk. The trio from Liberty University took the evangelical world by storm in the 1990s, becoming one of the dominant acts of the decade. Their influence could be measured in album sales (of which there were millions) but there was also a harder-to-quantify dimension to it. Put simply, in the evangelical youth culture of the 1990s, the cool kids listened to DC Talk. As one fond evangelical retrospective put it, "DC Talk was our Beatles."[55] When adoring crowds of white evangelical teenagers danced to DC Talk's songs, they heard Christian colorblindness delivered with an urban vibe and the powerful symbolism of a trio with a black evangelical member. In "Colored People" (1995) the group sang,

> We're colored people, and we live in a tainted place
> We're colored people, and they call us the human race
> We've got a history so full of mistakes
> And we're colored people who depend on a holy grace.

The music video showcased people of diverse backgrounds and featured a Holocaust remembrance theme. Only a brief shot of an elderly African American man holding an "I Am A Man" sign recalled a distinctly American experience of racism. The resolution offered by "Colored People" is a case study in Christian colorblindness. The group sang,

> Ignorance has wronged some races
> And vengeance is the Lord's
> If we aspire to share this space
> Repentance is the cure.[56]

One could hardly find a vaguer statement of the problem. Racism was a lack of knowledge more than a system of hierarchy. Those groups (conveniently unnamed) harmed by it should entrust themselves to God rather than demanding payback, knowing that repentance and spiritual rebirth was the only solution. As Hilde Løvdal Stephens has pointed out, the irony was that DC Talk delivered this colorblind message via a segregated Christian music market. The group's legions of white evangelical fans could consume an aura of diversity and urban cool without ever leaving the comfort and familiarity of their suburban church youth group.[57]

Racial Reconciliation and Evangelical Colleges

The racial reconciliation trend also made its presence felt on white evangelical college campuses across the country. If in the 1960s and 1970s a sense of Christian responsibility caused some white evangelical colleges to seek to help African American students, by the 1990s a growing number of institutions saw their own futures at stake. If they could not recruit and retain African American, Hispanic, and Asian students in the twenty-first century, the outlook for their institutions would be bleak. The Coalition for Christian Colleges and Universities (CCCU), an umbrella consortium of dozens of predominantly evangelical institutions, began to pay special attention to the racial progress of its member schools in the early 1990s. In these initiatives, a perception gap between college administrators and ordinary students paralleled the divide between clergy and laity seen in churches. While some college leaders sought to build more inclusive academic communities, many white evangelical students brought colorblind assumptions to campus and reacted against these efforts. At other institutions, administrators expressed a desire for diversity and racial harmony but did not pursue concrete reforms to match their rhetoric.

In 1991 the CCCU launched a project aimed at "developing and strengthening comprehensive diversity plans" at member institutions.[58] A survey of CCCU members indicated how much such plans were needed. Though black enrollment ticked up in the early 1990s, it was from a very low base.[59] Some evangelical institutions had fewer black students than they had enrolled a generation earlier. While some colleges had made significant gains in black recruitment, such as Howard Jones's alma mater Nyack College, many of the most prestigious evangelical schools stood out for their dismal record. At Wheaton and Messiah, black enrollment was 2 percent of the student body. At Calvin College, it was 1 percent.[60] The CCCU's diversity initiative devolved into controversy when the coalition suddenly shut down the office overseeing it in the summer of 1994 due to lack of funding. Some administrators of color believed the closure of the office "had betrayed their trust" and they vowed they would never work with the consortium again.[61] Administrators of color in white evangelical colleges were all too familiar with funding constraints. They viewed them as expressions of priorities.

Under its new president, Bob Andringa, the CCCU created a "Racial Harmony Council" to advance the cause of racial reconciliation at Christian colleges. In January 1996 the council sent a paper entitled "Affirmative Action and Racial Harmony in Christian Colleges" to all CCCU members. The document sought to build a theological and practical case for a distinctly Christian form of affirmative action among

CCCU member institutions. The paper argued that restitution was a well-attested biblical principle that ought to bear on the affirmative action debate. It contended that individualistic responses were inadequate to problems of generational and systemic sin. The council recommended that the CCCU issue a public "confession of the past and present sin of racism, and pledge to make every effort to remove any vestiges of the same from the campuses of its member institutions." Each member institution should approve the statement and "commit to carrying forward its implementation." The paper did not specify the form "restitution" ought to take. In an addendum of "optional recommendations," the report advised college presidents to conduct "comprehensive evaluations" of their efforts, including "admissions and scholarship plans; residence hall strategies; retention programs; courses" and much more. The paper offered a model apology and pledge of "reconciliation, restitution . . . and affirmative initiatives" to create a "Christian community . . . where unity in diversity is a cherished virtue."[62]

Fully embracing such a plan would have been risky for most predominantly white evangelical colleges. Their primary constituencies remained white colorblind Christians. Reforms seen as too liberal or race conscious could put at risk the financial and demographic underpinnings of the institutions. White evangelical college administrators' responses to the Racial Harmony Council's plan ranged from positive to ambivalent to hostile. Some colleges worried that a public confession of discrimination could open their institutions up to litigation. Others questioned the theological grounds of the project. In the end, few member institutions embraced the document as a viable model for their schools. The president of Campbell University in North Carolina didn't think outsiders "understand racial relations in the South." He claimed that "by not accentuating differences, we have been able to bring about a unified and harmonious campus." The president of Eastern Nazarene College in Massachusetts said he was all for increasing ethnic diversity but was adamantly against "quotas." He also worried that the proposed statement of repentance was unfair to earlier generations of evangelicals, who were not necessarily racist. Northwest College worked on the recommendations quite seriously but removed the word "restitution" from its final statement for fear of legal ramifications. An ad hoc committee at Taylor University warned that implementing the Racial Harmony

Council's plan could cause "further alienation" and "polarization" on their campus.[63] While national evangelical leaders spoke of restitution as a path to racial harmony, the closer one got to the ground in local contexts, the more resistance there was to such thinking.

More students and administrators on evangelical campuses were using the rhetoric of racial reconciliation in the 1990s, but its meaning remained contested. At times, students used the language of reconciliation as part of a John Perkins–style vision of social justice that made more conservative evangelicals queasy.[64] At other times, use of the term appeared almost farcical. At North Park College, even as the administration invited chapel speakers to call students to "reconcile" their "racial differences" and held a day-long event on "racial reconciliation," controversy arose anew, for it turned out that the college still had no black faculty.[65] A white faculty member claimed that the college was "trying to hire minority faculty but has been unable to do so" because of intense competition for evangelical professors of color.[66] The gap between the college's rhetoric and action displayed the continued pull of Christian colorblindness. Hiring a black professor was hard, but, in the meantime, students could be kind to each other. For many white evangelicals, racial reconciliation was a new term that rephrased rather than rethought their underlying colorblind theology. Talking about race remained controversial. Victor Mendoza, a Hispanic pastor of a suburban Chicago church, lamented that many racial reconciliation efforts were so shallow and slippery that they did not actually confront racism.[67] Yet it was precisely this malleability that made racial reconciliation a viable discourse for the colorblind campus.

On some campuses, the same old battles replayed as if little had changed since the 1960s. At Malone College in North Canton, Ohio, a new student group called Minority Students of Malone formed in 1990. But the following year the group changed its name to Unity Under Christ, an almost comically earnest effort to check all the boxes of appropriate theological framing for discussion of race on a Christian campus. The goal of the new name change was to "clearly state that it is not a club for minorities only." Said black student Angie Kirtdoll, "Some white people think they shouldn't attend meetings of Unity Under Christ, but the organization is open to everyone."[68] Tensions between colorblind white students and black students seeking change played out across the country. Celebrations of black history month and Martin Luther King Day became more prominent on white evangelical campuses, garnering predictable complaints from white students. One student at Houghton College grumbled that the school's black history month commemorations did not feature enough white people.[69] Eastern College became an evangelical leader in recruiting students of color in the 1990s, but as it did so tensions on campus rose. "There's a lot of talk about black and white, minority and majority," wrote one white student. "That kind of talk simply does not belong in a Christian community." He urged students to "realize that we are all blood relatives and *that* blood is the blood of Christ." This theological knowledge was the key that would empower them to "transcend black and white." But, in an echo of the 1970s radical moment, black students demanded changes in institutional culture and hiring of black faculty. "Most of you at Eastern profess to be Christians—how can you ignore the word of God and choose to be bigoted and prejudiced while claiming to be just," asked two black women in an open letter to the student body.[70]

While Eastern's campus in suburban Philadelphia became increasingly diverse, the racial reconciliation era seemed to have little effect on daily life at Messiah's Philadelphia campus. In 1995, Messiah hired five independent consultants to examine the urban campus with "fresh eyes." Their reports were bracing. The atmosphere of the campus, one consultant wrote, was "reminiscent of old time 'mission compounds' overseas, a small Christian enclave surrounded by the big, bad city."[71] Over two decades after Messiah had advertised the campus as a space much like a foreign mission field, these formative assumptions continued to shape the operation of the campus. Rather than seeing the campus as ideally situated for training in urban issues and social justice, the administration had allowed it to become a backwater. One consultant questioned why Messiah's 200-page college catalog featured the campus for all of one paragraph.[72] Another consultant, Dr. Willie Richardson, a black evangelical pastor in Philadelphia, reported that "most advisors willfully try to discourage students from taking courses in Philadelphia."[73] By the spring of 2001, staff working on recruitment for the Philadelphia campus were reduced to pursuing a simple but daunting goal: "Persuade President and other senior administrators of benefits of Philly Campus."[74] Remarkably, three decades after the founding of the Philadelphia campus, Messiah still did not actually have an urban studies major. Multiple consultants stressed the same factors that dogged the campus from its beginning: "anti-urban bias" and a pervasive fear among students and parents about safety.

Some observers tied the woes of the Philadelphia campus directly to the inadequacies of white evangelicals' turn toward racial reconciliation. Dr. Richardson bluntly warned that the program had to confront racial injustice directly in order to meet its potential. "I am not advocating racial reconciliation," he declared. The term had become so pervasive that Richardson wanted to make a point of pushing back against it. In his view, popular but vapid talk of racial reconciliation seemed to have produced little real change. Colorblind Christians remained ignorant of systemic racial injustice and continued to scorn the perspectives of Christians of color. How could there be reconciliation without justice and understanding? "Messiah College," Richardson argued, "could lead in educating white people in the truth about black people."[75] This idea was not new. In many ways, Dr. Sider had pursued it 20 years before and had run into a buzzsaw of resistance. A generation after the radical moment of the early 1970s, the college seemed to be in no mood to try again.[76]

As historically white evangelical colleges gradually became more diverse, some were beginning to realize that real racial reform in their institutions was the work of decades rather than a quick fix that could be implemented with a patina of racial reconciliation language. At Calvin College, after repeated failures to move beyond its Dutch heritage, a 1985 Master Plan called for turning the school into a truly "multicultural Christian community," and it established benchmarks for doing so stretching out to the new millennium. When Calvin's 11 "minority" faculty members were interviewed in 1995, they described ongoing challenges. "This community demands assimilation," wrote one professor. "There is little hope for integration." A staff person of color wrote, "I feel that my skin color makes me a trophy or a showpiece." Others pointed out that though Calvin claimed to desire diversity, it *required* its faculty to attend a Reformed church and enroll their children in Christian schools, a stricture rooted in the historically insular Dutch Reformed community, and one that carried significant "sticker shock" for some faculty.[77] The Christian schooling policy highlighted just how concrete the barriers to change could be, and it revealed an institutional preference for one set of (white) Christian values over another. "Does Calvin appreciate what it can mean to have worked long and hard to integrate public schools and then being now told that I must stay out of them?" asked one staff member. Wheaton College, too, began trying to brand itself as a "Multicultural community," even as administrators working on the Multicultural Affairs Committee admitted, "Unintentionally we are a racist college. The white student has no cultural awareness and needs it."[78]

If it was difficult and time-consuming to bring about institutional reform in churches and colleges, perhaps moving outside established channels altogether could produce the most racial progress. By the middle of the 1990s, it seemed that the greatest energy for racial reconciliation was in a new mass movement operating outside traditional networks and institutions. Evangelicals had a word for the sort of uprising that might awaken a nation from spiritual slumber and bring racial healing to their land: it was a revival.

Racial Reconciliation as Revival

Promise Keepers was the most aggressive and ambitious evangelical effort to confront racial division in the 1990s. At a moment when Americans feared dividing into hostile racial camps, PK seemed to be a godsend. Here was an organization that rejected separatism, promoted goodwill, and even called on white people to own up to racism. During PK's meteoric rise and fall, it embodied the successes and failures of evangelical racial reconciliation efforts. PK's sudden prominence produced an outpouring of commentary seeking to explain it. "Who are these guys, and what are they doing in our football stadiums?" asked the liberal Protestant *Christian Century*.[79] *CT*'s first long-form profile of PK was titled "Manhood's Great Awakening." The gendered aspect of the title was obvious, but alert evangelical readers would also notice the allusion to the eighteenth-century age of evangelical revival. For such readers the title called to mind luminaries of the evangelical tradition such as George Whitefield and Jonathan Edwards. Did PK's sudden success signal a new Great Awakening on the horizon? Though such hopes proved too optimistic, they correctly identified the animating impulse of Promise Keepers. It aspired to be an engine of mass revival. To those who worried PK was too political or not political enough, vice president Paul Edwards had a simple message: "This is a revival movement, not a reform movement."[80] This revivalist mode was a key factor in PK's popularity, but that also suggested its limits. PK did not envision a frontal assault on racial injustice. It sought to make better men.[81] Those spiritually invigorated men would in turn go to their communities and there engage in the grassroots interracial friendships that would change the country.

Promise Keepers was the creation of Bill McCartney, the national championship-winning coach of the University of Colorado football team. He was an unlikely evangelical hero, or perhaps a quintessential one, given his rocky road to redemption. A hard-charging alcoholic who lived and breathed football before his conversion, McCartney spoke openly about how his past failures had harmed his wife and children. This autobiographical authenticity added to his appeal. He launched Promise Keepers as a local initiative of Christian men in Boulder, Colorado, in 1991. PK challenged men to live by seven promises. The commitments centered on an ideal of Christian manhood. They promised to "Honor Jesus Christ . . . Build strong marriages and families . . . Practice spiritual, moral, ethical, and sexual purity," and so on. In 1992, the first national rally at the University of Colorado football stadium drew 22,000 men to participate in workshops with titles like "Healing the Masculine Soul." The language of healing was suggestive of the peculiar brand of masculinity PK promoted. *Real* men were not only breadwinners and leaders in their home; they were able to connect with their emotions and with others.[82] They weren't afraid to hug other men and form deep friendships with them. The following year attendance doubled. In 1994 the organization expanded with large rallies across the country. Evangelical media responded enthusiastically. Promise Keepers had "the feel of a movement." *Christianity Today* attributed the success to a dawning realization that American society was coming unglued and government couldn't repair the breach. "Movements like Promise Keepers get closer to the heart of the problem" than any political program, the magazine opined.[83]

From its earliest days, McCartney nursed a growing conviction that God had called PK to end racism in the church. He liked to tell the story of how God spoke to him as he looked upon an all-white crowd at a 1991 rally. "The absence of men of color somehow hit me between the eyes, and in that moment, the Spirit of God clearly said to my spirit, 'You can fill that stadium, but if men of other races aren't there, I won't be there, either.'" Driven by this experience, McCartney worked to make PK a multiracial movement. This was reflected in the diverse cast of speakers on the platform and in the organization's staffing. At the height of its popularity, Promise Keepers reported that 30 percent of its 437-member staff were people of color.[84] This was a remarkable achievement for an organization founded by white evangelicals. Garry Blackmon, a black Houston man who joined the staff in 1995, testified of the lifechanging impact of PK. "No other ministry, no other political agenda or group had ever dealt with my source of pain until I saw [McCartney] deal with the issue of racism. It really brought tears to my eyes because everybody else had just sort of skated over it, covered it or found another way to sidestep it."[85] Blackmon's experience was not entirely atypical. McCartney spent a great deal of time networking with Christians of color and visiting their churches to try to get them to join the PK movement. Attendees at PK events heard talks with titles like "Uniting Together as Brothers in Christ" and "Walking in Your Brother's Shoes: Embracing Diversity in the Body of Christ." PK sought to convince evangelical men that authentic Christian manhood included interracial friendship and harmony.

The widespread sense that the country had descended into a dangerous age of racial tension made Promise Keepers seem to some like a providential answer to the nation's troubles. In October 1995, Americans grappled in quick succession with the O. J. Simpson verdict and the Million Man March. The former suggested a huge gap in perception between white and black Americans, and the latter seemed to indicate that the appeal of racial separatism was growing. As one pundit wrote, these events warned Americans of "the dangers of segregated realities. We got an unvarnished glimpse into America's balkanized heart, and it wasn't pretty." The *Dallas Morning News* reported that the Million Man March gave added urgency to the racial reconciliation movement, as Christian leaders tried to head off "an increasing desire among African-Americans to separate from white society." News reports portrayed evangelical racial reconciliation efforts as signs of hope on the horizon.

The SBC's racial reconciliation resolution and the growing popularity of Promise Keepers indicated to some observers that a "shift of monumental proportions" was under way. Perhaps, amid all the animosity, a grassroots awakening, led by evangelical Christians, was reshaping the country. As the *Wall Street Journal* reported in 1997, "Across the country, conservative congregations and denominations . . . are embracing a concept called 'biblical racial reconciliation'—a belief that . . . they are required by Scripture to work for racial harmony." The paper marveled that conservative Christians seemed to be "the most energetic element of society addressing racial divisions."[86] Indeed, PK quickly became, in the words of sociologist John Bartkowski, "a media darling" that received positive coverage from mainstream outlets. "What makes this racial reconciliation movement different from those of the past is that it is so widespread," said the *Dallas Morning News*, and "it is being spearheaded not only by so-called liberal church groups but also by those who would consider themselves religious conservatives."[87] *CT* believed this evangelical leadership was as it should be. Government could not restore Americans' trust in each other; only the church, entrusted with the ministry of reconciliation, could do the job.[88]

PK's rise and the growing prominence of racial reconciliation occurred against a backdrop of reaction against race-conscious programs (such as affirmative action) and programs that were highly racialized in the public mind (such as welfare).[89] President Clinton had campaigned on the promise to "end welfare as we know it" and in 1994 Republicans swept into the House of Representatives pledging to shrink the size of government, ending the Democrats' 40-year reign in that chamber. In August 1996, President Clinton signed welfare reform into law. In November, California voters passed proposition 209, banning affirmative action in state institutions.[90] The *Houston Chronicle* marveled, "At a time when so-called 'angry white males' are publicly calling on government to repeal policies designed to heal historical effects of discrimination against minorities, a national movement of mostly white evangelical men . . . is promoting racial reconciliation in unostentatious fashion."[91]

These phenomena—interpersonal racial reconciliation and public racial reaction—were complementary rather than contradictory. Most white evangelicals perceived no conflict between these positions. Private initiative would replace public bureaucracy and personal friendship would substitute for institutional reform. As the *Dallas Morning News* perceptively noted, "Much of the [racial reconciliation] action is coming from groups that support the [proposed Republican] cuts" to government programs. *CT* described affirmative action as a failed experiment and called for racial reconciliation as a replacement for a government-driven "ideology of diversity."[92] Richard Land, who had done as much as anyone to push through racial reconciliation initiatives in the SBC, described welfare and affirmative action as "paternalistic" and "degrading to blacks."[93] Friendship, eye to eye and man to man, not government handouts, was the only way forward. "It's got to start between two men," wrote an evangelical pastor.[94]

Though many liberal voices could still be heard making the case for activist government to redress racial injustice, the palpable trend was toward skepticism of these solutions, as the politics of affirmative action and welfare reform indicated. Even major social scientists, including black intellectuals such as the University of Chicago sociologist William Julius Wilson and Boston University economist Glenn Loury, insisted that racism was no longer the decisive factor blocking black progress.[95] Evangelical media cheered on these trends. They saw American society coming around to their politics of church primacy. *CT* was not in the habit of doing major interviews with economists. But Loury—black, Christian, challenger of liberal orthodoxies—was worth the exception. Loury said the solution to the nation's problems was "the Christian faith." He admitted it was unusual for intellectuals to admit they hoped for "revival," but he believed "the circumstances require it" and the recent moves by the likes of the SBC and the Promise Keepers offered hope. "I really believe there's tremendous power there to get Americans to transcend their communal differences."[96] Mainstream media outlets gave such views a respectable hearing. Joe Maxwell's *Chicago Tribune* profile of evangelical racial reconciliation efforts in Mississippi was titled "Beating Racism, One Friendship at a Time." "It sounds simple, maybe even simplistic," admitted Maxwell, "but in Mississippi it seems to be working."[97] Only voluntary, spiritually driven solutions could make the kind of lasting moral change that would bring healing to American society. While other institutions could help, who was better positioned to deliver on the promise of racial reconciliation than the tens of thousands of evangelical churches spread across the country?

Promise Keepers imagined the work of racial healing as belonging to men in particular. This was partly because much of evangelicalism was patriarchal. Pastors were usually men, and many evangelicals taught that men should be the leaders of their home. But the push to make racial reconciliation *men's work* connected to broader angst about the role of men in American society in the 1990s. Commentators fretted about the alienated American male adrift in a postindustrial economy shaped by feminist movements and new challenges to men's prerogatives. When Timothy McVeigh bombed the Murrah Federal Building in Oklahoma City in the spring of 1995, killing 168 people, it became an occasion for some commentators to remark on the crisis of American manhood. Thomas Edsall declared, "The 27 years of Timothy James McVeigh's life have been the years in which Americans saw the end of the traditional culture of manhood."[98] "In deeply disturbing ways, he is a prototype of his generation," another article opined. He was a child of divorce who resented affirmative action and "began to feel shortchanged as a white male."[99] Maybe PK could step in where all else had failed. Comparisons between PK and the Nation of Islam–sponsored Million Man March were unavoidable.[100] Both movements relied on an ethos of male leadership and called on men to take up the roles they had supposedly shirked from occupying, with disastrous effects for their families and communities. "We're looking for a few good men is no longer the exclusive claim of the U.S. Marines," wrote Edward Gilbreath for *CT*. "More than ever, the estrangement of men from their roles as husbands, fathers, and moral leaders is being cited as reason for the breakdown of family and society."[101]

Promise Keepers' vision of Christian masculinity as the solution to the nation's crisis remained the centerpiece of its program, but the organization put a growing emphasis on racial reconciliation as a key aspect of Christian manhood. The question was whether white evangelical men who were enthusiastic about PK's gendered message would stay on board as the racial component of that message grew louder. The theme of the stadium rallies in 1996 was "Break Down the Walls." The phrase was inspired by a book by Raleigh Washington and Glen Kehrein. If there was a PK-approved racial reconciliation book, *Breaking Down Walls* was it. Raleigh was black, Kehrein was white, and both men were veteran ministers who had forged a close bond through their work on the west side of Chicago. One was a son of the Jim Crow South, the other a child of privilege. Both had felt the reconciling power of God's love and the transforming effect of interracial friendship. Published by Moody Press and blurbed by the likes of Chuck Colson and Bill Hybels, the book had the endorsement of the white evangelical mainstream.[102] Washington and Kehrein shared their very different stories as testimonies of how God could take white racism and black bitterness and create racial healing. Thousands of books described the problem, they wrote. But this book was different. It offered the solution: individual friendships. "Neither congress nor the president can apply a remedy to cure our country's ills. However, you, individually can apply the principles described in this book," they wrote. "Christians who are willing to pursue reconciliation through cross-cultural relationships may be the only hope for this country and for the effectiveness of our churches to demonstrate God's love in America today," they declared.[103] After being a featured speaker at PK conferences, Washington joined the organization as vice president of racial reconciliation and became an enthusiastic proponent of its vision.[104]

As major black evangelical leaders joined the Promise Keepers movement, others remained skeptical that its individualistic approach offered an answer for systemic injustice. When McCartney visited the 1995 convention of the National Black Evangelical Association, he faced searching questions. "What is Promise Keepers going to say about the anti–affirmative action atmosphere in this country?" asked one black evangelical.[105] Such questions directly confronted the individualistic theology of colorblind Christians. Some black evangelicals feared PK was blind to systemic issues. They believed it had good intentions—but precious few practical plans. Bill Pannell argued that the civil rights movement had shown that reconciliation needed to be paired with social justice. Without an anchor in the concrete experience of oppressed people, reconciliation could too easily devolve into sentimentality. He wondered how evangelicals could make racial reconciliation more than a "fad" so it wouldn't "depend on getting 6 million guys in a stadium someplace."[106]

When black evangelical leaders accused McCartney of not having a plan, he pushed back with his boldest idea yet. He intended to bring 100,000 pastors together in a single conference. "If reconciliation can happen among God's leaders," McCartney said, "it will happen in the church."[107] It was an audacious plan. If achieved, a significant percentage of the entire clergy of the United States would gather under PK's banner of racial reconciliation. In the spring of 1996, the conference kicked off in the Georgia Dome in Atlanta with 39,000 pastors in attendance. Though fewer in number than initially envisioned, it was by any measure a remarkable achievement. McCartney called it "the largest gathering of clergy in U.S. history."[108] *CT* credulously reported "a real breakthrough" in Atlanta as pastors of all colors and denominations worshipped together. "Pentecostals and Baptists prayed together; Anglos and men of color embraced. Suspicions had given way to respect, even love, for fellow believers with different beliefs." A Latino pastor declared, "Better than any other national or visible movement, Promise Keepers is not only preaching racial reconciliation, but they are doing something about it."[109]

During the summer of 1996, every single PK stadium rally—all 22 of them—presented an astonishing display that many black evangelicals never imagined they would live to see. From the platform, speakers railed against the sin of racism and challenged white men to repent for their own sins and those of their ancestors. Then the white men—invariably the large majority of the crowd—were told to find a person of color and ask for forgiveness. "The men often embrace in tears," reported one newspaper.[110] One reporter watched as "guys around me swarm on the only three African-Americans in our section," and "I wonder what is running through the black men's minds."[111] When racial reconciliation was a matter of the heart, its meaning, and whether it had even occurred, was always up for interpretation. But McCartney's sincerity was not in doubt as he spoke with growing candor about the sin of racism. He had traveled to dozens of cities, meeting with clergy of color in all of them. "What I have learned," he declared, "is that there is a spirit of white racial superiority that has oppressed, suffocated and strangled men and women of color."[112] Such earnest rhetoric and unusually robust efforts to include people of color drew praise from some black evangelicals, notably John Perkins. After decades of white evangelical indifference, Perkins looked at Promise Keepers and saw a group that was at least trying to do something.

As PK intensified its racial reconciliation work, it probed the boundaries of Christian colorblindness. When McCartney bluntly talked about white racism, he didn't just make white evangelicals wince. He operated outside the general tenor of 1990s white racial discourse entirely. When PK speakers called on white men to repent of racism and imagine themselves as inheritors of a generational legacy of racism, they challenged basic assumptions of white evangelical life. And PK leaders surely made other white evangelical leaders nervous when they boasted that their diverse staffing exposed the lie that qualified black Christians could not be found to serve in evangelical institutions.

And yet, for all its earnest efforts, PK had thoroughly embraced colorblind Christians' long-standing hostility to structural solutions. In the process, PK reframed the very meaning of racial reconciliation. Perkins's call for solidarity with the poor in opposition to the individualism and selfishness of the American Dream had become, in the hands of Promise Keepers, another in a long litany of evangelical calls for revival. This revival—mediated through interracial friendships—would supposedly fuel profound social change. McCartney declared that "the enduring solution to society's racial divisions lies in the conditions of our hearts, not laws alone." The "spirit of racial reconciliation" was not "engineered in the government offices of Washington or Denver." Jesus Christ was its source.[113] PK's president, Randy Phillips, said, "The key to reconciliation is relationships—and that means one at a time."[114] The stadium rallies, though sensational in their numbers and media attention, were designed to jump-start the quieter work of interpersonal relationships by which genuine change would occur. People who developed long-term interracial friendships as a result of PK spoke of how it transformed their lives.[115] But as a strategy for ending racism in the church, much less society, it was vulnerable to a familiar critique. As one black evangelical leader put it, "Tears and hugs and saying I'm sorry is a good first step, but for me, the question is not one of changing the hearts of individuals as [much as] it is dealing with the systems and the structures that are devastating African-American people."[116]

In the racial climate of the 1990s, "dealing with the systems and structures" was a minority point of view. The message of racial reconciliation rang out from the halls of Congress as well as from PK rallies. Republican congressmen Jack Kemp and J. C. Watts paired their limited-government vision of "community renewal" with a call for "real racial reconciliation—person to person, one heart at a time."[117] For liberals who conceived of America's racial problem as a matter of systemic injustice, these efforts sounded fatuous. But for colorblind Christians and Republican politicians alike, interpersonal solutions were effectively tailored to the nature of the problem. Friendship, personal responsibility, and local initiative were the best answers to a problem rooted in sinful human nature. They bet that Americans could be brought into a common moral and psychological world even if their economic circumstances remained far apart. And after all, the language of racial reconciliation had an almost intuitive appeal. Who didn't want people to get along? In June 1997, President Clinton announced that he wanted to promote a "national conversation on race." He signed an executive order establishing an advisory panel that would, among other things, "advise the President on matters involving race and racial reconciliation." American news organizations adopted the phrase "racial reconciliation" as a generic descriptor of the president's efforts and the nation's need.[118] The widespread embrace of a term so thick with evangelical connotations was an astonishing development that revealed how successful colorblind Christians had become in influencing the terms of American racial discourse.

In 1997, Promise Keepers launched its boldest move yet, a massive rally on the National Mall. PK leaders were quick to draw a contrast to the Million Man March and disavow any political purpose. "We are going to D.C. not to march," McCartney declared, "but to repent."[119] The Stand in the Gap rally aimed to start a national revival. "We're in a pre-revival state with little pockets springing up," said one PK vice president. "If we would confess our sin and repent, perhaps God would ignite the church to be what he wants it to be."[120] Raleigh Washington said the final goal was nothing less than to "eliminate racism as we now see it in the church of Jesus Christ."[121] The rally on October 4 was among the largest gatherings in American history. Conservative estimates put the crowd at over 400,000 men. For many, it was a memorable experience. "I cried my head off," said one man. "For the first time in our life, we could be real men of God."[122] The *Washington Post* reported that 14 percent of the crowd was black. PK faced criticism that it had conducted little more than a glorified "pep rally" but McCartney insisted the "fruit" of the gathering was on the way. PK leaders spoke in increasingly grandiose terms about both the revival they were ushering in and the astonishing social effects that were just over the horizon. McCartney announced plans for mass rallies at every state capitol on January 1, 2000, to declare "that the giant of racism is dead in the church of Jesus Christ."[123]

The question was whether Promise Keepers had the staying power to carry through these plans. One evangelical historian noted that there had been similar movements in decades past that had come and gone with little trace. But PK appeared to be different. "The thing that is noteworthy about Promise Keepers is that it is not fizzling."[124] He spoke too soon. The success of the Stand in the Gap rally helped to mask ominous signs of declining attendance at other PK gatherings that year. In fact, the rallies at state capitols to ring in the new millennium never happened. By then, Promise Keepers was a much-reduced organization. Declining donations and revenues, staff cuts, and diminishing interest from evangelical men left the organization a shadow of its 1994–1997 heyday. Positive talk of restructuring for a more focused mission only underscored the fact that the movement had not blossomed into the mass revival for which some evangelicals had hoped. Many causes have been proposed for the decline, but McCartney's own explanation was as convincing as any: he believed the organization's focus on racial reconciliation caused a backlash among white evangelicals.[125]

Even as the movement seemed to flourish, the warning signs of racial reaction were there all along. When McCartney told the first large gathering of men in 1991 that future rallies would have to be multiracial, it caused, in his words, "a minor firestorm of hate mail and caustic letters." Writers angrily demanded that McCartney focus on "the gospel" rather than racism. Looking back on the experience, McCartney said it provided his "first glimpse of the seething giant of racism lurking within the Christian church." In the early 1990s McCartney took his message of racial reconciliation on the road, visiting dozens of predominantly white churches. "I'd show up to churches filled with men eager to hear about the marvelous move of God called Promise Keepers," he recalled. Audiences were disturbed when instead McCartney gave them a message about "how a subtle spirit of white superiority has unwittingly alienated and wounded our brothers and sisters within the church." McCartney told white Christians to take responsibility for their own prejudices and the historic injustices of generations past. According to McCartney "it was the same story" in every church: "wild enthusiasm while I was being introduced, followed by a morguelike chill as I stepped away from the microphone." Such experiences left him "shaken and dejected," wondering if he was doing the right thing. After having the same experience in dozens of churches, one moment encouraged McCartney to remain faithful to the message of racial reconciliation. At a church in Portland, Oregon, he delivered his usual message to the stony-faced crowd, but before he left the stage, a black man with tears in his eyes approached him and said McCartney's words—words he never expected to "hear a white man say"—had given him hope. But the message that brought hope to some black Christians offended many white ones. As McCartney toured dozens of cities in 1996 and 1997, he found that pastors of color were "profoundly encouraged . . . while some among the white clergy remained aloof." In 1996, nearly 40 percent of all complaints from conference attendees were about the reconciliation focus.[126]

Racial backlash didn't account for the entirety of Promise Keepers' decline, but it did suggest the limits of Christian colorblindness. Even though most of PK's racial reconciliation work focused on friendship, any sustained attention to race raised the hackles of many colorblind Christians. When McCartney spoke of racism as a serious problem, he became a subject of suspicion in much the same way black evangelicals had been for decades. And he faced the same criticisms: if he was such a good Christian, why wasn't he focusing on the gospel? Promise Keepers was a Christian men's empowerment movement. As the racial reconciliation focus loomed larger and became more explicitly oriented toward white responsibility for racism, it began to threaten the core function of Christian colorblindness: the protection and perpetuation of evangelical whiteness. The vast majority of PK attendees came not as white people to reckon with racism, but as *men* seeking a revival of Christian manhood in a peculiar moment of social change and dislocation. McCartney's enthusiasm for racial healing as an essential part of Christian masculinity left many white evangelical men cold. When sociologists Michael Emerson and Christian Smith began asking white evangelicals about their opinions of racial reconciliation in the late 1990s, they were surprised to find that the movement had not entered the consciousness of most laypeople. "Despite the tidal wave of efforts to communicate the message of racial reconciliation, more than 60 percent of the white evangelicals we interviewed had not heard of racial reconciliation or did not know what it meant," they wrote.[127]

Conclusion

The new prominence of racial reconciliation in the 1990s did not show the declining influence of Christian colorblindness. On the contrary, it signaled that colorblind Christians successfully co-opted the language of racial reconciliation for their own purposes. For decades, black evangelicals like John Perkins and Clarence Hilliard had called on middle-class evangelicals—black and white alike—to choose to alter their material circumstances to such an extent that the concerns of the black poor would become their own concerns. In contrast, the interpersonal exchange envisioned in the popular brand of racial reconciliation was overwhelmingly a matter of consciousness and emotion. At PK rallies, men prayed together and asked for forgiveness. They promised not to overcome injustice as such, but to form interracial friendships that would bridge the alienation felt between black and white Christians. And yet even this revivalist and interpersonal approach couched in the language of evangelical theology alienated many white evangelicals. While evangelical elites swooned, ordinary white evangelicals asked why they should be made to think about race yet again, much less apologize for anything.

What, then, did stadiums full of Christian men really signify? Some pundits and scholars regarded the racial reconciliation phenomenon as the most salient feature of evangelical racial practices in the 1990s. It was supposedly an important turning point in which the desire to take racism seriously finally entered the white evangelical mainstream.[128] From the broader vantage point of the history of Christian colorblindness, the so-called racial reconciliation movement appears less as a turning point and more an appropriation. When colorblind Christians took up the language of racial reconciliation, shorn of Perkins's radical edge, they found the perfect vehicle for their long-standing message of racial harmony through unity in Christ. While the racial reconciliation era produced a lot of buzz and media coverage, there was less to it than met the eye.

It was a trend, not a groundswell. Racial reconciliation found its most devoted adherents among educated evangelicals, writers, clergy, professors, and administrators. These were important actors in the evangelical world, but as in every previous decade since the 1960s, their interest in racial matters risked putting them out of step with ordinary white evangelicals. The racial reconciliation wave crested and receded without overcoming colorblind Christians' core commitments to a gospel that invested in whiteness. Americans welcomed the new millennium without the promised crowds of evangelical men on the steps of 50 state capitols announcing the end of racism's reign. The racial reconciliation decade peaked with dreams of a Great Awakening and ended with the disillusionment felt after a fad has run its course.

Conclusion

In 2000, sociologists Michael Emerson and Christian Smith released a book that sent shockwaves through elite evangelical circles. *Divided by Faith: Evangelical Religion and the Problem of Race in America* explained that, despite white evangelicals' best intentions, their "religio-cultural toolkit" of "accountable freewill individualism," "relationism," and "antistructuralism" actually exacerbated racial division in American life.[1] Bill Hybels later said that reading the book was an "embarrassing" experience that left him "devastated." He admitted that at the time he launched Willow Creek, he had agreed with the church growth experts who said, "Don't dissipate any of your energies fighting race issues. Focus everything on evangelism."[2] Emerson and Smith's study was a sobering and nuanced snapshot of evangelical life in the 1990s. But some readers could also find grounds for optimism in it. Taking the authors' language about good intentions and cultural tools at face value, readers might conclude that evangelicals meant well, wanted to deal with racism, and had good theology with which to do so. The problem seemed to be that white evangelicals had allowed the individualism of American culture to overshadow their theological commitments.[3] In reality colorblind Christians had not failed to enact their intentions. They had succeeded at what was most important to them: growing the evangelical movement while keeping whiteness at its center in an age of colorblindness.

By the new millennium, the claims of Christian colorblindness had become common sense in most white evangelical communities. One's identity in Christ was supreme. Racial consciousness weakened this sense of Christian identity and divided believers from one another. Mature Christians emphasized unity in Christ and the power of the gospel to change hearts. Divisive racial talk, costly economic reforms, or institutional reorganizations failed to grapple with the underlying spiritual condition that produced racial animosity. These avowed colorblind claims protected an implicit identity, a peculiar way of being white in the United States. While acting as white people and being treated as such in America's racial hierarchy, most white evangelicals nurtured a self-conception as simple Christians taking the Bible as their cue for living. As white evangelicals listened to overwhelmingly white religious authorities, bought homes in white communities, and sent their children to white schools, they didn't merely insist that these decisions were not racial. They thought of them as normatively Christian. This was the essence of evangelical whiteness. The sacralization of whiteness, though less overt than in the Jim Crow era, remained stubbornly persistent in the twenty-first century.

The career of Southern Baptist megachurch pastor Rick Warren illustrated how Christian colorblindness had changed—and protected—evangelical whiteness. In contrast to an earlier Southern Baptist superstar, W. A. Criswell, the whiteness of Warren's evangelicalism was ecumenical, suburban, upwardly mobile. It was comfortable with a little diversity rather than lily-white, national instead of southern, even cosmopolitan in some respects. And yet it was an evangelical whiteness that still recoiled from serious scrutiny of evangelicalism's racial investments. In his influential 1995 book, *The Purpose Driven Church*, Warren wrote that there were two great inspirations for his career. One was Criswell, the onetime defender of sacred whiteness who later claimed to have had a change of heart when he became president of the Southern Baptist Convention. Criswell returned Warren's admiration by writing the foreword to his book. Warren's other hero was Donald McGavran. Warren might have been bothered by Criswell's and McGavran's most egregious statements if he was aware of them. But his ability to place these men with checkered racial pasts on a pedestal was symptomatic of a white evangelical movement that had not reckoned with its history and did not take black evangelical critiques seriously. In the world of white evangelicalism, a long record of advocating white supremacy was just water under the bridge, not a serious mark against one's pastoral judgment. Criswell said he had changed his mind, and so his past was not worth mentioning. Indeed, Warren called Criswell "the greatest American pastor of the twentieth century."[4] Was such effusive praise for a former advocate of sacred whiteness merely a regrettable indiscretion? Or was it an apt reflection of white evangelicals' ongoing investments?

Christian Colorblindness and the History of Evangelicalism and Race

Colorblind Christians' successful efforts to grow the evangelical movement suggest the need to rethink and retell the history of evangelicalism in the second half of the twentieth century. The well-known tale of partisan political mobilization is just one small part of the story that has too often stood for the whole. The recent transnational trend in the historiography of evangelicalism is a welcome development that casts evangelicals as major global actors and treats the internal dynamics of diverse evangelical communities as important in their own right.[5] The story of the Church Growth Movement (CGM) told here joins this transnational turn. Using race strategically, informed by transnational currents of missionary theory, evangelical denominations grew dramatically in the decades after the civil rights movement. Southern Baptists added over two million people to their member rolls between 1970 and 1985. The Assemblies of God and the Evangelical Free Church tripled their numbers.[6] Evangelical megachurches increased their market share with slick presentation and "seeker sensitive" approaches pioneered by CGM-trained pastors. These congregations made inroads into communities of color as well.[7] In short, white evangelicals appear not as baleful reactionaries seeking refuge in partisan politics but as successful religio-racial entrepreneurs in a time of rapid change. Evangelical institutions thrived, not despite their failure to become truly multicultural antiracist communities, but partly because of their adept colorblind balancing act in an era of racial ambiguity.

This balancing act was not the result of far-reaching plans laid down in advance. It was the negotiated outcome of a contest among evangelicals with opposing ideas for how best to be faithful to the gospel in a time of racial upheaval. Perhaps a clear evangelical theology of race could be theorized on paper, but in practice it emerged more through the exigencies of coalition management than ethical reflection. Throughout this process, black evangelicals insisted that they belonged in the evangelical coalition. The conflicts between black and white evangelicals were a powerful spur for change, even if white evangelical institutions rarely acted with the boldness black evangelicals desired. Indeed, black evangelicals experienced repeated frustrations and disappointments as progress often seemed glacial. They found through hard experience that when they read the Bible differently and found in its pages a call to liberate the poor from oppression, they ran headlong into colorblind Christians' investment in a theology colored white. They might be literally excluded, as at Houston '85, or more subtly silenced, as many black students at white evangelical colleges felt themselves to be, or they might face the psychological and spiritual toll of having the sincerity of their faith called into question by fellow Christians. Amid these hardships, the pressure white evangelicals felt to make their institutions more welcoming to people of color played a vital role in evangelicalism's successful positioning in the mainstream of post–civil rights movement America. When scholars fail to account for black evangelicals' crucial role in this story, they reproduce the very exclusion black evangelicals fought against.

Historians have frequently asserted that white evangelicals brought up the rear in America's civil rights revolution, reluctantly acceding to its legal and cultural changes after the fact.[8] Such claims are not wrong as far as they go, but they risk creating a broader distortion. Casting white evangelicals as principally southern and almost wholly reactionary—"the side of the conversation that lost"—inhibits our ability to see how white evangelicalism helped to form the boundaries of change in the civil rights era.[9] When scholars imagine white evangelicals as the people who are always on the sidelines coming to terms with the results after the game has been played, it becomes difficult to understand how the colorblind racial order of the post–civil rights years has had so much staying power. Among the many reasons for colorblindness's enduring appeal, none were more important than the vitality of an evangelicalism powered by a new theology of race that proclaimed equality while protecting implicit whiteness.

White evangelicals' creative religio-racial self-fashioning defies efforts to draw clear boundaries between winners and losers in the civil rights struggle.[10] In her exceptional study of southern white evangelicals in the civil rights era, Carolyn Renée Dupont wrote, "Rather than receiving the commands of God as fixed tablets of stone, people *make* and remake their religion, and white southerners crafted a faith divinely suited for white supremacy."[11] In the ensuing decades, white evangelicals nationwide remade their religion yet again, but not for white supremacy or for anti-racism. Instead, white evangelicals made a faith fit for white advantage in a colorblind era. The religio-racial order they helped to create was not the beloved community of racial equality and opportunity for all for which many civil rights activists labored. Nor was it a new iteration of sacred white supremacy that many southern white evangelicals wanted. It was something else altogether: a religiously infused colorblind order in which new opportunities went hand in hand with vast disparities; a colorblind evangelicalism in which whiteness had been dethroned in name but not decentered in practice.

White and black evangelicals alike believed that theology, when properly applied, was a vital pathway to racial change. They weren't wrong. Given the essential role of Christian theology in creating and contesting race in centuries past, it would be surprising indeed if theology did not continue to shape racialization in the United States.[12] When religion is removed from the picture, it is harder to understand the varieties and nuances of racist and antiracist discourse in American life. Scholars may readily recognize "colorblind racism" when they see it. But the racism conditioned by evangelical religiosity is a different matter. Understanding how a statement as quintessentially Christian as "you are all one in Jesus Christ" could take on racist or antiracist purposes requires careful attention to the intent of the speaker and the context in which the claim is made. Just as Martin Luther King's dream of a colorblind America was not inherently freeing, so, too, the Christian scriptures are latent with manifold possibilities that Americans have turned to their own contradictory purposes. Ideas voiced with the intent to liberate in one context can be repurposed to oppress in another. To say that evangelical religion has shaped the American racial order is not to suppose that in the absence of this religious force a more enlightened order would necessarily prevail. Evangelicalism has influenced the contours of race in complicated ways, perhaps mitigating some of its darkest passions while entrenching more subtle inequalities. As some commentators have suggested, a post-Christian American racism may be even more harsh and unyielding in its hatreds.[13]

Christian Colorblindness in the Era of New Racism

The implicit promise of Christian colorblindness as an evangelical theology of race was that it would help to hold together and grow a fractious coalition. A professed desire for racial harmony paired with opposition to substantial racial reform brought together a broad cross-section of evangelicals, including some evangelicals of color, around a vision of gradual racial progress rooted in spiritual rebirth. As late as the 1990s, Christian colorblindness seemed to be delivering impressive results in church growth and cultural influence. It was possible to imagine that evangelicalism was poised to go from strength to strength. But two decades of rapid change in the new millennium dealt a severe blow to this evangelical confidence. Church growth abated as the number of Americans claiming no religious affiliation surged. Sweeping cultural transformations from the election of Barack Obama and legalization of gay marriage to the rising salience of transgender rights and the emergence of the Black Lives Matter movement made many white evangelicals feel like strangers in their own country. For an evangelicalism whose racial posture had been premised upon putting people in the pews and growing the movement's power, stagnant membership rolls and lost cultural authority were nothing less than a crisis.[14]

Some black evangelicals saw the crisis coming. Christian colorblindness had been an engine of church growth as it placed evangelicalism strategically in the mainstream of white opinion. But if Christian colorblindness gave white evangelicals power for a time, it also enabled investments in whiteness to continue invisibly and unabated, delaying the day of reckoning. Bill Pannell, the longtime black colaborer with and critic of white evangelicalism, declared that the white evangelical movement had allied itself with "conservative, fundamentally racist politics." The scandal of white evangelicalism was that it had become "more American than Christian." Tony Warner, an area director for InterVarsity Christian Fellowship, wrote that "white evangelicals are more willing to pursue a white conservative political agenda than to be reconciled with their African-American brothers and sisters. It raises a fundamental question of their belief and commitment to the biblical gospel."[15] When Pannell and Warner made these claims in 1993, few white evangelicals took them seriously. Decades later, their words rang with eerie foresight.

Within evangelicalism, uncanny echoes of the 1960s and 1970s were everywhere to be found in the Black Lives Matter era. Debates that had raged for decades—between social justice and evangelism, racial consciousness and Christian unity—were renewed with explosive force. Black evangelicals became increasingly radicalized and race conscious as they watched footage of black people gunned down in the street. As in prior decades a key driver of black evangelical radicalization in the new millennium was the particularly painful experience of seeing fellow Christians dismiss their concerns and tell them to stop talking about their racial experiences. In an echo of their ancestors' response to the civil rights movement, white evangelicals insisted that they valued black lives and desired racial harmony but rejected the Black Lives Matter movement's tactics and ideology. A 2016 survey by the Barna Group found that just 13 percent of evangelicals approved of "the message of the 'Black Lives Matter' movement," while 94 percent believed "Christian churches play an important role in racial reconciliation." Here was a perfect distillation of what colorblind Christians' commitments to equality meant: yes to "racial reconciliation" enacted through the white-led church; no to social equality enacted through black protest and legal reform.[16] The racial politics of church primacy remained as strong as ever.

In a new era of protest and racial ferment, most white evangelicals supported the racist politics of Donald Trump even as they insisted that they valued unity in Christ and racial harmony. The persistence of an antiracist self-image among supporters of racism made the workings of their racial theology starkly visible. Christian colorblindness effectively protected white evangelical identity from self-scrutiny but did little to promote racial equality. Some observers supposed that social media and Fox News had somehow colonized the white evangelical movement. In fact, white evangelicals' own ecclesial practices primed them to see the resonance between the investment in white-dominated churches and a country supposedly threatened by black protest and the immigration of people of color. White evangelical pastors and church planters had been trained to think of church growth in ways that resonated with white nationalist political ideology, as McGavran's ruminations about "mongrel" congregations in the 1970s revealed. When more naked and brutal forms of bigotry became resurgent during the Trump presidency, most white evangelicals had few theological or ethical defenses against them. After all, their own churches had already taught them to invest in whiteness.

The popular black Christian rapper Lecrae provided a very public example of the heightened tensions between black and white evangelicals. Since the release of his first album in 2004, he had enjoyed a large and growing white evangelical audience. In his early songs, Lecrae rapped about the unimportance of racial identity in comparison to the common bond believers had in Jesus Christ. In his 2008 song "Don't Waste Your Life," Lecrae rapped:

> Your life ain't wrapped up in what you drive
> The clothes you wear, the job you work
> The color your skin, naw you're a Christian first.[17]

But beginning in 2014, Lecrae spoke out about police shootings. The blowback from his white evangelical audience was severe. By his own account, Lecrae sank into depression. In "Can't Stop Me Now" (2016), Lecrae said:

> Another murder on the television
> Man, somebody go turn it off
> I spoke my mind, I got attacked for it
> Thought these people had my back boy
> Then they tellin' me I asked for it
> I guess I'm just another black boy
> And then they killed Tamir Rice
> And they just go on with they life
> They tellin' me shut up talking 'bout it
> Like I should just talk about Christ.[18]

When Lecrae released a new album in 2017, it was marinated in black Christian consciousness. It was a declaration of independence from all those who wanted him to "shut [his] mouth and get [his] checks from evangelicals." In the song "Facts" he explored the dramatic disconnect in historical experience and identity between black and white Christians: "You grew up thinkin' that the Panthers was some terrorists, I grew up hearin' how they fed my momma eggs and grits." For Lecrae, the reconciliation he thought was happening between black and white evangelicals had been revealed as hollow. He rapped,

> You want unity?
> Then read a eulogy
> Kill the power that exists up under you and over me.[19]

Power was the rub. Amid widespread consternation about white evangelical support for Donald Trump, what was often lost in the conversation was that white evangelicals were enacting in politics what black evangelicals had already seen in the ecclesial realm. "The white Church considers power its birthright rather than its curse," wrote the black author and activist Austin Channing Brown. Esau McCaulley, a black theologian at Wheaton College, wrote that his "sojourn among the evangelicals" taught him that many looked with "disdain" on black culture and the black church, even as they eagerly welcomed black evangelicals willing to toe the white evangelical line. White evangelicals made silence about racism and whitewashing of American history essential "pillars" of their religion. But, McCaulley asked, "How could I accept a place in a community if the cost for a seat at the table was silence?" The black evangelical pastor Bryan Loritts agreed. "White evangelicalism has never played well, because she will only play with others by *her* rules," he wrote. "If she cannot sit at the head of the table, she won't sit at all. She won't even come into the house."[20] White evangelicals had spent decades learning within their own churches to sacralize white authority.[21] When American culture in the twenty-first century seemed to turn against them, they made a bid for power that was familiar to black evangelicals. In many cases, white evangelicals were prepared to write black evangelicals out of the movement rather than risk challenging the religio-racial identities of their white members.

But black evangelicals did not accept this policing of the movement's authority and borders. Loritts wrote, "White evangelicalism elevates the power of her limited perspective as a historical litmus test to vet the veracity of one's faith." It was a rigged religio-racial test. In white evangelical eyes, black evangelicals kept failing to pass it. White evangelicalism's troubled history and record of oppression seemed not to dent white evangelicals' confidence in the least. Somehow, they still owned the gospel and defined the proper evangelical way. Rebuking this presumption, black evangelicals insisted, as they had done for decades, that their own experience had something to teach the church. The story of the Christian scriptures was being replayed in America. It was right in front of white evangelicals' faces but they couldn't see it because God had put black people at the center of the narrative. Esau McCaulley recalled Christ's passion and the famous heroes of the faith described in the book of Hebrews when he blackened the scriptures to tell the history of black people in the United States: "We were despised and rejected by men, seen as cursed and abandoned by God. We were those from whom men hid their faces," McCaulley wrote. "And what more shall we say? For the time would fail me to tell of the lynching tree, the Red summer, the dogs and the water hoses, the sit-ins, Emmett Till, Medgar Evers, Martin Luther King Jr., the people who defied governors and presidents, braved mobs, and sang victory, people of whom the world was not worthy."[22] What might it take for white evangelicals to learn from the heroes of the faith in their midst?

Among black evangelicals in the Black Lives Matter era there was a palpable sense that the time had come to speak and act on their own terms and let the chips fall where they may. Austin Channing Brown remembered her experience working for racial reconciliation on a white evangelical campus as a time when she "contorted" herself "to be the voice white folks could hear." But now she was done with all that. "My story," she declared, "is about choosing to love my Black femaleness, even when it shocks folks who expected someone quite different." Brenda Salter McNeil, a pastor and professor at Seattle Pacific University, had devoted her career to the work of racial reconciliation among evangelical Christians. She carefully tailored her words to avoid offending white evangelicals. "For years," she wrote, "I tried to be biblical enough, nonthreatening enough, patient enough, persuasive enough, theologically rigorous enough, so that no one could say I had a hidden agenda." She thought that if she could show white evangelicals that she had a biblical motive rather than a political one they might act against racism. "I made my message easy for them to hear," she confessed. "But no more." In the face of white evangelicals' open collusion with racist politics, she resolved to "no longer preach, teach, or lead reconciliation on white-dominant culture's terms." From now on she was determined "to always remember and affirm that my truth, my spirituality, and my identity are rooted in the black community that raised me, nurtured me, and taught me to fight for a better world where all people can thrive."[23]

Jemar Tisby, after years of working to bring attention to racial justice in white evangelical spaces, published a book that became a surprise best-seller in 2020. He carefully constructed his history of racism in the church to answer white evangelical objections he had come to know so well. At the same time, he made no secret that though he might try to reach those who had ears to hear, he would not mince words or allow himself to be held back by the tired criticisms black evangelicals had faced for decades. "Christian complicity with racism in the twenty-first century," Tisby wrote, "looks like Christians responding to *black lives matter* with *all lives matter*. . . . It looks like Christians telling black people and their allies that their attempts to bring up racial concerns are 'divisive.' It looks like conversations on race that focus on individual relationships and are unwilling to discuss systemic solutions." Upon reflection, he wrote, "Perhaps Christian complicity in racism has not changed much after all." Pastor Tyler Burns, a colleague of Tisby's at The Witness: A Black Christian Collective, had a simple message for black evangelicals laboring in white evangelical churches where they did not feel at home: "Get out!"[24]

When Black Lives Matter protests spread across the country after the killing of George Floyd in the late spring of 2020, the evangelical coalition seemed on the verge of fracture. While majorities of white evangelicals expressed support for President Trump and opposition to protests for racial justice, some younger and more educated white evangelicals, along with evangelical elites in parachurch ministries, publishing, and higher education, formed a significant chorus for change. But evangelical elites had been saying similar things for decades. Billy Graham's 1957 *Ebony* interview seemed to be a clarion call for racial equality in the church. The ensuing years brought bitter disappointment. Would this time be any different? When *Christianity Today* supported President Trump's removal from office and reparations for racism, it did not signal a new direction for the white evangelical mainstream.[25] Instead, evangelicalism was splintering. The magazine founded by Billy Graham had finally given up any pretense of being the mouthpiece of most white evangelicals. How could the Black Lives Matter protestor and the Make

America Great Again enthusiast stay together in the same evangelical coalition? Though evangelical elites had a loud microphone, ordinary pastors quietly made the more influential and traditional calculation: the unity of the congregation had to be maintained, and there were far more MAGA enthusiasts in the pews than BLM activists. That meant a clear stand for racial justice would have to wait. While the evangelical mainstream continued its investment in whiteness in the name of Jesus, the *New York Times* reported on a "quiet exodus" of black evangelicals from predominantly white evangelical churches in the new era of racial polarization.[26] In the twenty-first century, black evangelicals remained the mirror that revealed colorblind Christians' investments in whiteness.

ACKNOWLEDGMENTS

A big thank you to Jennifer Hammer, Veronica Knutson, and the entire team at New York University Press. Thanks to the anonymous reviewers for making this a better book. I am also grateful for all the people who shepherded this project from its infancy, especially my advisor, Lila Corwin Berman, and committee members Harvey Neptune, Bryant Simon, and David Watt. So many people at Temple University helped in big and small ways over the years. I remember one fateful evening in a writing seminar when Devin Manzullo-Thomas said, "You know, you might find something useful in college student newspapers." Thanks to James Cook-Thajudeen, Sam Davis, Richard Kent Evans, David Farber, Holly Genovese, Petra Goedde, Steve Hausmann, Andrew Isenberg, Hilary Iris Lowe, Brian McNamara, Keith Riley, Travis Roy, and Ali Straub. I am grateful for a supportive scholarly community beyond Temple. I especially want to thank Paul Harvey, David Kirkpatrick, Mary Beth Swetnam Mathews, and David Swartz.

This book would not be possible without the often-unheralded work of librarians and archivists. Thanks to Keith Call, Katherine Graber, and the rest of the staff at the Billy Graham Center Archives. Thanks to Taffey Hall and her staff at the Southern Baptist Historical Library and Archives. Thanks to Glen Pierce at the Messiah College Archives; Anna-Kajsa Anderson at the F. M. Johnson Archives and Special Collections at North Park University; Hendrina VanSpronsen at Heritage Hall, Calvin University; Laura Habecker at the Willard J. Houghton Library, Houghton University; Corie Zylstra at the Crowell Library Archives, Moody Bible Institute; Sunya Notley at Bailey Library, Nyack College; Amy Yuncker at the Everett L. Cattell Library, Malone University; Melvin Hartwick at the Masland Library, Cairn University; and David Goss and Sarah Larlee at the Gordon College archives.

There is one special debt left. If it weren't for Alicia, I don't think I would have become a historian, much less come to know my tangled religio-racial inheritance. This book is one long-overdue result of my encounter with her.

NOTES

INTRODUCTION

1 Ironically, the meaning of the scripture Warren quoted to support his point was far from obvious. It had a long and contested history as a proof text for both evangelical integrationists and evangelical segregationists. Integrationists quoted the first line, "from one man" (often translated "from one blood"), to emphasize the unity of humanity created by God, while segregationists quoted the second half of the verse to argue that God had ordained segregation. As of this writing, Warren's August 13, 2015, post can still be seen on his page at www.facebook.com/pastorrickwarren.
2 In the 1960s some evangelicals used the phrase to oppose Martin Luther King's brand of civil rights activism (though Warren might not have known this).
3 Fredrickson, *Racism*, 6.
4 Major works on colorblind ideology include Doane and Bonilla-Silva, *White Out*; Brown et al., *Whitewashing Race*; Bonilla-Silva, *Racism without Racists*; Burke, *Racial Ambivalence in Diverse Communities*; Nilsen and Turner, *The Colorblind Screen*; and Gomer, White Balance. Major historical treatments of the rise of colorblindness have given relatively little attention to religion. See, for example, Lassiter, *The Silent Majority*; HoSang, *Racial Propositions*. The exception is found in Gordon, *From Power to Prejudice, 161–179*.
5 Fessenden, *Culture and Redemption*. "The secular is not an absence of religion," writes Kathryn Lofton; "rather, the secular is religion's kaleidoscopic buffet." Lofton, *Oprah*, 209.
6 See, for example, the near-total absence of religion in Harris, "Whiteness as Property"; Crenshaw et al, *Critical Race Theory*; Delgado and Stefancic, *Critical Race Theory*; and Lipsitz, *The Possessive Investment in Whiteness*.
7 McCutcheon, *Religion and the Domestication of Dissent*, 64–81. For examples of Christian scholars lamenting what they see as inappropriate mixing of religion and politics, see Balmer, *Thy Kingdom Come*; and Marsh, *Wayward Christian Soldiers*.
8 A helpful discussion of this outlook, which Samuel L. Perry calls "pietistic idealism," is found in Perry, *Growing God's Family*, 8–13. The crucial distinction I seek to make is that white evangelicals apply this pietistic approach in some contexts, especially when race is in view, while rejecting it in others. As Curtis J. Evans has argued, "evangelical individualism" is not a "sufficient explanation of their ap-

proach to race. Evangelicals have selectively applied an individualist ethic primarily to social practices with which they have disagreed." Evans, "White Evangelical Responses to the Civil Rights Movement," 250.

9 While evangelicals have often been described as antistatist, the idea of church primacy connotes the positive content evangelicals believed was inherent in their church-centric vision. As Steven Miller and Axel Schäfer have shown, white evangelical antistatism was not a negation of state power but an assertion of its proper role in support of evangelical institutions. See Miller, "The Persistence of Antiliberalism," 81–96; and Schäfer, *Piety and Public Funding*.

10 Few people, after all, escape the contradictions and hypocrisies inherent in trying to make their way through this confusing world. An evangelical might say, "Let he who is without sin cast the first stone" (John 8:7).

11 Barger, *The World Come of Age*, 253.

12 Frances FitzGerald's popular history of evangelicalism is symptomatic of this trend. It devotes hundreds of pages in the second half of the book to a small cadre of elite white evangelical political activists, leaving the internal worlds of evangelical communities largely unexplored. See FitzGerald, *The Evangelicals*, 291–623.

13 On white evangelicals, civil rights, and the rise of the Christian Right, see Williams, *God's Own Party*; Dochuk, *From Bible Belt to Sunbelt*; and R. Stephens, "'It Has to Come from the Hearts of the People.'" For scholars who have explored religion and race in the civil rights era beyond the familiar story of Christian Right politics, see Marsh, *God's Long Summer*; Emerson and Smith, *Divided by Faith*; Chappell, *A Stone of Hope*; Dailey, "Sex, Segregation, and the Sacred after Brown"; Curtis J. Evans, "White Evangelical Responses to the Civil Rights Movement"; Miles Mullin, "Neoevangelicalism and the Problem of Race in Postwar America," in *Christians and the Color Line: Race and Religion after Divided by Faith*, ed. J. Russell Hawkins and Phillip Luke Sinitiere (New York: Oxford University Press, 2014), 15–44; Mulder, *Shades of White Flight*; Dupont, *Mississippi Praying*; and Quiros, *God with Us*.

14 On the co-construction of religion and race, see Lum and Harvey, *The Oxford Handbook of Religion and Race in American History*, 1–19; and Goldschmidt and McAlister, *Race, Nation, and Religion in the Americas*, 3–34. A notably successful example of this framework in action is found in Blum and Harvey, *The Color of Christ*.

15 See, for example, Marsden, *Fundamentalism and American Culture*; and Carpenter, *Revive Us Again*.

16 Though Weisenfeld goes on to use the term in a more specific sense most applicable to her subject, she suggests its broader relevance, writing, "In some sense, all religious groups in the United States could be characterized as religio-racial ones, given the deeply powerful, if sometimes veiled, ways the American system of racial hierarchy has structured religious beliefs, practices, and institutions for all people in its frame." Weisenfeld, *New World A-coming*, 5.

17 Steven Miller has suggested that evangelicalism in the late twentieth century was no longer a subculture. It had entered the American mainstream. If this was so, its racial posture was a key prerequisite for this success. Positioned as not excessively reactionary yet inoffensive to the sensibilities of racially conservative whites, evangelicalism thrived in the post–civil rights era. S. Miller, *The Age of Evangelicalism*.
18 For decades David Bebbington's definition of evangelicalism based on four theological beliefs dominated the field, but it has faced growing scrutiny in recent years. The debate is summarized in Noll, Bebbington, and Marsden, *Evangelicals*. See also Bebbington, *Evangelicalism in Modern Britain*; and Dayton and Johnston, *The Variety of American Evangelicalism*.
19 Du Mez, "Evangelicalism Is an Imagined Religious Community"; Brenneman, *Homespun Gospel*, 11–17; Vaca, *Evangelicals Incorporated*, 1–12; Silliman et al., "The Imaginary Turn in Evangelical Scholarship"; Du Mez, *Jesus and John Wayne*, 5–9.
20 See, for example, Sinha, *The Slave's Cause*, 10–17.

1. WHAT DOES IT MEAN TO BE ONE IN CHRIST?

1 H. Jones, *Shall We Overcome?*, 124–125, 140.
2 Galatians 3:28.
3 Burkholder, *Color in the Classroom*; Gordon, *From Power to Prejudice*; Lassiter, *The Silent Majority*.
4 Keith M. Finley, *Delaying the Dream: Southern Senators and the Fight against Civil Rights, 1938–1965* (Baton Rouge: Louisiana State University Press, 2008); Kevin Kruse, *White Flight: Atlanta and the Making of Modern Conservatism* (Princeton, NJ: Princeton University Press, 2005); Curtis, "Remembering Racial Progress, Forgetting White Resistance."
5 On the effort to construct an imagined midcentury consensus around shared ideals, see Wall, *Inventing the "American Way."* In the most influential study of race in the era, the Swedish sociologist Gunnar Myrdal called this consensus the "American Creed" espousing individual liberty, opportunity for all, and equality before the law. Gunnar Myrdal, *An American Dilemma: The Negro Problem and Modern Democracy* (1944; New York: Harper & Row, 1962). Even if agreement on these principles was imagined more than realized, it gave to civil rights activists a powerful rhetorical tool to push for racial change.
6 Darren Dochuk has framed the rise of colorblindness among evangelicals as a product of Republican Party coalition building in 1960s Southern California. This narrative glosses over what evangelicals themselves found most concerning about racial change: how it affected their own institutions. Dochuk, *From Bible Belt to Sunbelt*, 274–281.
7 Historians have described white evangelicalism's turn toward racial moderation in these years, but most scholars have given relatively little attention to the very group that most exposed the racial boundaries and investments of the movement—black evangelicals. See, for example, R. Stephens, "'It Has to Come

from the Hearts of the People,'" 1–27; Mullin, "Neoevangelicalism and the Problem of Race in Postwar America," 15–44; and Curtis J. Evans, "White Evangelical Responses to the Civil Rights Movement," 245–273.

8. Carey Daniel to A. C. Miller, September 23, 1956, AR 138, Box 20, Folder 13, Southern Baptist Historical Library and Archives, Nashville, TN (hereafter cited as SBHLA).
9. On Catholics and the Mystical Body of Christ, see Johnson, *One in Christ*, 4, 52–56; and Newman, *Desegregating Dixie*, x, 83–84. On Protestant statements on race in the 1940s, see Emerson, *People of the Dream*, 19.
10. Carl Henry is quoted in Mullin, "Neoevangelicalism and the Problem of Race in Postwar America," 18.
11. The InterVarsity Christian Fellowship executive committee concluded, "Since colored people tend to relate segregation and the Christianity which we represent, we must demonstrate that in Christ there is neither black nor white." But the organization decided to implement this policy quietly and without "propaganda" since it was likely to have "serious repercussions, particularly among our constituency in the south." "1st Black Student Statement 1948," CN 300, Box 383, Folder 1, Billy Graham Center Archives, Wheaton, IL (hereafter cited as BGCA).
12. As Miles Mullin has noted, in the later 1950s evangelical magazines such as *His*, *Eternity*, and *Christian Life* increasingly featured articles supportive of desegregation and sometimes published black authors. Mullin, "Neoevangelicalism and the Problem of Race in Postwar America," 23–27.
13. On the National Council of Churches' shift to action in support of civil rights legislation, see Findlay, *Church People in the Struggle*, 3–75.
14. H. Jones, *Shall We Overcome?*, 121.
15. Reverend Montague Cook, "Racial Segregation Is Christian," September 8 and 15, 1963, AR 795-221, Box 59, Folder 10, SBHLA.
16. "Wrongs Do Not Make Civil Rights," *Eternity*, June 1964, 4.
17. See, for example, Gollner, "How Mennonites Became White."
18. Iola B. Parker, "Our Church's First Negro," *Christian Herald*, February 1964, 21.
19. Genesis 9:25, King James Version (KJV).
20. On the long and tangled roots of the Curse of Ham myth, see Goldenberg, *The Curse of Ham*.
21. Letter quoted in John Vander Ploeg, "The Christian Reformed Church and the Negro," *Banner*, October 4, 1957, 4.
22. "An Inventory of Race-Related Pronouncements and Programs of the Christian Reformed Church and Related Agencies," July 1971, 9, C2.1.8, Box 230, Folder 4, Heritage Hall, Calvin College.
23. Carl McIntire, "Open Letter to Martin Luther King," May 25, 1964, Carl McIntire Papers, Box 179, Folder 1, Princeton Theological Seminary Library. I am indebted to Paul Matzko for generously sharing his research and bringing McIntire's views to my attention. On McIntire's influence and the extraordinary reach of his radio show, see Matzko, *The Radio Right*.

24 Acts 17:26.
25 Carl Henry, "What of Racial Intermarriage," *Christianity Today*, October 11, 1963, 26–28.
26 On the racist practices and associations of early twentieth-century fundamentalism, see Mathews, *Doctrine and Race*, 11–40. As Matthew Avery Sutton has written, "Despite fundamentalists' talk of doctrinal purity as the foundation for Christian fellowship, the color line always trumped theology." Sutton, *American Apocalypse*, 109, 128–137.
27 Billy Graham was keenly aware of the negative connotations of fundamentalism. When asked whether he was a fundamentalist, Graham replied, "If by fundamentalism you mean 'narrow', 'bigoted', 'prejudiced', 'extremist', 'emotional', 'snakehandler' without social conscience—then I am not a fundamentalist. However, if by fundamentalist you mean a person who accepts the authority of the scriptures, the virgin birth of Christ, his bodily resurrection, his second coming and personal salvation by grace through faith, then I am a fundamentalist. However, I much prefer being called 'Christian.'" Quoted in McLoughlin, *Modern Revivalism*, 500–501.
28 This kind of constituent pressure is masterfully explored in Laats, *Fundamentalist U*.
29 Robert L. Smith, letter to the editor, *King's Business*, December 1957, 8; Jim Herring, letter to the editor, *King's Business*, February 1958, 8.
30 J. M. Baker to Brooks Hays, May 24, 1958, AR 97, Box 2, Folder 7, SBHLA. A persistent question in the historiography is whether southern white evangelicals were ambivalent segregationists or committed white supremacists. David Chappell has taken the former view and Carolyn Dupont the latter. While both authors are careful to note the divide between elites and laypeople, I find Dupont's argument more convincing because she pays closer attention to the extent to which race had become an inseparable part of religious identity among many white evangelicals. See Chappell, *A Stone of Hope*, 105–130; and Dupont, *Mississippi Praying*, 3–7.
31 H. Jones, *Shall We Overcome?*, 135–136.
32 Henry, "What of Racial Intermarriage," 26–28.
33 Harrison, *When God Was Black*, 27–29.
34 Ibid., 57.
35 Sarah C. Lewis, "The Black Mamba," *Pentecostal Evangel*, September 1962, 12.
36 C. Herbert Oliver, "The Christian Negro: What Should He Do?" *Eternity*, November 1960, 15–16. Oliver was a graduate of Wheaton College and went on to a long career of civil rights activism and pastoral ministry.
37 Howard Jones, "From the World of Jazz," CN 19, Box 80, Folder 34, BGCA; W. Jones, *Living in Two Worlds*, 9–15, 29.
38 Though often overlooked at the time, Wanda was every bit as much a missionary as Howard, and she had her own radio show and evangelistic campaigns with West African women. W. Jones, *Living in Two Worlds*, 33–39, 71, 76, 81, 96; H. Jones, *Gospel Trailblazer*, 71–77.

39. H. Jones, *Gospel Trailblazer*, 136.
40. Ibid., 141–142.
41. "No Color Line in Heaven," *Ebony*, September 1957, 99–104. The format of the article makes it unclear whether Graham himself used "colorblind" to describe God or if it was the interviewer's paraphrase.
42. Ibid.
43. "The Ministry of Howard O. Jones," CN 19, Box 80, Folder 34, BGCA. See also "Cleveland Minister Joins Billy Graham," *Atlanta Daily World*, July 16, 1958, 1.
44. For typical examples of Jones playing this role, see Howard Jones to Walter Smyth, November 15, 1961, and March 4, 1962, CN 19, Box 80, Folder 34, BGCA; Bob Ferm to Howard Jones, July 10, 1963, CN 19, Series 3, Sub-series 2, Box 3, Folder 8, BGCA.
45. H. Jones, *Gospel Trailblazer*, 134.
46. H. Jones, *Shall We Overcome?*, 139.
47. Ibid., 127–128.
48. Howard Jones, "Missions/Prejudice," *His*, January 1965, 1–4, 30.
49. M. R. Irvin to Donald L. Bailey, May 9, 1972, CN 17, Box 80, Folder 34, BGCA; John W. Dillon to Howard Jones, August 11, 1969, CN 17, Box 80, Folder 34, BGCA.
50. H. Jones, *Shall We Overcome?*, 122.
51. 1 John 3:11–17, KJV.
52. James 2:8–10, KJV.
53. H. Jones, *Shall We Overcome?*, 122–123, 139–140.
54. "America's First National Negro Evangelical Leadership Conference," CN 19, Series 3, Sub-series 2, Box 6, Folder 63, BGCA. On the founding of the NBEA, see A. Miller, "The Rise of African-American Evangelicalism in American Culture"; Rah, "In Whose Image," 182–195; W. Bentley, *The National Black Evangelical Association*; and Potter, "The New Black Evangelicals."
55. Homer Bigart, "Alabama Campus Accepts Negroes," *New York Times*, June 14, 1964, 65.
56. Marvin Printis to Howard Jones, March 26, 1963, CN 19, Series 3, Sub-series 2, Box 3, Folder 8, BGCA.
57. Howard Jones to Bob Ferm, March 29, 1963, CN 19, Series 3, Sub-series 2, Box 3, Folder 8, BGCA.
58. George M. Wilson to Walter Smyth, May 27, 1963, CN 19, Series 3, Sub-series 2, Box 3, Folder 8, BGCA.
59. "America's First National Negro Evangelical Leadership Conference," CN 19, Series 3, Sub-series 2, Box 6, Folder 63, BGCA.
60. William J. Petersen, "Evangelicals & the Race Barriers," *Eternity*, September 1963, 12–16, 48.
61. "National Group Formed by Negro Evangelicals," *Los Angeles Times*, April 27, 1963, 15.

62 Joseph Brown, "The Negro Evangelical and the Race Crisis," *Eternity*, September 1964, 17, 30.
63 W. Bentley, "Factors in the Origin," 311. In explaining the emergence of self-described black evangelicals, Albert G. Miller has emphasized the influence of black Protestants such as B. M. Nottage of the black Plymouth Brethren church, John Davis Bell of the Christian & Missionary Alliance, and Bentley himself, of the Church of God in Christ. Nottage was a mentor to Jones, Printis, and other key black evangelical leaders including Bill Pannell. Yet, when looking back on the emergence of the NBEA, many black evangelicals themselves emphasized the extent to which white evangelicalism had formed (or, indeed, deformed) their outlook. For background on black fundamentalism, see also Bare, *Black Fundamentalists*.
64 Potter, "The New Black Evangelicals," 303–304.
65 W. Bentley, "Factors in the Origin," 310.
66 "Let's Face Up to the Race Issue," *Eternity*, August 1963, 5–6.
67 George McMillan, "Silent White Ministers of the South," *New York Times Magazine*, April 5, 1964, 22, 114–115.
68 Quoted in Marsh, "The Civil Rights Movement as Theological Drama," 30.
69 Martin Luther King, "Letter from Birmingham City Jail," in Washington, *Testament of Hope*, 299.
70 See "Birmingham Negroes Given Differing Receptions at White Churches," *New York Times*, April 15, 1963, 1.
71 Floyd C. Delaney to Earl Stallings, no date; Harold Cummins to Earl Stallings, April 15, 1963; Jean V. N. DaCosta to Earl Stallings, April 16, 1963. All these sources are from AR 234, Box 1, Folder 3, SBHLA.
72 For more on Stallings, see Bass, *Blessed Are the Peacemakers*. See also Rieder, *Gospel of Freedom*.
73 Jim Marugg, "Evangelist Sees Need to Fill Void Left by King's Death," April 18, 1968, *Pasadena Star-News*, C-2.
74 McIntire, "Open Letter to Martin Luther King," May 25, 1964, Carl McIntire Papers, Box 179, Folder 1, Princeton Theological Seminary Library.
75 Jim Sexton, "Current News," *Trev-Echoes*, June 4, 1963, 2; "Graham Certain Forced Integration Won't Work," *Redlands Daily Facts*, August 28, 1963, 7.
76 "Graham Theory on Bias Draws Negro Attack," *Fresno Bee*, August 28, 1963, 47.
77 Wacker, *America's Pastor*, 125.
78 Martin Luther King, "I Have a Dream," in Washington, *A Testament of Hope*, 219.
79 On the voluminous literature documenting the appropriation of King's language, see especially Hansen, *The Dream*; Chappell, *Waking from the Dream*, 91–123; and Sokol, *The Heavens Might Crack*, 223–254.
80 Quoted in Quiros, *God with Us*, 85.
81 "The Washington March and the Negro Cause," *Christianity Today*, September 13, 1963, 27–28. See also "Desegregation," *Covenanter Witness*, September 11, 1963, 163.

82 See "Civil-Rights Legislation," *Christianity Today*, November 22, 1963, 31–32.
83 Martin Luther King, "Letter from Birmingham City Jail," in Washington, *A Testament of Hope*, 295.
84 "Let's Face Up to the Race Issue," *Eternity*, August 1963, 5–6.
85 Ibid.
86 Marlin Van Elderen, "300 Calvin Students Join in Protest March," *Calvin College Chimes*, September 27, 1963, 1; Harold Bontekoe, "The Alternative to Hate," *Calvin College Chimes*, September 27, 1963, 2.
87 Pannell, *My Friend, the Enemy*, 56–57.
88 William Henry Anderson Jr., "Evangelicals and the Race Revolution," *Christianity Today*, October 25, 1963, 6–8.
89 Sam Boyle, "An Apology to the Church in Japan," *Covenanter Witness*, November 13, 1963, 312–313; Galatians 3:28.
90 Brown, "The Negro Evangelical and the Race Crisis," 17.
91 John Herbers, "35,000 in Alabama at Biracial Rites," *New York Times*, March 30, 1964, 1; "Debate in the Senate; a Meeting in Birmingham," *Time*, April 10, 1964, 39; Benjamin E. Mays, "My View: Billy Graham and Birmingham," *Pittsburgh Courier*, April 18, 1964, 10; "Historic Crowd Stirred by Dr. Graham's Easter Sermon," *New York Amsterdam News*, April 4, 1964, 7.
92 H. Jones, *Shall We Overcome?*, 140.
93 "Billy Graham in Birmingham," *Christianity Today*, April 24, 1964, 38–39.
94 Harvey, *Christianity and Race in the American South*, 171–175. See also Haynes, *The Last Segregated Hour*.
95 Samuel Southard, a Southern Baptist professor, studied attitudes toward integration and concluded that concern about financial decline was the single biggest factor in churches' opposition to integration. William M. Dyal Jr., "A Strategy for Southern Baptists in Race Relations," AR 138-6, Box 1, Folder 12, SBHLA.
96 C. A. Roberts, "The Christian Ethic and Segregation," at Christianity and Race Relations Christian Life Commission Conference, August 1964, 25–37, AR 138-6, Box 1, Folder 12, SBHLA.
97 Iola B. Parker, "Our Church's First Negro," *Christian Herald*, February 1964, 21.
98 Judi C. Culbertson, "The Case of the Colorblind Church," *Eternity*, April 1964, 24–25, 47.
99 King A. Butler, "Black, White or God Supremacy," *Eternity*, July 1964, 17–18, 32–33.
100 Brown, "The Negro Evangelical and the Race Crisis," 17, 30.
101 L. Nelson Bell, "The Race Issue and a Christian Principle," AR 138, Box 20, Folder 12, SBHLA; Brown, "The Negro Evangelical and the Race Crisis," 17, 30.
102 "Integration and YOU," *Christian Herald*, February 1965, 26.
103 Leroy Gardner, "The Negro Needs the Gospel," *Evangelical Beacon*, September 1, 1964, 4.
104 Culbertson, "The Case of the Color-Blind Church," 47.
105 Mrs. B. Miller, "More Civil Rights," *Eternity*, August 1964, 3.
106 Mark Hatfield, "Wrongs and Civil Rights," *Eternity*, July 1964, 3.

107 Glenn Gohr, "For Such a Time as This: The Story of Evangelist Bob Harrison," *Assemblies of God Heritage*, Fall 2004, 5–11.
108 Robert E. Harrison, "These Things Shall Be," *Pentecostal Evangel*, October 22, 1967, 2.
109 It is important to note that this white evangelical woman claimed she was quoting the words of a local black pastor. Paradoxically, she understood her words might carry more weight if they came from a black pastor. Some black Christians did actively oppose the civil rights movement, a phenomenon that remains underexplored. Mrs. Hiram Gross to Hudson T. Armerding, May 1, 1968, RG-07-001, Box 1, Folder 30, Wheaton College Special Collections.
110 "Eutychus and His Kin," *Christianity Today*, May 8, 1964, 18.
111 Clyde W. Taylor to Herbert S. Mekeel, March 22, 1965; and "Memo for Dr. Taylor," March 12, 1965, both in SC-113, Box 52, Folder "Civil Rights 1965," Wheaton College Special Collections.
112 Just five years before, it had publicized its opposition to the election of the nation's first Catholic president. See also Kruse, *One Nation under God*, 87–92.
113 Though the SBC has acted at the highest levels of the convention to withdraw fellowship from LGBT-affirming churches in recent decades, I have been unable to find a single case of the SBC withdrawing fellowship from a racist church in the civil rights era. When a local SBC association disfellowshipped a church over racism in 2018, a prominent Southern Baptist pastor said he believed this was an unprecedented action. See David Roach, "'Third Way' Church Disfellowshipped from SBC," *Baptist Press*, September 23, 2014, www.baptistpress.com; Joe Westbury, "Association Disfellowships Church over Racism Charges," *Baptist Press*, April 4, 2018, www.baptistpress.com.
114 Howard Jones to Billy Graham, May 14, 1965; and Howard Jones to Walter Smyth, May 14, 1965, both in CN 17, Box 80, Folder 34, BGCA.
115 Walter Smyth to Howard Jones, May 21, 1965; and Billy Graham to Howard Jones, May 28, 1965, both in CN 17, Box 80, Folder 34, BGCA.
116 Interview with Howard Jones, *Eternity*, August 1968, 13–16; Marugg, "Evangelist Sees Need to Fill Void Left by King's Death," April 18, 1968, *Pasadena Star-News*, C-2.
117 "Graham Crusade Can Disturb the Blacks," *New York Amsterdam News*, April 18, 1970, 29.

2. CREATING THE COLORBLIND CAMPUS

1 "Bible Institute Grads Rip Diplomas; Protest Racism," *Jet*, March 19, 1970, 30; "The Mood at Moody," *Newsweek*, March 9, 1970, 51; "Ex-students Protest 'Moody White Racism,'" *Moody Student*, February 13, 1970, 1; "Time for Self-Examination," *Moody Student*, February 13, 1970, 2; "Dr. Culbertson Addresses Race Issue," *Moody Student*, February 27, 1970, 1; Dave Broucek, "Admin. Expresses 'Mood at Moody,'" *Moody Student*, March 13, 1970, 3.
2 Laats, *Fundamentalist U*, 1–11.

3 Nancy Hardesty, "Black Students in Christian Schools: Are We Trying?," *Eternity*, July 1969, 38–39.
4 Pannell, *My Friend, the Enemy*, 47–52.
5 Harrison, *When God Was Black*, 16–20.
6 Colossians 3:11 reads: "Here there is not Greek and Jew, circumcised and uncircumcised, barbarian, Scythian, slave, free; but Christ is all, and in all." Gordon S. Jaeck to V. Raymond Edman, July 11, 1960; and "Wheaton College Statement on Race Relations," both in RG-02-004, Box 7, Folder 17, College Archives, Buswell Library, Wheaton College.
7 Gordon S. Jaeck to V. Raymond Edman, July 11, 1960; and "Wheaton College Statement on Race Relations," both in RG-02-004, Box 7, Folder 17, College Archives, Buswell Library, Wheaton College.
8 V. Raymond Edman to Executive Council, July 22, 1960, RG-02-004, Box 7, Folder 17, College Archives, Buswell Library, Wheaton College.
9 Merrill C. Tenney to V. R. Edman, July 29, 1960, RG-02-004, Box 7, Folder 17, College Archives, Buswell Library, Wheaton College.
10 Laats, *Fundamentalist U*, 231–232.
11 William J. Petersen, "Evangelicals & the Race Barriers," *Eternity*, September 1963, 12–16, 48.
12 In a remarkably blunt self-assessment, the Christian Reformed Church studied the racial practices of its colleges and other institutions and concluded, "It appears to be more than coincidental that most if not all of the agencies which do have formal policies [of nondiscrimination] also have formal government contracts and associations of one type or another, thus *requiring* subscription to a fair employment policy." "An Inventory of Personnel Practices: A Final Report of Component E in the Study of Racism in the Christian Reformed Church," February 29, 1972, 8, C2.1.8, Box 230, Folder 4, Heritage Hall, Calvin College.
13 Roach, "The Southern Baptist Convention and Civil Rights, 1954–1995." For a compelling account of how colorblind theology helped to justify the integration of a southern school, Asbury College in Kentucky, see Swartz, *Facing West*, 65–96.
14 "An Inventory of Institutional Admissions Practices," 11.
15 Glen Pierce, "Notes on the Lecture Black Like Me," *Ivy Rustles*, May 9, 1967, 6–10; "Goal of $600 Reached in Negro Scholarship Fund Drive," *Ivy Rustles*, September 28, 1967, 1.
16 Joyce Suber, "Recruitment, Admission, Retention, and Success of Minority Students," February 18, 1981, 4, RG-02-005, Box 31, Folder 19, College Archives, Buswell Library, Wheaton College.
17 Memo from Dr. Kean M. Driscoll to President Karl A. Olsson, October 8, 1969, Series 9/1/26, Box 8, Folder 5, Committee on Disadvantaged Students 1969–1970, F. M. Johnson Archives and Special Collections, Brandel Library, North Park University.
18 Meehan, *Growing Pains*.
19 Robert Ottenhoff, "An End to Isolationism," *Chimes*, April 17, 1970, 5.

20 Joseph Ritchie, letter to the editor, *Chimes*, November 15, 1969, 6.
21 "Calvin Receives $15,000 Grant for Black Student Assistance," *Chimes*, September 11, 1970, 1; "Calvin College Enrollment of Minority Students, 1969–1977," C2.1.8, Box 230, Folder 5, Heritage Hall, Calvin College.
22 Steve Harris, "Blacks at Bethel, Part 1, 1969–1971: How Bethel Recruited Black Students," *Bethel Clarion*, March 21, 1975, 4.
23 "College to Aid Disadvantaged Students," *Spotlight*, December 16, 1968, 1.
24 Tim F. La Haye to Hudson T. Armerding, May 23, 1968, RG-02-005, Box 28, Folder 25, College Archives, Buswell Library, Wheaton College.
25 Mrs. Robert Peterson to Hudson Armerding, May 9, 1968, RG-02-005, Box 28, Folder 25, College Archives, Buswell Library, Wheaton College.
26 Mary Garnder, letter to the editor, *Bagpipe*, April 25, 1968, 2.
27 For example, Hudson T. Armerding to Mrs. Marian L. Wallace, January 3, 1969, RG-07-001, Box 1, Folder 30, College Archives, Buswell Library, Wheaton College.
28 Los Angeles Baptist College is now the Master's University.
29 Weary and Hendricks, *"I Ain't Comin' Back,"* 53–58.
30 Ibid., 59–62.
31 In 1974, Hardesty coauthored one of the first major efforts to take an interpretive approach to the Bible that was both evangelical and feminist. See Hardesty and Scanzoni, *All We're Meant to Be*.
32 Nancy Hardesty, "Black Students in Christian Schools: Are We Trying?," *Eternity*, July 1969, 38–39.
33 On the black student revolt and its enduring impact on mainstream colleges and universities, see Biondi, *The Black Revolution on Campus*.
34 Hardesty, "Black Students in Christian Schools," 38–39.
35 Ibid.
36 Ed Smith and Joyce Shimp, "Black Students Aim for Unity," *Scroll*, undated edition circa 1970, 1; Ralph Medley, *Scroll*, December 10, 1970, 2.
37 "AAC Also Open to White Students," *Nyack Forum*, December 20, 1968, 1.
38 "The Afro-American Society," *Spotlight*, November 7, 1969, 5.
39 Jacqueline Gibson, "B.S.U. Silent Minority Becomes Loud," *Ivy Rustles*, February 16, 1972.
40 "Quest for Acceptance," *Taylor University Magazine*, Winter 1970, 10, Ringenberg Archives and Special Collections, Taylor University.
41 Phil Jenks, "Racial Tokenism at Eastern Baptist College?," *Spotlight*, March 23, 1970, 2.
42 R. Ailes, "An Unholy War," *Covenant College Bagpipe*, January 14, 1972, 2–3.
43 Jenks, "Racial Tokenism at Eastern Baptist College?," 2.
44 Steve Heise, untitled editorial, *Ivy Rustles*, April 4, 1972, 2.
45 Fred Banzer, letter to the editor, *Nyack Forum*, February 11, 1971, 3.
46 R. E. Alexander, "Black Talk—No. 1 (General)," *Bagpipe*, December 10, 1971, 2; R. E. Alexander, "Black Talk—No. 3," *Bagpipe*, January 28, 1972, 2; Tim Belz, "Need for Clarity Cited," *Bagpipe*, January 14, 1972, 3.

47 Ed Carpenter, letter to the editor, *Bagpipe*, November 20, 1972, 6.
48 Steve Harris and Del Hampton, "Blacks at Bethel, Part IV, Future Blacks Will Need 'Blackness' at Bethel," *Bethel Clarion*, May 9, 1975, 5.
49 "Minutes of the Ad Hoc Committee on Discrimination," April 24, 1972, Discrimination Committee 1972–1974, XI—2–3.1, Archives of Messiah College.
50 "Minutes of the Messiah College Committee on Discrimination," November 27, 1972, Discrimination Committee 1972–1974, XI—2–3.1, Archives of Messiah College.
51 Cynthia Robinson, letter to the editor, *Bagpipe*, December 8, 1972, 5.
52 Barbara Bowser, "Editorial," *Houghton Star*, March 3, 1978, 2.
53 "Minutes of the Ad Hoc Committee on Discrimination," April 24, 1972, Discrimination Committee 1972–1974, XI—2–3.1, Archives of Messiah College.
54 Ailes, "An Unholy War," 3.
55 Hudson T. Armerding to Donald L. Fay, March 18, 1970, RG-02-005, Box 9, Folder 12, College Archives, Buswell Library, Wheaton College.
56 William Spoelhof memorandum to Dean Vanden Berg, September 27, 1970, Series 2.1.8, Box 230, Folder 6, Heritage Hall, Calvin College Archives.
57 Board of Directors minutes, April 18, 1970, Series 9/1/1, Box 10, F. M. Johnson Archives and Special Collections, Brandel Library, North Park University.
58 Jason Sokol calls this sensibility "the northern mystique." See Sokol, *All Eyes Are upon Us*, ix–xxvi.
59 D. L. Roberts to V. R. Edman, June 16, 1964, RG-02-004, Box 7, Folder 17, College Archives, Buswell Library, Wheaton College.
60 D. Ray Hostetter to various faculty, March 30, 1972, Discrimination Committee 1972–1974, XI—2–3.1, Archives of Messiah College.
61 "Final Report of the Committee on Discrimination in the Area of Race," May 1973, Discrimination Committee 1972–1974, XI—2–3.1, Archives of Messiah College.
62 "Frosh Learn Slave Trade," *Nyack Forum*, September 30, 1968, 3; "Black Students on Black Power," *Nyack Forum*, October 17, 1968, 6.
63 "'Slaves' for Hire," *Intercom*, March 30, 1978.
64 William Culbertson to John R. Rice, June 3, 1970; and John R. Rice to William Culbertson, June 8, 1970, both in President's Collection: Culbertson, Box 1, Folder "Rice: March–November 1970," Crowell Library Archives, Moody Bible Institute (hereafter cited as MBI).
65 "Dull Sword," *Christianity Today*, February 26, 1971, 39.
66 Anonymous letter postmarked December 6, 1970, President's Collection: Culbertson, Box 1, Folder "Rice: December 1970," Crowell Library Archives, MBI.
67 William Culbertson to John R. Rice, December 8, 1970, President's Collection, Culbertson, Box 1, Folder "Rice: December 1970," Crowell Library Archives, MBI.
68 William Culbertson to John R. Rice, unsent letter, December 7, 1970; William Culbertson to John R. Rice, December 8, 1970; handwritten notes on MBI

interoffice memo paper; all in President's Collection: Culbertson, Box 1, Folder "Rice: December 1970," Crowell Library Archives, MBI. Adam Laats suggests Culbertson's decision reflected pressure from core MBI constituencies. In my judgment, given the timing of the respective letters and the contents of Culbertson's handwritten memo, it appears highly likely that the anonymous threat was decisive in Culbertson's calculations. See Laats, *Fundamentalist U*, 239.

69 Numerous letters to Culbertson are found in the Rice folders in Box 1 of the Culbertson collection.
70 William Culbertson to Reverend Menno Harms, January 25, 1971, President's Collection: Culbertson, Box 1, Folder "Rice: January 1971," Crowell Library Archives, MBI.
71 Phyllis Mckoy, "Report on Black Solidarity Day," *Nyack Forum*, February 11, 1971, 4.
72 Memo from President Armerding to Dean of Faculty, March 26, 1970, RG-02-005, Box 9, Folder 12, College Archives, Buswell Library, Wheaton College.
73 Unsigned and undated document, RG-07-001, Box 4, Folder 1, College Archives, Buswell Library, Wheaton College.
74 John Skinner, "Insight on Blackness," *Nyack Forum*, February 17, 1972, 2; February 28, 1972, 2.
75 Ronald Earl Brown, "Blacks Do Not Need Paternalism," *College News*, December 1, 1969, 3; Ronald Earl Brown, "Help Wipe Out Fascist Oppressors," *College News*, September 29, 1969, 2, 5.
76 "This Is Then, That Was Now," fullerstudio.fuller.edu.
77 Pannell, *My Friend, the Enemy*, introduction.
78 Ibid., 120.
79 Ibid., 64–65.
80 Ibid., 66–68, 54.
81 Herbert E. Kyrk, review of *My Friend, the Enemy*, *Evangelical Beacon*, September 24, 1968, 25; *Brethren Missionary Herald*, September 7, 1968, 16; "Annette Griffiths, 'What's Wrong with Whites?'" *Moody Student*, May 8, 1970, 2.
82 Joyce Suber, "Recruitment, Admission, Retention, and Success of Minority Students," February 18, 1981, 4, RG-02-005, Box 31, Folder 19, College Archives, Buswell Library, Wheaton College.
83 Multi-cultural Relations Committee Minutes, May 9, 1983 and November 11, 1983, RG-07-08, Box 27, Folder 4, College Archives, Buswell Library, Wheaton College.
84 Unsigned and undated document circa 1970, Series 9/1/26, Box 8, Folder 5, Committee on Disadvantaged Students 1969–1970, F. M. Johnson Archives and Special Collections, Brandel Library, North Park University.
85 Hudson T. Armerding to Rev. Grover Wilcox, March 12, 1970, RG-02-005, Box 9, Folder 12, College Archives, Buswell Library, Wheaton College.
86 Memo from Alva Steffler to Donald Mitchell, February 1, 1974, RG-03-002, Box 15, Folder 2, College Archives, Buswell Library, Wheaton College.

87 Bud Ipema, "A Profile of the Minority Youth Served by the Christian Reformed Church: Results of a Pre-Conference Questionnaire," 36, C2.1.8, Box 230, Folder 8, Heritage Hall, Calvin College.
88 Unsigned and undated document, RG-07-001, Box 4, Folder 1, College Archives, Buswell Library, Wheaton College.
89 Anthony Diekema, "Race Relations—Which Way?," March 8, 1974, C2.1.8, Box 230, Folder 4, Heritage Hall, Calvin College.
90 William E. Pannell, *"Developing Evangelical Minority Leadership,"* in The Urban Mission, edited by Craig Ellison (Grand Rapids, MI: Eerdmans, 1974), 126.
91 R. Bentley, *Handbook for Black Christian Students*.
92 Ibid., 4–5.
93 Ibid., 37–38.
94 Ibid., 39–43.
95 Steve Harris, "Blacks at Bethel, Part 1, 1969–1971: How Bethel Recruited Black Students," *Bethel Clarion*, March 21, 1975, 4.
96 Steve Harris, "Blacks at Bethel, Part 2, First Bethel Blacks Faced Problems," *Bethel Clarion*, April 11, 1975, 4; Steve Harris and Del Hampton, "Blacks at Bethel, Part IV, Future Blacks Will Need 'Blackness' at Bethel," *Bethel Clarion*, May 9, 1975, 5.
97 "Calvin College Enrollment of Minority Students, 1969–1977," C2.1.8, Box 230, Folder 5; Steven Rhodes and Wilma Knoll to Anthony Diekema, October 9, 1976, C2.1.8, Box 230, Folder 5; Gordon D. Negen to Dean Donald Boender, December 19, 1974; William Spoelhof to Gordon D. Negen, December 17, 1974, C2.1.8, Box 230, Folder 6, Heritage Hall, Calvin College.
98 "An Inventory of Personnel Practices: A Final Report of Component E in the Study of Racism in the Christian Reformed Church," Table Two, February 29, 1972, C2.1.8, Box 230, Folder 4, Heritage Hall, Calvin College; Dawn DeHaan, letter to the editor, *Chimes*, September 23, 1970, 2.
99 "Christian Educators Face the Issues," *Christianity Today*, November 7, 1975, 8–12.
100 Anne Gilliam, "The Black Christian's Purpose: M.C. as a Mission Field," *Ivy Rustles*, October 17, 1973, 2.

3. GROWING THE HOMOGENEOUS CHURCH

1 The obstacles were legion, from differing styles of worship to perennial fears of interracial sex. See, for example, "Interracial Romance: Pastor's Dilemma," *Eternity*, April 1972, 12–13, 33; and Margaret Rowe, "Mom, What Does the Bible Say about Blacks Marrying Whites?," *Eternity*, August 1976, 29–31.
2 Despite the outsize influence of the Church Growth Movement, historians have not paid much attention to it. This began to change with the publication of Melani McAlister's book, *The Kingdom of God Has No Borders*. Though McAlister gives serious attention to the CGM, she conflates its influence with that of Billy Graham–style mass evangelism. This interpretation obscures important differences between Graham and the CGM, most notably in their approach to race and their strategies of evangelization. Other historians have generally ignored not

only the transnational influence of the CGM, but the movement in its entirety. Major recent works on twentieth-century evangelicalism ignore or barely mention the CGM. See, for example, Sutton, *American Apocalypse*; S. Miller, *The Age of Evangelicalism*; and FitzGerald, *The Evangelicals*. An exception is Molly Worthen's study of the battle between reason and revelation in evangelicalism. Worthen frames the CGM as an example of evangelicals' conflicted epistemologies. With respect to race, she argues that it gave evangelical leaders "a framework for coaxing their followers out of old prejudices" but "may have slowed the pace of integration." This seems an overly generous reading of the CGM's record on race. See Worthen, *Apostles of Reason*, 137, 140.

3 McGavran, *Understanding Church Growth*, 198.
4 C. Peter Wagner, "What Makes Churches Grow?," *Eternity*, June 1974, 56.
5 Perkins, *With Justice for All*, 107–108.
6 Hollinger, *Protestants Abroad*. Though Hollinger mostly focuses on liberal Protestants, he does mention McGavran briefly, describing his move "from liberal to conservative missionary theory" as "a striking exception to the general pattern of migration in the opposite direction" (74).
7 For representative contemporary examples, see Lindsell, *Missionary Principles and Practice*; and Maston, *The Bible and Race*, 94–95. Maston wrote, "What is said in North Carolina today is known in Nigeria tomorrow!"
8 Historian Brian Stanley describes the CGM as "possibly the most influential school of thinking in modern evangelical missiology" and argues that it "has shaped a whole family of approaches to evangelistic strategy, both in the western and non-western worlds. . . . Present-day 'seeker services' . . . all evangelistic strategies that pay particular attention to the need to express the gospel in terms of the prevalent cultural assumptions of the hearers can trace their origins to lessons learned outside Europe, usually through the medium of church growth theory." See Stanley, *The Global Diffusion of Evangelicalism*, 23.
9 The Student Volunteer Movement traced its origins back to an 1886 conference backed by the famous evangelist Dwight Moody. For more on the SVM, see Showalter, *The End of a Crusade*.
10 McIntosh, "The Life and Ministry of Donald A. McGavran," 8–15.
11 As Timothy Gloege has argued, both groups were in fact "equally modern." Gloege, *Guaranteed Pure*, 9.
12 McIntosh, *Donald A. McGavran*, 84–87.
13 Donald McGavran, "not sent," December 14, 1968, CN 178, Box 4, Folder 6, BGCA.
14 Though, as Jay Riley Case has pointed out, successful missionaries were often the first to push back against Western paternalism and adopt the cultural practices of the groups they were trying to reach. See Case, *An Unpredictable Gospel*.
15 McPhee, "Bishop J. Waskom Pickett's Rethinking on 1930s Missions in India."
16 Donald McGavran to "Dear Friends," September 6, 1936, CN 178, Box 25, Folder 10, BGCA.

17 Donald McGavran, "Mission Committees & Church Growth," CN 178, Box 25, Folder 9, BGCA.
18 "The Crisis Immediately Confronting Churches and Mission in Mid-India," CN 178, Box 25, Folder 9, BGCA. See also Donald McGavran, "Dear Herb," December 11, 1973, CN 178, Box 4, Folder 9, BGCA. In this letter McGavran describes the mid-1930s as a particularly formative period in the evolution of his thought. See also Pickett, "Donald A. McGavran."
19 Donald McGavran to "Dearest Mither and Gay," February 3, 1954, CN 178, Box 1, Folder 27, BGCA.
20 Donald McGavran to J. Waskom Pickett, March 13, 1954, CN 178, Box 1, Folder 27, BGCA.
21 Donald McGavran to "Dearest Family in India," April 10, 1954, CN 178, Box 1, Folder 27, BGCA.
22 Donald McGavran to "Dear Family," May 12, 1954, CN 178, Box 1, Folder 27, BGCA.
23 Donald McGavran to "Grace and Mother," April 27, 1954, CN 178, Box 1, Folder 27, BGCA.
24 For an overview of the Mau Mau revolt focused on British methods and atrocities, see Elkins, *Imperial Reckoning*. Other scholars describe the Mau Mau conflict as a Kikuyu civil war more than an anticolonial struggle. See Branch, *Defeating Mau Mau, Creating Kenya*.
25 Donald McGavran to Win & Pat, April 18, 1954, CN 178, Box 1, Folder 27, BGCA.
26 On British propaganda and perceptions of Mau Mau, see Lonsdale, "Mau Maus of the Mind," 398; Carruthers, *Winning Hearts and Minds*, 128–193; and Osborne, "'The Rooting Out of Mau Mau.'" On the political uses American conservatives made of Mau Mau, see Curtis, "'Will the Jungle Take Over?'"
27 Donald McGavran to Win & Pat, April 18, 1954, CN 178, Box 1, Folder 27, BGCA.
28 McGavran, *The Bridges of God*.
29 Ibid., 8–10.
30 One of McGavran's students later argued that the CGM could be usefully understood within the framework of modernization theory. See Read, "Church Growth as Modernization."
31 On the imagined midcentury consensus, see Wall, *Inventing the "American Way,"* 2008. For an influential contemporary account of the "American Way of Life" as a unifying national force, see Herberg, *Protestant, Catholic, Jew*.
32 "An Address by Dr. W. A. Criswell, Pastor, First Baptist Church, Dallas, Texas to the Joint Assembly," February 22, 1956, AR 795-221, Box 59, Folder 12, SBHLA.
33 J. P. Kretzmann, review of *Bridges of God*, *Concordia Theological Monthly* 28 (1957): 306–307.
34 Georg F. Vicedom, "Revolution in Missionary Methods," *International Review of Mission* (1956): 331–333.
35 Donald McGavran to Dr. J. Allen Ranck, March 29, 1958, Reviews and Critiques; 1955–1972, CN 178, Box 31, Folder 2, BGCA.

36 *Bridges of God* reviewed by Rev. A. J. Eastman, Missionary in Burma, Reviews and Critiques; 1955–1972, CN 178, Box 31, Folder 2, BGCA.
37 *Bridges of God* reviewed by Rev. B. L. Hinchman, Missionary in Japan, Reviews and Critiques; 1955–1972, CN 178, Box 31, Folder 2, BGCA.
38 General comments on *How Peoples Become Christian*, Reviews and Critiques; 1955–1972, CN 178, Box 31, Folder 2, BGCA. In his effort to quantify the cost of conversion, McGavran echoed the early twentieth-century American fundamentalist Mel Trotter, who calculated that his organization could convert one sinner for every $1.60 it spent. See Abrams, *Selling the Old-Time Religion*, 21.
39 Dr. Kraemer's comments on *The Church in the Ripening World*, ICG—Reviews and Critiques; 1955–1972, CN 178, Box 31, Folder 2, BGCA.
40 James K. Matthews to Donald McGavran, March 19, 1957, Reviews and Critiques; 1955–1972, CN 178, Box 31, Folder 2, BGCA.
41 Kruse, *One Nation under God*, 35–164; Hudnut-Beumler, *Looking for God in the Suburbs*, 29–84.
42 Sernett, *Bound for the Promised Land*; Best, *Passionately Human, No Less Divine*.
43 Mulder, *Shades of White Flight*; Dochuk, "'Praying for a Wicked City.'"
44 Watt, "Fundamentalists of the 1920s and 1930s"; Bendroth, *Fundamentalists in the City*.
45 Pierce, *Polite Protest*, 1–8; Bell, *The Time and Place That Gave Me Life*.
46 Donald McGavran, "A Profitable Next Step in Integration"; Donald McGavran to Ray McCready, January 30, 1977, both in CN 178, Box 5, Folder 55, BGCA.
47 Donald McGavran, "Defeating Segregation within the Congregations," 1958, CN 178, Box 5, Folder 55, BGCA.
48 Ibid.
49 Curtis J. Evans, *The Burden of Black Religion*; Weisenfeld, *Hollywood Be Thy Name*.
50 William J. Petersen, "Evangelicals & the Race Barriers," *Eternity*, September 1963, 12–16, 48.
51 Scott, *Contempt and Pity*.
52 Donald McGavran, "End Segregation in the Churches Now," CN 178, Box 47, Folder 8, BCGA.
53 Compare, for example, to another treatment of the problem of the church in an era of racial change published that same year, Gibson Winter's *The Suburban Captivity of the Churches*. The Episcopal priest and Harvard-trained sociologist proposed a model of "sector ministry" that would involve a pooling of church resources across boundaries of rich and poor, black and white, in the metropolitan area. Winter sought not only a change in consciousness, but also a practical redistribution of resources so that churches might arrest, rather than exacerbate, the growing racial and economic divides in American cities (140–159).
54 Donald McGavran, "End Segregation in the Churches Now," CN 178, Box 47, Folder 8, BCGA.

55 "The Institute of Church Growth" promotional pamphlet, CN 178, Box 27, Folder 3, BGCA.
56 "Foundation Grant," *NCC Bulletin*, January 1965, 2, CN 178, Box 28, Folder 2, BGCA.
57 Wade T. Coggins to Mahlon L. Macy, December 11, 1969; Mahlon L. Macy to Dr. Clyde Taylor, December 9, 1969, both in CN 165, Box 7, Folder 20, BGCA; Donald McGavran to Kenneth Johnston, April 28, 1965, CN 178, Box 27, Folder 10, BGCA.
58 WCC Department of Missionary Studies Statement, "The Growth of the Church," special consultation on church growth, July 31–August 2, 1963, CN 178, Box 28, Folder 1, BGCA.
59 McGavran, *Church Growth and Christian Mission*, 15, 22.
60 Donald McGavran to Wade Coggins, July 13, 1964; Clyde W. Taylor to Donald McGavran, July 23, 1964; Norman Cummings to Clyde W. Taylor, July 29, 1964; Clyde W. Taylor to T. K. Jackson, November 23, 1965, all in CN 165, Box 223, Folder 13, BGCA.
61 Marsden, *Reforming Fundamentalism*; D'Elia, *A Place at the Table*.
62 Clyde W. Taylor to Merrill C. Tenney, April 5, 1965, CN 165, Box 223, Folder 13, BGCA; Clyde W. Taylor to Norman L. Cummings, March 5, 1965, CN 165, Box 9, Folder 34, BGCA.
63 The definition of "church growth" used at Fuller during the 1980s is instructive: "Church growth is that science which investigates the planting, multiplication, function and health of Christian churches as they relate specifically to the effective implantation of God's commission to 'make disciples of all nations' (Matt. 28:19–20). Church growth strives to combine the eternal theological principles of God's Word concerning the expansion of the church with the best insights of contemporary social and behavioral sciences, employing as its initial frame of reference, the foundational work done by Donald McGavran." C. Peter Wagner to Elmer Towns, October 12, 1981, CN 178, Box 81, Folder 2, BGCA.
64 Gloege, *Guaranteed Pure*, 1–9.
65 Donald McGavran, "Advanced Church Growth," Winter 1979, CN 178, Box 31, Folder 3, BGCA.
66 On evangelicals as modernists and adopters of cutting-edge business and marketing strategies, see, in addition to Gloege, Pietsch, *Dispensational Modernism*; Sutton, *Aimee Semple McPherson*; and Cook, *Wanamaker's Temple*.
67 Donald McGavran to Martin Luther King, March 14, 1965, CN 178, Box 4, Folder 2, BGCA.
68 Donald McGavran to Martin Luther King, April 7, 1964, CN 178, Box 3, Folder 8, BGCA.
69 Donald McGavran to the Mayor of Grenada, MS, September 22, 1966, CN 178, Box 4, Folder 4, BGCA.
70 He even appears to have been friends with Allan Knight Chalmers, the president of the NAACP Legal Defense Fund. Allan Knight Chalmers to Donald McGavran, June 17, 1963, CN 178, Box 5, Folder 3, BGCA.

71 By 1970, in the face of rising crime rates and the militant protest tactics of antiwar and leftist groups, McGavran joined the law and order chorus. He wrote, "We are now reaping the bitter fruit of defining civil liberty in ways which permit tiny, well-organized minorities of extremists to tyrannize huge good-natured and bill-paying majorities. This must cease." Donald McGavran to Mr. Abernathy and Br. Brokaw, March 1, 1970, CN 178, Box 4, Folder 8, BGCA.
72 Donald McGavran, "The Entrepreneur in Modern Missions," January 5, 1979, CN 178, Box 31, Folder 3, BGCA; Donald McGavran, "Two Theologies of Mission Battle for Control," *Church Herald*, November 28, 1975, 10–12. See also Donald McGavran, "Will Uppsala Betray the Two Billion?," *Church Growth Bulletin*, May 1968, 1–6.
73 Donald McGavran, "not sent," December 14, 1968, CN 178, Box 4, Folder 6, BGCA.
74 Donald McGavran, "Two Theologies of Mission Battle for Control," *Church Herald*, November 28, 1975, 10–12.
75 WASPs are white Anglo-Saxon Protestants. Glazer and Moynihan, *Beyond the Melting Pot*; Novak, *The Rise of the Unmeltable Ethnics*. I rely here on Jacobson, *Roots Too*.
76 Quoted in Wagner, *Your Church Can Grow*, 15–16.
77 Donald McGavran to Cal Guy, October 10, 1969, CN 178, Box 4, Folder 7, BGCA.
78 "The Shepherd Role and Soul Winning in Texas," March 8, 1963, CN 178, Box 32, Folder 3, BGCA.
79 M. Wendell Belew, "Church Growth," 1978, AR 631-10, Box 44, Folder 17, SBHLA.
80 Quoted in David T. Britt, "Concepts of Church Growth in the Southern Baptist Convention," Research Division, June 1980, AR 631-10, Box 46, Folder 18, SBHLA. Major Southern Baptist church growth books of the era include Dubose, *How Churches Grow in an Urban World*; Chaney and Lewis, *Design for Church Growth*; and Hogue, *I Want My Church to Grow*.
81 Orrin D. Morris, "Comparison of Racial Ethnic Change to SBC Growth By States, 1970–1980," July 1981, 19, AR 631-10, Box 46, Folder 17, SBHLA.
82 Donald McGavran to Cal Guy, October 10, 1969, CN 178, Box 4, Folder 7, BGCA.
83 For contemporary examples, see Strong, *Our Country*; and Clark, *Leavening the Nation*, 262–282. As one historian has described Southern Baptist Home Missions' efforts in this period, "For immigrants, conversion was a call to become not only a Christian but an American as well." This would supposedly have the additional benefit of dispelling the attraction of radical political ideologies. See Harper, *The Quality of Mercy*, 23–24. Another historian wrote, "Home mission workers were agents of Christ, but they were also protectors of the state. 'The home mission problem . . . [was] to American and Christianize' immigrants, and frequently in that order." McDowell, *The Social Gospel in the South*, 69. For a broad overview of the Protestant encounter with immigration, see Davis, *Immigrants, Baptists, and the Protestant Mind in America*. See also Chang, *Citizens of a Christian Nation*; and Teasdale, *Methodist Evangelism, American Salvation*, 88–126.

84 The CGM's rise to prominence in the 1970s does suggest, however, an echo of the earlier period. Immigration led to anxious efforts to convert the immigrant masses, efforts that lost their urgency at midcentury as American society became more homogeneous. The CGM gained prominence as Americans took note of a new era of immigrant-led diversity after the Hart-Cellar Act of 1965 removed some of the most onerous restrictions of the 1924 Johnson-Reed Act. Though CGM leaders did not speak in the hysterical tones of racial panic and nation-building of the earlier era, they did stress the need to reach these new immigrant groups.
85 "Testimony: C. Peter Wagner," CN 178, Box 34, Folder 3, BGCA.
86 Waymire and Wagner, *The Church Growth Survey Handbook*.
87 Quoted in Orjala, *Get Ready to Grow*, 23.
88 Raymond W. Hurn, "Nazarenes . . . Is the Third Wave of a Religious Movement Commencing?," July 27, 1981, CN 178, Box 85, Folder 2, BGCA.
89 C. Peter Wagner, foreword to Schuller, *Your Church Has Real Possibilities*.
90 This description is found on the back cover of the paperback edition of Schuller, *Your Church Has Real Possibilities*.
91 Consumption—religious and otherwise—increasingly ordered Americans' lives and identities in the second half of the twentieth century. See Cohen, *A Consumer's Republic*; Moreton, *To Serve God and Walmart*; and Lofton, *Oprah*. For an evangelical critique of the nexus of consumerism and evangelicalism, and the Church Growth Movement that fostered it, see Metzger, *Consuming Jesus*. On Schuller, see Gerardo Martí and Mark T. Mulder, "Capital and Cathedral: Robert H. Schuller's Continual Fundraising for Church Growth," *Religion and American Culture: A Journal of Interpretation* 30 (2020): 63–107.
92 As Daniel Vaca notes, the CGM participated in and helped to propel the use of market segmentation practices in evangelicalism. See Vaca, *Evangelicals Incorporated*, 193–198.
93 "Revalidating the Homogeneous Principle," *Church Growth America*, Summer 1977, 2, AR 631-10, Box 15, Folder 10, SBHLA.
94 Win Arn, "The Pastor and Church Growth," *Church Growth America*, September–October 1977, 4, AR 631-10, Box 15, Folder 10, SBHLA.
95 "Wheat Graduate School Church Growth Seminar Final Exam," August 11, 1972, CN 165, Box 8, Folder 39, BGCA.
96 Wagner, *Your Church Can Grow*, 124–134.
97 Paul D. Simmons, "The Pastor as Change Agent," Churches in Racially Changing Communities Conference, April 23–25, 1979, AR 631-10, Box 18, Folder 15, SBHLA.
98 Since Yoder's death in 1997, his legacy has been the subject of significant reappraisal. For decades, Yoder sexually and spiritually abused dozens of women. Yet during this period, he influenced a generation of evangelicals with his writings on pacifism and other topics, and he was one of the most vocal critics of the Church Growth Movement. See especially Goossen, "'Defanging the Beast.'"

99 Yoder, "Church Growth Issues in Theological Perspective," 29.
100 Ibid., 35–38.
101 Ibid., 43–44.
102 "Four Spokesmen Answer Wagner," *Eternity*, September 1972, 18–19, 60.
103 Donald L. Robert, "The Meteoric Rise of the First Church of the American Dream," *Eternity*, June 1976, 24–26.
104 For more on Perkins's criticisms of the CGM, see chapters 5 and 6.
105 "Should the Church Be a Melting Pot? An Interview with C. Peter Wagner and Ray Stedman," *Christianity Today*, August 18, 1978, 13.
106 McGavran, *Understanding Church Growth*, 198.
107 Donald McGavran, "The Genesis and Strategy of the Homogeneous Unit Principle," CN 46, Box 13, Folder 24, BGCA.
108 The use of the word "mongrel" or "mongrelized" was such a staple of white supremacist rhetoric that it seems incredible that McGavran could be unaware of its connotations. One example will suffice. Amid the tumult of 1968, the Southern Baptist evangelist Vance Havner complained that Christians were living in "a day of unholy mixtures." Churches, religions, nations, even races—all seemed to be mixing, and this "opens the door to mongrelization." As in the days of Noah, the terrible judgment of God surely was not long in coming, he warned. Vance Havner, "As It Was . . . So Shall It Be," *King's Business*, May 1968, 11–13.
109 Robert T. Coote, "Church Growth: Shot in the Arm for Evangelism," *Evangelical Newsletter*, 1975, CN 338, Box 35, Folder 14, BGCA.

4. A MISSION FIELD NEXT DOOR

1 Bill Allen, "Messiah's Atmosphere: Springboard for the Good Life," *Ivy Rustles*, March 2, 1960, 3; Donald Keener, untitled editorial, *Ivy Rustles*, September 9, 1966, 2; D. Ray Hostetter, "Study Prospectus for a Messiah College Urban Center or College," October 10, 1967, Box XI 2-7.1, Messiah College Board of Trustees, Messiah-Temple Campus, Archives of Messiah College.
2 Dwight McMurrin, "The American Scene," *Glimmerglass*, April 19, 1963, 3.
3 "We Are Sick," *Christianity Today*, September 29, 1967, 34.
4 For a contemporary evangelical perspective on this point, see McKenna, *The Urban Crisis*.
5 See, for example, Mulder, *Shades of White Flight*; Dochuk, "'Praying for a Wicked City'"; and Conn, *The American City and the Evangelical Church*.
6 "Love with Skin on It," *Christianity Today*, December 19, 1969, 23.
7 Swartz, *Moral Minority*. See also Gasaway, *Progressive Evangelicals*.
8 David Swartz has attributed the decline of the evangelical left in the later 1970s to identity politics splintering the nascent coalition, but the Messiah College story reveals a more basic dilemma for left-leaning evangelicals like Dr. Sider: the more they pushed an antiracist agenda, the harder it became to stay connected to the crucial resources, institutions, and constituencies of the evangelical mainstream. Historians are right to note that the fractiousness of the evangelical left contrib-

uted to its decline, but equally important was its marginality from the power centers of evangelicalism.
9. On the Brethren in Christ becoming more like other evangelicals, see Manzullo-Thomas, "Born-Again Brethren in Christ."
10. On the early history of Anabaptists as a radical sect in Reformation-era Europe, see Goertz, *The Anabaptists*.
11. V. Raymond Edman, undated letter, RG-02-004, Box 3, Folder "communism," Wheaton College Archives.
12. "The 'Satellite' Campus: A Unique Program for College Education in the United States," Box XI—2-7.1, Messiah College Board of Trustees, Messiah-Temple Campus; Hostetter, "Study Prospectus for a Messiah College Urban Center or College."
13. Fred Bonaparte, "Epileptic Cripple Has Fit during Alleged Theft and Is Slain by Cop," *Philadelphia Tribune*, October 29, 1963, 1; "Tourigian Back on Duty in Police Radio Room," *Philadelphia Inquirer*, December 15, 1963, 33; Art Peters, "North Phila. Tension Seethes in Wake of Youth's Shooting," *Philadelphia Tribune*, October 29, 1963; Chris J. Perry, "False Killing Rumor Triggered Riot," *Philadelphia Tribune*, September 1, 1964, 1; Countryman, *Up South*, 154–164.
14. "The 'Satellite' Campus"; Hostetter, "Study Prospectus for a Messiah College Urban Center or College."
15. "The 'Satellite' Campus."
16. Philadelphia Faculty Minutes, September 25, 1970, Box T-13, Faculty Meeting, Archives of Messiah College. At the time of my visit to the Messiah College Archives, archival material from the Philadelphia campus was housed in large temporary boxes awaiting more systematic cataloguing after the 2014 closure of the Philadelphia Campus. I cite the temporary box number in the hope that future researchers will be able to trace the materials if they have been moved.
17. Floyd Stoner and Paul Heisey, "Cultural Virginity Undone," *Ivy Rustles*, October 3, 1968, 1.
18. E.A.P., editorial, *Ivy Rustles*, February 20, 1969, 2. See also Paul Heisey and Floyd Stoner, "Repentance Attempted," *Ivy Rustles*, October 31, 1968, 1, 4.
19. "Messiah College Philadelphia Campus Enrollment," Box T-13, Folder "Advisory Board: Davis' Oral Reports," Archives of Messiah College.
20. Marian Landis, "Come to Temple," *Ivy Rustles*, November 29, 1971, 3.
21. Ronald Sider, "Christian Cluster Colleges—Off to a Good Start," *Christianity Today*, May 24, 1974, 12–15.
22. Box T-11, Folder "Phila Campus Correspondence about This Model," Archives of Messiah College.
23. Linda Uhsemann, "Experiences in Newark," *Forum*, October 13, 1972, 1, 7; "Urban Field College Program," *Barringtonian*, May 1968, 1; "Barrington Urban Field College," *Barrington College Bulletin*, October 1971; "Newark Adventure for B.C. Students," *Barringtonian*, January 8, 1971, 1. For background on Bill Iverson, see Glenn Kittler, "Side Order of Love Reaches Teen-agers," *Lenten*

Guideposts, 1968. This syndicated column appeared in *Simpson's Leader-Times*, April 11, 1968, 4.
24 P. Reilly, "Inner-City Worker Iverson to Be Here," *Bagpipe*, November 17, 1970, 1.
25 Eunice and Donald Schatz and Lucille Dayton, "The Urban Life Center," in *The Urban Mission*, edited by Craig Ellison (Grand Rapids, MI: Eerdmans, 1974), 100–101.
26 Ronald M. Enroth, "The Westmont Urban Semester," in ibid., 109.
27 Philadelphia Campus Faculty Minutes, September 27, 1972, Box XI—4-1.5 Faculty Minutes (1968–1973), Folder "Faculty Minutes 1972–1973," Archives of Messiah College.
28 D. Ray Hostetter to James Dove and Tony Bryant, February 6, 1973, Box XI—4-1.5 Faculty Minutes (1968–1973), Folder "Faculty Minutes 1972–1973," Archives of Messiah College.
29 Minutes of Faculty Meeting, January 29, 1973; Minutes of Special Faculty Meeting, January 31, 1973; Minutes of Faculty Meeting, February 5, 1973, all in Box XI—4-1.5 Faculty Minutes (1968–1973), Folder "Faculty Minutes 1972–1973," Archives of Messiah College; Jacqueline Gibson, "B.S.U. Silent Minority Becomes Loud," *Ivy Rustles*, February 16, 1972.
30 Ronald J. Sider, "The Messiah Urban Satellite Campus," in *The Urban Mission*, edited by Craig Ellison (Grand Rapids, MI: Eerdmans, 1974), 93.
31 Quoted in Gasaway, *Progressive Evangelicals*, 78.
32 Messiah College Interoffice Correspondence, Merle Brubaker to Ray Zercher, June 24, 1972, Box T-13, Folder Summer-1972, Archives of Messiah College.
33 "Summer of 72," Box T-11, Folder "Summer Seminar—Advertising," Archives of Messiah College
34 "Models of Christian Ministry in the City—Mid-term Exam," Box T-13, Folder "Summer—1972," Archives of Messiah College.
35 President Johnson established the Kerner Commission to explore the roots of the 1967 urban uprisings. The commission's report famously declared, "What white Americans have never fully understood—but what the Negro can never forget—is that the white society is deeply implicated in the ghetto. White institutions created it, white institutions maintain it, and white society condones it." See McLaughlin, *The Long, Hot Summer of 1967*; and Hrach, *The Riot Report and the News*.
36 Ronald J. Sider to Rev. Robert Reasey, October 11, 1973; Ronald J. Sider to President Hostetter, October 1, 1973, both in Box T-13, Folder "Correspondence—Ronald J. Sider Phila. Campus 1973–1974," Archives of Messiah College.
37 Sider, "The Messiah Urban Satellite Campus," 94.
38 "A Seminar on Urban Problems," Box XI—2-7.1, Messiah College Board of Trustees, Messiah-Temple Campus.
39 Ronald J. Sider, "Does the Bible Teach the Equality of All Men? (Part II)," *Ivy Rustles*, November 21, 1972, 10–11.
40 Samuel Magesa, "Intercultural Experience," *Ivy Rustles*, November 21, 1972, 10.

41 Merle Brubaker, review of the Freshmen Weekend Seminars, Fall Semester, 1973, Box T-13, Folder "Freshman Weekend," Archives of Messiah College.
42 Minutes, Messiah College Philadelphia Faculty Meeting, December 4, 1973, Box T-13, Folder "Freshman Weekend," Archives of Messiah College.
43 Pam Bender, "Freshman Experience," *Ivy Rustles*, December 5, 1973, 10.
44 James W. Skillen to Ronald J. Sider, May 23, 1974; Ronald J. Sider to James W. Skillen, July 8, 1974, both in Box T-13, Folder "Correspondence—Ronald J. Sider Phila. Campus 1973–1974," Archives of Messiah College.
45 On the 1973 Chicago Declaration, see Sider, *The Chicago Declaration*; Swartz, *Moral Minority*, 170–184; and Gasaway, *Progressive Evangelicals*, 47–51.
46 Debbie Heacock, "The Summer of '71," *Ivy Rustles*, October 6, 1971, 4.
47 Enroth, "The Westmont Urban Semester," 111.
48 Uhsemann, "Experiences in Newark," 7.
49 Bill Iverson, letter to the editor, *Forum*, February 16, 1973.
50 Jan Whitworth, "Messiah at Temple in Philadelphia," *Ivy Rustles*, November 2, 1971, 4.
51 Randy Rhoad, untitled article, *Ivy Rustles*, December 20, 1977, 8.
52 "For 1973 Summer Seminar"; "Seminars on Urban Problems," Box T-13, Folder "Summer 1972," Archives of Messiah College.
53 "You Are Messiah College," *Ivy Rustles*, April 16, 1974, 10–11; Magesa, "Intercultural Experience," *Ivy Rustles*, November 21, 1972, 10.
54 Jay C. Basler, Director of Student Development, Campus at Philadelphia, Annual Report, 1973–1974, Box XI—14-7.1 General Files, Annual Reports: St. Dev. Archives of Messiah College.
55 McMurrin, "The American Scene," *Glimmerglass*, April 19, 1963, 3; Enroth, "The Westmont Urban Semester," 109.
56 Skinner, *Black and Free*, 54–65. In the retelling, this figure was sometimes inflated to 27.
57 An early *New York Times* account quotes Skinner saying he was converted in 1956, and *Christianity Today* also dated his conversion to "Columbus Day in 1956." This would have made him 14 years of age when he turned his back on gang life. His ministry's "Up from Harlem" comic later claimed he was 14 when he joined the Harlem Lords. McCandlish Phillips, "Evangelist Finds Harlem Vineyard: Son of Pastor Denounces Sin at Series of Rallies," *New York Times*, August 16, 1964, 78; "The Gospel with Candor," *Christianity Today*, October 14, 1966, 53–54.
58 In private, Jones wrote that he deliberately kept his distance from Skinner, in part because "I have not been able to accept the exaggerated version of his testimony concerning his conversion as a former gang leader in Harlem." Howard Jones to Walter Smyth, February 24, 1968, CN 17, Box 80, Folder 34, BGCA. For more on Skinner's conversion and relationship to white evangelicals, see Swartz, Moral Minority, 33–37; and Griffith, God's Law and Order, 76–77, 82–83, 90–92.

59 Skinner's ministry produced a colorful autobiographical comic book titled "Up from Harlem." Skinner, *Up from Harlem*.
60 Said one reviewer of Skinner's first book, "The power of the gospel was never more clearly seen than in this amazing transformation." David R. Enlow, "New Insights on the Race Problem," *Alliance Witness*, November 6, 1968, 10.
61 "What Will You Contribute?," *Moody Student*, March 25, 1970, 2.
62 "The Gospel with Candor."
63 One advertisement for Skinner's ministry featured a young black man behind prison bars. Beneath this striking image was a photo of Skinner himself. "Not everyone can reach him," the ad declared. "But this man can." *Eternity*, July 1978, 7.
64 "Summer of Racial Discontent," *Christianity Today*, July 21, 1967, 27.
65 "A Crippled People Cry Out!" blared an ad for Skinner's ministry in *Eternity* magazine. The ad promised "CRUSADES in black communities, penetrating to the back alleys." *Eternity*, June 1970, 1.
66 Tom Skinner, "Evangelicals and the Black Revolution," *Christianity Today*, April 10, 1970, 10–15.
67 Skinner, *Black and Free*, 45–53.
68 Ibid., 32.
69 "The Gospel with Candor." As Skinner's views evolved and he began to place more emphasis on social concern, he became too controversial for some white evangelicals. In 1971 Moody Radio took Skinner's show off the air. Norman B. Rohrer, "1971 Religion in Review," *Wesleyan Advocate*, January 10, 1972, 12.
70 Skinner, "Evangelicals and the Black Revolution," 10–15.
71 Skinner, "The U.S. Racial Crisis and World Evangelism."
72 "Inter Varsity Convention," *Ivy Rustles*, January 20, 1971, 3.
73 "A Statement Concerning the Crisis in Our Nation," June 5, 1968, AR 795-221, Box 59, Folder 31, SBHLA; draft of "A Statement Concerning the Crisis in Our Nation," May 1968, AR 631-3, Box 26, Folder 8, SBHLA.
74 "The Crisis in the Nation," *Covenanter Witness*, May 29, 1968, 344, 352.
75 Philip Leung, "Summary of Tentative Report of 'Churches in Transitional Areas' Study," September 1969, AR 631-3, Box 26, Folder 7, SBHLA.
76 Frank George, letter to the editor, *Campus Life*, May 1969, 16.
77 "By Their Fruits Shall Ye Know Them," *Chimes*, October 3, 1969, 5–6.
78 C. W. Scudder, "Southern Baptists and Changing Racial Patterns," February 14, 1966, AR 627-1, Box 2, Folder 26, SBHLA.
79 "Dialogue with Home Mission Board Staff and Negro Pastors," February 13, 1969, M, AR 631-10, Box 24, Folder 8, SBHLA.
80 Thomas Byron, "ICCA Report," January 27, 1965; "Christian Service Council Ministries" pamphlet, both in RG-02-005, Box 15, Folder "Christian Service Council 1964–1965," College Archives, Buswell Library, Wheaton College.
81 "Rescue Is Still Aim of City Missions," *Moody Student*, November 12, 1971, 3.
82 "Tares among the Social Wheat," *Moody Student*, May 12, 1967, 3.

83 The parable of the wheat and tares is found in Matthew 13:24–30.
84 Dean Berto, "Pinkerton Men Patrol Campus, Providing Security for Campus," *Moody Student*, February 25, 1966, 5.
85 Carol Stine and Rachel Goecking, "Can We Be More Effective?," *Moody Student*, May 24, 1968, 2.
86 "An Urban Anachronism—Fourth Pres," *Moody Student*, March 14, 1969, 3; Gary Havens, "Should We Overlook Our Own Neighbors?," *Moody Student*, May 21, 1965, 2; Denny Hollinger, "Small Town versus Chicago," *Moody Student*, November 1, 1968, 2.
87 "Buffalo Suburban Campus Report," September 25, 1981, Box 96-16, Folder "Buffalo Campus Development," Houghton College Archives.
88 "Buffalo Campus: The Shape of Things to Come," Box 93-9, Folder "1969–1968," Houghton College Archives.
89 "Houghton College—a Developing Institution (Institutional Narrative)," 3, Box 93-9, Folder "1970–1980," Houghton College Archives.
90 Wilber T. Dayton to Willa B. Player, July 31, 1974, Box 93-9, Folder "1970–1980," Houghton College Archives.
91 "Houghton College—a Developing Institution (Institutional Narrative)."
92 J. Craig Henry, "What Good Can Come out of Cleveland?" *Houghton Star*, February 1986, 2.
93 Henry Renn, "You Can Survive City Life!" *Ivy Rustles*, March 12, 1973, 14.
94 Kathy Brode, "The City," *Ivy Rustles*, December 13, 1976, 7; Chuck Burkett, "The Campus," *Ivy Rustles*, December 13, 1976, 6.
95 Debbie Houghton, "The New Cross-Cultural Courses," *Ivy Rustles*, February 19, 1974, 3.
96 Sider, "The Messiah Urban Satellite Campus," 99.
97 "1976 Evaluation of Philadelphia Campus of Messiah College at Temple University," Box XI—2-7.1 Messiah College Board of Trustees, Messiah-Temple Campus, Archives of Messiah College.
98 Susan Fredericks, "Social Work at the Center of God's Will," *Swinging Bridge*, January 28, 1993, 5.
99 Brent Fulton, "Philly Campus Celebrates!," *Swinging Bridge*, October 28, 1984, 1, 5; Sarah Wendell, "Plusses of Phila. Campus Not Threatened," *Swinging Bridge*, September 22, 1988, 4; Kristin A. Johnson, "Changes at Philadelphia Campus Support New Outward Focus," *Swinging Bridge*, November 16, 1989, 2.
100 Kim Barge, "J-Term in Philly Offers Rewarding Experiences," *Swinging Bridge*, March 26, 1987, 2.
101 Martha MacDonald, "Students Express Concern about Philly Safety," *Swinging Bridge*, April 9, 1987, 1.
102 Ibid.
103 Melanie Corey, "How Safe Is Philly Campus?," *Swinging Bridge*, October 3, 1991, 3; Amy Blough, "To Philly or Not to Philly," *Swinging Bridge*, September 24,

1992, 3; Michelle Camp, "New Faces on Broad Street," *Swinging Bridge*, February 6, 1992, 3.

104 Howard Tripp, "Healing the Inner City," *Swinging Bridge*, February 12, 1993, 5.

5. TWO GOSPELS ON A GLOBAL STAGE

1 C. René Padilla, "Evangelization and the World," CN 46, Box 26, Folder 20, BGCA.

2 In tracing this trajectory from Lausanne, I seek to complement, not overturn, David Kirkpatrick's excellent study of the rise of Latin American evangelical social Christianity and its growing influence around the world. The American story told here, set against the backdrop of Kirkpatrick's global story, highlights the multiple and contested trajectories of a diverse Lausanne movement. Kirkpatrick, *A Gospel for the Poor*.

3 On the genealogies of liberation theology in the United States and Latin America, see Barger, *The World Come of Age*. The most extensive account of the influence of liberation theology on Latin American evangelicals is found in Kirkpatrick, *A Gospel for the Poor*. For black evangelical engagement with liberation theology, see W. Bentley, "Factors in the Origin," 313–318.

4 Noll, *Turning Points*, 287–306. See also Swartz, *Moral Minority*, 113–134; Stanley, *The Global Diffusion of Evangelicalism*, 151–179; Dochuk, "Lausanne '74 and American Evangelicalism's Latin Turn"; and McAlister, "The Global Conscience of American Evangelicalism." For an admiring account from a Church Growth Movement activist that places the movement at the center of Lausanne, see McIntosh, *Donald A. McGavran*. Brian Stanley describes Lausanne as the moment American evangelicals reckoned with evangelicalism as a "multicultural global community." Dochuk, Swartz, and Kirkpatrick emphasize the decisive influence of social justice–oriented Latin American evangelicals at Lausanne. McAlister has perceptively argued that Lausanne had a contested legacy, with multiple actors claiming victory. The Latin Americans could point to the strong social justice plank the Congress produced; the Americans could point to the strong emphasis on evangelizing unreached people groups. Lausanne was all those things at once. But to a much greater extent than historians have appreciated, all these features of Lausanne were directly connected to the ideas of the Church Growth Movement.

5 Lausanne stood in stark contrast to the last major evangelical congress at Berlin in 1966, where white American men alone planned the proceedings. Social action was not high on their agenda. Kirkpatrick, *A Gospel for the Poor*, 8–9.

6 Brian Stanley allows that Lausanne "deserves to be remembered . . . as the occasion at which the single-minded emphasis of Donald McGavran and Ralph Winter . . . on the need to remember the 'unreached peoples' of the world first imprinted itself indelibly on the global evangelical conscience. Nonetheless," he continues, "the question of the relationship of social justice to Christian

mission was the dimension that attracted most press comment and provoked the most vigorous debates among participants." This dichotomous framing does not account for the ways the question of unreached peoples and the question of social justice were directly linked together, with the CGM thought at the center of both themes. Many participants saw these questions as two components of the same debate rather than separate issues. See Stanley, *The Global Diffusion of Evangelicalism*, 165. Similarly, Melani McAlister has framed Lausanne as a debate between Graham's "evangelism-first" approach and Latin Americans' "social concern." This interpretation misses the point that what Latin American leaders most objected to was not Graham's crusade evangelism as such but the implications the CGM's strategies had for the nature of the gospel and the unity of the church. See McAlister, "The Global Conscience of American Evangelicalism," 1197–1199.

7 Donald McGavran to Donald E. Hoke, February 5, 1973, CN 358, Box 10, Folder 3, BGCA.
8 Leighton Ford, "International Congress on World Evangelization Report by Leighton Ford," November 1974, CN 46, Box 35, Folder 3, BGCA; Billy Graham, "Why Lausanne?," CN 46, Box 26, Folder 20, BGCA; McAlister, "The Global Conscience of American Evangelicalism," 1205.
9 Stanley, *The Global Diffusion of Evangelicalism*, 165.
10 On the social gospel, see Christopher H. Evans, *The Social Gospel in American Religion*.
11 Graham, "Why Lausanne?"
12 Donald McGavran, "The Vast Dimensions of World Evangelization," CN 46, Box 26, Folder 20, BGCA.
13 Ibid.
14 On C. René Padilla, see Dochuk, "Lausanne '74 and American Evangelicalism's Latin Turn," 257–281; Swartz, *Moral Minority*, 118–125; Kirkpatrick, "C. René Padilla"; and Kirkpatrick, *A Gospel for the Poor*.
15 Stanley, *The Global Diffusion of Evangelicalism*, 165.
16 Padilla quoted the scriptures as follows: "Here there cannot be Greek and Jews, circumcised and uncircumcised, barbarian, Scythian, slave, free men, but Christ is all, and in all" (Colossians 3:11). "There is neither Jew nor Greek, there is neither slave nor free, there is neither male nor female; for you are all one in Christ Jesus" (Galatians 3:28).
17 Padilla, "Evangelization and the World," CN 46, Box 26, Folder 20, BGCA.
18 Ibid.
19 On Escobar, see Kirkpatrick, *A Gospel for the Poor*; and Swartz, *Moral Minority*, 113–134.
20 This is a paraphrase of Matthew 23:15. The subject of Jesus's wrath is usually rendered "scribes and pharisees," but Escobar changed it to "evangelists." Samuel Escobar, "Evangelization and Man's Search for Freedom, Justice, and Fulfillment," CN 46, Box 26, Folder 20, BGCA.

21 Kirkpatrick, *A Gospel for the Poor*, 154. I am indebted to David Kirkpatrick for sharing with me a copy of the letter from McGavran to Padilla, dated May 24, 1971, that is in his possession.
22 C. Peter Wagner's handwritten notes on Lausanne, CN 358, Box 4, Folder 9, BGCA.
23 On Winter's enduring influence, see Dochuk, "Lausanne '74 and American Evangelicalism's Latin Turn," 247–248; and McAlister, "The Global Conscience of American Evangelicalism," 1204–1209.
24 Ralph Winter, "The Highest Priority: Cross-Cultural Evangelism," CN 46, Box 26, Folder 20, BGCA.
25 Ibid.
26 "An Address by Dr. W. A. Criswell, Pastor, First Baptist Church, Dallas, Texas to the Joint Assembly," February 22, 1956, AR 795-221, Box 59, Folder 12, SBHLA.
27 Wagner, *Church Growth and the Whole Gospel*, 169.
28 This was the very church Wagner faulted for mixing with Zion Evangelical Free Church in his 1976 "autopsy" of a "dead" church. Wagner, *Your Church Can Grow*, 124–134.
29 For these and many other details of Hilliard's life, I am indebted to Soong-Chan Rah, an evangelical theologian at North Park University, who has done more than anyone to recover the overlooked story of Hilliard's career. To date, Rah's most extensive treatment of Hilliard is found in his dissertation. See Rah, "In Whose Image," 254–286.
30 Clarence Hilliard, "Urban Evangelization among the Poor," in Douglas, *Let the Earth Hear His Voice*, 920–922.
31 On American efforts to influence the Latin American Theological Fraternity and Wagner's history of clashes with Padilla, see Kirkpatrick, *A Gospel for the Poor*, 75–87. On the Radical Discipleship Group, see ibid., 23–27.
32 Stanley, *The Global Diffusion of Evangelicalism*, 173.
33 C. Peter Wagner's handwritten notes on Lausanne, CN 358, Box 4, Folder 9, BGCA.
34 "Theology Implications of Radical Discipleship," in Douglas, *Let the Earth Hear His Voice*, 1294–1296. On the drafting of the Covenant and Stott's crucial role, see Stanley, *The Global Diffusion of Evangelicalism*, 169–173.
35 Clarence Hilliard, "Open Letter to the Committee on the Lausanne Covenant," October 7, 1974, CN 590, Box 1, Folder 4.1, BGCA.
36 John Stott to Clarence Hilliard, November 14, 1974; Donald E. Hoke to Clarence Hilliard, October 23, 1974, both in CN 590, Box 1, Folder 4.1, BGCA.
37 Russell Chandler, "Evangelical Protestants Organize," *Washington Post*, July 26, 1974, D14; William J. Petersen, "Lausanne: Third World Speaks Out," *Eternity*, September 1974, 12.
38 "Continuation Committee Set Up," October 24, 1974, CN 358, Box 10, Folder 9, BGCA; A. Jack Dain to C. Peter Wagner, October 28, 1974, CN 358, Box 4, Folder 9, BGCA.

39. Samuel Escobar to A. Jack Dain, October 10, 1974, CN 46, Box 30, Folder 5, BGCA.
40. A. Jack Dain to Samuel Escobar, March 17, 1975, CN 46, Box 30, Folder 5, BGCA.
41. C. Peter Wagner, "Lausanne Twelve Months Later," *Christianity Today*, July 4, 1975, 7–9. This emphasis aligned with Billy Graham's wishes but was troubling to John Stott. See Kirkpatrick, *A Gospel for the Poor*, 128–130.
42. Samuel Escobar to A. Jack Dain, July 29, 1975, CN 46, Box 30, Folder 5, BGCA.
43. C. René Padilla, "Christianity American-Style," *Christianity Today*, October 10, 1975, 73–74.
44. Luke 4:18–19. Hilliard quoted the Revised Standard Version (RSV), used here.
45. See 1 Corinthians 1:18–31, RSV.
46. Clarence Hilliard, "How Black Is Our Valley," *The Other Side*, March 1984, 24–26 (originally published December 1976).
47. Clarence Hilliard, "Down with the Honky Christ—Up with the Funky Jesus," *Christianity Today*, January 30, 1976, 6–8.
48. Ibid.
49. Hilliard, "How Black Is Our Valley," 24–26.
50. Cone, *The Cross and the Lynching Tree*. Long before James Cone wrote *Black Theology and Black Power*, W. E. B. Du Bois, among others, anticipated these themes with stories featuring a counterculturual black Christ, most notably "The Riddle of the Sphinx" and "Jesus Christ in Texas." See Blum, *W. E. B. Du Bois*.
51. "Christ Recrucified" first appeared in *Kelley's Magazine*, October 1922, 13. See Rice, *Witnessing Lynching*, 220–222.
52. Hilliard, "How Black Is Our Valley," 26.
53. A version of the story appears in each of the synoptic gospels. See Matthew 19:16–30, Mark 10:17–31, and Luke 18:18–30.
54. Hilliard, "Down with the Honky Christ," 6–8.
55. Quoted in Cone, *The Cross and the Lynching Tree*, 132. On Moody and Wells, see Blum, Reforging the White Republic, 120–145.
56. "Eutychus and His Kin," *Christianity Today*, March 12, 1976, 30.
57. I rely here on Rah, "In Whose Image," 264–275.
58. Leighton Ford form letter, October 11, 1976, CN 358, Box 3, Folder 5, BGCA.
59. Memorandum from John Stott, "Lausanne Theology and Education Group Consultation on the Homogeneous Unit Principle," CN 46, Box 13, Folder 23, BGCA.
60. "Consultation on the Homogeneous Unit Principle Second memo to participants from John Stott," March 8, 1977, CN 46, Box 4, Folder 19, BGCA.
61. "The Homogeneous Unit Principle: Definition and Clarification," CN 46, Box 13, Folder 23, BGCA.
62. C. Peter Wagner, "How Ethical Is The Homogeneous Unit Principle?," CN 46, Box 13, Folder 24, BGCA.
63. Donald McGavran, "The Genesis and Strategy of the Homogeneous Unit Principle," CN 46, Box 13, Folder 24, BGCA.

64 This incident is described in Galatians 2:11–21.
65 Ralph Winter, "The Homogeneous Unit Principle in Historical Perspective"; Wagner, "How Ethical Is The Homogeneous Unit Principle?," both in CN 46, Box 13, Folder 24, BGCA.
66 Stott's handwritten notes on Charles H. Kraft, "Anthropological Perspectives on the Homogeneous Unit Principle," CN 590, Box 1, Folder 4, BGCA.
67 Victor E. W. Hayward, "The Homogeneous Unit Principle and the Record of Worldwide Missionary Expansion," CN 46, Box 13, Folder 23; Robert L. Ramseyer, "Anthropological Perspectives on the Homogeneous Unit Principle, II," CN 46, Box 13, Folder 24; Harvie M. Conn, "Reactions and Guidelines: The Praxis of a Covenant Ethnos," CN 46, Box 13, Folder 24, BGCA.
68 Padilla and Stott quoted in Kirkpatrick, *A Gospel for the Poor*, 154–155.
69 Gottfried Osai-Mensah, "Memorandum Re LCWE Consultation on the 'Homogeneous Unit Principle,' of Church Growth," June 9, 1977, CN 46, Box 4, Folder 19, BGCA; Russell Chandler, "World Evangelism Group Tallies Results," June 4, 1977, *Los Angeles Times*, A29; "The Pasadena Consultation (a Colloquium on the Homogeneous Unit Principle)," CN 46, Box 4, Folder 19, BGCA.
70 "The Pasadena Consultation."
71 "Theologians Debate Place of Ethnic Churches," June 13, 1977, CN 46, Box 4, Folder 19, BGCA.
72 Wagner, *Our Kind of People*, 107.
73 Wagner's use of Cone was opportunistic. On other occasions, Wagner saw "the paradigm or language of liberation theology" as something evangelicals ought to avoid. C. Peter Wagner to John Stott, June 29, 1982, CN 358, Box 10, Folder 5, BGCA.
74 Kenneth L. Smith, review of Wagner, Our Kind of People, *Review of Religious Research* 22 (1980): 100.
75 Tom Nees, "Evangelism without the Gospel: Church Growth in *Our Kind of People*," *Sojourners* (1980): 25–29.
76 Wagner, *Church Growth and the Whole Gospel*, 168–169.
77 Nees, "Evangelism without the Gospel," 25.
78 The language of disease and "ethnikitis" came directly from Wagner, *Your Church Can Grow*, 124–134.
79 Lynne Hybels later wrote that before starting Willow Creek, Bill read Schuller's book, *Your Church Has Real Possibilities* (see chapter 3). He later took his church staff to one of Schuller's pastors' conferences. Hybels and Hybels, *Rediscovering Church*, 51, 68–71. Rick Warren described his debt to McGavran in his best-selling *The Purpose Driven Church*, 25–30. On CGM influence and the early days of Warren's church, see Sheler, *Prophet of Purpose*, 139–141.
80 Warren, *The Purpose Driven Church*, 170.
81 Stanley, *The Global Diffusion of Evangelicalism*, 177; "A Statement of Concerns on the Future of the Lausanne Committee for World Evangelisation," CN 358, Box 10, Folder 5, BGCA.

82 "Conversation with a Legend," *Church Growth America*, 1981, CN 178, Box 62, Folder 6, BGCA.
83 Perkins, *With Justice for All*, 108.
84 C. Peter Wagner to Leighton Ford, October 24, 1984, CN 358, Box 6, Folder 4, BGCA.
85 "LCWE National Convocation on Evangelizing Ethnic America Minutes," May 15, 1982, CN 46, Box 97, Folder 18, BGCA.
86 C. Peter Wagner to Leighton Ford, April 10, 1982, CN 358, Box 6, Folder 2, BGCA.
87 William E. Pannell to J. Paul Landrey, September 22, 1983, CN 46, Box 97, Folder 18, BGCA.
88 C. Peter Wagner to Bill Hogue, October 11, 1983, CN 46, Box 97, Folder 18, BGCA.
89 Leighton Ford to Oscar Romo, September 27, 1984; Leighton Ford to Robert Coleman, September 27, 1984, both in CN 46, Box 97, Folder 18, BGCA.
90 C. Peter Wagner to Leighton Ford, October 24, 1984, CN 358, Box 6, Folder 4, BGCA.
91 See Jacobson, *Roots Too*, 1–71.
92 Wagner handwritten notes on *Time* article, CN 358, Box 6, Folder 4, BGCA.
93 Executive Committee minutes with Wagner cover letter, December 7, 1984, CN 46, Box 97, Folder 18; Leighton Ford to C. Peter Wagner, December 11, 1984, CN 46, Box 97, Folder 18; C. Peter Wagner to Robert Coleman, February 13, 1985, CN 46, Box 97, Folder 18; C. Peter Wagner to Bill Hogue, October 11, 1983, CN 358, Box 6, Folder 4; Bill Hogue to C. Peter Wagner, October 24, 1983, CN 358, Box 6, Folder 4; Robert E. Coleman to Leighton Ford, February 21, 1985, CN 358, Box 6, Folder 4, BGCA.
94 C. Peter Wagner to Billy Melvin, December 21, 1984, CN 358, Box 6, Folder 4, BGCA.
95 C. Peter Wagner to Oscar Romo, December 21, 1984, CN 358, Box 6, Folder 4, BGCA.
96 This rosy view of the conference as a multiethnic celebration has influenced historians. Darren Dochuk has described Houston '85 as an example of Latin American influence on American evangelicals. Dochuk argues that Wagner's "endorsement of a 'signs and wonders' theology and ambitions to restructure evangelicalism itself in accordance with the multi-ethnic dynamics of his day placed him within Escobar's and Padilla's theological purview." While Dochuk is right to suggest the turn toward Pentecostalism reflected Latin American influence, Wagner's ethnic evangelization strategies were predictable outgrowths of his McGavran-inspired church growth beliefs. These beliefs placed him firmly in *opposition* to Escobar and Padilla. Dochuk also erroneously concludes that Houston '85 was "co-led" by "Hispanic and African American pastors." While Hispanic leaders played important leadership roles in the conference, African Americans did not have any such positions. See Dochuk, "Lausanne '74 and American Evangelicalism's Latin Turn," 274–275.

97 Randy Frame, "Church Leaders Challenge the Notion That America Is a Melting Pot," *Christianity Today*, May 17, 1985, 40–42; Michael Tutterow, "Reaching the Real America," *Mandate* 1, no. 5, 2–3.
98 Dan Moul, "A Look at Ethnic Representation within NAE Denominations," June 1988, SC113, Box 99, Wheaton College Special Collections.
99 Raymond W. Hurn, "Nazarenes . . . Is the Third Wave of a Religious Movement Commencing?," July 27, 1981, CN 178, Box 85, Folder 2, BGCA; Raymond W. Hurn, "The Oregon Experiment," Church Growth America, January–February 1980, 6–7, 14, AR 631-10, Box 15, Folder 12, SBHLA; Orjala, *Get Ready to Grow*.
100 Moul, "A Look at Ethnic Representation."
101 Harrison quoted in Randy Frame, "Church Leaders Challenge the Notion."
102 "The Atlanta Response to Houston '85," November 22, 1985, CN 548, Box 3, Folder 12, BGCA.
103 S. Miller, *The Age of Evangelicalism*.
104 Pannell, *The Coming Race Wars?*, 20, 85.
105 Ibid., 86.

6. THE ELUSIVE TURNING POINT

1 Gilbreath later wrote a compelling memoir about his life as a black evangelical in white evangelical spaces, including becoming the first black staff member of *Christianity Today*. In part due to his influence, the magazine increased its coverage of racial issues in the 1990s. Gilbreath, *Reconciliation Blues*.
2 Edward Gilbreath, "Manhood's Great Awakening," *Christianity Today*, February 6, 1995, 21–28.
3 "Movement Generating Big Numbers," *Christianity Today*, September 11, 1995, 59.
4 Gilbreath, "Manhood's Great Awakening," 22.
5 Tony Norman, "Promise Keepers Echo Troubles and Triumphs of Million Man March," *Pittsburgh Post-Gazette*, July 16, 1996, D-1.
6 While passages about unity in Christ, such as Colossians 3:11 and Galatians 3:28, had been major texts for colorblind Christians since the civil rights movement, in the 1990s they increasingly turned to 2 Corinthians 5:18–19 as a text with racial implications. In this passage the Apostle Paul described God reconciling humanity to the divine and entrusting to Christians "the ministry of reconciliation."
7 On this colorblind consensus, see Curtis, "Remembering Racial Progress, Forgetting White Resistance"; and Gottlieb, "Sixth Avenue Heartache."
8 Michael Emerson and Christian Smith made this point in their foundational study of evangelical racial attitudes in the 1990s. They write, "As the message of reconciliation spread to a white audience, it was popularized. The racial reconciliation message given to the mass audience is individual reconciliation." *Divided by Faith*, 67.
9 Perkins, *A Quiet Revolution*, 10–11. Other scholars have also cited Perkins as a crucial vector of influence for later racial reconciliation movements. Newton,

From Panthers to Promise Keepers, 248–249; Emerson and Smith, *Divided by Faith*, 51–59. On Perkins's career and the Christian Community Development Association that grew out of his work, see Heltzel, *Jesus and Justice*, 160–177; and Marsh, *The Beloved Community*, 153–188.

10 Perkins, *With Justice for All*, 17.
11 Perkins, *A Quiet Revolution*, 26.
12 Perkins, *With Justice for All*, 21.
13 Will Norton, "A Day in the Life of a Black Fundamentalist," *Eternity*, September 1971, 23.
14 "The Mendenhall Model Answers the Black Muslims," *Christianity Today*, January 30, 1976, 13.
15 Perkins, *A Quiet Revolution*, 29.
16 Perkins, *With Justice for All*, 98–99. On the boycott and the story of Perkins's arrest, see Perkins, *Let Justice Roll Down*, 131–177. See also Lincoln Warren, Jr., "Take Rankin Case, U.S. Court Urged," Clarion-Ledger, February 13, 1970, A1, A4.
17 Perkins, *With Justice for All*, 59–188.
18 Perkins, *A Quiet Revolution*, 33–38.
19 Perkins, *With Justice for All*, 56.
20 John Perkins, "Something Is Wrong at the Root," *Christianity Today*, October 4, 1993, 18.
21 Darrel Anderson, "Report: Atlanta '88," August 22, 1988; Darrel Anderson, "Report: Destiny '87," July 20, 1987, both in SC113, Box 99, Folder "Social Action 1988–1989," Wheaton College Special Collections.
22 Anderson, "Report: Destiny '87."
23 Darrel Anderson, "Report—Consultation on Racism," June 14, 1989, SC113, Box 99, Folder, "Social Action 1988–1989," Wheaton College Special Collections.
24 Darrel Anderson, "Report—Consultation on Racism," October 19, 1989, SC113, Box 99, Folder, "Social Action 1988–1989," Wheaton College Special Collections.
25 "NAE, NBEA Groups Join to Condemn Racism," *Christianity Today*, March 5, 1990, 35; "Statement on Racism a Catalyst for Dialogue," *Christianity Today*, June 18, 1990, 57.
26 Robin Y. McDonald, "Stretch Your Racial Comfort Zone," *Christianity Today*, June 22, 1992, 14.
27 Pannell, *The Coming Race Wars?*, 64, 136.
28 Ibid., 19, 85.
29 J. Deotis Roberts, "Black Christians Love the Bible," *Christianity Today*, October 4, 1993, 27.
30 Morris E. Jones, "No Substitute for Love"; Glandion Carney, "I'm Pessimistic"; Peggy L. Jones, "Why Are We a Threat?"; Tony Warner, "Learn from Us"; Robert Suggs, "The Issue Is Sin," all in *Christianity Today*, October 4, 1993, 19–20, 24, 26.
31 "A Bus Ride beyond the Comfort Zone," *Christianity Today*, October 4, 1993, 22.

32 Ken Lewis and Richard E. Walton, letters to the editor, *Christianity Today*, January 10, 1994, 14, 12; Joel Solliday, letter to the editor, *Christianity Today*, December 13, 1993, 6.
33 On the rise of interracial churches—and their ambiguous effects on racial attitudes and racial inequality—see Edwards, *The Elusive Dream*; Wadsworth, *Ambivalent Miracles*; Christerson, Edwards, and Emerson, *Against All Odds*; and Hawkins and Sinitiere, *Christians and the Color Line*.
34 Ken Sidey, "Church Growth Fine Tunes Its Formulas," *Christianity Today*, June 24, 1991, 44-47.
35 Ibid.
36 Michael G. Maudlin and Edward Gilbreath, "Selling Out the House of God?," *Christianity Today*, July 18, 1994, 20–25.
37 Edward Gilbreath, "The Birth of a Megachurch," *Christianity Today*, July 18, 1994, 23.
38 James C. Hefley, "Richard Land on Racism," *Indiana Baptist*, April 11, 1989, 4.
39 Orrin D. Morris, "Comparison of Racial Ethnic Change to SBC Growth by States, 1970–1980," July 1981, 19, AR 631-10, Box 46, Folder 17, SBHLA.
40 Joe Maxwell, "Black Southern Baptists," *Christianity Today*, May 15, 1995, 27–31.
41 Memorandum from Jere Allen to State Executive Directors, April 7, 1994, AR 933, Box 173, Folder 13, SBHLA.
42 Jere Allen to Richard Land, April 6, 1994, AR 933, Box 173, Folder 13, SBHLA.
43 "Declaration of Repentance," April 6, 1994, AR 933, Box 173 Folder 13, SBHLA.
44 Dennis L. Sanders, "SBC to Be Challenged to Adopt Racism Repentance Statement," *Baptist Press*, May 24, 1994, 4–5.
45 Bill Merrell, "CLC Consultation Yields Proposed Stance on Racism," *Baptist Press*, May 25, 1995, 1–2.
46 Keith Hinson, "Resolution on Racism One of Eight Approved by SBC," *California Southern Baptist*, July 13, 1995, 10.
47 Eric Frazier, "Southern Baptists Repent; BOLD STEP," *Post and Courier*, June 21, 1995, 1; "Gayle White, "'A Great Day,' Black Pastors Agree," Atlanta Journal Constitution, June 21, 1995, B4.
48 "SBC Renounces Racist Past," *Christian Century*, July 5–12, 1995, 671–672.
49 Greg Garrison, "SBC Plans to Pursue Race Edict," *Birmingham News*, January 31, 1996, 3B.
50 Jolly E. Griggs, "No Need to 'Help God Out,'" *California Southern Baptist*, August 10, 1995, 14; Rick Warren, letter to the editor, *California Southern Baptist*, July 13, 1995, 14.
51 Mark A. Wyatt, "200+ California Messengers Take Part," *California Southern Baptist*, June 29, 1995, 8.
52 "News Briefs," *Christianity Today*, October 23, 1995, 85; Timothy C. Morgan, "Racist No More? Black Leaders Ask," *Christianity Today*, August 14, 1995, 53.
53 Maxwell, "Black Southern Baptists," 31.
54 Michael W. Smith, "Color Blind," *Change Your World*, Reunion Records, 1992.

55 Joel Heng Hartse, "A Peculiar Display," *Christianity Today*, November 1, 2015, 74–75.
56 DC Talk, "Colored People," *Jesus Freak*, Forefront Records, 1995.
57 This discussion of colorblindness in evangelical popular culture is thoroughly indebted to H. Stephens, "'Tearing Down the Walls of Segregation.'"
58 "The Model Site Project" brochure. The institutional origins of the project date back to 1989. See Deborah Bailey, "College/Church Partnerships: A New Resource for Educational and Social Change. A Proposal to the Pew Charitable Trusts," May 9, 1994, 3, SC-57, Box II B.1, Folder "CCCU Office of Racial/Ethnic Diversity (miscellaneous)," Wheaton College Special Collections.
59 "Enrollment at 1993 Members of CCCU and U.S. Four Year Colleges," SC-57, Box II B.1, Folder "Administrative Correspondence (etc) Regarding Diversity," Wheaton College Special Collections.
60 "Minorities and Christian Colleges: A Peak at 20 Liberal-Arts Schools," *Urban Family*, Fall 1994, 35.
61 Internal unsigned memo, August 31, 1994; Robert C. Andringa, "Our Ongoing Inclusiveness/Diversity Initiative," July 15, 1994, both in SC-57, Box II B.1, Folder "Administrative Correspondence (etc) Regarding Diversity," Wheaton College Special Collections.
62 "Affirmative Action and Racial Harmony in Christian Colleges: A Discussion Paper and Recommendations by Racial Harmony Council," SC-57, Box II B.1, Folder "Racial Harmony Council Discussion Paper & Recommendations," Wheaton College Special Collections.
63 Norman Adrian Wiggins to Robert Andringa, April 15, 1997; Kent R. Hill to Robert Andringa, May 12, 1997; Dennis A. Davis to Robert Andringa, May 16, 1997; Clintonia Barnes to Robert Andringa, April 24, 1997, all in SC-57, Box II B.1, Folder "Racial Harmony Council Discussion Paper & Recommendations," Wheaton College Special Collections.
64 Some black students embraced the term as well. At North Park, a black student helped launch a "Racial Reconciliation Bible Study." Erika Carney, "4 Students Honored for Achievements," *College News*, February 23, 1995, 2.
65 "Chapel Speakers," *College News*, January 28, 1994, 2; Rebekah Eklund, "Community Day," *College News*, February 23, 1996, 1.
66 Becky Eklund and Heidi Griepp, "'Millicent' Chapel Fuels Controversy: Faculty and Students Address Issues," *College News*, November 18, 1994, 1.
67 Mark Erickson, "I'm Not Racist," *College News*, November 10, 1995, 7.
68 Shelly Pruitt, "'Unity' Promotes Cultural Awareness," *Aviso*, February 22, 1991, 3.
69 Jamie Lindsay, letter to the editor, *Houghton Star*, February 24, 1989, 8.
70 Kevin Maness, "Transcend Black & White," *Waltonian*, February 23, 1990, 10; Kellie Goode and Jo Ann Logan, "African-American Students Voice Concerns," *Waltonian*, April 30, 1993, 5.
71 Consultant's Report: Roger S. Greenway, "Preliminary Report of the Ad-Hoc Committee for Review of the Philadelphia Campus," February 1996, Box XI—

2-7.2 Messiah College Board of Trustees, Messiah-Temple Campus, Archives of Messiah College.
72 Consultant's Report: Carolyn Adams, "Preliminary Report of the Ad-Hoc Committee for Review of the Philadelphia Campus," February 1996, Box XI—2-7.2 Messiah College Board of Trustees, Messiah-Temple Campus, Archives of Messiah College.
73 Willie Richardson, "Analysis and Recommendation Concerning Philadelphia Campus of Messiah College," June 16, 1995, 12, "Preliminary Report of the Ad-Hoc Committee for Review of the Philadelphia Campus," February 1996, Box XI—2-7.2 Messiah College Board of Trustees, Messiah-Temple Campus, Archives of Messiah College.
74 "Recruitment Strategies, Spring 2001," Box T-9, Folder "Recruitment for 2001–2002," Archives of Messiah College.
75 Richardson, "Analysis and Recommendation Concerning Philadelphia Campus."
76 Amid cost-cutting after the Great Recession, Messiah permanently closed the Philadelphia Campus in 2014.
77 "Survey of Minority Faculty and Staff," April 26, 1995. On the schooling policy, see "Clarification of Calvin College Faculty Membership Requirements and Procedures for Requesting Exceptions," November 1995, C11.24, Box 983, Heritage Hall, Calvin College.
78 Minutes of Multicultural Affairs Committee, October 14, 1986, RG-07-08, Box 27, Folder "Multicultural Affairs Committee Annual Reports 84–88," Wheaton College Archives; "Multicultural Community" brochure, RG-07-08, Box 23, Folder 30, Wheaton College Archives.
79 John D. Spalding, "Bonding in the Bleachers: A Visit to the Promise Keepers," *Christian Century*, March 6, 1996, 260.
80 "Standing in the Mall," *Christian Century*, October 22, 1997, 934–936.
81 Many scholars have studied Promise Keepers through the lens of gender and masculinity. I do not attempt to overturn this emphasis. Rather, my central claim is that race was the major dimension of PK's vision of Christian masculinity that didn't sit well with many white evangelical men—and that makes race extremely important. On Promise Keepers and gender, see Bartkowski, *The Promise Keepers*; White, *Lost in the USA*; Newton, *From Panthers to Promise Keepers*; and Du Mez, *Jesus and John Wayne*, 150–172.
82 On this "tender warrior" archetype, see Kristin Kobes Du Mez, "Donald Trump and Militant Evangelical Masculinity," in Noll, Bebbington, and Marsden, *Evangelicals*, 237.
83 Howard A. Snyder, "Will Promise Keepers Keep Their Promises?," *Christianity Today*, November 14, 1994, 20–21.
84 Jeff Coen, "Promise Keepers Out to End Racial Friction," *Chicago Tribune*, October 25, 1996, DA9; Ted Olsen, "Racial Reconciliation Emphasis Intensified," *Christianity Today*, January 6, 1997, 67.

85 Robbie Morganfield, "'Each One, Reach One': Growing Men's Group Promotes Racial Reconciliation," *Houston Chronicle*, May 29, 1995, 33.
86 Douglas A. Blackmon, "Racial Reconciliation Becomes a Priority for the Religious Right," *Wall Street Journal*, June 23, 1997, A1.
87 Salim Muwakkil, "Churches Give Blessing to Racial Reconciliation," *Chicago Sun-Times*, January 18, 1996, 27; Christine Wicker, "A Vision of Harmony," *Dallas Morning News*, January 6, 1996, 1A; Bartkowski, *The Promise Keepers*, 2.
88 Roberto Rivera, "Post-Simpson America," *Christianity Today*, November 11, 1995, 14–15.
89 See Tuch and Martin, *Racial Attitudes in the 1990s*; Harris, "Whiteness as Property"; Edsall, *Chain Reaction*; and Hancock, *The Politics of Disgust*.
90 HoSang, *Racial Propositions*.
91 Morganfield, "'Each One, Reach One,'" 33.
92 Wicker, "A Vision of Harmony," 1A; David Neff, "Dare We Be Colorblind?," *Christianity Today*, February 3, 1997, 14–15.
93 Wicker, "A Vision of Harmony," 1A.
94 Bob Price to Richard Land, May 6, 1996, AR 933, Box 173, Folder 18, SBHLA.
95 Wilson, *When Work Disappears*; Loury, *One by One from the Inside Out*.
96 Michael Cromartie, "Conquering the Enemy Within," *Christianity Today*, January 8, 1996, 17–20.
97 Joe Maxwell, "Beating Racism One Friendship at a Time," *Chicago Tribune*, November 3, 1993, 1. On the racial reconciliation initiative called "Mission Mississippi," see Slade, *Open Friendship in a Closed Society*.
98 Thomas B. Edsall, "Masculinity on the Run," *Washington Post*, April 30, 1995, 39.
99 Dale Russakoff and Serge F. Kovaleski, "An Ordinary Boy's Extraordinary Rage," *Washington Post*, July 2, 1995, A1.
100 See especially Newton, *From Panthers to Promise Keepers*, 27–31; and White, *Lost in the USA*, 54–64.
101 Gilbreath, "Manhood's Great Awakening," 22.
102 For a favorable review, see Edward Gilbreath, "Desegregating Our Hearts—and Pews," *Christianity Today*, November 8, 1993, 67–68.
103 Washington and Kehrein, *Breaking Down Walls*, 12, 30.
104 Larry B. Stammer, "Men's Group Strives for Racial Harmony," *Los Angeles Times*, April 20, 1996, 4; Bob Phelps, "A Prophet in His Own Hometown Hopes to Inspire Racial Harmony," *Florida Times Union*, October 18, 1996, A1.
105 Kevin A. Miller, "McCartney Preaches Reconciliation," *Christianity Today*, June 19, 1995, 43.
106 "Breaking the Black/White Stalemate," *Christianity Today*, March 2, 1998, 26–29.
107 Miller, "McCartney Preaches Reconciliation," 43.
108 Bill McCartney, "Reconciliation Part of Promise Keepers' Path," *Gazette*, September 25, 1998, 7.
109 Gayle White, "Clergy Conference Stirs Historic Show of Unity," *Christianity Today*, April 8, 1996, 88.

110 Ross Lilla, "McCartney: Racial Peace Soon Possible," *Florida Times Union*, October 20, 1996, A1.
111 Spalding, "Bonding in the Bleachers," 264.
112 Lilla, "McCartney: Racial Peace Soon Possible," A1.
113 McCartney, "Reconciliation Part of Promise Keepers' Path," 7.
114 Morganfield, "'Each One, Reach One,'" 33.
115 See, for example, Martha Sawyer Allen, "Promise Keepers: Racial Reconciliation Made a Difference," *Star Tribune*, May 9, 1996, 22A.
116 Steve Rabey, "Seedbed for Revival?," *Christianity Today*, September 1, 1997, 90.
117 Jack Kemp and J. C. Watts Jr., "Better Than Affirmative Action," *Washington Post*, July 8, 1997, A15.
118 For example, Sonya Ross, "President Seeks Road to Racial Reconciliation," *Philadelphia Tribune*, May 27, 1997, 1A.
119 Ted Olsen, "Racial Reconciliation Emphasis Intensified," *Christianity Today*, January 6, 1997, 67.
120 Rabey, "Seedbed for Revival?," 90.
121 Susan Hogan, "Promise Keepers Rally around Racial Reconciliation," *Star Tribune*, January 18, 1997, 5B.
122 Quoted in White, *Lost in the USA*, 23.
123 Joe Maxwell, "Will the Walls Fall Down?," *Christianity Today*, November 17, 1997, 62–65.
124 Ibid., 63.
125 Bartkowski attributes the decline to the "ephemeral character of American culture." For a brief moment, PK tapped into the cultural zeitgeist, but "today's novelties become yesterday's news" with remarkable speed. Bartkowski, *The Promise Keepers*, 151.
126 Bill McCartney, "The Coach's Burden," *Christianity Today*, May 18, 1998, 30–31.
127 Emerson and Smith, *Divided by Faith*, 127.
128 The historian Seth Dowland writes, "Conservative evangelicals in the 1990s saw the civil rights movement as a heroic moment in the nation's history. Most acknowledged white Christians' complicity in racial discrimination, and *they repented and set about trying to redeem their forebears' racial sins*" (emphasis mine). Dowland aptly describes the views of some Promise Keepers' leaders and white evangelical elites, but offers an exceedingly generous reading of mainstream white evangelical opinion. Dowland, *Family Values and the Rise of the Christian Right*, 208. See also Newton, *From Panthers to Promise Keepers*, 241–257.

CONCLUSION

1 Emerson and Smith, *Divided by Faith*, 76. The most basic statement of their argument, found in the preface, asserted that "evangelicals desire to end racial division *and inequality*" (emphasis mine). For a critical race theory critique of Emerson and Smith's book, see Tranby and Hartmann, "Critical Whiteness Theories."
2 "Harder Than Anyone Can Imagine," *Christianity Today*, April 2005, 38.

3 For evangelicals debating whether theology or culture was the culprit for the racial divide, see "We Can Overcome," *Christianity Today*, October 2, 2000, 43. My concern here is not to critique Emerson and Smith's book as much as to suggest how white evangelicals could find ways to sidestep its most difficult implications.
4 Warren, *The Purpose Driven Church*, 25–30. On Criswell's change of heart, see Freeman, "'Never Had I Been So Blind.'"
5 For example, McAlister, *The Kingdom of God Has No Borders*; Kirkpatrick, *A Gospel for the Poor*; and Swartz, *Facing West*.
6 Wuthnow, *The Restructuring of American Religion*, 192–193.
7 On the appeal of evangelical megachurches as a homogenizing religious force incorporating immigrant communities, see Kurien, *Ethnic Church Meets Megachurch*, 4–6.
8 For example, Dupont, *Mississippi Praying*, 231; and Newman, *Getting Right with God*, 209–210.
9 Dupont, *Mississippi Praying*, 3.
10 This has not stopped scholars from trying. David Chappell has written unambiguously of "the relative ease of the movement's victory," as though segregationists were comprehensively routed and then only found a way back to respectability and power through appeals to religion rather than race, as seen in the new Christian Right. In reality, during the civil rights era and beyond, religion and race, victors and losers, were never so easily separable. Chappell, *A Stone of Hope*, 153–178.
11 Dupont, *Mississippi Praying*, 7.
12 Carter, *Race*; Jennings, *The Christian Imagination*.
13 Beinart, "Breaking Faith."
14 On Black Lives Matter, see Taylor, *From #BlackLivesMatter to Black Liberation*. On the rapid shifts in American racial attitudes and their links to partisanship, see Sides, Tesler, and Vavreck, *Identity Crisis*. On the rising salience of whiteness and decline of colorblindness, see Jardina, *White Identity Politics*.
15 Pannell, *The Coming Race Wars?*, 79; Tony Warner, "Learn from Us," *Christianity Today*, October 4, 1993, 26.
16 Barna Group, "Black Lives Matter and Racial Tension in America." Other surveys found that white evangelicals were much more likely than other Americans to oppose interracial marriage and to reject the idea that African Americans continued to face significant discrimination in American society. Tobin Grant, "Opposition to Interracial Marriage Lingers among Evangelicals," *Christianity Today*, June 24, 2011, www.christianitytoday.com; Jones et al., "Who Sees Discrimination?"
17 Lecrae, "Don't Waste Your Life," *Rebel*, Reach Records, 2008.
18 Lecrae, "Can't Stop Me Now (Destination)," *All Things Work Together*, Reach Records, 2017.
19 Lecrae, "Facts," *All Things Work Together*, Reach Records, 2017.
20 Brown, *I'm Still Here*, 167; McCaulley, *Reading while Black*, 11–16; Loritts, *Insider Outsider*, 130.

21 As Lydia Bean has argued, evangelical churches in the United States forged implicit connections between religious and political identity. In these spaces, "Political conservatism takes on a sacred quality because it is woven into the fabric of everyday religious life." A normative whiteness was a key part of this fabric. Bean, *The Politics of Evangelical Identity*, 15.

22 Loritts, *Insider Outsider*, 130; McCaulley, *Reading while Black*, 121. The passages of scripture that McCaulley alluded to are found in Isaiah 53 and Hebrews 11.

23 Brown, *I'm Still Here*, 60, 23; McNeil, *Becoming Brave*, 22–23.

24 Tisby, *The Color of Compromise*, 190–191; Burns, "George Floyd and an Unjust Nation."

25 Mark Galli, "Trump Should Be Removed from Office," *Christianity Today*, December 19, 2019, www.christianitytoday.com; Timothy Dalrymple, "Justice Too Long Delayed," *Christianity Today*, June 10, 2020, www.christianitytoday.com.

26 Campbell Robertson, "A Quiet Exodus in White Evangelical Churches," *New York Times*, March 10, 2018, A1.

BIBLIOGRAPHY

ARCHIVES CONSULTED

Archives of Messiah College, Murray Library, Mechanicsburg, Pennsylvania
Billy Graham Center Archives, Wheaton, Illinois
Papers of Charles P. Wagner, Collection 358
Papers of Donald and Mary McGavran, Collection 178
Papers of John R. W. Stott, Collection 590
Records of InterVarsity Christian Fellowship, Collection 300
Records of the Atlanta '88 Congress on Evangelizing Black America, Collection 548
Records of the BGEA: Crusade Activities, Collection 17
Records of the BGEA: Papers of Robert O. Ferm, Collection 19
Records of the Evangelical Fellowship of Mission Agencies, Collection 165
Records of the Lausanne Committee for World Evangelization, Collection 46
Crowell Library Archives, Moody Bible Institute, Chicago, Illinois
Everett L. Cattell Library, Malone University, Canton, Ohio
F. M. Johnson Archives and Special Collections, Brandel Library, North Park University, Chicago, Illinois
Heritage Hall, Hekman Library, Calvin University, Grand Rapids, Michigan
Houghton College Archives, Willard J. Houghton Library, Houghton, New York
Masland Library, Cairn University, Langhorne, Pennsylvania
Nyack College Archives, Bailey Library, Nyack, New York
Southern Baptist Historical Library and Archives, Nashville, Tennessee
Brooks Hays Papers, AR 97
Christian Life Commission Administrative Files, AR 138
Christian Life Commission Seminar Proceedings Collection, AR 138-6
Clifton Judson Allen Papers, AR 795-221
Earl Stallings Papers, AR 234
Executive Committee Records, AR 627-1
Home Mission Board Executive Office Files, AR 631-3
M. Wendell Belew Collection, AR 631-10
Richard Land Papers, AR 933
Wheaton College Archives and Special Collections, Buswell Library, Wheaton, Illinois
Council for Christian Colleges and Universities (CCCU) Records, SC-057
National Association of Evangelicals Records, SC-113

Office of Academic Affairs Records, RG-03-002
Office of Development Records, RG-07-001
Office of Student Development Records, RG-07-08
Office of the President Records (Hudson T. Armerding), RG-02-005
Office of the President Records (V. Raymond Edman), RG-02-004

NEWSPAPERS AND PERIODICALS
Alliance Witness
Assemblies of God Heritage
Atlanta Daily World
Atlanta Journal Constitution
Banner
Barrington College Forum
Barringtonian
Bethel Clarion
Birmingham News
Brethren Missionary Herald
California Southern Baptist
Calvin College Chimes
Campus Life
Chicago Sun-Times
Chicago Tribune
Christian Century
Christian Herald
Christianity Today
Church Growth America
Church Herald
Clarion-Ledger
Colorado Springs Gazette
Concordia Theological Monthly
Covenant College Bagpipe
Covenanter Witness
Dallas Morning News
Eastern College Spotlight
Eastern College Waltonian
Ebony
Eternity
Evangelical Beacon
Florida Times Union
Fresno Bee
Glimmerglass
His
Houghton Star

Houston Chronicle
Indiana Baptist
International Review of Mission
Ivy Rustles
Jet
King's Business
Los Angeles Times
Malone College Aviso
Moody Student
New York Amsterdam News
New York Times
New York Times Magazine
Newsweek
North Park College News
Nyack Forum
The Other Side
Pasadena Star-News
Pentecostal Evangel
Philadelphia Inquirer
Philadelphia Tribune
Pittsburgh Courier
Pittsburgh Post-Gazette
Post and Courier
Redlands Daily Facts
Review of Religious Research
Scroll
Simpson's Leader-Times
Sojourners
Star Tribune
Swinging Bridge
Taylor University Magazine
Time
Trev-Echoes
Urban Family
Wall Street Journal
Washington Post
Wesleyan Advocate

PRIMARY SOURCES

Bentley, Ruth Lewis, editor. *Handbook for Black Christian Students*. Chicago: National Black Christian Students Conference, 1974. Revised edition, 1975.

Brown, Austin Channing. *I'm Still Here: Black Dignity in a World Made for Whiteness*. New York: Convergent Books, 2018.

Burns, Tyler. "George Floyd and an Unjust Nation 'on the Brink.'" Pass the Mic podcast. June 1, 2020. www.thewitnessbcc.com/pass-the-mic/.
Chaney, Charles L., and Ron S. Lewis. *Design for Church Growth*. Nashville, TN: Broadman Press, 1977.
Clark, Joseph Bourne. *Leavening the Nation: The Story of American Home Missions*. New York: Baker & Taylor, 1903.
Douglas, J. D., editor. *Let the Earth Hear His Voice*. Minneapolis, MN: Worldwide Publications, 1975.
Dubose, Francis M. *How Churches Grow in an Urban World*. Nashville, TN: Broadman Press, 1978.
Glazer, Nathan, and Daniel Patrick Moynihan. *Beyond the Melting Pot: The Negroes, Puerto Ricans, Jews, Italians, and Irish of New York City*. Cambridge, MA: MIT Press, 1963.
Hardesty, Nancy, and Letha Dawson Scanzoni. *All We're Meant to Be: A Biblical Approach to Women's Liberation*. Waco, TX: Word Books, 1974.
Harrison, Bob. *When God Was Black*. Grand Rapids, MI: Zondervan, 1971.
Herberg, Will. *Protestant, Catholic, Jew: An Essay in American Religious Sociology*. New York: Doubleday, 1955.
Hogue, C. Bill. *I Want My Church to Grow*. Nashville, TN: Broadman Press, 1977.
Hybels, Bill, and Lynne Hybels. *Rediscovering Church: The Story and Vision of Willow Creek Community Church*. Grand Rapids, MI: Zondervan, 1995.
Jones, Howard. *Gospel Trailblazer: An African-American Preacher's Historic Journey across Racial Lines*. Chicago: Moody Publishers, 2003.
———. *Shall We Overcome? A Challenge to Negro and White Christians*. Westwood, NJ: Fleming H. Revell Company, 1966.
Jones, Wanda. *Living in Two Worlds: The Wanda Jones Story*. Grand Rapids, MI: Zondervan, 1988.
Lindsell, Harold. *Missionary Principles and Practice*. Westwood, NJ: Revell, 1955.
Loritts, Bryan. *Insider Outsider: My Journey as a Stranger in White Evangelicalism and My Hope for Us All*. Grand Rapids, MI: Zondervan, 2018.
Loury, Glenn C. *One by One from the Inside Out: Essays and Reviews on Race and Responsibility in America*. New York: Free Press, 1995.
Maston, T. B. *The Bible and Race*. Nashville, TN: Broadman Press, 1959.
McCaulley, Esau. *Reading while Black: African American Biblical Interpretation as an Exercise in Hope*. Downers Grove, IL: IVP Academic, 2020.
McGavran, Donald. *The Bridges of God: A Study in the Strategy of Missions*. Eugene: OR, 2005. Originally published by World Dominion Press, 1955.
———, editor. *Church Growth and Christian Mission*. New York: Harper & Row, 1965.
———. *Understanding Church Growth*. Grand Rapids, MI: Eerdmans, 1970.
McGavran, Donald, and Win Arn. *How to Grow Your Church: Conversations about Church Growth*. Ventura, CA: Regal Books, 1973.
McIntire, Carl. "Open Letter to Martin Luther King," May 25, 1964. Carl McIntire Papers, Box 179, Folder 1, Princeton Theological Seminary Library.

McKenna, David L., editor. *The Urban Crisis: A Symposium on the Racial Problem in the Inner City*. Grand Rapids, MI: Zondervan, 1969.
McNeil, Brenda Salter. *Becoming Brave: Finding the Courage to Pursue Racial Justice Now*. Grand Rapids, MI: Brazos Press, 2020.
Novak, Michael. *The Rise of the Unmeltable Ethnics: Politics and Culture in the Seventies*. New York: Macmillan, 1971.
Orjala, Paul R. *Get Ready to Grow: A Strategy for Local Church Growth*. Kansas City, MO: Beacon Hill Press, 1978.
Pannell, William E. *The Coming Race Wars? A Cry for Reconciliation*. Grand Rapids, MI: Zondervan, 1993.
———. *My Friend, the Enemy*. Waco, TX: Word Books, 1968.
Perkins, John. *Beyond Charity: The Call to Christian Community Development*. Grand Rapids, MI: Baker Books, 1993.
———. *Let Justice Roll Down: John Perkins Tells His Own Story*. Glendale, CA: Regal Books, 1976.
———. *A Quiet Revolution: The Christian Response to Human Need: A Strategy for Today*. Waco, TX: Word Books, 1976.
———. *With Justice for All: A Strategy for Community Development*. Ventura, CA: Regal Books, 1982.
Perkins, Spencer, and Chris Rice. *More Than Equals: Racial Healing for the Sake of the Gospel*. Downers Grove, IL: InterVarsity Press, 1993.
Schuller, Robert H. *Your Church Has Real Possibilities*. Glendale, CA: Regal Books, 1974.
Sider, Ronald J., editor. *The Chicago Declaration*. Carol Stream, IL: Creation House, 1974.
Skinner, Tom. *Black and Free*. Grand Rapids, MI: Zondervan, 1968.
———. *Up from Harlem*. Old Tappan, NJ: Fleming H. Revell, 1975.
———. "The U.S. Racial Crisis and World Evangelism." www.urbana.org.
Strong, Josiah. *Our Country: Its Possible Future and Its Present Crisis*, revised edition. New York: Baker & Taylor, 1891.
Tisby, Jemar. *The Color of Compromise*. Grand Rapids, MI: Zondervan, 2019.
Wagner, C. Peter. *Church Growth and the Whole Gospel: A Biblical Mandate*. San Francisco: Harper & Row, 1981.
———. *Our Kind of People: The Ethical Dimensions of Church Growth in America*. Atlanta: John Knox Press, 1979.
———. *Your Church Can Grow: Seven Vital Signs of a Healthy Church*. Glendale, CA: Regal Books, 1976.
Warren, Rick. *The Purpose Driven Church: Growth without Compromising Your Message & Mission*. Grand Rapids, MI: Zondervan, 1995.
Washington, James Melvin, editor. *A Testament of Hope: The Essential Writings and Speeches of Martin Luther King, Jr*. New York: HarperOne, 1986.
Washington, Raleigh, and Glen Kehrein. *Breaking Down Walls: A Model for Reconciliation in an Age of Racial Strife*. Chicago: Moody Press, 1993.

Waymire, Bob, and C. Peter Wagner. *The Church Growth Survey Handbook*, 2nd edition. Santa Clara, CA: Global Church Growth Bulletin, 1980.
Weary, Dolphus, and William Hendricks. *"I Ain't Comin' Back."* Wheaton, IL: Tyndale House, 1990.
Wilson, William Julius. *When Work Disappears: The World of the New Urban Poor.* New York: Knopf, 1997.
Winter, Gibson. *The Suburban Captivity of the Churches: An Analysis of Protestant Responsibility in the Expanding Metropolis.* New York: Doubleday, 1961.
Yoder, John H. "Church Growth Issues in Theological Perspective." In *The Challenge of Church Growth: A Symposium.* Edited by Wilbert R. Shenk. Scottdale, PA: Herald Press, 1973. 25–48.

SECONDARY SOURCES

Abrams, Douglas Carl. *Selling the Old-Time Religion: American Fundamentalists and Mass Culture, 1920–1940.* Athens: University of Georgia Press, 2001.
Balmer, Randall. *Thy Kingdom Come: How the Religious Right Distorts the Faith and Threatens America: An Evangelical's Lament.* New York: Basic Books, 2006.
Bare, Daniel. *Black Fundamentalists: Conservative Christianity and Racial Identity in the Segregation Era.* New York: New York University Press, 2021.
Barger, Lilian Calles. *The World Come of Age: An Intellectual History of Liberation Theology.* New York: Oxford University Press, 2018.
Barna Group. "Black Lives Matter and Racial Tension in America." May 5, 2016. www.barna.com.
Bartkowski, John P. *The Promise Keepers: Servants, Soldiers, and Godly Men.* New Brunswick, NJ: Rutgers University Press, 2004.
Bass, S. Jonathan. *Blessed Are the Peacemakers: Martin Luther King Jr., Eight White Religious Leaders, and the "Letter from Birmingham Jail."* Baton Rouge: Louisiana State University Press, 2001.
Bean, Lydia. *The Politics of Evangelical Identity: Local Churches and Partisan Divides in the United States and Canada.* Princeton, NJ: Princeton University Press, 2014.
Bebbington, David. *Evangelicalism in Modern Britain: A History from the 1730s to the 1980s.* New York: Routledge, 1989.
Beinart, Peter. "Breaking Faith." *The Atlantic.* April 2017, online edition.
Bell, Janet Cheatham. *The Time and Place That Gave Me Life.* Bloomington: Indiana University Press, 2007.
Bendroth, Margaret Lamberts. *Fundamentalists in the City: Conflict and Division in Boston's Churches, 1885–1950.* New York: Oxford University Press, 2005.
Bentley, William H. "Factors in the Origin and Focus of the National Black Evangelical Association." In *Black Theology: A Documentary History, 1966–1979.* Edited by Gayraud S. Wilmore and James H. Cone. Maryknoll, NY: Orbis Books, 1979. 310–321.
———. *The National Black Evangelical Association: Reflections on the Evolution of a Concept of Ministry*, revised edition. Chicago: 1979.

Best, Wallace D. *Passionately Human, No Less Divine: Religion and Culture in Black Chicago, 1915–1952*. Princeton, NJ: Princeton University Press, 2005.
Biondi, Martha. *The Black Revolution on Campus*. Berkeley: University of California Press, 2012.
Blum, Edward. *Reforging the White Republic: Race, Religion, and American Nationalism, 1865–1898*. Baton Rouge: Louisiana State University Press, 2005.
———. *W. E. B. Du Bois: American Prophet*. Philadelphia: University of Pennsylvania Press, 2007.
Blum, Edward J., and Paul Harvey. *The Color of Christ: The Son of God and the Saga of Race in America*. Chapel Hill: University of North Carolina Press, 2012.
Bonilla-Silva, Eduardo. *Racism without Racists: Color-Blind Racism and the Persistence of Racial Inequality in the United States*. Lanham, MD: Rowman and Littlefield, 2003.
Branch, Daniel. *Defeating Mau Mau, Creating Kenya: Counterinsurgency, Civil War, and Decolonization*. New York: Cambridge University Press, 2009.
Brenneman, Todd M. *Homespun Gospel: The Triumph of Sentimentality in Contemporary American Evangelicalism*. New York: Oxford University Press, 2014.
Brown, Michael K., et al. *Whitewashing Race: The Myth of a Color-Blind Society*. Berkeley: University of California Press, 2003.
Burke, Meghan A. *Racial Ambivalence in Diverse Communities: Whiteness and the Power of Color-Blind Ideologies*. Lanham, MD: Lexington Books, 2012.
Burkholder, Zoe. *Color in the Classroom: How American Schools Taught Race*. New York: Oxford University Press, 2011.
Carpenter, Joel A. *Revive Us Again: The Reawakening of American Fundamentalism*. New York: Oxford University Press, 1997.
Carruthers, Susan L. *Winning Hearts and Minds: British Governments, the Media and Colonial Counter-Insurgency, 1944–1960*. New York: Leicester University Press, 1995.
Carter, J. Kameron. *Race: A Theological Account*. New York: Oxford University Press, 2008.
Case, Jay Riley. *An Unpredictable Gospel: American Evangelicals and World Christianity, 1812–1920*. New York: Oxford University Press, 2012.
Chang, Derek. *Citizens of a Christian Nation: Evangelical Missions and the Problem of Race in the Nineteenth Century*. Philadelphia: University of Pennsylvania Press, 2012.
Chappell, David L. *A Stone of Hope: Prophetic Religion and the Death of Jim Crow*. Chapel Hill: University of North Carolina Press, 2004.
———. *Waking from the Dream: The Struggle for Civil Rights in the Shadow of Martin Luther King*. New York: Random House, 2014.
Christerson, Brad, Korie L. Edwards, and Michael O. Emerson. *Against All Odds: The Struggle for Racial Integration in Religious Organizations*. New York: New York University Press, 2005.
Cohen, Lizabeth. *A Consumer's Republic: The Politics of Mass Consumption in Postwar America*. New York: Knopf, 2003.

Cone, James. *The Cross and the Lynching Tree.* Maryknoll, NY: Orbis Books, 2011.
Conn, Harvie M. *The American City and the Evangelical Church: A Historical Overview.* Grand Rapids, MI: Baker, 1994.
Cook, Nicole C. *Wanamaker's Temple: The Business of Religion in an Iconic Department Store.* New York: New York University Press, 2018.
Countryman, Matthew J. *Up South: Civil Rights and Black Power in Philadelphia.* Philadelphia: University of Pennsylvania Press, 2006.
Crenshaw, Kimberlé, et al. *Critical Race Theory: The Key Writings That Formed the Movement.* New York: New Press, 1995.
Curtis, Jesse. "Remembering Racial Progress, Forgetting White Resistance: The Death of Mississippi Senator John C. Stennis and the Consolidation of the Colorblind Consensus." *History & Memory* 29 (2017): 134–160.
———. "'Will the Jungle Take Over?' *National Review* and the Defense of Western Civilization in the Era of Civil Rights and African Decolonization." *Journal of American Studies* 53 (2019): 997–1023.
Dailey, Jane. "Sex, Segregation, and the Sacred after Brown." *Journal of American History* 91 (2004): 119–144.
Davis, Lawrence B. *Immigrants, Baptists, and the Protestant Mind in America.* Urbana: University of Illinois Press, 1973.
Dayton, Donald W., and Robert K. Johnston, editors. *The Variety of American Evangelicalism.* Knoxville: University of Tennessee Press, 1991.
Delgado, Richard, and Jean Stefancic. *Critical Race Theory: An Introduction*, 3rd edition. New York: New York University Press, 2017.
D'Elia, John A. *A Place at the Table: George Eldon Ladd and the Rehabilitation of Evangelical Scholarship in America.* New York: Oxford University Press, 2008.
Doane, Ashley, and Eduardo Bonilla-Silva, editors. *White Out: The Continuing Significance of Racism.* New York: Routledge, 2003.
Dochuk, Darren. *From Bible Belt to Sunbelt: Plain-Folk Religion, Grassroots Politics, and the Rise of Evangelical Conservatism.* New York: W. W. Norton, 2010.
———. "Lausanne '74 and American Evangelicalism's Latin Turn." In *Turning Points in the History of American Evangelicalism.* Edited by Heath W. Carter and Laura Rominger Porter. Grand Rapids, MI: Eerdmans, 2017. 247–281.
———. "'Praying for a Wicked City': Congregation, Community, and the Suburbanization of Fundamentalism." *Religion and American Culture: A Journal of Interpretation* 13 (2003): 167–203.
Dowland, Seth. *Family Values and the Rise of the Christian Right.* Philadelphia: University of Pennsylvania Press, 2015.
Du Mez, Kristin Kobes. "Evangelicalism Is an Imagined Religious Community." Anxious Bench blog. August 9, 2018. www.patheos.com/blogs/anxiousbench/.
———. *Jesus and John Wayne: How White Evangelicals Corrupted a Faith and Fractured a Nation.* New York: Liveright, 2020.
Dupont, Carolyn Renée. *Mississippi Praying: Southern White Evangelicals and the Civil Rights Movement, 1945–1975.* New York: New York University Press, 2013.

Edsall, Thomas Byrne. *Chain Reaction: The Impact of Race, Rights, and Taxes on American Politics*. New York: W. W. Norton, 1991.

Edwards, Korie L. *The Elusive Dream: The Power of Race in Interracial Churches*. New York: Oxford University Press, 2008.

Elkins, Caroline. *Imperial Reckoning: The Untold Story of Britain's Gulag in Kenya*. New York: Henry Holt, 2005.

Emerson, Michael O. *People of the Dream: Multiracial Congregations in the United States*. Princeton, NJ: Princeton University Press, 2006.

Emerson, Michael O., and Christian Smith. *Divided by Faith: Evangelical Religion and the Problem of Race in America*. New York: Oxford University Press, 2000.

Evans, Christopher H. *The Social Gospel in American Religion: A History*. New York: New York University Press, 2017.

Evans, Curtis J. *The Burden of Black Religion*. New York: Oxford University Press, 2008.

———. "White Evangelical Responses to the Civil Rights Movement." *Harvard Theological Review* 102 (2009): 245–273.

Fessenden, Tracy. *Culture and Redemption: Religion, the Secular, and American Literature*. Princeton, NJ: Princeton University Press, 2007.

Findlay, James F., Jr. *Church People in the Struggle: The National Council of Churches and the Black Freedom Movement, 1950–1970*. New York: Oxford University Press, 1993.

FitzGerald, Frances. *The Evangelicals: The Struggle to Shape America*. New York: Simon & Schuster, 2017.

Fredrickson, George. *Racism: A Short History*. Princeton, NJ: Princeton University Press, 2002.

Freeman, Curtis W. "'Never Had I Been So Blind': W. A. Criswell's 'Change' on Racial Segregation." *Journal of Southern Religion* (2007): 1–12.

Gasaway, Brantley W. *Progressive Evangelicals and the Pursuit of Social Justice*. Chapel Hill: University of North Carolina Press, 2014.

Gilbreath, Edward. *Reconciliation Blues: A Black Evangelical's Inside View of White Christianity*. Downers Grove, IL: IVP Books, 2006.

Gloege, Timothy E. W. *Guaranteed Pure: Fundamentalism, Business, and the Making of Modern Evangelicalism*. Chapel Hill: University of North Carolina Press, 2015.

Goertz, Hans-Jürgen. *The Anabaptists*. Translated by Trevor Johnson. New York: Routledge, 1996.

Goldenberg, David M. *The Curse of Ham: Race and Slavery in Early Judaism, Christianity, and Islam*. Princeton, NJ: Princeton University Press, 2005.

Goldschmidt, Henry, and Elizabeth McAlister, editors. *Race, Nation, and Religion in the Americas*. New York: Oxford University Press, 2004.

Gollner, Philipp. "How Mennonites Became White: Religious Activism, Cultural Power, and the City." *Mennonite Quarterly Review* 90 (2016): 165–193.

Gomer, Justin. *White Balance: How Hollywood Shaped Colorblind Ideology and Undermined Civil Rights*. Chapel Hill: University of North Carolina Press, 2020.

Goossen, Rachel Waltner. "'Defanging the Beast': Mennonite Responses to John Howard Yoder's Sexual Abuse." *Mennonite Quarterly Review* 89 (2015): 7–80.
Gordon, Leah N. *From Power to Prejudice: The Rise of Racial Individualism in Midcentury America.* Chicago: University of Chicago Press, 2015.
Gottlieb, Dylan. "Sixth Avenue Heartache: Race, Commemoration, and the Colorblind Consensus in Zephyrhills, Florida, 2003–2004." *Journal of Urban History* 39 (2013): 1085–1105.
Griffith, Aaron. *God's Law and Order: The Politics of Punishment in Evangelical America.* Cambridge, MA: Harvard University Press, 2020.
Hancock, Ange-Marie. *The Politics of Disgust: The Public Identity of the Welfare Queen.* New York: New York University Press, 2004.
Hansen, Drew D. *The Dream: Martin Luther King and the Speech That Inspired a Nation.* New York: Ecco, 2003.
Harper, Keith. *The Quality of Mercy: Southern Baptists and Social Christianity, 1890–1920.* Tuscaloosa: University of Alabama Press, 1996.
Harris, Cheryl I. "Whiteness as Property." *Harvard Law Review* 106 (1993): 1707–1791.
Harvey, Paul. *Christianity and Race in the American South: A History.* Chicago: University of Chicago Press, 2016.
Hawkins, J. Russell, and Phillip Luke Sinitiere, editors. *Christians and the Color Line: Race and Religion after Divided by Faith.* New York: Oxford University Press, 2014.
Haynes, Stephen R. *The Last Segregated Hour: The Memphis Kneel-Ins and the Campaign for Southern Church Desegregation.* New York: Oxford University Press, 2012.
Heltzel, Peter Goodwin. *Jesus and Justice: Evangelicals, Race, and American Politics.* New Haven, CT: Yale University Press, 2009.
Hollinger, David A. *Protestants Abroad: How Missionaries Tried to Change the World but Changed America.* Princeton, NJ: Princeton University Press, 2017.
Hopkins, A. G. *American Empire: A Global History.* Princeton, NJ: Princeton University Press, 2018.
HoSang, Daniel Martinez. *Racial Propositions: Ballot Initiatives and the Making of Postwar California.* Berkeley: University of California Press, 2010.
Hrach, Thomas J. *The Riot Report and the News: How the Kerner Commission Changed Media Coverage of Black America.* Amherst: University of Massachusetts Press, 2016.
Hudnut-Beumler, James. *Looking for God in the Suburbs: The Religion of the American Dream and Its Critics, 1945–1965.* New Brunswick, NJ: Rutgers University Press, 1994.
Jacobson, Matthew Frye. *Roots Too: White Ethnic Revival in Post–Civil Rights America.* Cambridge, MA: Harvard University Press, 2006.
Jardina, Ashley. *White Identity Politics.* Cambridge: Cambridge University Press, 2019.
Jennings, Willie James. *The Christian Imagination: Theology and the Origins of Race.* New Haven, CT: Yale University Press, 2010.
Johnson, Karen. *One in Christ: Chicago Catholics and the Quest for Interracial Justice.* New York: Oxford University Press, 2018.

Jones, Robert P., et al. "Who Sees Discrimination? Attitudes on Sexual Orientation, Gender Identity, Race, and Immigration Status." Public Religion Research Institute. June 21, 2017. www.prri.org.

Kirkpatrick, David C. "C. René Padilla: Integral Mission and the Reshaping of Global Evangelicalism." PhD dissertation, University of Edinburgh, 2015.

———. *A Gospel for the Poor: Global Social Christianity and the Latin American Evangelical Left*. Philadelphia: University of Pennsylvania Press, 2019.

Kruse, Kevin. *One Nation under God: How Corporate America Invented Christian America*. New York: Basic Books, 2015.

Kurien, Prema A. *Ethnic Church Meets Megachurch: Indian American Christianity in Motion*. New York: New York University Press, 2017.

Laats, Adam. *Fundamentalist U: Keeping the Faith in American Higher Education*. New York: Oxford University Press, 2018.

Lassiter, Matthew D. *The Silent Majority: Suburban Politics in the Sunbelt South*. Princeton, NJ: Princeton University Press, 2006.

Lipsitz, George. *The Possessive Investment in Whiteness: How White People Profit from Identity Politics*, 20th anniversary edition. Philadelphia: Temple University Press, 2018.

Lofton, Kathryn. *Oprah: The Gospel of an Icon*. Berkeley: University of California Press, 2011.

Lonsdale, John. "Mau Maus of the Mind: Making Mau Mau and Remaking Kenya." *Journal of African History* 31 (1990): 393–421.

Lum, Kathryn Gin, and Paul Harvey, editors. *The Oxford Handbook of Religion and Race in American History*. New York: Oxford University Press, 2018.

Manzullo-Thomas, Devin. "Born-Again Brethren in Christ: Anabaptism, Evangelicalism, and the Cultural Transformation of a Plain People." *Mennonite Quarterly Review* 90 (April 2016): 203–237.

Marsden, George. *Fundamentalism and American Culture*. New York: Oxford University Press, 1980.

———. *Reforming Fundamentalism: Fuller Seminary and the New Evangelicalism*. Grand Rapids, MI: Eerdmans, 1988.

Marsh, Charles. *The Beloved Community: How Faith Shapes Social Justice, from the Civil Rights Movement to Today*. New York: Basic Books, 2004.

———. "The Civil Rights Movement as Theological Drama." In *The Role of Ideas in the Civil Rights South*. Edited by Ted Ownby. Jackson: University Press of Mississippi, 2002. 19–38.

———. *God's Long Summer: Stories of Faith and Civil Rights*. Princeton, NJ: Princeton University Press, 1997.

———. *Wayward Christian Soldiers: Freeing the Gospel from Political Captivity*. New York: Oxford University Press, 2007.

Mathews, Mary Beth Swetnam. Doctrine and Race: *African American Evangelicals and Fundamentalism between the Wars*. Tuscaloosa: University of Alabama Press, 2017.

Matzko, Paul. *The Radio Right: How a Band of Broadcasters Took on the Federal Government and Built the Modern Conservative Movement*. New York: Oxford University Press, 2020.

McAlister, Melani. "The Global Conscience of American Evangelicalism: Internationalism and Social Concern in the 1970s and Beyond." *Journal of American Studies* 51 (2017): 1197–1220.

———. *The Kingdom of God Has No Borders: A Global History of American Evangelicals*. New York: Oxford University Press, 2018.

McCutcheon, Russell T. *Religion and the Domestication of Dissent*. Oakville, CT: Equinox, 2005.

McDowell, John Patrick. *The Social Gospel in the South: The Women's Home Mission Movement in the Methodist Episcopal Church, South, 1886–1939*. Baton Rouge: Louisiana State University Press, 1982.

McIntosh, Gary L. *Donald A. McGavran: A Biography of the Twentieth Century's Premier Missiologist*. Boca Raton, FL: Church Leader Insights, 2015.

———. "The Life and Ministry of Donald A. McGavran: A Short Overview." American Society for Church Growth Annual Meeting. November 2005. 8–15.

McLaughlin, Malcolm. *The Long, Hot Summer of 1967: Urban Rebellion in America*. New York: Palgrave Macmillan, 2014.

McLoughlin, William G. *Modern Revivalism: Charles Grandison Finney to Billy Graham*. New York: Ronald Press, 1959.

McPhee, Art. "Bishop J. Waskom Pickett's Rethinking on 1930s Missions in India." *International Journal of Frontier Missions* 19 (2002): 31–38.

Meehan, Christopher. *Growing Pains: How Racial Struggles Changed a Church and School*. Grand Rapids, MI: Eerdmans, 2017.

Metzger, Paul Louis. *Consuming Jesus: Beyond Race and Class Divisions in a Consumer Church*. Grand Rapids, MI: Eerdmans, 2007.

Miller, Albert G. "The Rise of African-American Evangelicalism in American Culture." In *Perspectives on American Religion and Culture*. Edited by Peter W. Williams. Malden, MA: Wiley-Blackwell, 1999. 259–269.

Miller, Steven P. *The Age of Evangelicalism: America's Born Again Years*. New York: Oxford University Press, 2014.

———. "The Persistence of Antiliberalism: Evangelicals and the Race Problem." In *American Evangelicals and the 1960s*. Edited by Axel R. Schäfer. Madison: University of Wisconsin Press, 2013. 81–96.

Moreton, Bethany. *To Serve God and Walmart: The Making of Christian Free Enterprise*. Cambridge, MA: Harvard University Press, 2009.

Mulder, Mark T. *Shades of White Flight: Evangelical Congregations and Urban Departure*. New Brunswick, NJ: Rutgers University Press, 2015.

Newman, Mark. *Desegregating Dixie: The Catholic Church in the South and Desegregation, 1945–1992*. Jackson: University Press of Mississippi, 2018.

———. *Getting Right with God: Southern Baptists and Desegregation, 1945–1995*. Tuscaloosa: University of Alabama Press, 2001.

Newton, Judith. *From Panthers to Promise Keepers: Rethinking the Men's Movement.* Lanham, MD: Rowman and Littlefield, 2005.

Nilsen, Sarah, and Sarah E. Turner, editors. *The Colorblind Screen: Television in Post-Racial America.* New York: New York University Press, 2014.

Noll, Mark. *Turning Points: Decisive Moments in the History of Christianity,* 3rd edition. Grand Rapids, MI: Baker Academic, 2012.

Noll, Mark, David W. Bebbington, and George Marsden, editors. *Evangelicals: Who They Have Been, Are Now, and Could Be.* Grand Rapids, MI: Eerdmans, 2019.

Osborne, Myles. "'The Rooting Out of Mau Mau from the Minds of the Kikuyu Is a Formidable Task': Propaganda and the Mau Mau War." *Journal of African History* 56 (2015): 77-97.

Perry, Samuel L. *Growing God's Family: The Global Orphan Care Movement and the Limits of Evangelical Activism.* New York: New York University Press, 2017.

Pickett, J. Waskom. "Donald A. McGavran: Missionary, Scholar, Ecumenist, Evangelist." In *God, Man and Church Growth.* Edited by A. R. Tippett. Grand Rapids, MI: Eerdmans, 1973. 1-9.

Pierce, Richard B. *Polite Protest: The Political Economy of Race in Indianapolis, 1920-1970.* Bloomington: Indiana University Press, 2005.

Pietsch, B. M. *Dispensational Modernism.* New York: Oxford University Press, 2015.

Potter, Ronald C. "The New Black Evangelicals." In *Black Theology: A Documentary History, 1966-1979.* Maryknoll, NY: Orbis Books, 1979. 302-309.

Quiros, Ansley L. *God with Us: Lived Theology and the Freedom Struggle in Americus, Georgia, 1942-1976.* Chapel Hill: University of North Carolina Press, 2018.

Rah, Soong-Chan. "In Whose Image: The Emergence, Development, and Challenge of African-American Evangelicalism." PhD dissertation, Duke University Divinity School, 2016.

Read, William R. "Church Growth as Modernization." In *God, Man and Church Growth.* Edited by A. R. Tippett. Grand Rapids, MI: Eerdmans, 1973. 188-198.

Rice, Anne P., editor. *Witnessing Lynching: American Writers Respond.* New Brunswick, NJ: Rutgers University Press, 2003.

Rieder, Jonathan. *Gospel of Freedom: Martin Luther King, Jr.'s Letter from Birmingham Jail and the Struggle That Changed a Nation.* New York: Bloomsbury Press, 2013.

Roach, David Christopher. "The Southern Baptist Convention and Civil Rights, 1954-1995." Dissertation, Southern Baptist Theological Seminary, 2009.

Schäfer, Axel R. *Piety and Public Funding: Evangelicals and the State in Modern America.* Philadelphia: University of Pennsylvania Press, 2012.

Scott, Daryl Michael. *Contempt and Pity: Social Policy and the Image of the Damaged Black Psyche, 1880-1996.* Chapel Hill: University of North Carolina Press, 1997.

Sernett, Milton C. *Bound for the Promised Land: African American Religion and the Great Migration.* Durham, NC: Duke University Press, 1997.

Sheler, Jeffery L. *Prophet of Purpose: The Life of Rick Warren.* New York: Doubleday, 2009.

Showalter, Nathan D. *The End of a Crusade: The Student Volunteer Movement for Foreign Missions and the Great War.* Lanham, MD: Scarecrow Press, 1997.

Sides, John, Michael Tesler, and Lynn Vavreck. *Identity Crisis: The 2016 Presidential Campaign and the Battle for the Meaning of America.* Princeton, NJ: Princeton University Press, 2018.

Silliman, Daniel, et al. "The Imaginary Turn in Evangelical Scholarship." Roundtable at the *American Society of Church History* Winter Meeting. New York, NY, January 4, 2020.

Sinha, Manisha. *The Slave's Cause: A History of Abolition.* New Haven, CT: Yale University Press, 2016.

Slade, Peter. *Open Friendship in a Closed Society: Mission Mississippi and a Theology of Friendship.* New York: Oxford University Press, 2009.

Sokol, Jason. *All Eyes Are upon Us: Race and Politics from Boston to Brooklyn.* New York: Basic Books, 2014.

———. *The Heavens Might Crack: The Death and Legacy of Martin Luther King Jr.* New York: Basic Books, 2018.

Stanley, Brian. *The Global Diffusion of Evangelicalism: The Age of Billy Graham and John Stott.* Downers Grove, IL: IVP Academic, 2013.

Stephens, Hilde Løvdal. "'Tearing Down the Walls of Segregation': Race, Conservatism, and Evangelical Rap." *Journal of American Studies* 52 (2018): 1043–1065.

Stephens, Randall J. "'It Has to Come from the Hearts of the People': Evangelicals, Fundamentalists, Race, and the 1964 Civil Rights Act." *Journal of American Studies* (2015): 1–27.

Sutton, Matthew Avery. *Aimee Semple McPherson and the Resurrection of Christian America.* Cambridge, MA: Harvard University Press, 2009.

———. *American Apocalypse: A History of Modern Evangelicalism.* Cambridge, MA: Harvard University Press, 2014.

Swartz, David. *Facing West: American Evangelicals in an Age of World Christianity.* New York: Oxford University Press, 2020.

———. *Moral Minority: The Evangelical Left in an Age of Conservatism.* Philadelphia: University of Pennsylvania Press, 2012.

Taylor, Keeanga-Yamahtta. *From #BlackLivesMatter to Black Liberation.* Chicago: Haymarket Books, 2016.

Teasdale, Mark R. *Methodist Evangelism, American Salvation: The Home Missions of the Methodist Episcopal Church, 1860–1920.* Eugene, OR: Wipf and Stock, 2014.

Tranby, Eric, and Douglas Hartmann. "Critical Whiteness Theories and the Evangelical 'Race Problem': Extending Emerson and Smith's *Divided by Faith*." *Journal for the Scientific Study of Religion* 47 (2008): 341–359.

Tuch, Steven A., and Jack K. Martin, editors. *Racial Attitudes in the 1990s: Continuity and Change.* Westport, CT: Praeger, 1997.

Vaca, Daniel. *Evangelicals Incorporated: Books and the Business of Religion in America.* Cambridge, MA: Harvard University Press, 2019.

Wacker, Grant. *America's Pastor: Billy Graham and the Shaping of a Nation*. Cambridge, MA: Harvard University Press, 2014.

Wadsworth, Nancy D. *Ambivalent Miracles: Evangelicals and the Politics of Racial Healing*. Charlottesville: University of Virginia Press, 2014.

Wall, Wendy L. *Inventing the "American Way": The Politics of Consensus from the New Deal to the Civil Rights Movement*. New York: Oxford University Press, 2008.

Watt, David Harrington. "Fundamentalists of the 1920s and 1930s." In *Fundamentalism: Perspectives on a Contested History*. Edited by Simon A. Wood and David Harrington Watt. Columbia: University of South Carolina Press, 2014. 18–35.

Weisenfeld, Judith. *Hollywood Be Thy Name: African American Religion in American Film, 1929–1949*. Berkeley: University of California Press, 2007.

———. *New World A-coming: Black Religion and Racial Identity during the Great Migration*. New York: New York University Press, 2016.

White, Deborah Gray. *Lost in the USA: American Identity from the Promise Keepers to the Million Mom March*. Urbana: University of Illinois Press, 2017.

Williams, Daniel K. *God's Own Party: The Making of the Christian Right*. New York: Oxford University Press, 2010.

Worthen, Molly. *Apostles of Reason: The Crisis of Authority in Evangelicalism*. New York: Oxford University Press, 2014.

Wuthnow, Robert. *The Restructuring of American Religion: Society and Faith since World War II*. Princeton, NJ: Princeton University Press, 1988.

INDEX

abortion, 5
Africa: college students from, 54; McGavran's travels in, 81–83; as mission field, 21–22, 25, 27, 29, 44. *See also specific countries*
Alexander, Rod, 64
Allen, Jere, 185
American Bible Society, 91
Anderson, Darrell, 177
Anderson, William Henry, Jr., 38
Andringa, Bob, 190
apartheid, 147, 157, 159
Armerding, Hudson T.: and black students, 66, 69, 73; remarks at King memorial service, 57–58
Arn, Win, 100–102
Asbury College, 232n13
Assemblies of God, 51, 91; authority of whiteness in, 21–22; discriminatory practices of, 21, 44; growth of, 211

Barrington College, 115, 122
Basler, Jay, 124
Belew, M. Wendell, 96–97
Bell, Nelson L., 43
Bentley, Ruth Lewis, 30; advice to black evangelical college students, 74; participant in the Chicago declaration, 121
Bentley, William H., 31–32
Bethany Bible College, 51–52
Bethel College: black students at, 64–65, 75; recruitment of black students, 57
Bible Institute of Los Angeles, 20, 110.

Billy Graham Evangelistic Association: black evangelicals in, 24, 27–28, 31, 44. *See also* Graham, Billy
Birmingham, 46, 94; civil rights campaign in, 32–34; church bombing in, 37–38; Graham crusade in, 39–40. *See also* Sixteenth Street Baptist Church
blackness: 29, 48; and the black evangelical experience, 14, 25, 27, 74, 126; as gift from God, 64, 119; as marker of spiritual inferiority, 21–22; as metaphor for following Christ, 139, 152–154, 156; stereotypes about, 66, 88
black evangelicals: and Billy Graham, 27, 35–36, 47–48; challenging Christian colorblindness, 7, 47–48, 50, 139, 212; criticisms of the homogeneous unit principle, 78, 104–106; demanding reforms in white evangelical institutions, 2–3, 9, 48, 61–63, 211; exclusion of, 51–54, 138, 140, 162–170; 212; increasing prominence of, 24; origins of, 229n63; and Lausanne Congress, 147–150; and Promise Keepers, 200–203; and racial reconciliation, 11, 173–182; views of Dr. King, 34; using colorblind theology, 13–15, 23–24, 42–43, 45. *See also* National Black Evangelical Association; *names of specific individuals*
Black Lives Matter, 3, 11, 218; 2014–2015 protests, 1; 2020 protests, 219–220, evangelical views of, 214–215
Blackmon, Garry, 197
black nationalism, 70, 74

Black Panthers, 68, 120
black power: black evangelical promotion of, 69–72, 74, 174; and the Church Growth Movement, 95–96; and environment on white evangelical college campuses, 50, 55, 64
Black Solidarity Day, 63
black theology, 70, 74, 117, 152
Bob Jones University, 51, 68–69
Boyle, Sam, 38.
Bradford, Odessa, 113
Brethren in Christ Church, 109, 111
Brown, Austin Channing, 217–218
Brown, Joseph, 39, 42–43
Brown, Michael, 1
Brown, Ronald, 70
Brubaker, Merle, 117, 119–120
Buffalo Bible Institute, 131, 148
Burns, Tyler, 219
Butler College, 80, 86
Butler, King A., 42

Calvin College, 37, 110; black students at, 66, 73; dominance of whiteness at, 190, 194–195; Dutch ethnicity of, 75, 194; recruitment of black students, 56–57
Campbell University, 191
Campus Crusade for Christ, 51
Carmichael, Stokely, 70, 74
Carney, Glandion, 180
Catholicism, 140
Chaney, Charles, 98
Chicago Declaration, 121
Christian colorblindness, 9–11; and the American city, 108, 110–111, 123, 137; as challenge to segregated churches, 41; as coalition management, 47–48, 214; on college campuses, 50, 61, 63–64, 77, 192; definition of, 2–3; as motivation for race-conscious reform, 60; origins of, 8, 14; in popular music, 188–189; as a racial order, 3–6, 212–213; and racial reconciliation, 172, 178, 203, 207; as reactionary tool, 61, 77, 170, 206, 209–210, 215; relationship to Church Growth Movement, 79; relationship to colorblind ideology, 4, 212; as shaper of evangelical identity, 6–8; as wedge between fundamentalists and neo-evangelicals, 19. *See also* colorblindness
Christian and Missionary Alliance, 85
Christian Reformed Church, 18, 56, 75, 232n12
Christian Right, 5–6, 262n10
Church Growth Movement, 9–10; characteristics of, 93; church segregation and, 78, 103, 107, 161, 185; criticisms of, 103–106, 143–145, 151–153, 156–159, 161–163, 179; expansion to the United States, 95–107; influence of, 150, 156–159, 161–162, 182–184, 211, 237n8; investment in whiteness, 79, 107–108, 156; origins of, 78–86; at Lausanne Congress 138–148, 249n6. *See also* homogeneous unit principle; McGavran, Donald; Wagner, C. Peter)
church primacy: 199, 215; definition and function of, 5, 224n9; during the civil rights movement, 27–29, 32, 37
Circle Church, 148; as CGM case study, 103; racial controversy at, 155. *See also* Hilliard, Clarence
Civil Rights Act of 1964, 28, 55
civil rights movement, 1–6, 9–10; aftermath of, 108, 136, 139, 160, 179, 187; as antecedent of Black Lives Matter era, 215; effects of, 14, 23, 27, 49, 54, 64, 67–68, 78–79, 96, 99, 109; evangelical support for, 93–94, 111; lessons of, 165, 185, 201; reaction against, 73, 169; white evangelical resistance to, 32, 37, 40, 43–46, 79, 147, 170; winners and losers of, 211–213, 262n10
Clark, Jim, 94
Cleveland, 25

INDEX | 283

Clinton, Bill, 198, 204
Coalition for Christian Colleges and Universities, 190–192
Coggins, Wade, 91, 96
Cold War, 86, 138
Coleman, Robert, 165–167
colorblindness: growth of, 13–14; relationship to Christian colorblindness, 4, 172, 209, 212, 225n6; used to protest Jim Crow, 8. *See also* Christian colorblindness
Colson, Chuck, 201
Columbia University, 80
communism, 14, 58, 86, 107, 184
Cone, James: Church Growth Movement's appropriation of, 159, 253n73; influence on black evangelicals, 70, 117, 152
Congo, 82, 110
Conn, Harvie, 158
Connor, Bull, 94
Convocation on Evangelizing Ethnic America, 138, 163–169
Cook, Montague, 16–18, 46
Coote, Robert T., 107
Covenant College, 58, 64, 115
Criswell, W.A., 102; defense of segregation, 84, 147; influence on Rick Warren, 210
Crowell, Henry, 93
Culbertson, Judi, 41–42, 44
Culbertson, William, 68–69
Cullen, Countee, 153
Cummings, Norman, 92
Curry, Edna, 56, 67
Curse of Ham, 18

Dain, A. J., 151
Davidson College, 115
DC Talk, 188–189
decolonization, 14, 23, 138
Des Moines, McGavran's experience in, 87–89, 96

Disciples of Christ, 80
Divided by Faith, 209
Dordt College, whiteness of, 55, 75
Drake Divinity School, 87
DuBose, Francis, 98
Duke, David, 172

Eastern Baptist College: black students at 62–63; recruitment of black students, 57, 193
Eastern Baptist Seminary, 180
Eastern Nazarene College, 191
Edinburgh Missionary Conference, 141–142
Edman, V. Raymond, interracial dating policy at Wheaton College, 52–53
Edwards, Jonathan, 195
Escobar, Samuel: at Lausanne Congress, 141, 145–149; reaction to Lausanne Congress, 150–152
Evangelical Foreign Missions Association, 91–92, 96
Evangelical Free Church, 211
evangelicals: *See* black evangelicals; white evangelicals
evangelical whiteness: ascendance of, 169; meaning of 2–4, 6–7, 210; protection of, 123, 206
Evans, Tony, 177

Federal Council of Churches, 15
feminism, 59, 200, 233n31
Ferguson, Missouri, 1
First Baptist Church of Birmingham, 33
First Baptist Church of Dallas, 84
First Baptist Church of Tallahassee, 40
Floyd, George, 219
Ford, Leighton: and Convocation on Evangelizing Ethnic America, 164–168; on homogeneous unit principle, 159
Fort Wayne Bible College, 51
Frost, Gary, 186

fundamentalism, 14, 16, 51; black varieties of, 31; influence on white evangelical colleges, 76, 112; negative connotation of, 227n27; sacred whiteness as marker of, 19–20, 227n26; success in cities, 86

Fuller Theological Seminary: black evangelicals at, 30, 51, 164; and the Church Growth Movement, 92–93, 100–101, 140–141, 156–159, 162, 240n63; School of World Mission, 92, 141

Garden Grove Community Church, 101
Gardner, Leroy, 43
Georgetown College, 55
Gilbreath, Edward, 171, 200, 255n1
Gilliam, Anne, 77
Glazer, Nathan, 96
Golden Gate Baptist Theological Seminary, 98
Grand Rapids, 37, 56, 181
Grant, John, 130
Gray, James, 93
Gratton, John, 155
Great Migration, 7, 25, 86
Gregory, Dick, 166
Griffin, John Howard, 55–56
Graham, Billy, 13, 43–44, 159, 219; in Birmingham, 39–40; black evangelical criticisms of, 47–48, 155; and Christian colorblindness 46–48; Christian nationalism of, 86; fundamentalist criticisms of, 68; and Lausanne Congress, 140–142, 149–150; Los Angeles crusade, 31, 35–36; membership at First Baptist Church of Dallas, 84; New York crusade, 24–27; relationship with Jones, Howard, 24–28, 35–36, 46–47
Guy, Cal, 99

Hamitic Curse. See Curse of Ham
Hardesty, Nancy, 59–61
Harlem: New York Crusade, 26–27; Skinner, Tom, and, 125–126, 246n57-n58

Harrison, Bob, 44–45, 126, 158; discrimination faced, 21, 51–52
Hatfield, Mark, 44, 91
Heise, Steve, 63
Henry, Carl, 16, 19–21
Hillegas, Lyle, 76
Hilliard, Clarence, 121, 158, 207; criticisms of the Church Growth Movement, 152–155; education of, 148; firing of, 155; at Lausanne, 148–150; theological blackness, 139, 153, 156; theological whiteness, 153, 161–162, 170
homogeneous unit principle: Consultation on, 156–159; critics of, 98, 104–105, 144, 148, 160; definition of, 98, 156; as protector of diversity, 146, 160, 167; racial implications of, 102–104, 107, 160–161; revisionist history of, 183–184
Hostetter, D. Ray: conflicting visions of Philadelphia Campus, 116, 118, 133–134; planning of Philadelphia Campus, 109–110, 112–114; support for Philadelphia Campus, 124, 137
Houston '85. See Convocation on Evangelizing Ethnic America
Houghton College, 75, 148, 193; black students at 65; "Buffalo" campus, 131–132
Hybels, Bill, 201; church growth and, 184, 209; helped by Robert Schuller, 101, 161, 253n79

India: as focus of McGavran's thought, 89, 107; McGavran's career in, 80–83, 86; as precedent for the CGM in the United States, 10, 78, 84–85, 89
Indianapolis: changing racial climate of, 86–87; McGavran's experiences in, 80, 86–87, 89, 96
Institute for American Church Growth, 100–101
Institute for Successful Church Leadership, 101

Institute of Church Growth, 90–92
integration, 20, 26, 68, 94, 99, 129; of churches, 40–42, 78, 87, 90, 102–103, 146, 161, 170, 183; of colleges, 50, 54, 56, 58–60, 75, 77, 194; "forced," 35–36
International Foreign Mission Association, 91
International Lausanne Congress on World Evangelization, 10, 138; Lausanne Covenant, 149; Theology and Radical Discipleship Group, 148–149; planning of, 140–141; reactions to, 139, 150–154; speeches given at, 141–147. See also Lausanne Movement
interracial marriage, 20, 52–53, 107, 262n16
InterVarsity Christian Fellowship: black evangelicals in, 30, 180, 214; integration of, 16, 226n11; Latin American evangelicals in, 143, 145; Urbana conference, 127
Iverson, Bill, 115, 122–123

Jackson, Joseph H., 166
Jenkins, Leona, and protest at MBI, 49–50
Jenks, Phil, 62–63
Jones, E. Edward, 187
Jones, Howard, 44, 67, 85, 190; criticisms of white evangelicals, 16, 20, 28–30, 47; discrimination experienced by, 13, 25–26, 28; and the National Black Evangelical Association, 30–32, 36; proponent of colorblind theology, 13–15, 29–30, 33, 39, 42, 48, 72, 104–105, 172; relationship with Billy Graham, 24–28, 46–47; skepticism of Tom Skinner, 126, 246n58; view of Martin Luther King, 34, 45
Jones, Morris E., 180
Jones, Peggy L., 180
Jones, Randy, 117
Jones, Wanda Young, 85; discrimination experienced by, 25–26; missionary career of, 227n38

Kampala Cathedral, 82
Kehrein, Glen, 179, 200–201
Kemp, Jack, 204
Kennedy, John F., 36
Kenya, 78; McGavran's observations of, 82
Kerner Commission, 118, 245n35
King, Martin Luther, 56, 218; Body of Christ language, 8, 33; colorblind language and appropriation of, 36, 213, 229n79; evangelical reactions to, 34–35, 45, 57–59, 69, 93–96, 170, 223n2; holiday for, 193; "Letter from Birmingham City Jail," 33, 35, 37; New York crusade, 26–27
King, Rodney, 178
Kraft, Charles, 158

LaHaye, Timothy, 57
Land, Richard, 184–186, 199
Landrey, Paul, 164, 166
Latin American Theological Fraternity, 143, 148
Latourette, Kenneth Scott, 85
Lausanne Movement: accused of racism, 169; battles for control of, 139–140, 150–151; endorsement of the homogeneous unit principle, 159; Pataya Consultation, 162; role in Houston '85, 138, 163–168. See also International Lausanne Congress on World Evangelization
Lawson, James, 36
Lecrae, 216–217
Legion Field, 39
"Letter from Birmingham City Jail," 33, 35, 37
Lewis, Ron, 98
Liberia, Howard Jones in, 26, 30, 46
Loritts, Bryan, 217
Los Angeles: founding of National Black Evangelical Association in, 30; Graham crusade in, 31, 35; uprising in, 172, 178–179

Los Angeles Baptist College, 58–59
Loury, Glenn, 199

Macedonia Assembly of God Church, 180
Madison Square Garden, 26
Mains, David, 155
Malcolm X, 117
Malone College, 192
Manila, 169
March on Washington for Jobs and Freedom, 32, 35–36
Mau Mau revolt, 82
McCartney, Bill: background and conversion of, 196; explanation of Promise Keepers' decline, 205–206; efforts to make PK multiracial, 197, 202–203; founding of PK, 196; meeting with NBEA, 201; Stand in the Gap rally, 204–205; view of racial reconciliation, 203
McCaulley, Esau, 217–218
McCulloch, Bob, 1
McDonald, Robin, 178
McGavran, Donald, 86–88, 154–155; African travels 81–83; *Bridges of God*, 83–85; church integration plan, 89–90; death of, 183; education of, 80; founding of the Institute of Church Growth, 90–91; homogeneous unit principle 78, 98, 102–103, 106–107, 156–158; influence of, 79–80, 168, 183–184, 210, 215; at Lausanne 140–145, 148; missionary to India 78, 80–81; move to Fuller Seminary, 92; opposition to liberal Protestants 95–96; support for the civil rights movement, 93–94; transfer of church growth ideas to the United States, 96–100; view of black church 162–163; warnings against integrated churches, 107, 157
McGovern, George, 121
McIntire, Carl: opposition to Dr. King, 35; segregationist reading of scripture, 18

McKenna, David, 76
McNeil, Brenda Salter, 218–219
McVeigh, Timothy, 200
Messiah College: black students at, 62–63, 65, 67, 77, 116, 190; integration of, 55–56; racial climate of, 67, 75. *See also* Philadelphia Campus of Messiah College
Mexico City, 151
Million Man March: compared to Promise Keepers, 200, 204; and fear of racial division, 172, 197
Missions Advanced Research and Communication Center, 141
Mississippi, 104; black college students from, 56, 58; black SBC church in, 187; civil rights movement in, 94; John Perkins in, 173–174; racial reconciliation in, 199
Montgomery, 46–47
Moody Bible Institute, 75; black students' protest at, 49; John R. Rice controversy, 68–69; urban environment of, 130–131
Moody, Dwight L., 49, 154
Moore, Earl, 129
Moynihan, Daniel Patrick, 96, 100
Mystical Body of Christ, 15

National Association of Evangelicals, 91, 128; compared to NBEA, 31–32; dialogue with NBEA, 176–178; neutrality of during civil rights movement, 45–46
National Baptist Convention, 166, 187
National Black Evangelical Association, 39, 42, 51; challenging white evangelicals, 35–36, 47–48, 176–178; early conservatism of, 31–32, 229n63; founding of, 24, 30–31
National Council of Churches, 92; support for civil rights movement, 15–16, 35

National Negro Evangelical Association. *See* National Black Evangelical Association
Nation of Islam, 172, 200
Nazarenes: embrace of Church Growth Movement, 101, 162, 168
Newark: uprising, 110; Urban Field College, 115, 122–123
North Park College, 75, 192; black students at, 66, 70, 72; recruitment of black students, 56
Northwest Christian College, 90
Novak, Michael, 96
Nyack College: black students at, 61, 67, 70; Christian colorblindness at, 63–64; Howard and Wanda Jones at, 13, 25–26; increasing diversity of, 190

Obama, Barack, 11, 214
Oliver, C. Herbert, 23, 227n36
Olivet Nazarene University, 109
Orange County, CA, 101, 162

Padilla, C. René: at Consultation on the Homogeneous Unit Principle, 156, 158–159; criticisms of the Church Growth Movement, 104, 140–141, 143–145, 151–152, 156, 158–159; at Lausanne Congress, 138–141, 143–148
Pannell, Bill, 121, 147, 157; college experience of, 51; criticisms of Lausanne Movement, 169–170; critiques of white evangelicals, 74, 105, 164–165, 214; *My Friend, the Enemy*, 70–71; reaction to Birmingham bombing, 38; view of racial reconciliation, 179–180, 201
Pasadena, 151, 156, 173
Paul (apostle), 19, 88, 100, 152, 157; as authority for colorblind theology, 8, 13, 29, 255n6
Perkins, John, 121, 147; activism of, 174; childhood and conversion of, 173; criticism of Church Growth Movement, 78, 106, 162–163; founding of Voice of Calvary, 174; philosophy of racial reconciliation, 175–177, 179, 192, 203, 207; support for Promise Keepers, 202
Perkins, Spencer, 179
Perkins, Vera Mae, 176; childhood of, 173; Head Start program of, 174,
Perry, George M., 47–48
Petersen, William J., 88–89; advice for white evangelical colleges, 53–54
Philadelphia: uprising in, 112–113
Philadelphia Campus of Messiah College, 10; closing of, 259n76; colorblind reaction against, 120, 133–134, 136–137; culture shock at, 114, 123; during the "racial reconciliation" era, 193–194; fear of crime at, 132–133, 135–136; as model for others, 115, 131; opening of, 114; planning of, 109–114; racial controversy at, 116–121, 124; racial paternalism at, 118–119, 123
Philadelphia College of Bible, 61, 110
Philyaw, Willie, 112
Pickett, J. Waskom, influence on Donald McGavran, 80–83
Pittsburgh, 17–18, 41, 171
Potter, Ronald, 31, 74
Printis, Marvin L. 30; criticism of Graham, 35–36
Promise Keepers: Christian masculinity, 196, 200, 259n81; decline of, 205–206, 261n125; founding of, 196; and racial reconciliation, 171, 195–207; as revival movement, 195–196, 203–205

racial reconciliation, 11, 170; and black evangelicals, 176–182; on college campuses, 189–195, 218; and John Perkins, 106, 175–177, 179, 192, 203, 207; as expression of Christian colorblindness, 172, 178, 203, 207, 215; as method of church growth, 182, 184–188; popularization of, 171–172; and Promise Keepers, 195, 197–208

Ramseyer, Robert, 158
Reeb, James, 45
Reformed Presbyterian Church of North America, 38
Republican Party, 79, 198–199; and racial reconciliation, 204; white evangelicals in, 5–6, 172
Richardson, Willie, 193–194
Rhoad, Randy, 123
Rice, John R., 68–69
Rice, Tamir, 216
Roberts, J. Deotis, 180
Romo, Oscar, 163, 165–167
Roosevelt University, 115

sacred whiteness: on college campuses, 53, 69, 76; definition of, 16; during civil rights era, 15–23, 32, 40, 42, 47; and interracial sex, 20–21, 90; persistence of, 210
Saddleback Church. *See* Warren, Rick
San Diego, 57
San Francisco, 51, 115, 122
Schuller, Robert H., 101–103, 162
Scott, Manuel L., 151
Scudder, C. W., 129
Seattle Pacific College, 76, 218
Second Christian Church, 87
secularization, 4
Selma Campaign: evangelical response to, 45–46, 93–94
Sider, Ronald, 139, 194; director of Philadelphia Campus, 115–121, 123, 133–134; challenging colorblind Christians' view of the city, 117, 125, 128, 136–137; leader of evangelical left, 110–111, 121
Simmons, Paul D., 103–104
Simpson, O. J., 172, 197
Sixteenth Street Baptist Church, bombing of, 17, 37–38
Skinner, John, 70

Skinner, Tom, 30, 51, 177; conversion of, 125–126, 246n57; relationship with white evangelicals, 126–128
Smith, Michael W., 188
Smyth, Walter, 46
Southern Baptist Convention, 9–10; "A Statement Concerning the Crisis in Our Nation," 128–130; colleges, 55; engagement with Church Growth Movement, 91, 96–99, 162; ethnic church planting of 97–98, 140; growth of, 211; influence on Convocation on Evangelizing Ethnic America, 163, 167; racists welcome in, 46; Resolution on Racial Reconciliation, 184–188; sacred whiteness in, 20, 84, 210
Southern Baptist Theological Seminary, 103
Southern Christian Leadership Conference, 94
South Main Baptist Church, 167
Southwestern Baptist Theological Seminary, 129
Spoelhof, William, 66, 75
St. John's Missionary Baptist Church, 42
Stott, John: as chairman of the Consultation on the Homogeneous Unit Principle, 156, 158–159; work on Lausanne Covenant, 149
Students for a Democratic Society, 68
Student Volunteer Movement, 80
Suggs, Robert, 181

Taylor, Clyde W., 45–46, 92
Taylor University, 62, 115, 191
Temple University, partnership with Messiah College, 109, 112–114
Tenney, Merrill C., 53
Tenth Presbyterian Church, as model for integration, 41–42
Tisby, Jemar, 219
Trinity Baptist Church, 16

Trinity College, 115
Trinity Evangelical Divinity School, 148
Trump, Donald, 11, 215, 217, 219

Union Theological Seminary, 80
University of Alabama, integration of, 30
University of Oregon, 91
Upsalla, 95, 140
Urban Field College, 115, 122

Vietnam War, 73, 95
Voice of Calvary, 174. *See also* Perkins, John

Wagner, C. Peter: church integration as threat to church growth, 78, 102–103, 106; critics of, 104–105; decision to exclude black evangelicals, 164–166; defense of the homogeneous unit principle, 156–157, 159–161; at Lausanne Congress, 145–146, 148; planning of Houston '85, 163–167; reaction to Lausanne Congress, 150–151; spreading the Church Growth Movement in the United States, 100–102, 162, 168. *See also* Convocation on Evangelizing Ethnic America
Walker, Jimmie, 58–59
Warner, Tony, 214
Warren, Melvin: as pastor at Circle Church, 148; protest at MBI, 49–50, 68
Warren, Rick, 187; Church Growth Movement influence on, 162, 183, 210; critique of Black Lives Matter, 1–3
Washington, Raleigh, 179, 200–201, 204
Watts, J. C., 204
Wayland Baptist College, 55
Weary, Dolphus, 58–59
Wells, Ida B., 154
Wesleyan Church, 132
Westmont College, 76, 115, 122

Wheaton College, 31, 102, 111, 143, 155, 217; dominance of whiteness at, 69, 73, 190, 195; interracial dating controversy, 52–53, 69; memorial service for Dr. King, 57–58, 69; ministry in Chicago, 66, 115, 130; recruitment of black students, 56, 75
white evangelicals: appropriation of racial reconciliation, 11, 176, 207–208; and church integration, 17, 40–42, 78, 87–90, 102–103; and college integration, 54–60; definition of, 6–8; opposition to black lives matter, 214–215; religio-racial identity of, 7–8; response to civil rights movement, 2–3, 32, 36–39, 40, 43–46, 79, 147, 170; support for Trump, Donald, 215, 217–219; views of the city, 110–112, 124–126, 129–137; views of King, Martin Luther, 34–35, 37, 45, 57–59, 69, 93–96, 170. *See also* Christian colorblindness; evangelical whiteness; sacred whiteness
Whitefield, George, 195
whiteness: on college campuses, 49, 64–65, 72–73, 77; contested meaning of, 10, 108; discovery of, 120, 122; and ethnic revival, 166; as heresy, 152–154, 161; investment in, 2–5, 24, 49, 77, 133, 137, 156, 170, 208, 214, 216, 220; invisibility of, 79, 108, 184; as peoplehood, 108, 140, 157; as shaper of evangelical identity, 6–8, 84, 209–213; theological connotations of, 88. *See also* evangelical whiteness; sacred whiteness
white supremacy: investment in, 4, 79; as racial order, 14, 23, 99, 108, 152; theologies of, 2, 16, 27, 84, 210, 212–213
Whitworth, Jan, 123
Willow Creek. *See* Hybels, Bill
Wilson, George, 31
Wilson, William Julius, 199
Wingert, Don, 135

Winter, Gibson, 239n53
Winter, Ralph: at Consultation on Homogeneous Unit Principle, 156–157; ideas used to support apartheid, 147–148; influence of, 249n6, 251n23; role in planning Lausanne Congress, 140–141; speech at Lausanne Congress, 146–147
Westminster Seminary, 158

World Council of Churches, 91–92, 95, 120
World Vision, 141

Yale Divinity School, 80
Yoder, John Howard: criticisms of Church Growth Movement, 104, 139, 156; sexual abuse committed by, 242n98

Zion Evangelical Free Church, 103

ABOUT THE AUTHOR

JESSE CURTIS is Assistant Professor of History at Valparaiso University.

www.ingramcontent.com/pod-product-compliance
Lightning Source LLC
Chambersburg PA
CBHW020357080526
44584CB00014B/1061